THE HISTORY
OF THE
SOUTH ATLANTIC
CONFLICT

Map 1
The Falkland/Malvinas Islands

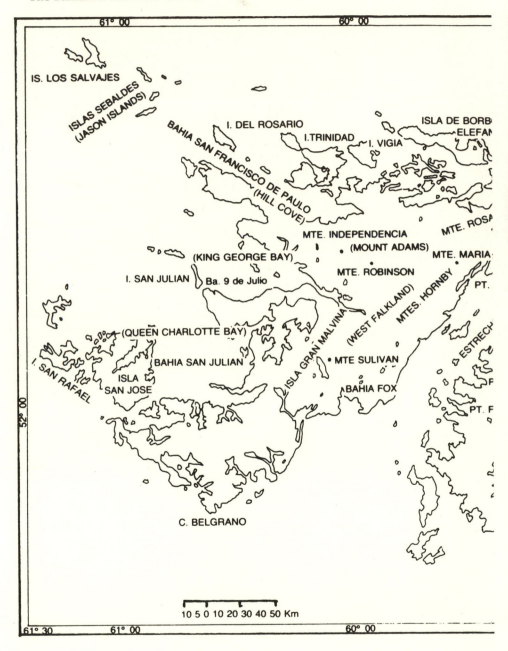

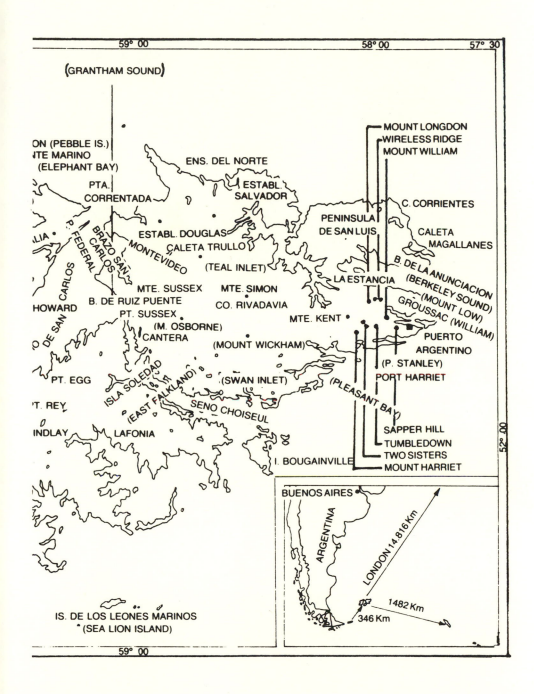

59° 00   58° 00   57° 30

(GRANTHAM SOUND)

ON (PEBBLE IS.)
NTE MARINO
(ELEPHANT BAY)

PTA.
CORRENTADA

ENS. DEL NORTE

ESTABL.
SALVADOR

MOUNT LONGDON
WIRELESS RIDGE
MOUNT WILLIAM

C. CORRIENTES

PENINSULA
DE SAN LUIS

CALETA
MAGALLANES

LIA

P. FEDERAL

BRAZO SAN CARLOS

ESTABL. DOUGLAS
CALETA TRULLO
MONTEVIDEO
(TEAL INLET)

B. DE LA ANUNCIACION
(BERKELEY SOUND)
(MOUNT LOW)
GROUSSAC (WILLIAM)

LA ESTANCIA

HOWARD

DE SAN CARLOS

B. DE RUIZ PUENTE
PT. SUSSEX
(M. OSBORNE)
CANTERA

MTE. SUSSEX
CO. RIVADAVIA

MTE. SIMON

MTE. KENT

PUERTO
ARGENTINO
(P. STANLEY)
PORT HARRIET

PT. EGG

ISLA SOLEDAD

(EAST FALKLAND)

(MOUNT WICKHAM)

(SWAN INLET)

(PLEASANT BAY)

'T. REY

SENO CHOISEUL

NDLAY   LAFONIA

I. BOUGAINVILLE

SAPPER HILL
TUMBLEDOWN
TWO SISTERS
MOUNT HARRIET

52° 00

BUENOS AIRES

ARGENTINA

LONDON 14.816 Km

1482 Km

346 Km

IS. DE LOS LEONES MARINOS
(SEA LION ISLAND)

59° 00

THE HISTORY OF THE SOUTH ATLANTIC CONFLICT

The War for the Malvinas

RUBÉN O. MORO

PRAEGER

New York
Westport, Connecticut
London

Library of Congress Cataloging-in-Publication Data

Moro, Rubén O. (Rubén Oscar)
   [Guerra inaudita. English]
   The history of the South Atlantic conflict : the war for the
Malvinas / Rubén O. Moro.
       p.   cm.
   Translation of: La guerra inaudita.
   Bibliography: p.
   Includes index.
   ISBN 0–275–93081–5 (alk. paper)
   1. Falkland Islands War, 1982.   I. Title.
F3031.5.M6713   1989
997'.11—dc19   88–38300

Library of Congress Catalog Card Number: 88–38300
ISBN: 0–275–93081–5

First published in 1989

Praeger Publishers, One Madison Avenue, New York, NY 10010
A division of Greenwood Press, Inc.

Printed in the United States of America

The paper used in this book complies with the
Permanent Paper Standard issued by the National
Information Standards Organization (Z39.48–1984).

10 9 8 7 6 5 4 3 2 1

Contents

Illustrations

Abbreviations

ARA	Argentine Republic Armada
BRP	parachute delayed bomb
CAP	combat air patrol
EEC	European Economic Community
ELMA	Argentine Maritime Line
FIC	Falkland Islands Company
FO	flight order
GMT	Greenwich Mean Time
IATRA	Inter-American Treaty for Reciprocal Assistance
LADE	Argentine state airline
NATO	North Atlantic Treaty Organization
NCO	non-commissioned officer
NM	nautical mile
OAS	Organization of American States
RAF	Royal Air Force
RFA	Royal Fleet Auxiliary
RRS	Royal Research Service
SAS	Special Air Service
SATO	South Atlantic Theater of Operations
SBS	Special Boat Squadron
TEZ	total exclusion zone
TRALA	tug, repair, and logistics area

Translator's Note

When I was first approached to translate this work, I balked at the enormity of the task, as well as the heavy responsibility I would bear in trying to re-create such a recent event. Still, the author convinced me of the need for the issue, and the narration of events, to be aired in English from the Argentine perspective. This would be a first. As chief interpreter at the Inter-American Defense Board (IADB) in Washington, I had enjoyed a ringside seat, from an interpreter's booth, as I watched, and rendered succeeding interventions into English or French, while history was being made. I interpreted my Argentine colleagues' ringing appeals for U.S. understanding of their quest for what they believe to be rightfully theirs, a land wrested from them in the name of "empire" in 1833, barely ten years after James Monroe enunciated his famous doctrine. I became as fascinated by the drama as I became surrounded by a feeling of aloneness as, one by one, my Latin colleagues grew cold. I could not share their enthusiasm for what I regarded to be the precipitate act of the junta, but as the growing cries of "The British are coming" rang throughout the halls of the IADB and the Organization of American States, I found it increasingly difficult to fathom my government's increasingly unabashed support of our one-time masters in what amounted to a colonial war. Shades of Paul Revere! It all had an eerie sense of déja vu.

For seven weeks the media tracked the task force on its grim quest, while we turned a deaf ear to the pleas of a hemispheric ally. "The British are coming" seemed to echo down from our own fight for freedom. Where were we going wrong?

Then it happened! Screaming out of the skies like avenging eagles, the daring pilots of the Argentine Air Force rewrote the book on naval air warfare, chalked up crushing blows against the oncoming foe, and came back again and again. What had been touted by the British as a "walkover" became a proud page in one air force's history that earned it worldwide admiration, even from its adversaries.

In order for the American, or even the British, reader to get a better grasp on the events as they unfolded, historical references and vignettes have been woven into the narrative, with the author's permission. It is a modest attempt to put into a more familiar perspective what this fight meant for the Argentine side, and how they felt about the defense of the rights of all those who share our hemisphere.

This is their story, seen through the eyes of a senior Argentine Air Force officer and told in English. Rubén Moro, as we worked tirelessly on his original and my rendition, has earned my friendship and respect. I dedicate my translation to him, to his family, and to all the brave men, on both sides, who are the true authors of these chapters, which were written with their blood.

The lights dim, the drums roll, the curtain rises on this latest drama in mankind's eternal tug of war. Let the countdown begin . . . to D-Day in the Falklands!

Michael Valeur

Preface

God had the will that this book come into the hands of readers, not from any known reporter, author, or even a lover of literature. There has been no attempt here to seek literary prowess, or to resort even to the most modest of literary flourishes.

As I began to gather data regarding the South Atlantic conflict, in the autumn of 1982, I did so with an awareness that for us Argentines, the most significant chapter of our history in the twentieth century had just been written. The scope of the information that luck seemed to be pouring into my hands led me to develop this study in which events, as well as political, diplomatic, and military circumstances, are entwined. But what drove me most relentlessly to the task was the nature of the accounts being published about these events, especially in Great Britain, most notably the distortion with which certain agencies reported the facts of the war, something that did not end with the taking of Puerto Argentino, but is going on as I write these lines.

I have enjoyed the cooperation of valuable, reliable Argentine sources, as well as British and others, who all contributed vital information that has enabled me to shed some light on circumstances that the United Kingdom has endeavored to conceal by passing the Military Secrecy Act, thereby clamping a lid on the story of the conflict.

Since historical research is continuing, under no circumstances should this work be regarded as the final or most accurate account. The historical background, as well as the juridical bases for Argentina's claim to the Malvinas (Falklands), South Georgia, and South Sandwich islands, are not delved into in this study because they are deemed to be well known. The story starts with the events immediately preceding April 2, 1982.

Times for all events are given in official Argentine time (GMT–3) unless otherwise stated. The ranks of all military personnel named in this account are those they held at the time of the events.

I wish to dedicate this work to all those who served in the South Atlantic Theater of Operations, and to pay special tribute to those who fell in battle, particularly my fellow Argentine air force officers and enlisted men. History will record their names on the roll of honor. They will be a shining example to generations of my countrymen yet unborn—indeed, to all of Latin America. The struggle for the independence of the remaining shackled lands of the New World has yet to end.

Acknowledgments

This rendition of the story of the Falkland/Malvinas war has come into the hands of English-speaking readers thanks to men and women of goodwill, without whose assistance the tale would never have been told in the English language.

My proud salute of admiration goes to those unsung heroes behind the typewriter, the dictionary, the word processor, and the typesetting device, whose combined efforts have given this book its place in the sun.

To Jose Theiler and his wife, Anne, as much for their steadfastness as for their dedication in getting the final typed manuscript out in practically record time, my endless thanks.

To my friend and fellow officer Jorge Belarmino Fernandez, whose unwavering assistance was crucial in achieving this feat, my eternal gratitude.

To Michael Valeur, the translator whose enthusiasm brings to the English-speaking world, especially to U.S. readers, a work enhanced by historical parallels and quotes that bring the events of this conflict into sharper focus by comparing them, sometimes quite directly, with other milestones in the history of both the United States and Great Britain, victories and defeats alike—often against each other—praise for an effort that was beyond the mere translation of words, and sought to convey the gripping saga of the most swirling of human storms: war.

To my publisher, to all who share in this task, the undying expression of my deepest indebtedness for their having enabled me to make my voice heard by the English-speaking world at large, and especially by the United States of America, to which we appealed our righteous cause in the South Atlantic as our lookout was sounding the historical cry: "The British are coming . . . !"

THE HISTORY
OF THE
SOUTH ATLANTIC
CONFLICT

1

The Seeds of War

... those wretched islands, the scene of struggle and mayhem, and seed for heated argument among our Nations....
Robert Fitzroy, March 1, 1833.

The British occupation of 1833 was at the time an act of unjustifiable aggression....
Official memorandum, British Foreign Office, September 17, 1946.

HASTENING DECISION

On March 26, 1982, at 1915 hours, the Military Committee, supreme joint decision-making body for the conduct of military strategy, held one of its regular meetings in the Libertador Building, army command headquarters. The three members of the ruling military junta, the foreign minister, and the chief of the Joint Staff were there, along with other officials.

General Leopoldo Fortunato Galtieri, Admiral Jorge Isaac Anaya, and General Basilio Arturo Ignacio Lami Dozo—commanders in chief of the army, navy, and air force—their faces betraying no clue as to the extraordinary business at hand, entered the conference room. The agenda for that day included an option that had been kept under tight wraps for about three months: the possible use of military force as a means of bringing about a change in the course of the ongoing talks with Great Britain dealing with the issue of sovereignty over the South Atlantic island groups known as the Falkland/Malvinas, the South Georgia, and the South Sandwich islands. In the course of this meeting, the Military Committee mulled over the events on South Georgia, where, it seemed, an Argentine work crew had raised their national flag at Port Leith (San Pedro Island/South Georgia), thereby triggering an overreaction by Great Britain, which may well have grasped this opportunity as an excuse for increasing its naval presence in the area.

This assumption was supported by the announcement that the British nuclear submarine HMS *Superb* and the polar vessel *Endurance*, carrying marines taken on board at Port Stanley (shortly to become Puerto Argentino), capital of the Falklands, had been developed to retake the Grytviken garrison (South Georgia Island), events that were widely reported by the British press and brought a prompt reaction from Parliament. Noteworthy at this point is the fact that the diplomatic talks held under the auspices of pertinent U.N. resolutions since 1965 were at a complete stalemate.

The military junta considered their options: pursue negotiations, bring charges before the Security Council, or take the islands by force. The first would in no way preclude an increase in the British naval presence in the area, nor would it constitute any guarantee for the least of Argentina's aspirations. Prospects for the second were regarded as dismal, since it appeared unlikely that the Security Council would convene to consider an alleged threat of this sort. The third, in the junta's thinking, would be the most likely to force the British back to the negotiating table while giving Argentina the upper hand. It had the added advantage of preempting the islands' fortification by the British.

The goal pursued was in no way aimed at cutting off the talks or triggering a battlefield confrontation with a world power; rather, it sought to encourage the United Kingdom to return to the negotiating table with a more serious-minded approach to Argentina's claim to the disputed territories. There was no set target date for carrying out the plan that was beginning to take shape, nor was such a plan envisioned in any standing staff study on national war hypotheses. It had further been determined that should the implementation of such a plan prove necessary, the earliest date by which the armed forces could be fully prepared to stage such an operation would be May 15, provided they had a fortnight's minimum advance notice.

But in view of the events on South Georgia, the military junta was faced with an option as critical as it was flawed: either the date for retaking the Malvinas had to be moved up in order to head off the arrival of the British vessels, or all hope of achieving any change in the course of negotiations had to be abandoned for a long time to come. In so doing, they let a third option slip by. Minimizing the importance of the issue in order to avoid an adverse reaction would, in all probability, have been the wiser course of action.

The junta decided—for reasons both political and military—that the operation should be carried out no later than early April in order to gain the all-important ingredient for success: surprise. This required no less than absolute secrecy right up to H-hour and, in order to lessen probable enemy response, it had to be completely bloodless.

While the state of readiness of Argentina's armed forces could be deemed less than ideal at that time, with the possible exception of its air force, the operation was carried out flawlessly on April 2, 1982. But the British government's reaction, which had been badly misjudged, came to play a crucial role, far afield from the hopes and forecasts of Argentina's political leadership. London's established political objective was to maintain control and administration of its colonial possessions, and its strategic resolve was to wrest the islands back from Argentina's bloodless takeover by the most violent of military means.

Decisions were beginning to take shape within the leadership on both sides, but whether there was a clear understanding of such decisions remained to be seen.

GREAT EXPECTATIONS, SCANT RESULTS

The seeds of the dispute that has pitted Argentine and Briton against one another were sown as far back as 1833, when British troops—by force of arms—took the islands and expelled the Argentine settlers and their leaders. There had been, for all intents and purposes, from that time until 1965 no negotiations to speak of between the two countries regarding the status of the Malvinas, in spite of Buenos Aires's regular entreaties. Such claims were given short shrift by the British Foreign Office, which continued to turn a deaf ear.

With the founding of the United Nations in 1945, a worldwide decolonization process was initiated that brought about a change in the status of the archipelago. The United Kingdom, which, along with Argentina, is a signatory of the U.N. Charter, in 1946 submitted to that group, at its request, a list of 43 territories that it pledged to decolonize. The Malvinas Islands were on that list. In 1960, the United Nations adopted Resolution 1514 (XV), which established guidelines for granting independence to those countries and peoples who remained under colonial rule. Two basic principles were set forth: the right of all peoples to free self-determination, and any attempt to break up the territorial unity of any state was inconsistent with the principles of the U.N. Charter. It can be inferred, therefore, that the right to self-determination may serve as an instrument for dismembering a territory, which flies in the face of the very principles for which the United Nations stands.

In 1964, the Argentine government decided to take part in the debates of the U.N. Special Commission on Decolonization, with the stated purpose of setting forth its sovereign rights over the Malvinas, South Georgia, and South Sandwich islands. The opposition of the United Kingdom notwithstanding, the Special Commission on Decolonization acknowledged, in essence, the validity of Argentina's claims. The following year, Argentina achieved another victory with the adoption of U.N. Resolution 2065 (XX), which by an overwhelming majority acknowledged that the islands should come under the provisions of Resolution 1514. It followed that Great Britain should be bound to decolonize the archipelago even if the islands' small population desired to remain under British rule. Moreover, the General Assembly established, in precise terms, that the dispute concerned sovereignty over these territories, and invited the parties to follow through on negotiations without delay, taking into account the provisions of the U.N.

Charter and of Resolution 1514, as well as the interests of the inhabitants. Great Britain stopped short of voting against the resolution by abstaining.

In 1966, British Foreign Secretary Michael Stewart traveled to Buenos Aires to open talks. By 1968, both parties had reached an agreement in principle. Great Britain would recognize Argentina as sovereign and would turn the administration of the islands over within not less than four, nor more than ten, years. Publicity over this agreement in the British press and parliamentary infighting were, by and large, responsible for the failure of this proposal. As a portent of things to come, H. S. Ferns, professor of political science at the University of Birmingham, wrote at the time: "As events are shaping out, however, it is impossible to foresee a situation in which Argentina will force the solution, as it can, . . . and thus do something the Argentine Government has no wish to do, i.e. to humiliate Britain. If this happens the British will have no one to blame but themselves" (*Argentina*, p. 260).

The British Conservative Party assumed power from the Labourites in 1970. From that time on, London turned a deaf ear to the U.N. resolutions—which had been unanimously in favor of Argentina's position in 1966, 1967, and 1969— and there ensued a five-year de facto stalemate in negotiations. In July 1971, a communications agreement was signed. This document, known as the Buenos Aires Joint Declaration, was the first positive result of the talks. Argentina agreed to establish air and maritime communications, make health and educational facilities available to the islanders, grant technical and logistical assistance, and be a supplier—at discount prices—of liquid fuels and bottled gas. It further agreed to build an airstrip near Port Stanley and to establish postal, telephone, and telegraph service.

In 1973, the U.N. General Assembly again expressed its concern over the lack of progress in the sovereignty talks due to Britain's unyielding stance, and so stated through Resolution 3160 (XXVIII). While recognizing the Argentine government's efforts to promote the welfare of the islanders, it again skirted the possibility of applying the principle of self-determination. In the face of all this, the United Kingdom held fast to its position.

Meanwhile, in 1974, the Organization of American States (OAS) stated, through the Inter-American Juridical Committee, its concern over the fact that in spite of repeated claims filed by Latin American nations for redress, there remained within the confines of the Americas areas that were still under foreign rule. The same committee declared in 1976 that Argentina had justifiable claim to sovereignty over the Malvinas Islands, thereby reducing the basic issue to that of establishing the procedure for the territory to change hands. That same year the OAS General Assembly echoed this sentiment, adding that the presence in American waters of British warships, as well as the United Kingdom's veiled threat to send more, constituted a threat to the peace and security of the Western Hemisphere. In 1975 and 1976, the conferences of the foreign ministers of the nonaligned countries, meeting in Lima and in Colombo, respectively, sided with Argentina.

About this time the British research vessel *Shackleton* was in waters adjacent to the Falklands, ostensibly prospecting for natural resources. In the absence of any Argentine government permission for such activities, there was an incident involving the British vessel and the Argentine Navy destroyer ARA *Almirante Storni*. This brought about the withdrawal of both nations' ambassadors, and the talks were cut off. The *Shackleton* report concluded that exploitation of the area's resources would be neither rational nor economically feasible without the cooperation and goodwill of the Argentine government.

The lobby for the Falkland Islands Company (FIC)* in Parliament played up the economic potential of the area in order to bring about a hardening of the British position, despite the fact that Great Britain was attempting to gain Argentina's cooperation for the future development of natural resources. The FIC, fearful of any accommodation with Argentina, orchestrated a movement aimed at discrediting Buenos Aires's efforts to gain the goodwill of the Kelpers. Its goal was to seek independence for the area, under a British protectorate, by means of the principle of free self-determination. The role played by British attorney Bill Hunter Christie, who acted as spokesman before Parliament for the interests of both the FIC and the more radical faction of the Kelpers (through an entity known as the Falkland Islands Commission), was noteworthy in this respect.

These activities, which ran counter to the current of thinking at the Foreign Office, the sense of which was to seek accommodation with Argentina, successfully brought about the reform of the islands' Legislative Council, giving way to broader Kelper representation within this body that shared in the decision making by the government at Port Stanley. Great Britain in turn sought to link any talks on the future of the territory to the wishes of the islanders, as a nonnegotiable demand, which would effectively sound the death knell for any attempt at transferring sovereignty to Argentina. The fact of the matter is that the inhabitants were never consulted through any referendum or other such public airing of the issue, decisions having been confined to a small minority handpicked by the FIC, thus serving the interests of the colonial company ahead of those of the community they represented, and even more so those of the Crown.

While all this was going on, Argentina had patiently built the airport, established air service, and created other facilities that had gained it friendship and support among the Kelpers. In 1976, Argentina established a scientific station on Thule Island, in the South Sandwich group, which was the only populated base on that desolate outpost. British reaction to this was practically nil.

In 1977, British Foreign Secretary David Owen (a Labourite) submitted a written report to the House of Commons stating that both governments had

---

*FIC enjoys a monopoly over trade with the islands, which is mostly in sheep's wool, the only significant export. Mrs. Thatcher's husband sits on the FIC board of directors and has reaped fat profits from its operations.

agreed to conduct talks on the political future—to include the issue of sovereignty—of the Falkland, Georgia, and South Sandwich islands. Cooperation in the economic development of those territories and the Southwest Atlantic was also on the agenda, but the dilatory tactics went on. Using alleged Argentine maneuvers as an excuse, Great Britain deployed a nuclear submarine and two frigates to the South Atlantic in secrecy. They remained on station in the vicinity of the islands.

By 1979, both countries had agreed to a new exchange of ambassadors, which was carried out in 1980. In May 1979, the Conservative Party, under the leadership of Margaret Thatcher, assumed power from the Labourites. In June, the new under secretary for the Foreign Office, Nicholas Ridley, paid a visit to Port Stanley. Stopping over in Buenos Aires, he met with Argentina's deputy foreign minister, Commodore Carlos Cavandoli. Both parties stated their interest in improving bilateral relations and breathing new life into the negotiations.

Ridley and Cavandoli met several times that year and raised the interesting possibility, following their talks, of solving the issue by entering into a lease and joint stewardship arrangement. Sovereignty over the islands and adjoining waters would be transferred to Argentina at the signing of the agreement. In order to ensure the Kelpers' way of life, a shared administration under both flags would be agreed to, for a term of 99 years—as proposed by Ridley—or three generations—as suggested by the Argentine deputy foreign minister. The current inhabitants would continue to be British, their children would enjoy dual citizenship, and the third generation would be Argentine citizens. Buenos Aires pledged to ensure and guarantee the well-being of the Kelpers.

During the U.N. General Assembly session held in September 1979, Argentine Foreign Minister Carlos W. Pastor met in New York with his British counterpart, Lord Carrington. He informed the latter of the urgency of the Malvinas problem for Buenos Aires. Carrington, for whom the Falklands issue was far down on his list of priorities, was quite shaken.

In November 1980, Ridley paid a second visit to the islands. In Buenos Aires, he personally assured Cavandoli that he favored the lease option but that the prime minister did not share his views. In spite of this, he had received Cabinet go-ahead to submit a basic plan for a leasing arrangement for the islanders' approval. In Port Stanley, the Kelpers were presented with three options; joint stewardship; transfer and lease for a period of time to be agreed upon; and freezing of the status quo for an indefinite period. These proposals were given the cold shoulder, much to Ridley's consternation. Yet the younger people, and most of those living in Port Stanley, seemed to acknowledge the need for long-term stability in relations with Argentina.

It was felt that between a third and half of the Kelper population would be amenable to some form of lease arrangement; but as the Legislative Council hard-liners consolidated their position, negotiations were stonewalled in favor of freezing the status quo. According to British historian Peter Beck, Ridley's negotiations and proposals signaled a turning point in the dispute, since the

British government had, for the first time, publicly acknowledged its wish to consider transferring sovereignty to Argentina (Del Carril, *El Futuro de las Malvinas*, p. 42). Those behind the failure of these proposals are responsible for erecting the greatest single obstacle that pushed the Buenos Aires government over the brink and laid the groundwork for the military option that would lead to an avoidable, painful war.

On his return from Port Stanley, the British diplomat reported somewhat ambiguously to Colonel Cavandoli that he was not yet in a position to confirm the results of his trip, and that the solution to the problem required both time and forbearance. When Ridley submitted his proposals to Parliament, he was met with a wave of invective, the likes of which, the London press reported, had not been heard in years in the House of Commons. The Falklands lobby had struck again.

In February 1981, a new round of talks was held in New York. This meeting was distinguished by the fact that the British Delegation included Kelpers, who thus became de facto negotiators. Ridley explained that the islanders were seeking a ten-year freeze of the status quo. This was rejected by the Argentine delegation, which contended that the first issue to be resolved must be the return of the islands to Argentine sovereignty, followed by which British demands could be taken up. Obviously, the political clock was winding down.

At the close of 1981, there was a change of government in Buenos Aires, and Dr. Oscar Camilion was named foreign minister. He called for a speedup of the process, pointing out that "this colonial situation is as outdated as it is unacceptable for the dignity of Argentina." Nicholas Ridley left the Foreign Office in September of that year. From then on, no one on the British side did anything to head off the fast-approaching events.

London gave no priority to the Falklands issue. Years of efforts had brought about nothing but a standoff. Buenos Aires, on the other hand, went out of its way to demonstrate its goodwill. In August 1981, it had airlifted supplies to the islands in the face of an emergency shortage. In mid-December, both houses of Parliament voted, at the insistence of the Island Council, to increase British naval presence in the area, under the guise of protecting the Antarctic approaches to the archipelago. In the course of these debates, pushed by small pressure groups with vested interests, the decision to decommission the polar vessel HMS *Endurance* at Port Stanley, as a part of a scheduled Royal Navy surface fleet reduction that affected the British Antarctic Survey, came under fire.

Shortly before Christmas 1981, General Galtieri was sworn in as the new president of Argentina. His new foreign minister, Dr. Nicanor Costa Mendez, sought to renew the talks, but his efforts were doomed to failure. At the same time, the government decided to seek alternative means to induce the British to resume serious negotiations without, however, discarding the military option should all others fail. The first seeds of such an option saw light during a meeting of the military junta held on January 5, 1982.

The Junta met again a week later, and a working committee was established to initiate the planning phase of the military option, the premise being that the eventual use of military force should be the subject of an analysis, in view of the lack of any improvement on the diplomatic front. The working committee consisted of three senior officers: Army Major General Osvaldo Jorge Garcia, Navy Vice-Admiral Juan Jose Lombardo, and Air Force Major General Sigfrido Martin Plessl. Its work was cloaked in utmost secrecy.

The last talks to be held between the two nations' delegations took place at New York in February 1982 and proved fruitless. On March 2, 1982, in closing out the round of talks, Foreign Minister Costa Mendez made known the position of the Argentine government through a communiqué that stated:

For over 15 years, Argentina has negotiated with Great Britain with forbearance, loyalty, and in good faith, within the spirit of the pertinent U.N. Resolutions, in search of a solution to the sovereignty dispute over these Islands. The new system represents a step forward for a prompt solution of this dispute. Furthermore, should it be otherwise, Argentina reserves the right to put an end to this process and freely elect whatever path may serve her interests.

The closing line of the communiqué served warning on the British government.

THE INCREDIBLE DAVIDOFF EXPEDITION

Every war has its trigger—the spark that sets off the fuse, sometimes with malice aforethought, at other times random. And so it was in the South Atlantic conflict, in the person of one Constantino Davidoff, an Argentine businessman. To seek the circumstances that set off our fuse, we turn the clock back to 1976, when Mr. Davidoff was salvaging undersea cables. At the time, a foreman hired for the job remarked to Mr. Davidoff that upon visiting South Georgia Island, he had spotted a large number of abandoned metal implements that could turn a sweet profit, considering Argentina's relatively favorable location for obtaining them. Since scrap metal was not beyond the scope of Davidoff's activities, he sounded out the British embassy in Buenos Aires, which proved reluctant to deal with him. His persistence led him in 1978, to the governor of the Falkland Islands, through whose good offices he eventually succeeded in cutting a deal with the Edinburgh firm of Salvensen Ltd., proprietor of the facilities to be dismantled.

Davidoff signed an agreement whereby the firm transferred ownership of "all equipment and installations pertaining to the leasing of our abandoned whaling stations." The agreement was dated September 19, 1979. The contract was duly notarized following a cash payment of £10,000, along with an option for the extraction of available metals, for a total payment of £105,000. This contract had an expiration date of March 31, 1983. Salvensen informed the authorities at Grytviken of the existence of the contract in October 1980.

Following this, Davidoff set up the corporation South Georgia Islands, S. A.

in 1980. He then sought to lease the *Endurance*, but was turned down by the British authorities. In August 1981 he was called upon by the Foreign Ministry in Buenos Aires to explain the nature of his contacts with the British. Their curiosity satisfied, the Argentine officials—who had been apprised of Davidoff's activities since Dr. Camilion's tenure—decided to support his efforts through the Naval Transport Service, a state-owned shipping concern, which had occasion to sail in the South Atlantic. The South Georgia Islands Company's basic needs were to carry out a survey; to land personnel and equipment necessary to dismantle the abandoned whaling station; and to ship the scrap back to the mainland. The Argentine Navy, acting in coordination with the Foreign Ministry, decided to support the Davidoff operation and, to this effect, provided passage for Davidoff and six other persons aboard the icebreaker *Almirante Irizar*, which docked at San Pedro Island on December 20, 1981, on its way to Argentina's Antarctic bases. The Davidoff party remained ashore for six hours to survey the area.

Meanwhile, the military junta's evaluation of the situation in early January was that the negotiation process with Great Britain should be maintained, whatever the cost. The South Georgia Islands Company was informed by the Naval Transport Service, after a long delay, that all personnel and paperwork had to be cleared with the British embassy and ready for boarding on March 11. Formalities were completed on March 9, and on March 11, complement of 41 employees of the Argentine firm sailed on the *Bahia Buen Suceso*. Of them, 39 remained on South Georgia to carry out their operations. Advice of the Argentine vessel's sailing, with an estimated date of arrival of March 28, was radioed to Port Stanley, and from there to Grytviken, which received the message on March 12. The *Buen Suceso* sighted the desolate South Georgia coast on March 17, sounded the harbors at Stromness Bay the next day, and anchored at Port Leith on March 19. It did not put in at Grytviken (20 kilometers to the south) because the whaling station to be dismantled by the Davidoff crew was located at Stromness Bay. The only populated spot on South Georgia was King Edward Point, near Grytviken and, according to British authorities, the obligatory point of entry. Since this territory was in dispute, the Argentine vessel flew no flag and did not land within sight of British authorities at King Edward Point.

Once the ship's company and the work party had landed, they improvised a mast, ran up the Argentine national flag, and, in a spontaneous and simple gesture, sang the Argentine national anthem. At Port Leith, a three-member team from the British Antarctic Survey had monitored the arrival of the ship and, within two or three hours of its dropping anchor, had presented its captain with a verbal invitation to lower the flag, not alter signals, load the material already deposited on the dock, and steam toward Grytviken in order to fulfill the normal formalities required there, the island's port of entry. The captain, who had carried out a risky and difficult maneuver to dock the ship in a location where heavy loads had already been stockpiled, felt that these requirements exceeded the bounds of his authority, and informed the British party that he would consult Buenos Aires on the matter.

While this was going on, the flag had been lowered from its staff and could in no way be considered an obstacle of any sort. The British Antarctic Survey party left the ship and made camp for the night. According to British sources (Heathland, *The Island of South Georgia*, p. 244), this party had left King Edward Point on the previous day and had come upon the *Buen Suceso* by chance, a circumstance just short of unbelievable if one considers that the survey had received advance notification of the ship's arrival.

Communications that weekend were garbled, and it was impossible to establish contact between the vessel and the Buenos Aires office. Therefore, the following morning, the captain informed the survey party, that his orders were to land at Stromness Bay and that, in view of this, he would not put in at Grytviken. The British again presented their request, this time in writing; declined to reboard the vessel; and withdrew from the area.

A short time later, news was flashed from King Edward Point to Port Stanley, and on to London, that a party of Argentine civilians and military personnel had invaded South Georgia Island. In London, the sensation-seeking tabloids scrambled to reap a bumper harvest sown by the seeds of the imagination. To an objective observer, the British reaction was totally unforeseen.

In view of the facts stated here, it can be deduced that both governments sought to turn to their political advantage a venture, in this case Operation Davidoff, that had originally been conceived as a private business dealing.

1. Argentina tried to gain leverage by using the Davidoff party to establish precedents that would allow it to formalize acts, whether for the long or the medium term, of physical presence on the islands. Since the idea of regaining the Malvinas was already in the works, one operation should not have dovetailed with the other. The end result was to render the master plan a slave to the incidental, the events on South Georgia, as it precipitated the moving up of D-Day in the Falklands.

2. Great Britain showed its colors in two ways. First, the Foreign Office gave the appearance, in a measured reaction, of having been willing to talk. Second, a group of vested interests headed by persons within the Royal Navy, the FIC, and the British Antarctic Survey, well aware of what would happen on South Georgia, orchestrated a scenario, blew the incident out of proportion in Parliament, and influenced the British media in order to trigger a domestic public outcry that was completely incommensurate with the true scope of the issue. Not the least of these was Rex Hunt, governor of the islands, who aligned himself with this pressure group, thus placing his own interest ahead of that of the Crown.

The South Georgia incident had the following immediate consequences:

1. Argentina was put at a disadvantage, for the South Georgias were not the main objective, and it found itself forced to act on the spur of the moment.

2. The British gained the advantage, since these events were blown up into an incident that played to the advantage of their political designs, even though the war that soon

came surpassed all expectations, as much in its scope as in its toll in material and human lives.

A South Atlantic replay of Pearl Harbor had taken place. If someone had planned it thus, it could not have been better carried out. Nevertheless, the consequences of acts of war can get away from those who set them up.

REACTION VERSUS REACTION

London's response was not long in coming. On March 20, a protest note was received expressing much surprise that Argentina would allow an act of "such gravity" at such a "critical" juncture of the negotiations, and that the Foreign Office deemed such actions "most serious." London's grievance centered on the landing of "civilian and military personnel" at Port Leith, their having raised the Argentine flag and tampered with British signal markers, their not having gone through immigration formalities at Grytviken, and the discharge of firearms. To complete the picture, British Ambassador Williams, in Buenos Aires, delivered a message from the Foreign Office to the Argentine Foreign Ministry stating that all personnel who had landed on South Georgia must leave immediately or the British government would take whatever action it deemed necessary. It further expressed the "wish" for a prompt response.

Argentina's response was immediate and was issued in a calm tone, in keeping with reality and the circumstances at hand. It stated the following:

1. That the *Bahia Buen Suceso* was a vessel well known to British authorities, and that it would sail from Leith the following day, as soon as its cargo had been unloaded.

2. That transport was being effected by the aforesaid vessel in the absence of other means.

3. That no military personnel were on board, and therefore no military personnel had landed on South Georgia, and that no weapons of war were possessed by the crew or passengers.

4. That the configuration of the receiving dock was such that existing equipment had to be moved about on it.

5. That Mr. Davidoff's contract was well known by British authorities, who had granted their permission.

6. That the events on South Georgia were of no significance or importance, so there was no reason for them to have any effect on negotiations.

Ambassador Williams insisted that the ship should put in at Grytviken. At this point he was made aware that the United Kingdom should be mindful of the fact that it had acknowledged that this was disputed territory that Argentina regarded as its own. Williams promised his cooperation. On March 21, Mr. Fearn of the Foreign Office informed the Argentine chargé d'affaires in London, Mr. Molteni, that his government was satisfied with the explanations received, that he was confident that the *Bahia Buen Suceso* would depart the islands on March 22, and that he hoped there would be no recurrence of such action.

But almost at the same time, the offices of LADE (the state-owned airline that operates between the mainland and the islands) in Port Stanley were defaced by locals who scrawled on a British flag draped over an Argentine flag, "Tit for Tat, Buggers." Aside from the sheer gall and narrow-mindedness of these scoundrels, such behavior toward a company that for years had spared no effort to alleviate the problems inherent to the isolation of the islanders while asking nothing in return except, perhaps, a little better understanding and joint sense of purpose from those benefiting from such services, was a source of deep hurt to Argentina.

Also on March 21, on a scant two hours' notice, 22 British Marines posted at Port Stanley boarded the *Endurance*, which sailed for Port Leith to enforce Britain's demands on Argentina. This was on orders from Governor Hunt, who acted without consulting the Foreign Office. The next day, Buenos Aires instructed its chargé d'affaires in London to file a complaint regarding the incident at the Port Stanley LADE office. Mr. Fearn's response was conciliatory in tone, concluding that, with the departure of the *Buen Suceso* and the work crew, his government considered the issue closed. Mr. Molteni in turn informed Mr. Fearn that, while he had certain knowledge of the *Buen Suceso*'s departure, he was unable to confirm that the work crew was in fact on board. Fearn then concluded that he could no longer keep these events from the press.

The Foreign Office issued a communiqué on March 22, reporting the undocumented landing of a work party at Port Leith, and that the Argentine government had given its assurances that they had left the previous day—there being, however, no confirmation of the latter. That evening, Londoners read the big "scoop" in *The Standard*, which reported an Argentine invasion of the South Georgia Islands and quoted the Foreign Office release, while omitting the incident at the Port Stanley LADE office and the fact that the *Bahia Buen Suceso* had left South Georgia Island. A later Argentine release underscored this fact, adding that the ship had sailed from Port Leith, leaving ashore a work party in accordance with the provisions of a private business contract signed by a private firm.

On March 23, the London morning papers bannered the story and made much of two events: (1) there appeared to be a consensus that the incident was "premeditated by Argentina" and therefore an act of aggression; (2) not a single mention was made of the incident at the Port Stanley LADE office. British television echoed the news in much the same terms. There remains, then, the question of how all these independent media were able to draw identical conclusions while making the same omissions. What is more, no voice of restraint was raised among responsible British news circles stating that, after all, what it boiled down to was a small group of laborers who had raised a flag on a remote, deserted beach on a disputed piece of territory; that they had been landed there rather than at the normal port of entry because of this dispute; and that the

Almirante Irizar had done likewise in December without giving rise to the beating of breasts and cries of ''outrageous aggression.''

It can be assumed that the press may react spontaneously to a given event; but governmental and parliamentary circles should temper the flow of information to stay in tune with the facts. No such thing happened in Parliament. What was heard was angry voices crying out against the ''invasion of sovereign British territory,'' demands for explanations, affirmations of the need for keeping the *Endurance* on patrol in the area, and support for the ''self-determination'' of the islanders. Conservative M.P. John Stokes was particularly shrill in his statements, the clear intent of which was to overplay the incident; he affirmed, for reasons clear only to himself, that the ''landing of a group of Argentines has the gravest of implications, even if they already had left the islands by that time.'' Naturally, the anger zeroed in on the Foreign Office and Lord Carrington, who was obliged to go before the Parliament with an explanation.

In the meantime, in Buenos Aires, Ambassador Williams was delivering a note to the Foreign Ministry informing Argentina that the HMS *Endurance* would be anchoring at Leith on March 24 to remove the Argentine laborers and that the ''cooperation'' of the authorities was expected.

On March 23, the Argentine Foreign Ministry stated that the South Georgia Island Company was operating under a private contract, that Mr. Davidoff had made a similar journey in 1981 without incident, and that British authorities had been duly apprised thereof and had granted their permission. At 1800 hours, London time, Mr. Molteni was called to the Foreign Office, where Minister Fearn outlined to him the serious turn of events since, in spite of his best efforts, the press had blown the issue out of proportion, which in turn brought about the need for the *Endurance* to evacuate the work crew. Mr. Molteni stated that he was aware of the reaction in Parliament because he had been present in the House of Commons; that the British government was misreading the status of the workmen, who were on South Georgia legally; and that if the *Endurance* were to proceed with the proposed evacuation, the reaction in Argentina might trigger unforeseeable consequences. Following consultation with their respective foreign ministries, each legation received instructions to avoid widening the breach.

Meanwhile, the *Endurance* was approaching South Georgia Island with orders to evacuate the Argentine contingent. But as the ship hove in sight of land, and a result of Lord Carrington's orders to avoid the use of force, it was directed to make for Grytviken and anchor there. As the ship passed eight miles off the coast, a helicopter left the polar vessel in order to reconnoiter the Argentine encampment and survey its activities. Note was taken of the lack of anything special on the ground, as well as of the removal of the flag.

At the same time, in the face of increasing pressure being brought upon the British government, as much from policymakers as from the media, London requested Buenos Aires to order the return of the *Buen Suceso* to Port Leith to pick up the work crew. Obviously, the Foreign Office was making clever use of the problem created by the sensationalistic press. It exploited the turmoil stirred up in the House of Commons by the incident in order to press its demands on Argentina.

THE HOUR OF DECISION

At 0930 hours on March 23, the military junta held a meeting at navy head-quarters to ponder the news from South Georgia. This problem had become a full-blown controversy because such a turn of events complicated previously established plans and called for charting a change in the course of anticipated action.

The junta decided against the option proposed by Lord Carrington. They should protect the Argentine workers and deploy the ARA *Bahia Paraiso* to Port Leith for this purpose, since this vessel was currently assigned to the antarctic expedition then off the South Orkneys (relatively close by, if one takes the distances involved into account). As for the Malvinas, plans for all contingencies were ordered activated, including the South Georgia Islands option—something that until that time had not been envisioned. The overall operation to occupy the islands given the code name Azul (blue).

Great Britain's attitude and intentions also took the South Georgia incident into account, since London's obvious exaggeration of it, as well as the possible underlying motives, had been a source of great alarm to the military junta. Two especially preoccupying motives stood out: the intent not to negotiate the future of the islands, and the plan to maintain a strong naval presence in the area. Cable traffic from London concerning the news of March 23 was not encouraging: The *Daily Telegraph* trumpeted on page 1, "Ships sail to expel intruders"; *The Guardian*, "Great Britain sends Royal Navy"; others reported that the *Endurance* was on its way to eject the workers. The House of Lords took up the issue for the first time on the night of March 23. Its debate was overall more balanced and devoid of sensationalist innuendo, but the weight given the issue was mainly due to the presence of former Prime Minister Callaghan and the other opposition leader, Mr. Healy, during the debates.

In Buenos Aires, Dr. Costa Mendez had informed Ambassador Williams that the Argentine work crew would not be removed from Port Leith and that their expulsion by force would not be permitted.

Talks continued on March 24 and 25 while the British press continued to label the incident an "invasion." News from Parliament continued to be a rising source of concern for Buenos Aires. In the House of Commons, the secretary of state for defense made it known that the Royal Navy—and not just the *Endurance*—would ensure the future of the islands and even suggested the possibility of forming a SATO (South Atlantic Treaty Organization) in view of the "strategic importance" of the area. A motion submitted to the House of Commons began to gather an alarming number of backers. This motion called

on the government to declare in no uncertain terms that sovereignty over the
Falkland Islands would never be handed over to any foreign government without
the express consent of the islanders, and that sufficient naval forces must be
maintained in the area to repel any attempt by the Argentine government to
annex this British colony.

On March 25, the South Georgia Island Company presented a note to the
British ambassador in Buenos Aires outlining, once again, the origin of its
contract and the legitimacy of its actions. In London, Commodore Frow, resident
commissioner of the Falkland Islands, was calling for the militarization of the
islands. Parliament was shaping its "hard ball" policy in the face of Argentina's
claims while it scored the Foreign Office for its "soft" approach. Confirmation
had been received from Montevideo the previous day of the sailing of the *John
Biscoe* with a contingent of Royal Marines for the Falklands military garrison,
and it was reported that the *Bransfield* was steaming toward Port Stanley from
Punta Arenas.

It became obvious that the Argentine leadership was facing the following
defining factors:

1. Great Britain's arbitrary and overblown handling of the South Georgia incident

2. Britain's obvious intention to reinforce its military presence in the South Atlantic, as
   well as its beleaguered stance, through the deployment of the *Biscoe*, the *Bransfield*,
   and a nuclear submarine to the area

3. The intention of indefinitely freezing any talks regarding sovereignty over the islands,
   and granting priority to the islanders' wish for self-determination

4. The negative repercussion in terms of domestic policy that these circumstances would
   bring for the deteriorating "National Reorganization Process," of which the leaders
   themselves were a part.

These were the circumstances that moved the junta to decide to occupy the
islands by force in early April. The date was set for the early hours of April 1,
with the possibility of moving the operation up to 1800 hours on March 31.
Underscored was the condition that the operation must be bloodless. Once reoc-
cupation had been achieved, the intent was to leave a reduced garrison on the
islands and then restart talks as quickly as feasible. For the period between March
26 and April 2, Foreign Minister Costa Mendez received instructions to do
nothing that would compromise the negotiations.

In London, the South Georgia dilemma was front-page fare for the Sunday
papers. The *Sunday Express*, boasting the largest readership, bannered "Argentina sends the Marines" and labeled the action as a deliberate challenge to British
sovereignty.

On March 28, Operation Azul shifted into phase three. General Mario Benjamin Menendez learned he would become the governor of the Malvinas Islands.
Naval vessels were weighing anchor at Puerto Belgrano to sail toward that long-

awaited objective—reclaiming Argentine sovereignty over territory that had been wrested away by force of arms over 149 years before.

On March 30, the military junta held two meetings. Gen. Osvaldo Jorge Garcia was appointed operation commander. His mission was to recapture the Malvinas by D-Day + 5, at which time the task force should complete its evacuation, leaving behind a new government with a reduced garrison for the purpose of maintaining security, law, and order.

Lord Carrington's message to the House of Lords, read concurrently by Mr. Luce to the House of Commons, boded ill for Buenos Aires's intent: "We have no doubt as to British sovereignty over the Falkland Islands and the dependency of the Georgias. We maintain that the unauthorized presence of Argentine nationals in the Georgias is unacceptable." The planned deployment of forces became the word of the day, and the media took up the cry, reporting the sailing of the nuclear submarine *Superb* along with another naval vessel of the same class, a tender, and the destroyer HMS *Exeter*, which steamed from Belize.

On the other side of the Atlantic, the *New York Times* picked up the story and ran it next to Lord Carrington's address to the House of Lords. The hardening of London's stance, as well as the seriousness of this turn of events, was becoming even more obvious.

In the midst of this situation, Lord Carrington, with the obvious intent of buying time for the arrival of the Royal Navy in the disputed area, proposed sending a negotiator to discuss the incident with the authorities in Buenos Aires. On April 1, the Argentine Foreign Ministry responded that it felt this action unnecessary, since the South Georgia incident did not carry sufficient weight, but that the sending of a representative would be acceptable if Great Britain would agree to further discussion of the problem of sovereignty. It was stated, moreover, that the deployment of warships to the area was unacceptable. At the same time, Argentina instructed its ambassador to the United Nations to deliver a note to the Security Council, in light of British reaction to the South Georgia incident. A few hours later that day, Britain denounced before the Security Council an imminent Argentine invasion of the Falkland Islands, and called an emergency session of that body.

The military junta met on April 1 to frame the position Argentina would present to the United States and the United Kingdom. It was resolved that the government would agree to negotiate on the basis of the explicit premise of the transfer of sovereignty over the three archipelagos to the Argentine Republic. At 2210 hours, four hours and ten minutes past the time deemed the point of no return for Operation Azul, President Galtieri received a telephone call from President Reagan, who made clear his deep concern about the use of force, advised against the risks being taken, and offered to send Vice-President Bush to help seek a solution. Argentina's chief of state couched his answer in words as courteous as they were unwavering. Argentina, he said, was a sovereign nation whose patience was at an end. Its rights had been acknowledged by international bodies, but Great Britain's obstinate refusal to negotiate sovereignty over the islands had induced his government to this extreme step.

A deadly determination emerged from the expression and tone of his words. The die was cast.

THE SOUTH ATLANTIC

The geopolitical space of the South Atlantic is far-reaching. It bathes sweeping coastal areas of three landmasses (South America, Africa, and Antarctica) and spans one of the largest stretches of water on Earth. The American side is shared by Brazil, Uruguay, and Argentina. The African coast, on the other hand, is a diverse, politically unstable region, consisting of 20 states of every ideological color. Outstanding among this group is South Africa, which, both for its economic and technological development and for its commanding strategic position astride the passage linking the South Atlantic and the Indian Oceans, dominates that area. The southern front, Antarctica, is politically neutral because of the Antarctic Treaty, which effectively internationalizes the whole continent as well as the surrounding waters south of the 60th parallel until 1991.

But geography serves only as the stage for the playing out of political events. In order for them to acquire geopolitical significance, they must be touched by human activity.

The most commonly exploited natural resource of the area is fishing. Trawlers flying the flags of the Soviet Union, Japan, and Poland, to name but a few, take around 4 million tons annually. Also high on the list of recoverable resources are algae, south of the 42nd parallel. Krill also are gaining increasing importance in a world ever in search of novel sources of food. As for hydrocarbons, there are proven reserves off the coasts of Brazil, Angola, Benin, and Ghana. Because of geological continuity, oil could lie under the Argentine continental shelf. As for mineral resources, precise evaluations do not go beyond potential estimates.

It is its sea-lanes that give the South Atlantic its strategic importance. This area contains the main shipping routes for crude oil around the Cape of Good Hope—30 percent of the oil consumed by Western Europe and over 25 percent of that imported by the United States must round the Cape of Good Hope en route from the Persian Gulf.

The two privileged areas of this region owe their strategic importance to the position of South Africa, which stands guard over the southern tip of Africa, and the Atlantic Narrows (defined by a straight line linking Natal, Brazil, and Dakar, Senegal). Of lesser weight is the Drake Passage (due to the light traffic through the area) linking the South Atlantic to the Pacific around Cape Horn. It can be assumed, however, that in the event of a worldwide conflict, in which the neutralization of the Panama Canal would be almost assured, control over these two vital sea-lanes would become crucial.

In this regard, the coastal states of the Southern Cone area of South America that border on the South Atlantic, as well as the neighboring islands and archipelagos, would play a major role as the location of operational bases for aircraft, ships, or submarines. It is in this respect that the Malvinas gain their significance for nations that lack support points in the Southern Cone area. The presence of the United Kingdom in the South Atlantic island chains implies territorial aspirations on Antarctica and, because of their geographic proximity, the potential for those islands' serving as bases to support its operations in the area. The two superpowers, located far from this area of the world, have sought to maintain a presence in the region. The Soviet Union has bases in Angola and Cuba. The United States operates out of ports or air bases in friendly countries and from Ascension Island, where, thanks to arrangements with Great Britain, it enjoys landing facilities.

In terms of belligerent action, the South Atlantic is far removed from historical flash points and has not, until recent times, been a theater for active warfare. Aside from those of privateers, the only clashes in the area have been between Britain and Germany, with the sinking of the German vessels *Scharnhorst* and *Gneisenau* in World War I, and of the *Graf Spee* in World War II.

But, if the Panama Canal were to be affected, the strategic importance of this area would undergo substantial change. This area comes under the provisions of the Inter-American Treaty for Reciprocal Assistance (IATRA), also known as the Rio Treaty, signed in 1947. It is the supreme hemispheric juridical instrument, and its purpose is the preservation of peace and security in the Americas. Its genesis is the Monroe Doctrine, laid before Congress by President James Monroe in 1823 as a means of dealing with threats to the American continent arising from the actions of the Holy Alliance and the aggressive activities of Russia, which had sent expeditions as far south on the west coast as San Francisco Bay. Monroe affirmed that the American republics should not be the target of colonial aims of any European nation, and that such action would be regarded by the United States as hostile to its interests.

The United States has put this doctrine into practice on two occasions: in 1895, when the U.S. secretary of state protested to Great Britain when it changed the border between Venezuela and what is now Guyana; and in 1898, when the United States declared war against Spain. In the first instance, Britain rejected Washington's protest, the issue was closed, and Venezuela had to accept the British dictate, which generated a still unresolved conflict. In the second instance, the dispute ended in Spanish withdrawal from Cuba and the ceding of Puerto Rico, Guam, and the Philippines to the United States.

World War II brought an awareness of the need to safeguard the hemisphere against all outside incursions. Riding on the crest of U.S. interests, the IATRA was signed at Rio de Janeiro on September 2, 1947. In view of its importance with regard to the South Atlantic conflict, some of its provisions, especially Article 3, are summarized below:

1. An attack by any state against any American state shall be considered an attack against all the American states.

2. At the request of the state that has been attacked, each country will determine the measures it will take in order to carry out the above provisions.

3. These provisions shall be applicable in the event of an armed attack within the area outlined by the treaty, or within the territory of any of its members. (The Malvinas, South Georgia, and South Sandwich islands are located within the area covered by the IATRA.)

4. Member states may adopt appropriate measures for their self-defense as long as the U.N. Security Council has not taken steps to preserve international peace and security.

This last point constitutes the weak link in its provisions, since IATRA is subject to the action of another body—the Security Council—whose effectiveness in solving problems is compromised by the interests of the five great powers, which have veto power and a permanent seat within that body. Under these circumstances, the only hemispheric country to have its rights guaranteed is the United States.

Article 8 lists measures suggested by the Organ of Consultation to be applied against the aggressor state: withdrawal of the chief of the diplomatic mission, breaking of diplomatic relations, breaking of consular relations, partial or total interruption of communications, and, finally, the use of armed force. The confrontation between Argentina and the United Kingdom put both the validity of the treaty and American solidarity to the test. They were found wanting north of the Rio Grande. The spirit, however, remains and continues to serve as a beacon for the nations of Latin America.

The Malvinas, outcroppings on the Argentine continental shelf, are surrounded by waters less than 100 fathoms deep, and lie about 400 nautical miles (NM) from Rio Gallegos, capital of Santa Cruz Province. The nearest landfall from the archipelago is Staten Island, 180 NM south (see Map 1). The area of the islands is about 4,500 square miles, slightly larger than Jamaica. The two main islands are Gran Malvina (West Falkland), which lies closer to the mainland, and Soledad (East Falkland), site of Port Stanley, scene of the main land engagements of the conflict. The two landmasses are separated by San Carlos Strait, which is about 62 miles long and 13 miles wide. The following harbors are noteworthy:

1. On Soledad (East Falkland), there is Port Louis, seat of the former French government of the islands, and Port Soledad, seat of the former Spanish government. Both are on Annunciation Bay. Port Groussac (Port William) is at the far east of Soledad, which also contains Stanley Bay and Port Stanley.

2. In San Carlos Strait, on the west coast of Soledad Island lie Port San Carlos and San Carlos Bay. To the west of the northern entrance to San Carlos Strait lie Borbon (Pebble) Island, one of the largest islands after the two main ones, and Sea Elephant Bay.

These islands have unique topography. The terrain, which is geologically similar to that of Patagonia, is largely made up of peat bogs that, due to their roughness and instability, as well as their dampness, are practically impassable. The winds, which blow strongly from the west, along with almost daily rains during the winter, make the local weather one of the worst enemies for anyone who is not properly acclimated, equipped, and trained to withstand its test. And for the air force, fall and winter are the worst seasons for operations, since conditions for offensive air operations are the most unfavorable: short daylight hours, low ceilings, low visibility, and frequent rain and fog.

It becomes obvious, when comparing the United Kingdom's military might with that of Argentina, that there is a great difference between the two. In the equation of power, only one factor was favorable to Argentina: its strategic location, which presented Britain with a tremendous challenge, for it had to stretch its supply lines to the very limit. The United States, by making available its facilities on Ascension Island, as well as myriad other supplies and materiel, enabled the British task force to carry out what otherwise might well have proved to be South Atlantic: Mission Impossible.

Great Britain had the capability to wage war, both conventional and nuclear, under the NATO alliance, with the Warsaw Pact countries. Argentina, on the other hand, had armed forces of far more modest proportions, and was limited to conventional warfare. Furthermore, it was hobbled by U.S.-imposed restrictions, thanks to the Humphrey-Kennedy amendment, in its efforts to resupply from the United States or to procure vital spare parts for weapons systems, especially for the air force. What is more, its land and naval combat experience dated back to the nineteenth century, and the air force had yet to be tested under fire. And, finally, Argentina's strategic planning had never envisioned the possibility of a war involving Great Britain as an adversary. The military junta's decision to occupy the South Atlantic islands entailed an overwhelming drawback: facing off with a world power without advance planning.

Great Britain is 8,000 NM (14,816 km) from the Falkland Islands and 4,225 NM (7,816 km) from Ascension Island. Its closest base to Port Stanley is at Gibraltar, 6,000 NM (11,100 km) away. The shortest distance between the Argentine mainland and the islands (400 NM) would prove to be the only advantage held by Argentine armed forces against those of a formidable adversary that enjoyed almost unrestricted materiel, logistical, and diplomatic support from the United States, and that of both NATO and the European Economic Community (EEC) insofar as economic and diplomatic measures were concerned.

On its side, Argentina had the diplomatic support of the OAS and the invocation of the IATRA, which, in the absence of any effective economic or military measures, was limited to the field of diplomacy. The Soviet Union, contrary to what the British would have had their allies believe, did nothing for Argentina in the way of facilities or intelligence, nor did it exercise its veto power when U.N. Security Council Resolution 502 was adopted.

Seldom has a nation gone to war under such unfavorable conditions, almost alone and completely bereft of third-party assistance. It was Argentina's great shortcoming, but also to its great credit. Argentina owes no debts to anyone, save in diplomatic terms to Latin America. And, in view of the final outcome, in the cold light of impartial analysis, had luck been just a bit less on the British side and a bit more on Argentina's, the fortunes of war might well have been different. While this is more than could reasonably be expected from a Southern Hemisphere nation, the final result of the conflict does not bear out the evaluation the balance of power would tend to indicate. The British are now well aware of this, and it is only their effective propaganda that made a victory of what in fact was, from a historical viewpoint, a political-military folly.

ARGENTINE WINGS OVER THE SOUTHERN ISLANDS

In 1970, both governments opened talks and laid the groundwork for the establishment of communications between the Argentine mainland and the Malvinas. The proximity of the mainland would permit more frequent service, less conditioned by distance, and relieve the isolation in which the islanders lived. The Kelpers were entirely dependent on the infrequent visits of the steamship *Darwin*, out of Montevideo, for which reservations had to be made almost a year in advance. Thus was born the idea of establishing air service by means of Argentine Air Force Albatross hydroplanes—the only practical means of linking Port Stanley by air, since there was no landing strip there, and this craft could land and take off within the confines of the bay. On February 13, 1971, the first Albatross made the flight, in order to evacuate a seriously ill patient. A curious crowd of Kelpers lined up along Ross Road, just west of Port Stanley, to watch the successful landing of the amphibious aircraft. Shortly thereafter, the plane lifted off from the bay, the patient safely on board, and winged its way toward the mainland without further ado.

The benefits to be gained from the establishment of direct air service with Argentina, due to the losses incurred by operating the *Darwin*, were not lost on the British government, which promptly opened talks with Argentina. They culminated in the Joint Buenos Aires Declaration of July 1, 1971. Two day after the agreement was signed, shuttle service was inaugurated with the first of what would prove to be regular commercial flights operated by LADE, thus ending the centuries-long isolation of the island population.

For the first time, mail delivery could be assured in a matter of days rather than months. Fresh fruits and vegetables were flown in from the mainland for the first time. The agreement provided for weekly passengers air service, and bimonthly or quarterly surface transport through the ELMA shipping company was established. In addition, tourist facilities were made available, temporary travel documents were issued, medical assistance was provided, Argentine teachers went to Port Stanley, scholarships were granted to students from the archipelago in Argentina, and exemption from taxes and compulsory military service was assured, along with other facilities that would improve the quality of life for the Kelpers. The cost of this was borne almost entirely by Buenos Aires.

Thirty flights were completed by Albatross aircraft. Each trip held its share of adventure, experienced by passengers and crew alike. The flights offered advantages to the parties involved: Argentines saw this as a chance to get closer to the island people; the British government had found a very economical means of improving the lot of the inhabitants, both British and Kelpers; FIC kept its trade relations and profits up; and the Kelpers had a window on the world that considerably improved the quality of their lives.

In May 1972, Argentine and British authorities decided to go one step further in the integration process: a landing strip was to be built for twin-engine turboprop passenger aircraft. But the terrain presented a challenge. Damp peat bogs did not make the job easy, nor did the scarcity of vehicles in Port Stanley and the absence of roads outside the town limits. The Argentine Air Force designed the project. The strip would be 720 meters long by 30 wide, built entirely of aluminum matting laid over a compacted base to keep the aircraft from sinking into the bog under their own weight. The site chosen—on Cape Pembroke, three miles from the capital—required the construction of a road. It was completed in six months, the work having been done by Argentine workers and engineers, and the landing strip went into service in November.

Due to the short length and width of the runway, along with unfavorable weather conditions that prevailed most of the time, operating conditions were, at best, difficult. Every possible precaution was taken to ensure the safety of the flights, which were made for several years on a regular basis and without incident. With the construction of a new, longer, and paved runway on the Freycinet Peninsula, LADE was able to offer improved service to the islanders, thereby achieving, it was hoped, an improved relationship with them.

On May 17, 1978, the first twin-jet Argentine Air Force F–28 operated by L.A.D.F. made the flight to Stanley, thus reducing flying time from Comodoro Rivadavia to just under two hours. From there, the Kelpers could make connections to Buenos Aires, and then on to Europe in 24 hours, a goal that had appeared beyond reach a few years before. The last flight was completed on March 31, 1982, as Argentina had already set in motion its operation to reclaim the islands by force of arms. LADE's operations record was as follows: total number of flights, 1,515; passengers carried, 21,597; cargo shipped, 465,763 kg.; hours of flight time, 3,553; Albatross, 203 hours; F–27, 2,709 hours; F–28, 639 hours; C–130, 2 hours.

It was a long way from the landing of the first Albatross. A tradition of responsibility and a vocation for service had been set in motion for the benefit of the islanders by all—crew members and others—who had sought to lift the curtain of isolation behind which a handful of Kelpers lived, cut off from the world and practically forgotten by their motherland on a desolate island chain unknown to the vast majority of the British public.

The wishes expressed by the Argentine government representative, so full of hope that November 15, 1972, the day Port Stanley Airport was inaugurated, were not to be: "The people of these islands, as well as the people of the Argentine mainland, seek to come together in fruitful dialogue. . . . May God grant that this airport, dedicated to such noble aims, may ever serve as a beacon of peace, harmony, and give and take among men of good will." On April 2, 1982, many of those who had actively extended the hand of brotherhood to the Kelpers found themselves crew members aboard the Argentine Air Force planes carrying to the Falklands the implements of war for the forces that had reclaimed the islands. The memory of other times, and the noble intentions that had moved them then, filled their minds. Their hearts were heavy with frustration, discouragement, and irritation, but also lifted by fierce determination.

2

The World Turned Upside Down

The right flag flies over the wrong goods.

James Morgan

D-DAY FOR "OPERATION AZUL"

Our mission is to land on the Malvinas Islands, to dislodge the British forces and authorities stationed there. That is our objective.

Destiny has made it our lot to see justice is done for these almost 150 years of usurpation.

We shall find on these Islands a population that deserves special treatment. They live on Argentine soil; therefore they should be treated as anyone who lives in Argentina would be treated. Strict respect must be shown at all times for the integrity of both persons and property. No private residence shall at any time be entered unless by necessity for reasons of combat. Women, children, and men, both old and young, shall be respected.

You shall show the enemy no leniency, but be courteous, respectful, and friendly toward the inhabitants of our territory, which we are bound to protect. Tomorrow the world shall see an Argentine force worthy of victory. May God be with us. Let us all now say together: Long live our country!

The squawk boxes aboard the ARA *Cabo San Antonio*, steaming south, fell silent following this announcement by Rear Admiral Carlos A. Busser, commander of the landing force. It took by surprise the ship's company of 542 officers and men, who had boarded the vessel at Puerto Belgrano on March 28 without the slightest idea of the mission about to be undertaken.

The amphibious landing force, commanded by Rear Admiral Gualter O. Allara, brought together the following units:

—The landing force, composed of the 2nd Marine Battalion, an amphibious commando group, an army rifle company, and reserves

—The transport group, with the troop carrier ARA *Cabo San Antonio*, the icebreaker ARA *Almirante Irizar*, and the transport *Isla de los Estados*

—A support, escort, and landing group, made up of the Class 42 destroyers *Hercules* and *Santisima Trinidad*, and the corvettes ARA *Drumond* and *Granville*

—A special task force group, the Guppy Class submarine ARA *Santa Fe*.

The ships had weighed anchor on March 28, in keeping with the decision to move up the date of the occupation of the islands; April 1 was D-Day, with backup dates of April 2 and 3, if warranted by weather conditions. In accordance with the decision of the military junta, the commander for theater operations was Maj. Gen. Osvaldo Jorge Garcia. Heavy storms sweeping the Argentine Sea had forced a 24-hour delay in landing operations, but on the night of April 1, all ships were at their assigned positions for the final assault.

The task force's assigned mission was to occupy Port Stanley, capture the airstrip, and keep the inhabitants under control, in order to complete the reclaiming of the islands and the establishment of a provisional government. For political reasons, all this was to be done without enemy casualties.

The air force scrambled its Air Transport Command and made ready its attack squadrons should their use prove necessary. Shortly thereafter, they were ordered to make ready for takeoff. Argentina was poised to retake the islands, which was tantamount to a declaration of war against the United Kingdom. An airlift would have to be established to resupply the occupation troops. Soon the heavy Hercules C–130s lumbered down the runway one by one and climbed into the sky.

Meanwhile, in Port Stanley, Governor Rex Hunt had been alerted on the morning of March 31 by London that an Argentine submarine was sailing toward the archipelago. The following day, he was advised that a large landing force was headed toward Port Stanley, intent on invading. Unfortunately for Hunt and his Royal Marines, the closest British vessel was the HMS *Endurance*, over 400 NM away, assigned to remove the Argentine work crew from Port Leith on South Georgia Island. The only available ship was the 91-foot freighter *Forrest*, which was dispatched, to the consternation of its captain, to stand guard at the entrance to the outer bay as a radar picket, to sound the warning at the approach of the Argentine flotilla.

Major Mike Norman of the Royal Marines made ready the defenses. Following evaluation of the most probable Argentine invasion sites, he positioned 67 marines at the spots deemed fittest for resisting any attempted landing. With the command post at Government House, the general plan called for resisting the Argentine landing and advance, falling back to Government House and, if feasible, fleeing inland to establish an alternative command post. Fortunately for both sides, the landings were not carried out at any of the points deemed most likely by the defenders.

At 0030 hours, and according to plan, Task Force 40's auxiliary landing craft were already unloading the amphibious commando group at Port Harriet, some four miles south of Port Stanley. The commandos landed without opposition and began their overland march toward their previously assigned objectives: the marine barracks at Moody Brook and vital points of the island capital. They were followed three hours later by frogmen at Cape Pembroke (San Felipe), where they had been dropped off by the submarine *Santa Fe*, with the objective of occupying the lighthouse and supporting the landings from the transport *Cabo San Antonio*, which would soon be leaving the 2nd Marine Battalion on the beach, along with a rifle company from the 25th Infantry Regiment. Their objective was to take the airport and advance toward objectives in Port Stanley in a classical pincer movement aimed at Government House while sealing off the withdrawal route of the defenders toward the interior of East Falkland.

The Royal Marines, realizing they were at the wrong location—if indeed they intended a serious defense—resolved to fall back toward the town to join their companions. In fact, the proper thing to do, from a tactical standpoint, would have been to take up defense positions at the airport, since this was a vital objective for the occupation forces, and any delay in securing it would have constituted a serious obstacle to the invaders.

At about the same time, an action in the gardens of Government House produced the first casualty of the war. Marine Lt. Cmdr. Pedro Eduardo Giachino, who had advanced with his column of commandos from the south, proceeded to surround the governor's mansion and, seeing the great numerical disadvantage of the defenders, decided, in an excess of professional zeal and temerity, to force his way into the building without further delay. He ordered his men to cover his attack and made for one of the entrances. The defenders, who could not know that the Argentines were under orders to secure the objective without incurring enemy casualties, could only see a heavily armed and grimly determined commando. As they opened fire, Giachino fell in the courtyard. When he was finally recovered, he was beyond help. Shortly thereafter, upon the arrival at Government House of a column of armored vehicles that had been landed by the *Cabo San Antonio*, Governor Hunt decided the time had come to call for a truce. A cease-fire was arranged, and at 0915 hours the governor surrendered to the Argentine commander, Major General Garcia.

Thus it was that, following 149 years under British rule, political power was once again exercised in the Malvinas by an Argentine governor, albeit temporarily. Meanwhile, Rex Hunt followed in the footsteps of Juan Carlos Pinedo, who on January 3, 1833, was illegally removed from his office of provisional governor and, accompanied by his officers and the island's Argentine settlers, deported to Montevideo aboard a British sloop. At 1120 hours, the British Union Jack was solemnly lowered from its mast, and in its place rose the sky-blue and white banner of the Argentine Republic, to the emotional salute of a company of soldiers at rigid attention.

As the day wore on, the landing of troops and equipment was completed, aircraft droned in and out, and the *Almirante Irizar* completed deployment of army troops at Darwin, Goose Green, and Port Fox, in order to secure the recapture of the islands at the main geographical points. The operation was carried out with clockwork precision. All that remained was the transfer of power and the reembarkation of most of the troops, since the plans called for the removal, by D-Days + 5, of all but the governor and a small contingent to reinforce his authority. That same afternoon, April 2, 1982, and into the evening, marine contingents were being loaded aboard transports and flown back to their home bases.

This final phase of the operation remained unconcluded. At 1145 hours, the Security Council met in New York—at the behest of the United Kingdom the day before—to deal with the South Atlantic crisis. The news from London and Washington was anything but encouraging for Buenos Aires. Something had gone terribly askew in the Argentine political leadership's carefully laid calculations.

The Fall of Grytviken

When the junta had decided to guarantee and protect the task being carried out at Port Leith, South Georgia Island, by an Argentine work crew, the ship closest to that point was the ARA *Bahia Paraiso*, attached to the Antarctic campaign (a yearly operation to support Argentine bases and scientific activity on Antarctica). The vessel received orders to weigh anchor at the Argentine base in the South Orkneys and immediately head north to Port Leith in order to ensure that protection. Its captain appointed a company of ten men, under Lt. Alfredo Ignacio Astiz, to land at Port Leith and carry out the task as assigned. At 2340 hours on March 24, the *Bahia Paraiso* dropped anchor in Stromness Bay and proceeded to land the Aztis Group, which immediately set up camp alongside the party from the South Georgia Island Company.

The news coming over the wires at that time indicated a steady deterioration of the situation: the *Endurance* had steamed from Port Stanley at 0830 hours on March 21, on Governor Hunt's orders, to remove the Argentine work crew from Port Leith; the RRS *John Biscoe*, which was in port at Montevideo to pick up the relief detachment for the Royal Marines at Port Stanley, had to return to the archipelago with the men on March 24, and the RRS *Bransfield*, anchored at Punta Arenas, would sail the following day.

Meanwhile, in order to secure the objective at Grytviken, the Argentine command ordered the cutter *Guerrico* to proceed to that location with a rifle company that, after linking up with the *Bahia Paraiso* and Lieutenant Astiz's group, would form a task force. The transport, which was equipped for the Antarctic campaign, had two helicopters aboard: a Navy Alouette and an army Puma. Since none of this deployment had been provided for in advance, both the captain of the *Guerrico* and the commander of the rifle company were hard put to prepare their men. The *Guerrico* had been in dry dock for overhaul and was forced to put to sea on 48 hours' notice, come what may, no later than March 29, while the rifle company, made up mostly of conscripts, was far from an optimum level of preparedness.

The cutter sailed on April 1. The *Endurance* had dropped anchor the day before at Grytviken, and had most certainly landed its company and prepared a defense. During its passage through the heaving Atlantic, the *Guerrico* had no means of making up for lost time nor could the men and materiel be prepared, since it was bounced about by storms all the way to Cumberland Bay, where it made landfall at 1700 hours on April 2. In view of the unfavorable weather conditions and the advanced hour (1700), it would not be feasible to attempt taking Grytviken that day, and the operation was postponed to the morning of April 3, thus losing all the advantage of surprise, since by then the news of the British surrender to Argentine forces at Port Stanley had blanketed the radio waves.

At first light on April 3, the two task force vessels weighed anchor at Stromness Bay and made their approach to Cumberland Bay, where Grytviken lies. At about 1000 hours, the commander of the task force established radio contact with Grytviken and informed it that Port Stanley had surrendered unconditionally, and that it was hoped Grytviken would follow suit, in order to avoid bloodshed.

The chief of the British Antarctic Survey base, Stephen John Martin, radioed back that he was under orders to resist and that no landing should be made. But time was running short for the Argentine skipper; at that moment the Security Council was considering this very issue in New York, and it was paramount that he secure his objective prior to the close of that meeting. He ordered the *Alouette* to reconnoiter the area. It was followed by the army Puma, which landed the first marine contingent on the beach. This first landing was without incident, but while the Puma was hovering for its second landing attempt, the Royal Marines, who were holding a fortified position on the side of the mountain, opened fire and forced the helicopter which sustained both human casualties and extensive damage, to make an emergency landing on the opposite side of the cove.

In the meantime, the first wave of marines came under heavy enemy fire. The landing operations were continued by the Alouette helicopter. Faced by this turn of events, the cutter—which could make only limited use of its armament—entered the narrow and treacherous cove in an attempt to pin down the defenders, who returned the fire with light rifles and antitank rockets, inflicting casualties and causing damage that obliged the cutter to withdraw to a prudent distance.

On the second assault, at 1322 hours local time (1022 GMT), the Royal Marines laid down their arms. Shortly thereafter, the Astiz group—which had been held in reserve aboard the *Bahia Paraiso*—was landed in order to process the prisoners and deactivate the mine fields that had been laid prior to engagement.

The task force had accomplished its mission: to take Grytviken with the least possible losses to the enemy. It did, however, pay an exceedingly heavy price: three killed and seven wounded, the Puma helicopter destroyed, and the cutter

Guerrico damaged; the British counted one man wounded (flesh wound in the arm). The enemy made good on their government's order to oblige Argentina to use force.

Meanwhile, the Security Council adopted Resolution 502, which gave Mrs. Thatcher carte blanche to throw the full might of her task force against Argentina. Davidoff's work crew and a reduced marine detachment remained on South Georgia Island to wait out the coming events.

Ironically, the results achieved by the Argentine task force were as Pyrrhic as those gained by the British task force. Both secured their objectives, but the price was high indeed, as much in the consequences as in the cost.

Reaction on the Home Front

On the morning of April 2, Argentina awoke to the news that its armed forces had retaken the Falkland Islands, the beloved Malvinas.* Considering that such an action would be viewed as a legitimate and historical national aspiration, massive popular approval of an action no government had dared until then to undertake was a foregone conclusion. But popular reaction went beyond mere approval: a wave of indescribable joy and contagious festivity spread like wildfire throughout the land.

Reasons for such good cheer were far from lacking: since 1833 the nation had nourished the dream of consolidating its territory. It was a reaction to an endless string of frustrations even a military government could no longer contain. It was the natural expression of patriotism, of a national sentiment held dear, an animosity toward colonialism, or even the liberalism that, for many Argentines, was the source of all evil in Argentina. Such joyous outpourings were blind to any thought of the consequences of war—especially in terms of human cost—but most assuredly, Argentines from every social and national background were brought together as never before in their history.

At 0700 hours Argentina's president, General Galtieri, called a Cabinet meeting attended by the chairman of the Joint Chiefs of Staff and the future governor of the islands, General Menendez. The president spoke at length of the retaking of the archipelago and of the feats of the armed forces, how the theater of operations had been laid out, the chain of command, the preparations. He was followed by Foreign Minister Costa Mendez, who briefed the group on the events in the South Georgias and the Reagan-Galtieri telephone exchange. He also presented an evaluation of what could be expected of the Security Council.

The Plaza de Mayo, the esplanade in front of the presidential mansion, began to fill with people who came to share their joy, their approval. The pyramid that

---

*Malvinas, the traditional Spanish name for the islands, is derived from the French Malouines, as they were known in the seventeenth century. It referred to the home port of many of the early inhabitants, who hailed from St. Malo, on the northern coast of France.

stands in its center was witness once again to an important historical event in the life of the nation . . . possibly the happiest in many, many years. A heady spirit of joy over Argentina's triumph moved through every stratum of society on those cool autumn days. It was not just those enthusiastic supporters who jammed the Plaza de Mayo that day, nor was it the faceless throngs who were there in spirit. The media—with their snowball effect—spread this excitement both to the governed and, what is worse, to those who govern, and by and large made even the most reflective lose sight of reality. The "exclusive" photo of British Marines spread-eagled on a beach at Port Stanley—which became Puerto Argentino—as they were frisked by our own marines were published not only in an Argentine picture weekly but made front pages around the world—all the better excuse for Mrs. Thatcher to dispatch the Royal Navy. Not only could those images have justified such a decision, they made it, for all purposes, politically mandatory.

To put things into perspective, we Argentines had not truly reclaimed the Falkland/Malvinas on April 2. For that to be so, international recognition was basic—and, to begin with, that of Great Britain. What we did on that day was to slap a colonial power in the face, and what better excuse could a beleaguered prime minister have to distract her people from the more pressing and crucial problems that endangered her remaining in office? Something not unlike that must have also crossed the minds of the military junta, for whom reclaiming the Malvinas, an aspiration as pure as it was legitimate for the Argentine people, was made to order to shore up a government that was coming apart from its own contradictions.

To sum things up, our leadership became totally blinded by the popular reaction and, although they did not realize it, they were to lose the political elbow room that would have allowed them to seek a diplomatic solution—which was, after all, what had been sought in the first place. While the nation's president was busy issuing binding promises from his balcony at the Casa Rosada, Argentina's diplomats were assuming postures that those who had no interest in negotiating would find hard to accept.

Reaction in Britain

If news of the invasion was given banner headlines and multicolumn coverage in the Argentine press, the British were not to be outdone. The morning editions of April 3 ran headlines with gargantuan type: "SHAME,"tolled the *Daily Mail;* "HUMILIATION," cried the *Daily Telegraph.* The others reverberated with righteous indignation.

As for the British public, they knew little or nothing about these Falkland Islands, far removed in the wastes of the South Atlantic. But the very fact that a third-rate power had dared tweak the British lion's whiskers served to whet their curiosity, on the one hand, and their warrior instinct, on the other. The British public is to a great extent conditioned to war. Its history is the story of one conflict after the other. Due to economic problems, social unrest, and rising unemployment at home, this conflict came to Mrs. Thatcher as a tailor-made alternative with which to distract from the realities that were eating away at the foundation of her Conservative government, and she was not about to let it slip by. She was faced with a dilemma: she was not really sure what Argentina was capable of, and yet she believed that, as should be typical of a South American country, it could not be much. The islands, on the other hand, were so far off the beaten track that the Soviet Union and the United States could see a conflict there as being in their own interests, which gave her the green light to follow her own devices—which she immediately set about doing. She did not, however, reckon with one crucial factor: the significance of those islands to Argentina. Margaret Thatcher's main difficulty lay in figuring out how to win over the opposition, overcome the tough obstacles the Labourites were sure to throw in her way at every turn. And here is where luck played into her hands.

Within minutes of the confirmation of Governor Hunt's surrender at Port Stanley, Labour leaders were accosted by the media for instant commentary. John Silkin, Labourite spokesman for the House of Commons' Subcommittee on Defense, went on the important "World at One" radio broadcast, favoring a warlike stance. The following day—Saturday, April 3—Parliament met in emergency session for the first time in the past quarter-century. Officialdom, seemingly given a green light by the opposition, endorsed the adoption of a strong response by sending a powerful task force to the South Atlantic. Had the islands been taken on a Monday, the House's response would surely have been different. And once Michael Foot, head of the Labour Party, had made a stand, the immediate reaction in an emergency session was to rally to that position. Furthermore, the meeting was scheduled for a scant three hours (1100 to 1400 hours) rather than the five that would have been necessary to hear the statements of all those members who had requested the floor. If not for the monopolization of those three hours by the prime minister and Messrs. Foot, Silkin, and Nott (the defense secretary), the results might well have been different (had the House sat for its customary eight-hour session).

In the diplomatic arena, the British government had played a brilliant hand before the U.N. Security Council. On March 31, three hours following delivery by the Argentine delegate of a note denouncing the British threat against the work party on South Georgia Island, Ambassador Roca had been caught by surprise by Britain's call for a Security Council meeting to examine the evidence that Argentina was about to move on the Malvinas—an issue on which he had received no advance notice.

But all did not go smoothly during the emergency session in Parliament. Many issues went unclarified, many questions went unasked, and many charges had yet to be leveled. Lord Carrington was nailed to the witness stand as if the defendant in a criminal case, for someone had to answer for the carelessness that had allowed Britain to be caught with its guard down. Defense Secretary Nott was not beyond reproach, although he put up a skillful defense while laying responsibility for the business at hand at the foreign secretary's doorstep by stating that he was a mere instrument of policy.

The head of the Foreign Office was meant to be the sacrificial lamb. A circumspect gentleman of great moderation, Lord Carrington had incurred the distrust of the right wing of his party following the settlement of the Rhodesian question, which gave birth to the nation of Zimbabwe. All of this notwithstanding, the cross was not his alone to bear. As a matter of principle, the lack of foresight with regard to the Argentine government's designs fell squarely on the Joint Intelligence Committee, a body that no longer accounted to the Foreign Office for its actions, but to the Cabinet Office. But things had been allowed to go too far, and the price had to be paid by a top-ranking official. Following some misgivings, Margaret Thatcher found it best—lest she, too, be sucked into the gathering tornado—to accept Carrington's resignation, along with that of the Foreign Office's second and third in command, Humphrey Atkins and Richard Luce. So it came to be that Peter Alexander Rupert Carrington, P.C., K.C., M.P., G.C.M.E., became the second man to lose his job in the wake of the fall of Port Stanley, following Rex Hunt, although, unlike the latter, he did not regain his post after the Falklands were regained.

John Nott's resignation was rejected, and with the blood of three victims on their hands, the main spectators in the grand circus were satiated and Mrs. Thatcher could, as of that moment, go about the business of dispatching the fleet—preparations had been under way since March 31—to fight for ill-defined principles, and its men to die for the decisions of those who only spoke of dying. The words of the pirate James Morgan took on new meaning: "The right flag flies over the wrong goods."

That Argentine soldiers would soon die to keep their territory whole and their nation's dignity unblemished, while British soldiers would not enjoy such a clear view, there is no doubt.

Reaction in The United States

Any scholar of U.S. foreign policy could assume the reaction of that nation in the face of such a conflict. Historical and political considerations could only lead to the conclusion that when the chips are down, the old allies of two world wars and pillars of the Atlantic Alliance would close ranks and act as one, at the expense of hemispheric relations.

However that may be, the government of Argentina had harbored a glimmer of hope for a somewhat broader support from the United States in the conflict, if only by virtue of the following:

—Inter-American solidarity and the spirit of the Monroe Doctrine

—The support given by Argentina's military government to President Reagan's Central American policies

—Assistant Secretary of State for Latin American Affairs Enders, during a visit to Buenos Aires on March 8, 1982, on being questioned about his country's position regarding the Falklands issue, had responded, "Hands off!"

—The general course being taken by relations between both countries, which, while they had been beset with problems during the Carter administration, had brightened under the Republican administration.

But, as soon as news of the landing of Argentine troops on the Malvinas had been confirmed, Great Britain launched an effective mass media campaign that it used to marshal all of its influence both in the diplomatic arena and in Washington political circles. This action was soon translated into editorial commentary that ran in the most influential and widely circulated news media, followed shortly thereafter by U.S. Senate endorsement of a pro-British resolution, which passed with a single nay from Senator Helms, who was thoroughly familiar with the long history of the dispute. A skillful observer of the U.S. Congress was quick to note that when the senators vote massively for or against a given proposal, it is because they do not understand the issue. Otherwise, there are always differences of opinion and of positions.

But, no matter. When faced with the initial fait accompli, the United States stood ready to mediate, to be a friend to both parties, just as President Reagan had stated in his telephone call to President Galtieri. Nevertheless, on April 1, at 1700 hours, Secretary of State Haig called on Argentine Ambassador to the United States Esteban Takacs to inform him that, in the event of conflict, the United States would, of necessity, have to stand side by side with the British. This news was flashed to Buenos Aires that same night, when it was already too late to steer a new course, or even sound the warning of danger dead ahead.

U.K. Ambassador Henderson's activities were both vigorous and effective, and he found in Secretary of State Haig a unique ally, for they engaged in frequent consultations and constantly compared notes. In this way, Secretary Haig became ever further entwined in the Malvinas problem. Henderson tilted the balance of opinion in high Washington political circles in favor of the British position, not only through these contacts but also through his readiness to go on television with prepared statements. He was the delight of the producers, who reveled in the interesting interviews he granted, which were broadcast live by the U.S. networks. Thus was U.S. public opinion shaped to fit Margaret Thatcher's view of the conflict: Argentina had committed a treacherous and bare-faced act of aggression; it should be taught a lesson and made to pay. As far as evenhanded respect for international law was concerned, Argentina's cause counted for naught. It simply did not exist.

The Argentine embassy, which had been caught unprepared for such a contingency, was able to issue releases on television during off-hours, when few people were watching. It is therefore not surprising that 70 percent of the U.S. public sided with Britain, while the other 30 percent were, at best, "misinformed."

But not all of the current of thought ran against Argentina in the stereotyped atmosphere of Washington foreign policy. U.S. Ambassador to the U.N. Jeane Kirkpatrick was the main defender of a more evenhanded position. A woman endowed with great political wisdom, she moved with ease in her country's diplomatic circles and proved to be one of the few high-level officials within President Reagan's cabinet who was well versed in the politics of Latin America, and who had the president's ear. She was the complete opposite of Alexander Haig, former NATO supreme commander in Europe, who enjoyed a broad range of relationships and friendships. As for Assistant Secretary Enders, his counsel to the White House was most objective, in defense of U.S. interests in the hemisphere.

Reaction Throughout the World

Latin America came down almost as one on Argentina's side. One of the first surprises on the diplomatic front came from Panama, since no previous openings had been made in that direction. In the Security Council, Panama assumed a clear and courageous position as it outlined the anachronistic and colonial nature of the conflict. Peru also aligned itself stalwartly on Argentina's side, while Venezuela went a step further, assuming a leadership role in orchestrating political and diplomatic support for its sister republic. These were not just the solemn pronouncements of these nations' governments—which were two of the few Latin American governments accountable to an electorate—but the echo of a widespread popular constituency that took to the streets and public squares by the thousands to express their support, to the surprise of the Argentine public, which had not expected such fraternal accord.

The lack of support on the part of the government of Paraguay made that country look pale in comparison with others. Argentina had expected a warmer understanding. Even more surprising was the stance assumed by Colombia, whose government distanced itself from the rest of Latin America—and from the feelings of its own people—to seek avenues of contact with the United States.

Our brothers in Uruguay—the great majority of them—rose to the occasion and echoed the common historic tie linking the Rio de la Plata nations even though that country's media—apparently under British influence—gave clear indications of an anti-Argentine posture.

Bolivia, true to its common historic and territorial ancestry, voiced its brotherhood and solidarity. Chile was completely taken by surprise by its neighbor's action. Until it could get a firm grasp on events, and chart a course for what could come at the conclusion of the confrontation, it adopted a wait-and-see attitude. In hindsight, the Chilean government must have been aware that Argentina had at no time entertained any notion of resolving the territorial dispute in which they had been involved since 1978 by any means other than through negotiations. Chile's diplomatic position was that of a neutral, but it showed different colors in the field of operations.

Brazil joined the rest of Latin America in proclaiming solidarity with Argentina, which was politically significant. It stopped short, however, of endorsing Buenos Aires's claims on the South Georgia and South Sandwich Islands. Ecuador sided earnestly and squarely with Argentina.

In Central America, besides Panama, Guatemala made a valuable contribution, for it, along with Nicaragua, offered to send troops, while El Salvador and Honduras joined the concert of nations that sided with Argentina. Costa Rica's stance was more neutral, while Mexico became the linchpin of which the expression of solidarity south of the Rio Grande. As for the Caribbean, the former British colonies remained aloof, casting their lot with the Commonwealth and turning a blind eye to the geopolitical reality that makes them part and parcel of the New World. Jamaica, Trinidad and Tobago, St. Lucia, Barbados, and Guyana were as reluctant as Canada to show any support for Argentina.

Cuba, whose ideology keeps it in a state of semi-isolation from the rest of the hemisphere, came out decidedly in favor of Buenos Aires's position, and unselfishly offered assistance. To round out the Americas, Haiti and the Dominican Republic offered their assistance to Argentina, while leftist Grenada assumed an ideological and diplomatic posture similar to Cuba's.

The picture in the Old World was very different. Ill-disposed toward Argentina because of the human rights issue, and slaves to their economic or political interests, the EEC rallied almost as one round the British lion, which had growled loudly and thrown its political and economic weight about, clasping the banners of NATO and the EEC between its teeth.

Spain shrugged off the link of history and kinship in order to better serve its Old World interests. While Gibraltar is the same historical thorn for Spain as the Malvinas are for Argentina, it opted, in its quest for spoils (mainly that of being admitted to the EEC), to play the European card. The British government repaid the favor by showing the task force, on its victorious return from the South Atlantic, off Gibraltar, in an ominous warning, just in case Spain had any notions of its own.

In the Far East, the broad support shown by the People's Republic of China is noteworthy, although its reaction was not swift enough to head off the adoption of Resolution 502. Japan, on the other hand, was an early sympathizer of the British position but experienced a change of heart more in harmony with the background of the conflict. India played a waiting game, for it has a geopolitical problem with the Andaman and Nicobar Islands, which are India's but, because of their location near Sumatra, are in a situation similar to that of the Malvinas in relation to Argentina and Great Britain.

Israel backed the Argentine government's position, not only in consonance with its economic interests (it sells arms and other goods) but also because Argentina is among the few nations of the world that opened its borders during World War II to give refuge to the Jews persecuted by the Nazis, to the extent that Buenos Aires boasts the third largest Jewish community in the world, following New York City and Tel-Aviv.

The Arab countries, which have inherited a blood feud that pits them against Israel in the Middle East (and which is due in large part to Britain's sponsoring the creation of the Jewish state in Palestine, which they had also promised to the Arabs if they helped Britain expel the Turks from those lands), took various stances. As noteworthy as it is unprecedented, Libya offered a wide range of assistance with no strings attached, although it may be said it acted thus more out of Colonel Qaddafi's aversion to Great Britain than out of any sympathy for the military junta. At the opposite end of the spectrum was Jordan, which at the time of the conflict was a member of the Security Council and a nonaligned country, but which flew in the face of these countries and clinched the vote in favor of Great Britain for adoption of Resolution 502.

New Zealand's position also was totally unexpected. It was the only country—aside from Great Britain—unilaterally to break diplomatic relations with Argentina in the wake of the reclaiming of the Malvinas. Such an action was undeserved by Buenos Aires, which had initiated a policy of rapprochement with the former British colony through the establishment of air service linking Rio Gallegos and Auckland, which eliminated these two nations' status as "end-of-the-line" countries because of their locations.

As for international bodies, the OAS, the top inter-American deliberative organ, threw its full support to Argentina, and even went so far as to invoke the Rio Treaty.

Structured to cater to the interests of the powerful, the United Nations, through the good offices of the Security Council, was the scene of events such as ignoring an Argentine note denouncing a British threat against its people in the South Georgias, adoption of Resolution 502 (which was weighted in Britain's favor), and the veto of a cease-fire proposal.

NATO gave its support to one of its main members, Great Britain, whose naval forces in the North Sea and the Mediterranean were stripped clean in order to press them into service in the punitive expedition to the South Atlantic.

The EEC, in spite of this being a bilateral conflict between one of its members and a client nation, applied economic sanctions against Argentina in order to placate Britain, which had advocated them. Such measures would have no major effect other than applying an embargo on arms shipments to Argentina and creating difficulties in other areas, such as trade between nations, as well as commercial and cultural or technological cooperation. For whatever reason, the EEC's reaction was not limited to mere rhetoric in condemning the action of a given country, but was translated into tangible measures that were immediately applied against a South American nation—an action that constituted a first, for there had been far more violent and less fair situations that had not been dealt with in this manner.

SECURITY COUNCIL RESOLUTION 502

The United Nations is an organization of peculiar characteristics. In the General Assembly, all nations are entitled to a vote and to equal rights, but their recommendations bear only a relative weight, for they normally cannot be enforced. Such is not the case in the Security Council, which does enjoy political clout, since resolutions adopted are binding on the parties involved. The Security Council is composed of 15 members, 10 of which change every 2 years, and 5 of which enjoy permanent status. These are the United States, the Soviet Union, the United Kingdom, France, and China. These "Big Five" not only have permanent seats but also enjoy a very exclusive privilege: they can veto any resolution that may run counter to their interests or aspirations. This right ensures that no resolution will ever be adopted against any of these five members against its will. This essentially means that the United Nations is set up in such a way as to apply sanctions to the rest of the world community, unless one of the "Big Five" uses its veto.

But this is not the only contradiction. It is well known in the field of justice that one cannot be both judge and party to a case, and this is outlined in the legal codes of every country of the world. It is therefore surprising that the Security Council is not bound by this basic tenet of law, since if one of its permanent members becomes embroiled in a conflict with a country that does not enjoy equal privileges, or is not represented within the Council, that permanent member continues to enjoy its right to veto.

If the South Atlantic conflict had only one virtue, it served to underscore these absurdities within the framework of international law. And it will be seen that the "rules of the game" are not alone in shouldering the blame. During the conflict, the Council considered three resolutions: 502, which enjoined the parties to cease hostilities and Argentina to withdraw its forces from the islands; 505, which was an inconsequential text referring peace negotiations to the secretary general of the organization; and a resolution enjoining both parties to a cease-fire. This resolution was vetoed both by the United Kingdom and the United States.

It is said that improvisation is the enemy of perfection, and this is especially true in the field of diplomacy. As Argentina's decision to reclaim the islands was taking shape, Ambassador Roca journeyed to New York on March 24, while still recovering from an operation, to assume his new duties as chief of the Argentine delegation to the United Nations. An excessive zeal for secrecy cloaking the operation kept the new ambassador in the dark as to what was brewing, and by the same token kept the Foreign Ministry from taking appropriate preventive steps in the arena of international relations, where the fate of Argentina's political goals would be played out.

The delegation of the United Kingdom to the United Nations was in a completely opposite situation. Far from being a newcomer, British Ambassador Sir Anthony Parsons, a veteran member of the Foreign Service, had been posted to the United Nations for over two years, and he was fully familiar with the prevailing atmosphere there, where both professional finesse and personal charm can be so crucial to the successful fulfillment of one's duties. Parsons knew all the ins and outs of this diplomatic circle, and was well known by all. He could move as smoothly as silk in this rarefied sphere of international relations, and what is more important, he was a mover and a shaker who was thoroughly at home in crisis situations.

At 1145 hours on April 2, the Security Council convened a meeting called by Great Britain. The makeup of the Council was as follows:

—Permanent members: United States, Soviet Union, Great Britain, France, and China
—Nonaligned countries: Panama, Jordan, Guyana, Togo, Uganda, and Zaire
—Other countries: Japan, Ireland, Spain, and Poland

A two-thirds majority was needed for the British proposal to pass. This is the not inconsiderable number of ten votes. From a standpoint undisturbed by circumstantial elements, it would appear that the British proposal would be in for some rough sailing: The Council was made up of six nonaligned countries, three Eastern bloc nations, three iffy countries, and only three decidedly pro-British countries: the permanent members that were also NATO members.

With the cards thus laid on the table, British diplomacy was faced with the formidable task of garnering the votes of nine members whose willingness to back the proposal offered by the United Kingdom hung in the balance. The British plan was to move as swiftly as possible to head off an Argentine diplomatic parry that might bring about a more in-depth study of the issue, which would reveal the legal flaws in Britain's stance. The issue should be presented squarely as an act of aggression and a clear violation of international law on Argentina's part, which called for the use of every possible guise and device with those member nations that could be susceptible to such measures.

Confident that Great Britain would be incapable of achieving the majority needed to impose the resolution, Argentine diplomacy did not act with the necessary speed and effectiveness. No advance contacts or overtures were made toward countries that could have used their veto power (the Soviet Union and China) or those which may have looked favorably on Buenos Aires's intent, whether for reasons of affinity or because their ideology or policies were at odds with London's. Between a recently accredited representative to that body and a foreign minister who arrived at the Council meeting under a deadline to read a prepared statement, the delegates remained unconvinced, at the hour of decision, to vote against the British proposal.

Another factor that operated in Britain's favor was the fact that as of March 31, the chairmanship of the Council had rotated out of the hands of the U.S. representative to that body, Ambassador Jeane Kirkpatrick, into those of Kamanda wa Kamanda, of Zaire. Had Jeane Kirkpatrick still been chairing the Council, it is safe to assume that the issue would not have been given such short shrift, and there would have been sufficient time to allow the facts of the case, especially Argentina's side of the story, to be properly aired.

Having garnered the votes of the United States, France, and Guyana (the latter in view of its border dispute with Venezuela), and those of Japan and Ireland in view of the fact that Argentina had resorted to the use of force, British diplomacy worked its charm successfully on the delegate from Zaire (and chairman of the Council), while France softened up the delegation from Togo. The score stood at eight . . . two short of the minimum necessary to carry. Leaving aside the socialist bloc countries, but adding Spain (due to Gibraltar) and Panama, which was Argentina's leading supporter, the outcome for Britain swung on the votes of two nonaligned nations: Uganda and Jordan. Parsons maneuvered deftly with the delegate from Uganda, while the Foreign Office worked its "outside lines" on that nation's capital. Between them, they were successful in extracting instructions from Kampala to its ambassador to cast a "yea" vote for the British initiative. That left Jordan.

The Jordanian representative had instructions to support Argentina's position. Parsons instructed his backup to make contact with Lord Carrington in London and get Amman (Jordan's capital) to change those orders. He was tended to by no less than Mrs. Thatcher, who, taking matters into her own hands, phoned King Hussein personally. She kept the king on the line for 45 minutes. Possibly overwhelmed by the urgency of this call and flying in the face of his nonalignment, he agreed to change his delegate's instructions, thus chalking up that tenth crucial vote that would bring Britain's proposal, so vital to the conflict from both a military and a political standpoint, to fruition.

When it came time to count hands, the British delegate had only one doubt: which way would the Soviet Union and China go? Would they use their veto? But the bureaucracy in Communist countries is exceedingly slow moving, and there was not enough time for the Soviet delegate to obtain a change of instructions, which was not atypical of Soviet conduct under similar circumstances.

By this time, there was no ringing speech that could sway the wills, the decisions that had been hammered out on the sidelines and molded over the phone lines.

Argentine Foreign Minister Costa Mendez summed up an extensive appeal to the Council in the following words:

The Republic of Argentina is not carrying out hostilities against anyone; we have no interest in an armed confrontation with anyone, and we are willing to negotiate all our differences with the United Kingdom on the diplomatic front. All, Mr. Chairman, except sovereignty. That is nonnegotiable.

Various speakers followed him to the podium, among them the representatives of Bolivia, Peru, Brazil, the Soviet Union, and Panama. All came out against the British position. But the British representative's deft maneuvers had won him the votes of the nonaligned countries on which the outcome swung.

The final vote was as follows: Great Britain, the United States, France, Ireland, Guyana, Togo, Zaire, Uganda, Japan, and Jordan voted yea; Panama voted nay; and the Soviet Union, China, Poland, and Spain abstained. The complete text of Resolution 502 appears below:

Adopted by the Security Council at Its 2350th Meeting
on 3 April 1982

The Security Council,

Recalling the statement made by the President of the Security Council at the 2345th meeting of the Security Council on 1 April 1982 (s/14944) calling on the Governments of Argentina and the United Kingdom of Great Britain and Northern Ireland to refrain from the use of threat of force in the region of the Falkland Islands (Islas Malvinas),

Deeply disturbed at reports of an invasion on 2 April 1982 by armed forces of Argentina,

Determining that there exists a breach of the peace in the region of the Falkland Islands (Islas Malvinas),

1. Demands an immediate cessation of hostilities;

2. Demands an immediate withdrawal of all Argentine forces from the Falkland Islands (Islas Malvinas);

3. Calls on the Governments of Argentina and the United Kingdom to seek a diplomatic solution to their differences and to respect fully the purposes and principles of the Charter of the United Nations.

This was all Great Britain needed to justify the dispatching of the largest military armada since World War II. No further resolution would stay its hand. It was poised to use all its might, all the strength it could muster to dislodge those Argentine troops.

Nobody summed up the situation better than Panama's delegate, Dr. Illueca, who made the following statement after the votes had been counted:

What will happen when the aircraft carrier *Invincible* and other British naval units arrive in Argentine territorial waters is inevitable. There will be hostilities, and what the Council is doing here today is simply to establish the framework for hostilities which are not being dealt with here.

But the words of a delegate from a small nation, no matter how true they may ring, bear little weight when the interests of the powerful are hanging on the opposite side of the scales. Great Britain had already won its first major battle, one whose military and political implications were perceived by few at that juncture. For with Resolution 502, the British government had solved its domestic problem, on the one hand, while on the other, in the foreign arena, it could justify the sending of a retaliatory force under the guise of the provision of Article 51 of the U.N. Charter, which establishes the right of self-defense and the use of discretionary military force, since Argentina had been branded the aggressor.

The general surprise that Argentina's reclaiming of the southern islands had caused in the world was immediately followed by the psychological action of the United Kingdom, which, moving with deftness and speed in every possible area of endeavor (the political, economic, military, and psychosocial fields), confounded world public opinion by painting Argentina as the aggressor, by claiming legitimate sovereignty over the islands, by picturing the islanders as hostages, by branding the military government as an atrocious dictatorship because of its alleged human rights record, and by glorifying the task force as a liberating quest to set things right in a remote corner of the globe.

So it was that the task force steamed southward, plying the waves toward a lightning-quick military triumph that would surely fill the British public with jubilation and cover their government with political glory.

The Security Council—the world's supreme peacekeeper—had handed Mrs. Thatcher the keys to warfare.

3

The Haig Initiatives: Mission Impossible?

I am wholeheartedly committed to a peaceful settlement of this dispute.

Ronald Reagan

If they wish to come, let them come. We will meet them in battle.

Leopoldo Fortunato Galtieri

The United States will respond positively to the material needs of the British forces.

Alexander Haig

ARGENTINE DIPLOMACY SEEKS REDRESS

In the aftermath of that frustrating session in the Security Council, the Argentine Foreign Ministry turned to Latin America for support. Diplomacy had to be conducted in such a way as to make Great Britain acknowledge the de facto situation created and dissuade it from the use of armed force, while at the same time seeking U.S. support as well as that of the American republics by invoking the Rio Treaty.

The Argentine mission to the OAS put in a request on April 3 for a meeting on April 15 in order to present a statement with regard to the events in the Malvinas. Foreign Minister Costa Mendez traveled to Washington on April 5 to state the basic premise that Argentine sovereignty over the islands was a non-negotiable issue. It was hoped that Washington would be kindly disposed to achieving a settlement of the dispute. What Argentina's diplomats did not know was that at that very time, Great Britain was successfully maneuvering for a priceless bit of U.S. assistance: the use of Ascension Island as support base for the task force. If Resolution 502 represented the key to war in political terms, the use of the facilities at Ascension Island was the key to war in operational terms.

In the meantime, cable traffic from London indicated that Francis Pym had resigned as defense secretary, but the resignation had been declined, and John Nott assumed Lord Carrington's post as head of the Foreign Office. In Buenos Aires, on the other hand, the least popular government in our recent history was receiving the broadest possible support from citizens in every walk of life: labor unions, industry, business, every level of society poured out unabashed approval for the decision to reclaim the islands, settling once and for all a long-standing historical grievance.

Foreign Minister Costa Mendez met with OAS Secretary General Orfila in Washington on April 5. He was accompanied by the U.S. representative to the OAS, Ambassador Middendorf. His objective was to outline Argentina's position and intentions to that body. When it came time for Costa Mendez to address the assembled representatives of the American republics, he couched his nation's position in the following terms:

Great Britain bases her case for opposing negotiations on the issue of sovereignty over the Malvinas, South Georgia, and South Sandwich Islands on the following premise: the wishes of the islanders.

The United Nations have dealt with the interests of the islanders in every resolution bearing on this issue, and the Argentine government has demonstrated, throughout the years, its full respect for such interests, and has always heeded the call of the General Assembly. Just who are these islanders? They are the 1,800 descendants of Britishers who were sent there in 1833 to replace the Argentine settlers, who were forcibly removed. . . .

Is it possible to consider these few people, who were transplanted, the majority of whom spend only part of their lives in the islands, the true inhabitants in the sense of the term as defined by international law? Can these persons become an obstacle to negotiations between governments over territorial sovereignty as ordained by resolutions adopted by the General Assembly of the United Nations? . . . I affirm unto you, I reiterate unto you, that Argentina is willing to comply fully with the resolutions of the General Assembly and cater to the interests of the islanders in the fullest, most absolute, most unreluctant, most unrestricted way possible.

Foreign Minister Costa Mendez's words were met with thunderous applause.

Shortly after the Argentine foreign minister's address, Ambassador Takacs received a call from Assistant Secretary Enders, informing him that Secretary of State Haig was anxious to meet with Dr. Costa Mendez. The meeting was held the following day, April 6, in Washington. In the most cordial of atmospheres, the secretary of state offered—on behalf of President Reagan—the assistance of the United States in the conflict, stating that it was neither mediation nor good offices but "assistance" to both parties. The lengthy interview between the two statesmen can be synthesized as follows:

Costa Mendez: We are aware that a way out must be found in order for the United Kingdom, as well as the governing party, to save face. But they simply do not understand what is at stake in the Malvinas Islands question because they have not taken the time to delve into the issue.

Haig: I do not quite see how it is possible for the British to save face if you will not compromise on the issue of sovereignty. Perhaps there could be some sort of joint administration for a time until transfer is effected, but I somehow do not believe such a solution would sit too well with Mrs. Thatcher.

Costa Mendez: They have been willing to make concessions on the issue of sovereignty on other occasions. It would not be the first time.

Haig: It is possible. It is something more clear and direct. These issues need to be handled in a certain way. Perhaps the provisional administration could be shared with two or three friendly countries.

Costa Mendez: Yes, but that would just complicate things. Perhaps it would be easier were the United States to act as arbitrator for the parties in the event of any disagreements.

Haig: Fine, but I need an affirmative answer from you on my offer of assistance; once I have that, although I can make no promises, I will go to London.

At 2200 hours that evening, Dr. Costa Mendez contacted President Galtieri and presented an account of his talks with Secretary Haig. The president seemed amenable, although he underscored the fact that the Argentine government should in no way be committed, and that Great Britain must halt the fleet as a first step toward initiating talks.

Things appeared to be moving in the direction the military junta had hoped. The United States, in its role of big brother to Argentina and to the concert of Latin nations, as well as that of "cousin" and ally to the British, surely would not abdicate its responsibility. If it could not pressure Great Britain, then who could? On the other hand, it was also fair to recognize that the United States owed a small debt of gratitude to Argentina for its support of President Reagan's Central American policies. And then, there was the hemisphere to think of. How could the United States possibly turn against the whole of Latin America to support Great Britain and its Conservative government. Surely it wouldn't. . . .

Meanwhile, in Buenos Aires, the British community in Argentina sent a wire to Mrs. Thatcher that read as follows:

On behalf of the Council for the Community of British Subjects and their descendants who reside in Argentina, who number over 100,000 persons, we should respectfully wish to point out to you that we feel that our situation has not been duly taken into account in the difficult problem which has arisen between Argentina and Great Britain.

Argentina has always shown herself to be kindly disposed towards the British Community, allowing them to maintain their own schools, churches, hospitals, old people's homes, etc. Furthermore, members of the British Community have come to share in all of the Nation's activities, and play a significant role particularly in the fields of industry and agriculture.

The President of the Republic of Argentina has repeatedly stated that, in spite of the difficult times we are passing through, both the Community and its institutions will be respected. Furthermore, the population is showing the Community every consideration.

We therefore urge you to seek a peaceful solution to the current situation and be mindful of the strong British presence in Argentina and the size of the resident community here. We pray the Lord to grant you guidance in your quest for peace.

The British descendants of the Anglo-Argentine community, who make up a noticeable and appreciated social group within Argentine society, felt that the prime minister would take their interests and their views to heart. After all, the island population amounted to only 1,800 Kelpers, while they were 100,000 strong, with vested economic interests that surely could not be ignored.

But Mrs. Thatcher had other plans. She would reap no political benefit by bowing to the demands of 100,000 Anglo-Argentines, but the 1,800 Kelpers, toward whom the fleet sailed, were another matter.

The Argentine Cabinet met at the Casa Rosada, where they mulled over the daily events, not the least of which was Haig's assistance to the two beleaguered nations and the scope of the Security Council's Resolution 502. Thought was first given to raising objections to the resolution, but this was ruled out by the Foreign Ministry, since the document did in fact include the following favorable aspects:

1. Argentina was not singled out as the "aggressor."
2. The first point made reference to "ceasing hostilities," which Argentina had already done. It remained for Great Britain to do the same.
3. No reference was made to the issue of sovereignty.
4. In referring under Point 2 to the "withdrawal of Argentine forces," no mention was made of an established deadline.
5. The third point implied negotiations, which was exactly what Argentina sought.

SECRETARY HAIG GOES TO LONDON

On April 8, Secretary Haig arrived in London on the first leg of his diplomatic shuttle as go-between. On that same day, and as a portent of the final outcome of his efforts and of what was to be expected of the British, the Swiss embassy in Buenos Aires received the following cable from the United Kingdom, for delivery to Argentine officials:

As of 0400 hours Greenwich Time on April 12th 1982, a maritime exclusion zone will be established round the perimeter of the Falkland Islands. The outside boundary of this zone shall be a circle radiating out 200 nautical miles from a point 51'40"S and 59'30"W which is approximately at the center of the Falkland Islands. As of that moment, any Argentine warship or Argentine auxiliary craft found within that zone shall be deemed hostile and subject to attack by British forces.

This news broke in Buenos Aires just as General Menendez was taking office as governor of the Malvinas. At this time, the squares, streets, public buildings, and most private homes in Buenos Aires, as well as throughout the country, were bedecked with Argentina's sky-blue and white flag.

The foreign minister's report was received in government circles upon his return from the United States, and the position to be assumed with regard to Secretary Haig's offer of assistance was studied with care. It was decided that a working committee should be established to support and keep the military junta abreast of events, and to assist the Foreign Ministry in the business at hand.

The basic guidelines for initiating talks with Great Britain would be as follows:

—The Republic of Argentina, having reclaimed the islands without bloodshed, had effectively ceased hostilities in accordance with the provisions of Resolution 502 (unlike the United Kingdom, until it decided to halt the fleet and lift the blockade).

—Argentina would reduce its troop presence in the islands once the fleet had turned around.

—Once these conditions had been met, talks would be opened with regard to government, forces, the citizenship of the islanders, the economy, suppliers, and other matters, excluding any discussion of the issue of Argentina's sovereignty over the islands.

These basic guidelines appear both overly optimistic and not too realistic if one takes into account the grim determination of the contenders, although they could reasonably serve as opening chips in the bargaining that is implicit in any negotiated settlement.

The news from London indicated that Secretary Haig was encountering sizable hurdles because of the stance being taken by the British government:

—A free people had been subjected to unjustified aggression.

—British public opinion was adamant in its demand that measures be taken.

—No act of aggression like that perpetrated by the dictatorship in power in Buenos Aires could be allowed to go unpunished.

It was obvious that if Secretary Haig thought acting as intermediary in the South Atlantic conflict was a sparkling opportunity to give political luster to his career, he was to be sadly disappointed.

In the face of Britain's determination to keep the task force on its southerly heading, the Argentine Foreign Ministry sought support within the Latin American community through the possible invocation of the Rio Treaty, which would require a two-thirds majority vote of the Assembly (14 out of 21).

SECRETARY HAIG COMES TO BUENOS AIRES

Accompanied by Assistant Secretary of State for Latin American Affairs Thomas Enders, Secretary Haig and his retinue arrived in Buenos Aires at 2200 hours on April 9. Meanwhile, at the United Nations, document no. 24,963, which consisted of a note addressed to the chairman of the Security Council by the acting chargé d'affaires for the British delegation, had been received. It advised the Council of the blockade imposed by the United Kingdom around the operational area of the islands, an act that had been denounced by Argentina the day before. At the same time, Ambassador Roca submitted to the Council a note stating Argentina's reaction to the establishment of a 200-nautical mile exclusion zone around the islands.

On the morning of April 10, in addition to Secretary of State Haig's visit, the Cuban ambassador to Argentina, who had been absent from his post for over two years, requested an audience with the chief of state. The meeting with the delegation from the United States opened at 1030 hours in the situation room at the Casa Rosada, clouded by the announcement of the British blockade of the islands. The talks went on all afternoon and into the evening; and as things began to take shape, it became increasingly clear to the Argentine side that its point of view was not being driven home, that the U.S. position appeared to be sidestepping it. Meanwhile, that afternoon, work continued at the Foreign Ministry, with the objective of making ready a list of points of agreement. But the gap widened steadily between the two sides as they took turns expounding their views, and this objective disappeared into the twilight. It was becoming clear to the Argentine negotiators that the U.S. diplomats were not weighing Argentina's statements in the balance and were trying to make their own opinions and options prevail.

The main stumbling block to agreement between the two delegations was the U.S. requirement that Argentina withdraw its troops from the islands as an initial step that would lead to further discussion, while Argentina's stance was couched in the wording of Resolution 502, which it interpreted as being a binding instrument on both parties to the dispute. If the troops stationed in the islands were to be withdrawn without a compensatory move on Britain's part, then Argentina would lose its only bargaining chip, the only card it held that would incline London to resume negotiations.

In the wee hours of April 11, General Galtieri and Secretary Haig held a private meeting where they weighed the risks being taken at that moment in the light of the increasingly entrenched Argentine position, which could trigger a confrontation nobody wished. Secretary Haig expressed his concern on behalf of the United States, about the invocation of the Rio Treaty. The meeting broke up at 0115 hours, and each delegation drew up a draft outlining the conclusions of the past 24 hours of talks.

The two positions were summed up as follows:

U.S. Draft Proposal

1. Demilitarization of the islands and withdrawal of forces by both sides within two weeks
2. Lifting of sanctions and restrictions
3. Establishment of a transition period through December 31, 1982, during which the local government of the islands would be maintained, overseen by a commission to

ratify the decision of the local body, such commission to be made up of a representative of the United States, one from Argentina, and one from Great Britain.

4. Reestablishment of communications facilities

Argentina's Draft Proposal

1. The governor is to be appointed by Argentina.

2. The Argentine national flag should continue to fly over the islands, with the assurance that once negotiations were finalized, Argentina's sovereignty would be acknowledged.

3. Native Argentines and islanders shall enjoy equal rights.

4. Demilitarization is to be understood within the framework of Resolution 502.

Considering that points 1 and 2 of the Argentine position were sine qua non conditions, there remained a broad gap between the two proposals, and Great Britain had yet to offer its opinion or agreement. By midmorning of April 11, the U.S. delegation was leaving Ezeiza Airport.

FROM THE BALCONY AT THE CASA ROSADA

While the U.S. and Argentine delegations were hammering out the makings of a tentative agreement within the confines of the presidential mansion, the Plaza de Mayo began to buzz with boisterous crowds that had come to vent their feelings. The rejoicing people of Argentina wanted to celebrate this unique milestone in their history. The crowds began to call for the president to come out on the west balcony of the Casa Rosada. Caught up in the contagious enthusiasm of his people, he improvised some allegorical words for the events that had taken place. But emotions can be the enemy of politicians, especially when verbalized from a balcony. What the president had effectively tried to say was that the idea had been to "occupy in order to negotiate," and that the troops would be withdrawn once this objective had been achieved and the new government in the islands had been installed. This was a change in the strategic-military game plan. But Britain's firm intent to send the fleet, and the clear indication that the Argentine people were giving their broad support to the action, made that basic premise change to "occupy in order to deter," thereby sending more troops and hardening the negotiating position. Ironically, when General Galtieri stepped in from the Casa Rosada balcony, he had, in strategic terms, lost considerable leverage, for he had made public pledges that dangerously narrowed his leeway in talks with an adversary whose entrenched position was becoming increasingly unassailable.

By that time, the London media were reporting that the prime minister was enjoying full backing for her hardline handling of the crisis, and were commenting favorably on the possibility of fulfilling Resolution 502 and negotiating the future of the islands with Argentina by means of a Hong Kong or New Hebrides-style solution.

A Cabinet meeting was held on April 12 in Buenos Aires during which a full analysis of the situation was undertaken, including the widespread support of the population. During this meeting, a call came through from Secretary Haig in London stating that he had been unable to make headway and asking that the calling of the IATRA meeting be delayed. He was told no such decision would be forthcoming so long as the fleet steamed toward the South Atlantic. But no change had been elicited in the British position regarding the islands. They were holding out for a return to the status prior to April 2.

The secretary of state's position from that time on was to apply increasing pressure on the Argentine government to see the dispute his way, which was far from satisfying the least of Buenos Aires's aspirations. Haig went so far as to threaten withdrawal from the negotiations, evidence of which was made public in a U.S. newspaper on April 14, thus betraying the firm U.S. determination to cease its assistance and take Great Britain's side in the dispute. (This had in fact been the situation from the very beginning, although the United States had maintained a de jure position of neutrality.)

At the United Nations, Argentina circulated document S/14,268 on April 12:

The Government of the Argentine Republic believes that the operative part of the . . . resolution constitutes a text that must be considered as a unified whole . . . .

Respect for cessation of hostilities is something to be demanded of both parties.

My government is prepared to comply with paragraph 2, on condition that the United Kingdom fully complies with the provision of paragraph 1 and does not attempt to use Resolution 502 as an instrument for justifying a return to the previous colonial situation. . . .

The government of the Argentine Republic also wishes to reaffirm its understanding to consider with an open and receptive mind the situation of 1,800 residents of the islands, which interests Argentina will respect.

In the meantime, the *London Times* had this headline on its front page on April 13: "Let them fly their flag on the Islands, says Owen." That day Mr. Henderson revealed Britain's bad faith for all to see when he submitted a note (published as document 14,973) rejecting the Argentine position regarding violation of Resolution 502 by the establishment of a naval exclusion zone by arguing that Argentina had been the first to violate it by occupying the South Georgia Islands on April 4. (In fact the occupation occurred on April 3 at 1122 hours New York time, the exact moment of the British garrison's surrender, such action having taken place prior to adoption of Resolution 502.) The Argentine government focused its diplomatic strategy on the support it could garner from the OAS as well as on the chances of the Haig initiatives in pressuring Britain in order to forestall hostilities. It was on April 13 that the U.S. ambassador to Buenos Aires, Mr. Schlaudemann, delivered a note from Secretary Haig to Foreign Minister Costa Mendez declaring that, in order to preserve the dignity of nations with which the United States shared both common roots and common interests, faith was not to be lost and trust in him should be maintained. That was all the encouragement Buenos Aires needed to continue keeping the faith both in Secretary Haig's initiatives and in the United States.

On April 14, a note signed by the European Common Market countries condemning Argentina's position was circulated within the Security Council. The following should be noted about this document:

1. For the first time a nonpolitical entity, whose purpose was commercial, had adopted political measures against a nonmember nation that had a dispute with one of its members.

2. The unanimity, speed, and enmity with which a country struggling for its own territorial integrity—and that had offended no one save Great Britain—had been slapped with sanctions was noteworthy.

3. The fact that sanctions would be applied in such a discriminatory fashion against a pro-Western, American nation whose population was overwhelmingly of European extraction was surprising in the face of the absence of similar measures against others deemed guilty of like offenses.

Meanwhile, at the OAS, support for Argentina was growing and draft resolutions calling for a negotiated settlement of the dispute were taking shape. Application of IATRA was being held back until Secretary Haig could wind up his initiatives. Noteworthy was the amendment proposed by St. Lucia and Barbados, Caribbean nations that are members of the Commonwealth and that had received backing from Argentina on more than one occasion, that the term Malvinas be replaced by Falkland—a proposal doomed to oblivion though it had the support not only of St. Lucia and Barbados but also of Antigua, Grenada, Jamaica, St. Vincent, and Trinidad and Tobago.

The OAS resolution, approved by consensus, bore witness to the good faith, the confidence in a peaceful resolution of international disputes, and the hope of a whole continent. It read as follows:

The Permanent Council of the Organization of American States,
WHEREAS:
The dispute between the Republic of Argentina and the United Kingdom of Great Britain and Northern Ireland in relation to the Malvinas Islands is endangering the peace of the Hemisphere,
RESOLVES:
1. To express its profound concern over the serious situation that the Republic of Argentina and the United Kingdom of Great Britain and Northern Ireland now face.
2. To express its fervent hope that a rapid, peaceful solution can be found to the disagreement between the two nations within the context of the rules of international law.
3. To offer its friendly cooperation in the peace efforts already under way, in the hope of contributing in this way to a peaceful settlement of the dispute that will avert once and for all the danger of war between the countries that deserve the respect of the international community. (CP/RES 359 [490/82])

THE SECOND COMING OF ALEXANDER HAIG

While the U.S. secretary of state was concluding his second round of talks in London and then stopping off in Washington on his return trip to Buenos Aires, options were being discussed for the next meeting. It was felt that the Argentine position should not be made public until the British position had been received and analyzed.

On April 14, information was received from the United States to the effect that ABC News, through the office of its director, Mr. Karel Berestein, had broadcast that the United States had come down on the British side of the conflict, and had offered the following:

1. Satellite communications support between the fleet and the nuclear submarines already on station in the South Atlantic

2. Logistics support through delivery to Ascension Island of 2 million gallons of fuel for the task force

3. Intelligence on the movement of Argentine troops and interception of their communications.

ABC News went on to question whether the Haig initiatives would have any effect since the United States had sided with Great Britain. Both the Pentagon and Gen. Vernon Walters (U.S. Army, Retired) would deny the truthfulness of this information in individual communications to Buenos Aires. But it is common knowledge today that the information was accurate and that Washington officials were either in the dark or at odds with the truth. In any event, this was a serious responsibility for the leader of the free world, which had pledged to remain neutral in the face of a conflict between members of its own camp. Not only should the United States have played a neutral role in assisting two friendly nations to resolve a conflict, it should have taken the lead as the Western superpower and the cradle of the way of life that has been the choice of the nations of the free world.

Secretary Haig telephoned Foreign Minister Costa Mendez that same afternoon at 1350 hours, giving assurances that he would be making a public statement on the subject on ABC News and that the British fleet would not sail beyond Ascension. He appeared both surprised and upset to learn that Mrs. Thatcher had gone before Parliament to state that there could be no negotiations with Argentina, since he had asked her to avoid making such statements public. Dr. Costa Mendez was surprised to learn from Secretary Haig that the truth of the matter was that the British government had—as of that date, April 14—made no proposal except the original ultimatum demanding the withdrawal of Argentine forces and a return to the status quo prior to April 2.

It became painfully obvious at this stage of the game that Secretary Haig's initiative had come to naught, since not only had he been unable to modify the British posture, but he had failed to halt the task force at Ascension, the halfway point to its rendezvous in the South Atlantic. That Alexander Haig could have been acting in bad faith in order to buy time for one of the contenders to improve its chances on the battlefield is not something that could be seriously considered as a calculated U.S. objective.

In later communications that same day with Buenos Aires, the U.S. secretary of state gave his assurances that he would be bringing new British options on April 15, to be laid out the following day. He also sent a formal letter to President Galtieri on President Reagan's behalf, calling for confidence, patience, and mindfulness of the need to keep this situation from becoming a North-South conflict.

While Secretary Haig was flying to Buenos Aires, General Galtieri received a second telephone call from President Reagan on April 15 at 1900 hours. This conversation was couched in terms of the sincerity and goodwill of two statesmen in search of a settlement to a conflict. There was an understanding, a commonality of purpose, and a mutual respect that had seldom have been voiced in the history of relations between the United States and Argentina.

But it was not enough. There was a third party to the dispute, and hidden interests can be more powerful than the noble intentions of presidents, even the president of the United States. Late that evening, Secretary Haig and his team landed at Ezeiza Airport. He appeared optimistic, and the meeting with President Galtieri at the Casa Rosada was set for 1000 hours the next morning. As if to torpedo the second round of talks between Secretary Haig and the government in Buenos Aires, the British government distributed a note dated April 16 to serve notice that any ship or aircraft approaching the task force, whether civilian, commercial, or military, would be deemed hostile and subject to attack. To add to this state of affairs, news was received that same day that the task force had weighed anchor at Ascension and was steaming south.

Argentina reacted by delivering a note to the Security Council in which it stated:

1. It was willing to implement Resolution 502.

2. Its goodwill was demonstrated by the negotiations it had been carrying on through the good offices of the United States.

3. The adoption of the use of force by the United Kingdom made the situation worse, in that it was unreasonable to expect one of the parties to implement Resolution 502 unilaterally, thus placing it in an absolutely defenseless position.

4. Britain's actions were inconsistent, for it heeded international organizations on the one hand while on the other it employed force, a position it appeared to justify in the framework of an outmoded concept of punitive expeditions, through a subjective interpretation of international law, the likes of which had been brought into question even in the harshest days of colonialism.

5. The current situation was an act of "recolonization" through the use of force, an unprecedented event in the history of the United Nations.

6. It was the British government that had threatened to use force to expel an Argentine work crew from Port Leith.

7. The announced sailing of the fleet, which bore witness to Britain's unwillingness to implement Resolution 502, obliged Argentina to resort to legitimate self-defense, as provided for under Article 51 of the U.N. Charter.

8. Argentina had ceased all hostilities, and had not in any manner threatened the United Kingdom with a hostile act.

Secretary Haig arrived at the Casa Rosada at the appointed hour to meet with General Galtieri, who proceeded to outline the Argentine position, which contained seven main points:

1. Halt the fleet.

2. Maintain the Argentine flag over the islands.

3. Broaden Argentina's role in the islands during the transition phase.

4. Guarantee that negotiations would be concluded in Argentina's favor by year's end.

5. Guide the process in accordance with the principles of decolonization.

6. Reestablish normal communications between the islands and the mainland.

7. Lift the sanctions and guarantee U.S. support throughout the process.

The talks were continued at San Martin Palace, which houses the Foreign Ministry, and a document was drawn up framing the Argentine position, although at that time there was no similar document outlining Britain's intent. All the Argentine side was able to elicit from Secretary Haig's collaborators was a paper listing those points they felt might be acceptable to the United Kingdom.

Attention was then turned to the draft Argentine proposals, in which changes suggested by the United States were made—everything of course subject to the final wishes of Great Britain, a very unorthodox manner of conducting serious negotiations over a matter such as this. At 1900 hours, the foreign minister left San Martin Palace and made public the three points that were still at odds with the Argentine position: the issues of government, the rights of Argentine inhabitants, and the final status of the islands (sovereignty). He also noted the risk that the U.S. position might harden, that the threat of war was looming ever higher, and that Argentina could lose support within the international community. The changes Argentina had hoped to introduce into the three critical points of the draft had been labeled "unacceptable to Great Britain" by Secretary Haig, who added the comment that were he to send such proposals to London that night, there would be war.

The next day, Saturday, April 17, at 1000 hours, Secretary Haig met with the military junta. The secretary of state stated his fear of a broadening of the conflict and the dire consequences to U.S. good relations with Latin America. He had tried to structure some changes in the proposals. He underscored the fact that Argentina should have every confidence that the United States could achieve a settlement that would satisfy its national aspirations. He insisted on maintaining an ambiguous political stance and that it should be clear that the long-term intention was the return of the islands to Argentina. Secretary Haig gave every indication that he was truthful and sincere, but events were conspiring against his apparent good intentions. The United States' making available the facilities at Ascension, Caspar Weinberger's statements, the ABC News report, the sailing of the fleet south from Ascension, and other signals had completely undermined any faith Argentine diplomats could have entertained with regard to a deal they regarded as dubious at best, as well as toward a go-between who had come down on the opponent's side.

The military junta decided to make it known to Secretary Haig that each people has its own historical icons; that for Argentines, the Malvinas were such a icon; that it was not feasible to come to terms at gunpoint; and that, aside from halting the British fleet's southward advance, broader assurances should be given that sovereignty over the islands would be transferred to Argentina as of December 31, 1982. Secretary Haig noted that Great Britain attached great interest to the paragraph dealing with government, at which the working committee busied itself about coming up with a new wording for the points in question.

The talks continued into the afternoon. Argentina's foreign minister expressed doubts as to what would happen if no transfer of sovereignty had been effected by December 31. He stated that the military operation had brought the diplomatic freeze to a full boil and that now was not the time to concede on the diplomatic front that which had been gained on the battlefield. Secretary Haig replied that in terms of international law, the use of force to change the status of a dispute was untenable; that Great Britain—as well as the United States—could not swallow such a contention; and that, for the British, it was sufficient reason to go to war. Foreign Minister Costa Mendez agreed, but pointed out that when it came to grabbing lands by force of arms, Great Britain was the undisputed world champion. At 2200 hours, Secretary Haig and his team left the Casa Rosada.

While the working committee put the finishing touches, including some of the requested amendments, on a final version of a memorandum of agreement to be submitted to Secretary Haig on the morning of April 18, the military junta, faced with the imminent arrival of the British fleet in waters under the jurisdiction of the IATRA security zone, and in the absence of any foreseeable agreement, decided to invoke the Rio Treaty as of Monday, April 19.

At 1430 hours on the afternoon of April 18, another meeting was held. At first, Secretary Haig seemed pleased with the progress made in the new wording of the draft agreement. But he later proposed some changes that proved unacceptable, under the guise that, in order to meet with Mrs. Thatcher's approval, everything had to be vague. In fact, these changes were tantamount to a return to the existing status prior to the initiation of hostilities, and they further underscored the issue of self-determination for the islanders.

The Argentine delegation withdrew to deliberate in private. They returned with a new proposal: that sovereignty should be transferred to Argentina no later than December 31. Secretary Haig shook his head. He warned of the impending arrival of the fleet, of the consequences of a military confrontation. He predicted the fall of the Argentine government and, finally, he threatened to call off the talks altogether. As a final touch, he explained that the only position Mrs. Thatcher had ever espoused was that of full withdrawal of Argentine forces and the reestablishment of British authority. Then there could be talks. Thus did the intentions of the British finally come into focus. They had tried to mask their own intransigence while Argentina bargained through the U.S. delegation, the better to gain time for the fleet to position itself for the attack, and charge that it was Argentina that had broken off the talks by refusing to accept the terms proposed. Everything would thus appear neatly wrapped up. Could one expect better of Perfidious Albion? ("Perfidious Albion" is a French poet's reference to England in a 1793 work.)

Finally, while the talks were still going on, Secretary Haig received a message that caused him to break off the meeting and state that he had to leave at 1600 hours to deal with an emergency. Foreign Minister Costa Mendez saw him off at Ezeiza Airport, where he delivered Argentina's latest proposal and made a short statement. Buenos Aires did not see General Alexander Haig as U.S. secretary of state again. The foreign minister received a message on April 20 that indicated London's rejection of the proposals on demilitarization and sovereignty, and pointed out that the rights of the islanders were not sufficiently ensured. Suffice it to say that the whole Haig initiative, at least from the Argentine standpoint, had been in vain.

ARGENTINA INVOKES THE RIO TREATY

The military committee met on April 20 to decide on a course of action following the failure of Secretary Haig's efforts. The British fleet's estimated time of arrival in the theater of operations was on or about April 25, and the decision was made to go ahead and invoke the Rio Treaty. About the same time in Washington, Argentine ambassador Raul Quijano was preparing his address to the OAS. The U.S. representative to that body appeared surprised at this turn of events, in light of the progress Secretary Haig apparently had made in the talks (according to the U.S. representative's statements).

The OAS paid close attention to the words of Argentina's representative as he outlined Buenos Aires's position, Argentina's rights to the islands, its complete willingness to discuss everything except the issue of sovereignty. Several speakers followed him to the podium, and then the ballots were cast. The vote was 18 yeas, 0 nays, and 3 abstentions: the United States, Colombia, and Trinidad and Tobago. As a result of that vote, the 21 signatory nations of the Rio Treaty held the twentieth meeting of consultation of foreign ministers to deal with one of the most serious issues ever submitted to that body. And while the political and diplomatic world of Washington was caught up in the swirl of such activity,

7,000 miles to the south, Argentine Air Force craft had picked up the task force as it entered the IATRA security zone and began to assume proper battle stations.

On April 23, Haig wired Buenos Aires that his talks with Pym were at a stalemate because of British rejection of the various points, while the media revealed that the first units of the task force were 50 miles off the South Georgia Islands and that Pym had stated that there was still "a broad margin for talks." In London, the press picked up on reports of internal dissension within the Cabinet between those who favored an immediate military response and those who felt irreparable damage would be done to Britain's international position. The *Washington Post* pointed out on its editorial page that Haig's bold diplomacy, deemed ridiculous by some Americans and labeled by London as treacherous, was "what it was because Margaret Thatcher wants it that way." In Buenos Aires, public opinion polls indicated continued strong support for the decision to reclaim the islands, that they should not be returned at any price, and that suspicion toward the United States was on the rise.

During the military junta's meeting of April 23, basic guidelines for the invocation of the Rio Treaty were drawn up, with a view to ensuring that the wording of any resolution would avoid calling for drastic measures such as a joint breaking of diplomatic relations with Great Britain or participation of troops from the American republics in the conflict. Also to be avoided was any overly radical confrontation between the United States and the rest of Latin America. Furthermore, there should be a consensus for any measures adopted, for the less drastic the resolution, the more support it would elicit, even though only 14 votes out of a possible 21 were needed to carry the day.

On April 23, the Argentine delegation left Buenos Aires for Washington, heavily laden with instructions for the big meeting of the OAS. Two days later, news was received that Great Britain had proclaimed an air and sea exclusion zone around the task force, which was already within the IATRA security zone, and that the Argentine garrison on South Georgia Island had come under attack by British forces. Argentina presented a firm protest to the Security Council against both of these acts of aggression (note no. 14,999). Upon its arrival in Washington, the delegation from Buenos Aires was apprised of the events described above. They were also informed that the secretary of state wished to meet with Foreign Minister Costa Mendez. This invitation was declined because the United Kingdom had committed acts of aggression during ongoing talks with the United States, actions that had caused a very negative reaction in the international community, especially within the OAS. Through its actions, Britain was being disloyal to the United States and underhanded with regard to the recommendations of the Security Council. Once again it bore witness for all to see, to its lack of good faith in seeking a negotiated settlement, in spite of Argentina's best efforts in that direction.

Secretary Haig, in a later telephone conversation with Argentina's foreign minister, expressed his deep concern over this turn of events. He pledged his ongoing efforts, and those of President Reagan, in the search for a negotiated settlement in order to avoid what could be a deep tragedy for the Western world.

Mrs. Thatcher went before Parliament to give assurance that the attack against an Argentine submarine at Grytviken was justified because the vessel had constituted a threat against the fleet, and that in the process of retaking the South Georgia Islands, no losses had been incurred. (The task force lost two helicopters during this first action. This fact, now acknowledged, is proof that the British government bent the truth and hid its losses from the very outset.) She expressed confidence, moreover, that negotiations would continue with Secretary Haig's assistance. She added that time was running out, that the fleet was approaching the Malvinas and that Argentina alone must shoulder responsibility for the consequences.

There was obviously enough leeway in the wording of Resolution 502 for Great Britain to turn it to its own advantage, to justify the aggression deemed necessary by the governing party to achieve a military solution to the problem, and to allow its diplomats to press their demands on Argentina for unilateral compliance on some points while reserving the right not to comply with points not to Britain's advantage. It appears inexplicable that the Security Council, in the face of diverse interpretations of words that could mean the difference between war and peace, between life and death for several hundred men, did not intervene to clarify concepts and establish priorities for compliance with the points it propounded, as well as a timetable for carrying them out.

Britain's response also betrayed its overwhelming interest in stalling the negotiations, for had it wished otherwise, there can be no doubt that the conflict would have been brought to a standstill in the very first days, considering that a solution was both planned and desired by Argentina, which had steadfastly rejected the ultimatum it was being compelled to accept, and was fighting for what it regarded as rightfully its own, as well as for its dignity as a sovereign nation.

On April 26, the coordination bureau for the nonaligned nations, headquartered in Havana, came out in favor of Argentina's claim of sovereignty over the Malvinas and expressed support for a peaceful, lasting, and fair negotiated settlement within the framework of Resolution 502 of the Security Council. As the date for the twentieth meeting of consultation of the Rio Treaty countries neared, the U.S. secretary of state played every chip on the U.S. political game board to head off this event. While the U.S. ambassadors in every Latin American country maneuvered in vain to block the meeting, Foreign Minister Costa Mendez was receiving personal telephone calls from Secretary Haig, whose aim was the same and who seized upon these opportunities to issue dire warnings (or were they threats?) of a fearful attack to be mounted against Argentine positions on Malvinas at a very early date.

At long last, the foreign ministers of the American republics, brought together for this momentous assembly, heard these words from Argentina's foreign minister:

The facts are clear and known by all. The Argentine people suffered a century and a half of usurpation in silence. Short shrift was made of a 17-year effort to negotiate this dispute. And, finally, the Argentine nation was jolted by a British act of force as inexplicable as it was overblown: a group of civilian workers from Argentina, who were going about their business on South Georgia Island, under the terms of a private contract agreed to by commercial interests in both countries, with the prior consent of the British government, were threatened with forcible eviction by the United Kingdom, which backed up her threat by summarily dispatching vessels of war.

Once Argentina had fully reestablished her sovereignty over the Malvinas Islands, my government made known its full willingness to implement Resolution 502, as approved by the U.N. Security Council, with the understanding that its three main clauses constituted a whole. It was the United Kingdom, and not Argentina, that violated that mandate by threatening the initiation of hostilities, as she soon proceeded to do, by sending out a powerful war fleet. How could Argentina be expected to withdraw her forces when the bulk of Britain's naval might was headed for our shores?

Mr. Chairman, the use of force against an American state by a foreign extracontinental power is being perpetrated before your very eyes. Peace in the Americas is in grave danger, and with it the territorial integrity of Argentina. . . .

We cannot stand by while silence or ambiguous statements hinder a decision, wherefore speed is of the essence. A colonial venture backed by a powerful military machine should not be allowed to materialize at this juncture of history in any part of the world. Much less should such an action pose a grave threat to the peace and security of America. It is illicit, it is immoral, it is a historical fluke. Our proposal, as I have stated, should be both clear and immediate. The British fleet has its place in another part of the world, and colonialism has no place anywhere in the world. It is a tragedy of another time. . . .

The historical process of the emancipation of the Americas shall not have ended for as long as there remain within our hemisphere peoples or areas under colonial rule, or territories occupied by non-American nations.

Foreign Minister Costa Mendez's closing words were met with a thundering standing ovation that was without precedent in the annals of the IATRA. All the foreign ministers were on their feet—all, that is, except Secretary of State Haig.

When it came Secretary Haig's turn to speak, he stated that the United States follows the rule of international law, and that changes brought on by the use of force between nations cannot be accepted. He added that the United Kingdom was the United States' closest ally, and that Mrs. Thatcher had been seeking a peaceful settlement, while pointing out that Argentina had rejected a U.S. proposal. At the conclusion of his speech, there was silence throughout the chamber. Secretary Haig had just played out the most disastrous role of his career. Not only that, his words were flawed.

The Argentine delegation had not had so much as a peek at the latest U.S. proposals, much less the chance to reject them.

When votes were counted, the draft resolution was adopted by a yea vote of 17, no objections, and 4 abstentions (the United States, Colombia, Trinidad and Tobago, and Chile). The resolution called for an immediate cessation of hostilities and a peaceful settlement of the conflict; it deplored the stance of the EEC; it stated that Argentina's undeniable right to sovereignty over the Malvinas Islands, as provided for by the Inter-American Juridical Committee, should be taken into account; it further provided for the resolution's being submitted to the Security Council; and, finally, it called for keeping the meeting of consultation open with a view to overseeing compliance with the terms of the resolution, as well as taking any additional steps that might prove necessary.

SCOPE OF THE IATRA RESOLUTION

The wording of the final point of the resolution gives rise to serious reflection. What was its true scope in regard to the lifting of sanctions and cessation of hostilities, as well as to the final settlement of the dispute? The crux of the matter is that it had no teeth whatsoever. The Security Council stood pat; Great Britain was not so much as ruffled. It showed a total lack of concern, and turned a cold shoulder to the call from the foreign ministers of a whole continent. What was of significance at this stage was not so much the legitimate claim of a member nation regarding its territorial integrity as the respect due to a recognized body in the international community. We in this part of the world were to learn that validation of a people's rights is not endorsed by the legitimacy of their scrolls or by the eloquence of their orators, but by the severity of the sanctions leveled against them. What would have come to pass had 20 American nations joined together in breaking diplomatic and trade relations with the aggressor? What would have happened had the nonaligned nations taken up the cause? And, in this particular instance, what if the Eastern bloc nations and Arab League had joined in?

It should be pointed out that this meeting, which had been largely justified by the British attack on the South Georgia Islands, made no mention thereof in its resolution, nor did it refer to the South Sandwich Islands.

SECRETARY HAIG'S FINAL EFFORTS

Following the meeting of consultation, Secretary of State Haig met with Foreign Minister Costa Mendez in the office of the secretary general of the OAS. At this time, a proposal from President Reagan was laid on the table, an entreaty to both nations in a last ditch-effort to head off the final showdown. The proposal was delivered to the U.S. embassy in Buenos Aires and to Dr. Costa Mendez in Washington in the early hours of April 27. The document was accompanied by a statement from the secretary of state that called upon Argentina to give an answer by midnight that same day. These documents were digested by Argentine officials in both capitals. They concluded that the new conditions were even less favorable than those rejected in the April 19 proposal.

Argentina couched its response in general terms, in the sense that more time would be required for proper evaluation; that certain points were conducive to further negotiations while others did not meet basic requirements; that the Argentine government was in every way willing to seek a peaceful settlement, as long as the opposing side did not impose impossible demands for a solution. Appreciation was expressed to the U.S. government for its efforts to achieve a negotiated settlement, especially in light of the fact that an attack by the United Kingdom against the islands was imminent. This response was worded so as not to be interpreted as a rejection, in order to avoid Argentina's taking the blame for the collapse of the talks and thus paving the way for the British attack—which already was practically under way—as well as the United States' making good on its announced intention of granting aid to the United Kingdom.

It was obvious that, faced by a mediator who had lost the confidence both of the negotiators and the public, officials in Buenos Aires, whose position had hardened in light of these events and the show of bad faith by the opposing side, could not fathom that acceptance of such a proposal might have called a halt to the coming onslaught, entrusting the fate of the islands' status to further talks in which the United States promised assistance, but with no assurance as to the outcome.

But there remained yet another element to weigh in the balance: were Argentina to accept the draft proposal, how would it be received by the British? Based on the hard experience of the talks until then, the London solution as framed by the Conservative government—which appeared to be aimed at ensuring its survival in power—was the military solution: kick the invaders out! Once the fleet had been sent on its way, could it conceivably return empty-handed? By the same token, Argentina had never been handed a hard proposal by London other than an ultimatum to remove its troops from the islands—pronto. Moreover, the latest U.S. proposal apparently had been rejected by London on April 23, and had been submitted to Buenos Aires as a token action to underscore that rejection and single out Argentina as responsible for the breakdown of the talks—which, in turn, gave the British the green light to proceed with the attack.

On that same day, April 28, as if in response to the IATRA resolution, Great Britain notified the Security Council, by means of document no. 15,006, that it was establishing a total exclusion zone around the islands, adding the surrounding air space to the naval exclusion zone that had been in place since April 12.

ARGENTINA TAKES THE FALL

On April 28, Dr. Costa Mendez met with Secretary Haig at the State Department. The latter pointed out that the British fleet could not turn about without some justification, and that war appeared inevitable. The British would almost certainly launch their attack on April 30 and, with that, the opening of hostilities, the United States would support Britain. He also forecast that the Argentine government would cave in under the pressures brought to bear. Costa Mendez replied that this was the cause of a nation and not of a military government. The nation had received the unwavering support of the OAS; the American republics acknowledged Argentina's sovereignty over the islands; and a negotiated settlement should continue to be sought. He also inquired as to the United Kingdom's answer to President Reagan's proposal.

Secretary Haig responded that Mrs. Thatcher's government, which affirmed that the crisis had been triggered by Argentina, had not been satisfied. He added that the document was a good option for Argentina and, were it to accept it, the United States would get Britain's acceptance. It was a question of trust, for the United Kingdom could not face another crisis similar to the current one.

Costa Mendez reminded Secretary Haig that, as strong as the ties of kinship binding the United Kingdom and the United States may be, the latter should be mindful that its interests in Latin America are at least of the same weight as those in Europe. The negotiations boiled down to three central issues: sovereignty, government, and the wishes of the islanders. Haig stated that, when the chips were down, one of the sides had to take the fall for the breakdown of the talks; and the United States, for political considerations, could offer no assurances to the Argentine government regarding final sovereignty over the Malvinas Islands.

Meanwhile, in London, the Cabinet sat on the U.S. proposal without issuing an answer, hoping that Argentina would reject it and thus shoulder the blame for the collapse of negotiations.

On April 29, Argentina presented its formal answer to the latest U.S. proposal. The Department of State responded in terms that indicated it would issue a public statement holding Argentina responsible for the failure of the talks, that Great Britain would accept the proposal, and that the United States would apply severe sanctions against Argentina and would advise U.S. citizens to leave that country.

At noon the next day, U.S. Secretary of State Haig issued the following press release:

The South Atlantic crisis is about to enter a new and dangerous phase in which large-scale military actions are likely. We have made a determined effort to restore peace. . . .

We made this effort because the crisis raised the vital issue of Hemispheric solidarity at a time when a Communist adversary seeks positions of influence on the mainland of the Americas . . . .

The United States made this extraordinary effort because the stakes in human lives and international order require it.

. . . We acted as well because the United States has the confidence of both parties. The United Kingdom is our closest ally. . . . We have also recently developed a better relationship with Argentina, as part of our success in revitalizing the community of American States.

The British Government has shown complete understanding for this position. Now, however, in light of Argentina's unwillingness to accept a compromise, we must take steps to underscore that the U.S. cannot and will not condone the use of unlawful force to resolve disputes.*

*This was not the policy followed by the United States in 1983 in Grenada. It is quite plain, therefore, that principles are respected or interpreted in accordance with what is expedient at the moment.

The President has therefore ordered the suspension of all military exports to Argentina, the withholding of certification of Argentine eligibility for military sales, the suspension of new Export-Import Bank credits and guarantees and the suspension of Commodity Credit Corporation guarantees.

The President also directed that the United States will respond positively to requests for material support for British forces. There will, of course, be no direct U.S. military involvement. American policy will continue to be guided by our concern for the rule of law and our desire to facilitate an early and fair settlement . . . .(*The Times* [London], May 1, 1982, p. 4)

The analysis of the document from an abstract, logical perspective reveals serious contradictions arising from confusing and enigmatic intentions that are at variance with the administration's stated policies. The section spelling out the resolutions (the adoption of sanctions against Argentina and the granting of almost unbridled support to the United Kingdom) also expresses the sincere desire to do the following:

—Prevent "large scale military actions"

—Avoid "the stakes in human lives"

—Preserve "the international order"

—Not jeopardize "the vital issue of Hemispheric solidarity"

—Revitalize "the community of American States"

—Enjoy "the confidence of both parties"

—Develop "a better relationship with Argentina"

—Achieve " . . . our desire to facilitate an early and fair settlement"

—Counter a Communist adversary who "seeks positions of influence in the mainland of the Americas."

Is it to be concluded from all this that these feelings are in consonance with the fact that " . . . the United Kingdom is our closest ally" and that "The British Government has shown a complete understanding for this position"?

What more could Mrs. Thatcher's government want? Washington was giving full backing to her decision to reclaim the islands by force while throwing its policy of hemispheric solidarity to the winds, along with its responsibilities toward the Rio Treaty and the future outcome of the struggle against Marxist penetration in Central America, to which the Buenos Aires government had given broad support, not only on the diplomatic front but also by sending military advisers to this area where U.S. strategic security was in jeopardy. In this regard, columnist John M. Grasho made a wise observation: "The first casualty of President Reagan's decision to side openly with Britain in the Falkland Islands dispute is the hope of enlisting Argentina as a key ally of the U.S. campaign to build an inter-American front against Communist penetration in the Western Hemisphere" (*Washington Post*, May 2, 1982, p. 4).

As time pressed inexorably on, the Argentine government released a statement through the OAS, in which it made the following points:

The United States, a member country of the Organization of American States, and a state party to the Inter-American Treaty of Reciprocal Assistance, took part in the sessions of the Twentieth Meeting of Consultation under your able Chairmanship on April 26th, 27th, and 28th. In the remarks of Secretary of State Haig, at no time did the United States state, or even suggest or hint at, the possibility of taking the coercive measures . . . indicated. They were announced the day after the American Ministers of Foreign Affairs had left Washington, D.C.

The economic measures [U.S. sanctions against Argentina] . . . indicated are included in the censure that similar measures taken by states not parties to the Inter-American Treaty of Reciprocal Assistance received from the Organ of Consultation in operative paragraph 5 of the resolution on the serious situation in the South Atlantic adopted on April 28th, 1982. In this instance, the measures are even more reprehensible because they come from a state party to the Treaty in reference which is obliged to comply with the decisions of the Organ of Consultation.

Although this situation is highly serious, even more serious is the announcement of military support to an extracontinental state that is in conflict with an American State and which the Organ of Consultation has urged immediately to cease the hostilities it is carrying on within the security region defined by Article 4 of the Inter-American Treaty of Reciprocal Assistance and also to refrain from any act that may affect inter-American peace and security.

Equally serious is the fact that, while the Organ of Consultation urges both Governments immediately to call a truce that will make it possible to resume and proceed normally with the negotiation aimed at a peaceful settlement of the conflict—a mandate that my government accepted and so informed Your Excellency—a state party to the Inter-American Treaty of Reciprocal Assistance announces that it will lend military support to one of the parties in conflict.

The decisions of the Organ of Consultation have been set aside by the Government of the United States of America in its declaration of yesterday, in which it openly sides with the extracontinental aggressive power.

We deplore this position of the United States Government because it can mean a real split in the inter-American system by ignoring the commitments involved in the Organization of American States. (Doc. 36/82, OAS).

On April 30, the British fleet was sighted off the Malvinas Islands. This act, as tragic as it was unrestrained in light of its historical genesis, was being played out by a leading Western nation whose way of life had served as a blueprint for our own, while in the wings stood the U.S. secretary of state.

We would like to believe that Secretary Haig was sincere in his efforts to mediate the dispute, but in attempting to impose the solution of one contender without heeding the least of the legitimate aspirations of the other, he made a serious error, for if the Haig initiatives' intent had been to seek a negotiated settlement by every possible means, the failure had been complete. But if the objective was to buy time, the better to allow the British fleet to position itself for the attack while standing in the way of any further attempt to find a way out, then truly, "Mission Impossible" had become "Mission Accomplished"!

4

Deployment

I believed that America's moral fiber, alone among free countries,
was sufficiently powerful to ensure global security.

Henry Kissinger

BRITISH READINESS

Although British armed forces had not actually been engaged in a shooting war
since the 1956 Suez crisis, Great Britain was nevertheless prepared to meet any
contingency arising from its Atlantic Alliance obligations. For this purpose, a
high level of preparedness and professionalism was found within the ranks of
all its military forces, and especially within the Royal Navy.

But the Royal Navy's NATO role was being steered on a course that was
clearly at odds with the Admiralty's aspirations. If one considers that NATO
strategic military concepts are merely defensive, Britain's role was to ensure
that strategic deterrent (Polaris and Trident weapons systems), and in such a
framework aircraft carriers did not make a lot of sense. In spite of this, the Royal
Navy had defended the continued existence of its carriers by modifying current
strategic doctrines in order to justify their use as helicopter platforms in antisubmarine warfare.

Along with aircraft carriers, a significant number of surface vessels would
soon become the object of a reduction in force (from 66 vessels in mid 1981 to
44 in 1985). In keeping with these planned cutbacks, the first ship to feel the
scrapper's torch would have to be the HMS *Endurance*, a polar patrol vessel
normally assigned to the Antarctic and the South Atlantic. Its retirement had
been confirmed by Parliament as early as June 30, 1981, following bitter arguments between the proponents of the measure (Defense Ministry) and its foes
(the Foreign Office, the Islands Council, and its defenders in Parliament). In

this regard, Lord Hill Norton, admiral of the Royal Navy and chief of defense operations, stated: "In two more years, we would have been unable to stage the task force, and we would have been defeated had we so tried."

Under these circumstances, the South Atlantic conflict took the British government by surprise at an ideal moment for the Admiralty: Here were aircraft carriers and a part of the fleet scheduled for decommissioning just when a military situation arose whose solution would of necessity require the use of this very type of vessel if there was to be any hope of a successful outcome in a confrontation with a land-based air force. Furthermore, at the time Argentina's forces reclaimed Port Stanley, part of the fleet was on annual maneuvers in the Mediterranean. This not only shortened their voyage by 1,200 miles but also meant that these units, both surface and undersea, were operational and available for immediate action.

By the same token, there had been much speculation as to the amount of warning the United Kingdom had to prepare for a possible invasion of the islands by Argentina. In this a distinction must be made, within official British circles, between two opposing camps: the British government and the Admiralty. Intelligence reports available at that time to British government circles speculated that Argentina would take no military action to reclaim the islands anytime soon (Franks Report, para. 149), although on March 10 (Franks Report, para. 151), a defense intelligence official warned the Foreign Office that recent statements published in the Buenos Aires press had the backing of the Argentine Navy, which was pressuring for a diplomatic offensive—"break diplomatic relations with Great Britain and launch a military offensive against the Islands"—while concluding that other government circles in Buenos Aires were more inclined to a negotiated settlement, and that the military option was out of the question. Nevertheless, a unilateral communiqué published by the Foreign Ministry following the round of talks in New York toward the end of February 1982, which was made public on March 2, put the British government on alert and the prime minister ordered up contingency plans. As early as March 8, Mrs. Thatcher is known to have spoken with Defense Minister John Nott, inquiring as to the time it would take for the Royal Navy to reach the islands should the need arise. The answer was 20 days (Franks Report, para. 153).

By all accounts, the taking of the islands on April 2 took the British public completely by surprise, to the point that news reports in that morning's Buenos Aires papers were discounted as false, even though there had been an inkling of the impending invasion as early as March 31, when Governor Hunt was informed that the Argentine submarine ARA *Santa Fe* was steering a course toward the islands. He had also received confirmation on April 1 that Task Force 40 had been sighted off the islands.

With regard to how forewarned the Royal Navy had been, available sources indicate that it suspected more than did the government. Chilean journalist Raul Sohn, based in Great Britain, has published articles stating that the Royal Navy had access to the best intelligence in this regard. It had been fighting a running battle with the government, in light of the prime minister's stated policy of reducing public expenditures, to the extent that the Royal Navy would suffer a 50,000-man reduction as well as the decommissioning of 20 vessels, which would reduce it to one aircraft carrier on active duty. All of this ran counter to the thinking of numerous ranking admirals, who felt that only a conflict on the seas in a far-off place would return the Royal Navy to its former prominence.

Also of great interest was a statement by Virginia Gamba, an Argentine analyst with degrees in Latin American and foreign affairs earned in Great Britain, affirming that the Royal Navy has always been able to defend itself in the face of any threat to its existence, protecting the alleged usefulness of its aircraft carriers according to the circumstances, whether as a shock force (1957), as an antisubmarine weapon (1966), or as the unbeatable means of extending the long arm of empire (1982).

The Royal Navy's state of readiness was described by Commander Nick Kerr, of that service, a member of the British Defense Ministry's Operations Center, in the following terms:

. . . only by accident were the two light carriers available. HMS *Hermes* and HMS *Invincible* had just completed exercises and were about to put into their home ports and send their crews home on liberty. Another group, which had just completed NATO exercises, were about to sail from Gibraltar. Other units were heading towards their home bases to observe the Easter Holiday. In another 24 hours, these crews would have scattered throughout Britain, and many would have gone on holiday abroad.

But the staging of the Task Force on Thursday and Friday of that week (April 1 and 2) caught them just before liberty. Such was the case of the 3rd Royal Marine Commando Brigade, which had just made home port at Plymouth.

. . . all records [for making ready] were broken, planes were flown, stockpiles were made ready, and men sent to their ships in record time. ("The Falkland Campaign," *Naval War College Review*, Nov.–Dec. 1982, pp. 14–15)

In the same vein, British M.P. Tom Dalyell stated in his book *One Man's Falkland*: " . . . the Navy wanted to sail to the South Atlantic, among others, in order to justify its belief in the future of capital ships such as the *Invincible*, which the Government wanted to sell off. . . . "

What the facts bear out in regard to the British reaction to Argentina's reclaiming of the Malvinas Islands is that by April 3, the British government had decided to send a huge task force to the South Atlantic. A short 48 hours later, on April 5, a powerful fleet weighed anchor at Portsmouth and set its course to a rendezvous, 8,000 miles from home, with an aircraft carrier slated for the scrap heap as its flagship.

A surprising split-second reaction indeed. Almost too surprising on such a short notice.

ARGENTINE READINESS

It could be supposed that since the initiative in retaking the islands had been Argentina's, its armed forces must have had sufficient warning for the approaching campaign. It was not so. Contingency planning for use of the military option had been cloaked in such secrecy that even Argentina's intelligence services had been kept in the dark until the last few hours prior to the landings in the islands.

At the time of the incident on South Georgia, all the military junta had decided was to plan for a bloodless takeover of the Malvinas—in case the talks became deadlocked. The establishment of these plans had been entrusted to three general officers who were to draw them up without letting any other person or agency in on them, all papers to be written in longhand. These plans specified that the armed forces would need until May 15 to prepare for such an operation, and that they would need at least 15 days' advance notice.

It was the landing of the Argentine work crew at Port Leith that triggered the British reaction which came as such a surprise both to the members of the military junta and to the foreign minister. At first, it was decided to play the incident down, an idea that prevailed on March 20–22. But surprise became alarm with the cable traffic from London that revealed the British Parliament was openly discussing protection of the islanders, their territory, and their wishes, as well as the growing swell against transfer of sovereignty and for the sending of a fleet to the South Atlantic. Britain's implementation of any one of these actions would be a dangerous setback to Argentina's dream of reestablishing its claim to the islands. After conferring, the commanders in chief decided to carry out Operation Azul on April 1, with April 2 and 3 being backup dates. This agreement was made official during the military junta's March 26 meeting.

The armed forces had to be at the peak of readiness. The army had yet to complete processing the military draft class of 1963, and most of the young draftees had just entered basic training. The navy had yet to complete refitting several key vessels. Installation of the Super Etendard-Exocet weapons system, half of which was sitting in crates on the docks at Marseilles, following France's embargo of weapons shipments to Argentina in the wake of the invasion of the islands, was incomplete. The air force's ongoing state of readiness allowed it to play an active role in the conflict with acceptable operational standards, although its men were not sufficiently trained or properly equipped to come to grips with such a skilled adversary as the British task force. All of this reinforces the fact that the armed forces had never given so much as a thought to establishing a war hypothesis for a conflict with Great Britain, for such had not been envisioned as a possibility.

The British fleet received its sailing orders on March 28, as did the units that constituted Argentina's Task Force 40, heading to points unknown. The Argentine army learned of the retaking of the islands on April 2, while the Argentine Air Force received the news on the evening of April 1. But until then, nobody had given the possibility of a battlefield confrontation with the British a minute's thought. Operation Azul had been conceived as a bloodless takeover of the islands, the establishment of a military government, and the withdrawal of the bulk of the troops in order to follow up on the dispute at the diplomatic level. "Occupy to negotiate" had been the concept.

So it was that the men who landed on Malvinas on and following April 2 were serenely convinced they would never fire a shot and that things would be worked out at the negotiating table. This mentality boded ill, for the opponent sailing toward them was a highly trained professional spoiling for a fight. This sadly flawed thinking spread down from the top. It began at the very pinnacle of the military government, for all political and military planning, as well as the basic concepts and suppositions, had been mistakenly grounded on two premises:

1. The British government would not respond militarily to the taking of the islands.

2. The United States would bring its weight to bear in this conflict, and not allow it to escalate.

TASK FORCE 317—HEADING: THE SOUTH ATLANTIC

At the opening of the South Atlantic conflict, the Royal Navy had the following inventory: 2 antisubmarine aircraft carriers, 16 destroyers, 44 frigates, and 31 submarines. Of these, about a dozen frigates and as many submarines either were in dry dock for overhaul or were being refitted. As for the amphibious landing fleet, there were 2 assault vessels, 6 logistical landing ships, and some 70 small landing craft. This force, although smaller than the 1956 Royal Navy (14 carriers, 20 cruisers, 69 destroyers, 186 frigates, and 54 subs), was nevertheless a formidable fleet. It held the second spot in the free world and ranked third after the United States and the Soviet Union. It was equipped with the latest in sophisticated missilery. Its fleet of state-of-the-art submarines carried the Polaris nuclear warhead.

The first naval units to be moved by the British government at the very outset were those affected by the South Georgia incident: the HMS *Endurance*, which had sailed from Port Stanley at 0830 hours on March 21 with 22 marines on board. The mission had been to remove the Argentine work crew from Port Leith. This assignment had gone unfulfilled, since the ARA *Bahia Paraiso* had beat the marines to the punch. Then, on March 24, the RRS *John Biscoe*, out of Montevideo with relief for Royal Marine contingent 8902, set its course for the Malvinas, along with the RRS *Bransfield*, which sailed from Punta Arenas on April 25. Britain announced the sailing from Gibraltar of the nuclear submarine *Superb* on the same day, although it was later sighted off the coast of Scotland. Shortly thereafter, on March 30, ITV Thames in London announced that two nuclear subs had been dispatched to the South Atlantic—no names given—one of which allegedly weighed anchor at Gibraltar on April 25. The same day, London made public the sailing of the HMS *Exeter*, a Class 42 frigate, from

Belize, on a course for the South Atlantic. The following day, news was received that another auxiliary craft would join the fleet on the way to the war zone.

On March 31, prior to the Argentine landing, the British Admiralty had already decided to send a sizable naval force. Orders had already been issued: the two carriers were to be made ready, and the necessary administrative steps were being taken to requisition merchant marine vessels. Mobilization would be completed by May 1, as the United Kingdom came to realize that the war effort would entail much more than had originally been imagined. Britain marshaled its fighting forces from the war room, to which the Defense Staff reports, and to which, in turn, the commander in chief of the Royal Navy, headquartered in Northwood, reports. Units deployed to the South Atlantic would be under the command of Admiral Sir John Fieldhouse, and would be as follows: the battle group of the task force under Rear Adm. John Moore, the amphibious forces under Commodore Michael Clapp, and the auxiliary fleet under Capt. S. C. Dunlop.

The task force would be made up of vessels attached to the Royal Navy, the auxiliary fleet, or requisitioned craft. The only two carriers, available at that time were beefed up for action in the South Atlantic, in order to provide air cover for the fleet. Both were fitted to receive a larger contingent of Sea Harriers: 12 aboard the *Hermes*, 10 aboard the *Invincible*. The destroyer arm was formed of two County-Class vessels: the *Antrim* and the *Glamorgan*. The advance force was rounded off with the Class 42 destroyers HMS *Sheffield, Exeter, Glasgow*, and *Coventry*, which were built between 1975 and 1982. They were state-of-the-art fighting ships, armed with the antiaircraft Sea Dart missile. Losses suffered by the Royal Navy early in the engagement forced Britain to dispatch two replacement vessels, the Class 42 HMS *Cardiff* and the *Bristol*, the latter being larger than the others.

The vanguard of the frigate fleet was made up of the latest addition to the British naval arsenal: the Class 22 vessels HMS *Broadsword* and *Brilliant*, of recent design and freshly armed with the Sea Wolf missile system, specially built to shoot down low-flying aircraft or missiles (unlike the Sea Dart system, aimed mainly at high-flying targets). Sailing with the first wave of ships were the Class 21 *Arrow* and *Alacrity*, along with the older Rothesay Class *Plymouth* and *Yarmouth*. Later came the Class 21 *Antelope, Ambuscade, Active*, and *Avenger*, along with the *Minerva* and *Penelope*. The latter, modified Leander Class vessels, were ordered to the war zone on an emergency basis, as replacements. Practically the whole Royal Navy inventory of Class 21 frigates saw action in the South Atlantic.

But without a doubt, the deadliest weapons Great Britain deployed to the South Atlantic were its submarine forces. Six units of an available 31 were sent in groups of three. In the first were the *Conqueror*, the *Spartan*, and the *Valiant*, all nuclear powered. The second was made up of the *Splendid*, the *Courageous*, and the *Onyx*, the latter being the only conventional diesel-powered sub.

The amphibious force brought together the assault landing vessels *Fearless* and *Intrepid*, equipped with landing craft. This contingent also included the auxiliary fleet transports RFA *Sir Galahad, Sir Bedidere, Sir Geraint, Sir Lancelot, Sir Tristram*, and *Sir Percival.*

In addition to the above, a broad range of ships were sent to the war zone for various assignments. There were patrol boats (three), minesweepers (two), hospital ships (four), oilers (ten), and resupply and maintenance (six). Private merchant vessels also were requisitioned and pressed into service to cover the vast logistical needs of a fleet operating in waters 8,000 miles from its home base. The bulk of these ships sailed from their home ports in the British Isles on April 5. As they steamed past Gibraltar, they were joined by units that had been on maneuvers in the Mediterranean. Later, following the initial engagements and the losses incurred as of May 1, an additional ten warships joined the fight. The requisitioned units were sent on their way as soon as they had been modified and refitted as backups, or to replace vessels lost in action. Ascension Island became an almost compulsory landfall, since it lies about halfway between Portsmouth and the disputed islands. A supply line of support shipping stretched between the British Isles and this little dot of land, so strategically located for the task force, while other vessels closed the loop to the battlefront. U.S. vessels shuttled back and forth to Ascension laden with fuel and supplies, which were reloaded for the long run to the fleet. An airlift moved men and essential materiel between Britain and Gibraltar—the closest British base to the conflict—and Wideawake Air Station on Ascension, which, as of April 4, was used with the blessings of the United States.

During operations in the South Atlantic, the Royal Navy stripped its home front practically bare, since the few ships remaining in the United Kingdom—except for the submarines—were either out of service or maintaining a symbolic presence in the home waters.

To sum up, after adding the three units that happened to be in the area at the initiation of hostilities, the British expeditionary force was made up of 121 ships. It was the first time in many years that such a vast flotilla had plied the waves. It was the stuff of dreams for more than one British admiral, who envied "Sandy" Woodward, the admiral whose lot it was to leave behind the dreary drudgery of a staff position to face into the wind at the head of a mighty armada, sent to the rescue of a distant colony. Perhaps even the members of the military junta could puff their chests, if only a bit, for in their grandest dreams they had never conjured up the staging of such a formidable naval juggernaut as this, set in motion by their decision alone.

The Naval Air Arm of the Task Force

The Sea Harrier, which became the backbone of the task force's air might, was not an aircraft particularly well suited to the area or proven in combat at the opening of hostilities in the South Atlantic. Its main characteristic, being a vertical takeoff and landing aircraft—which eliminates the requirement for a conventional airstrip—also imposes, by its very design, serious limitations on its performance, with the exception of its superior maneuverability. These limitations, mainly the small payload and its low speed, put it at a disadvantage against more conventional attack aircraft of its own generation, such as the French Mirage 2000, the U.S. F–14, the Russian MIG–23, or even the British Jaguar. But none of the latter could fly from the Royal Navy's light carriers, which is why the Sea Harrier became the only aircraft available to do the job.

Naval Air Squadrons 800 and 899 delivered aircraft (six each) to the light carrier HMS *Hermes*, and Squadrons 801 and 899 delivered aircraft (five each) to the *Invincible*, the latter having to make the delivery after the carrier had sailed to join the task force and was steaming through the English Channel. During combat operations, the *Hermes* Squadron 800 was reinforced—to make up for losses—by aircraft from recently formed Squadron 809, along with Squadron 1(F) GR–3 Harriers assigned to the Royal Air Force (RAF). The Invincible's inventory of Sea Harriers was replenished with aircraft from Squadron 809.

Preparations included the transfer from the British base at Yeoviltown of a large number of AIM–9 Sidewinder air-to-air missiles. These would be mounted on external struts under the wings of the Sea Harrier in its interceptor configuration to fend off attacking Argentine fight-bombers.

The Royal Navy Helicopter Force, those workhorses of modern warfare that can operate just about anywhere under any conditions, had six types of craft available: the Sea King, Wessex, Lynx, and Wasp, along with some Scouts and Gazelles attached to the British Army Command and to the Royal Marines. The RAF also pressed its search-and-rescue Sea Kings and its Squadron 18 Chinooks into service. Over 200 helicopters were mustered by Great Britain for action in the war. The scope of their duties was enormous: the attack configuration, antishipping, antisubmarine warfare, search and rescue, logistics support, troop carrying, artillery range adjusting, commando operations, medical evacuation, land support, radar picket, and so on. Nineteen of the requisitioned vessels had been fitted with helicopter pads.

The RAF performed a broad range of services, considering how far removed the theater of operations was. Its squadrons, normally numbering 12 aircraft, operated out of Wideawake at Ascension. Some 120 aircraft saw action during the conflict and over 400 operations were recorded in a single day at that base, whether on route to Gibraltar or to the war zone. Preparing airborne equipment for operations 8,000 miles from their home bases was no simple task. Although Ascension Island reduced the flying range by half, the distances involved were nevertheless a great challenge to the RAF, which quickly set about seeking efficient solutions to the various technical and operational problems, for the success of the task force's mission hung in the balance.

Ground Forces

The ground forces assigned to the task force were the best and most highly trained available in the United Kingdom. They were provided by the Royal

Marines and by the British Army (Airborne). The British Royal Marine 3rd Commando Brigade, composed of 13 highly trained units, joined the fight along with the British Army's 5th Royal Infantry Brigade with elements picked from 35 different units. Making available such a large and diverse land force on such short notice had not been easy. The men's Easter leaves had to be canceled; they had to be made ready, staged, and moved to the war zone. As the rosters were completed, the men boarded military or requisitioned shipping, or were airlifted to Ascension, where they were transferred to surface vessels on route to their final destination.

A Long, Long Journey to the South

The first British troop movements were carried out by the RAF. As early as April 3, a VC–10 from Air Transport Squadron 10 lifted off from Brise Norton Base on its first leg of the long flight to Montevideo to pick up deposed Governor Rex Hunt and his retinue, and a first flight of eight C–130s took off for Ascension Island, almost before the United States granted permission. On board these aircraft were the advance companies whose duty it would be to make Wideawake ready for the crucial role British strategists had in mind for it: the staging area for both task force vessels and support aircraft.

The first ships weighed anchor on April 5. They included the carriers and several escort units, followed by the SS *Canberra* with the 42nd Commando Battalion and the 3rd Airborne Battalion, followed by the RFA *Stromness* transporting the 45th Battalion, along with other auxiliary fleet units and requisitioned vessels. The 2nd Airborne Battalion was moved aboard the *Europic Ferry* and the motor launch *Norland*, while the Blue and Royals boarded the *Elk* along with two light Scorpion tanks and four Scimitar armored vehicles and their full complement of weaponry. Throngs brimming with emotion saw the combatants off at the docks as military bands struck up "Anchors Aweigh" and "Don't Cry for Me, Argentina," sarcastically retitled "Don't Pull One on Me, Argentina." Many would never return. More, in fact, than anyone had planned for or expected.

The liners *Canberra* and *Uganda* were ordered to cease their cruise operations and offload their passengers. The first returned to the British Isles, and the second unloaded at Gibraltar. On May 1, the British government caused a sensation when it ordered the requisitioning of the *Queen Elizabeth II*, which was converted posthaste into a troop carrier and fitted with a helicopter pad. This majestic ship set sail on May 12, laden with troops from the 5th Infantry Brigade, which included Welsh Guards, Scots Guards, and Gurka riflemen. The enormous liner hugged the coast of Africa at a speed of 30 knots, the better to avoid Argentine submarines. It transferred its troop contingents to other units in the waters off the South Georgias for the final run to the hostile beaches of the Malvinas.

The combined effort of the Royal Navy and the merchant marine was best described by the British military representative at NATO, who stated, following the conflict: "It may quite possibly not have been feasible to handle the huge volume of material and personnel to be moved to the South Atlantic with the navy and the auxiliary fleet alone, although we used 85 percent of the latter. But, thanks to the fine cooperation of the Commerce Department, it was possible to charter or requisition all the ships we needed." Worldwide, over 100,000 tons of supplies were moved in this fashion, as well as 400,000 cubic meters of fuel to cover the task force's fuel requirements.

Over 9,000 military professionals (6,000 soldiers and 3,000 marines), fully equipped and trained, kept in fighting trim as they sailed to accomplish the mission set by the British government, whose political objective was dictated more by circumstantial than by structural precepts. The goal, of course, was to retake the Falklands and the South Georgias.

COUNTERORDER FOR REDEPLOYMENT

Once the military junta had been warned of the British decision to break diplomatic relations and send a naval task force to retake the islands, troop evacuations were ordered halted and units were made ready to return to the theater of operations. This decision, which was at odds with the original plans, denoted a change in the initial strategic objective, which had been "Occupy in order to negotiate," to "reinforce in order to deter Great Britain from retaking the islands by force, and then negotiate." The necessary diplomatic and military groundwork had not been laid for this objective. Meanwhile, Brig. Gen. Mario Benjamin Menendez, who had been appointed governor, would also have command of the Malvinas military garrison.

As of 1000 hours on April 3, a company of the 25th Infantry Regiment took up positions at Darwin and Goose Green. The following day, the Argentine Air Force deployed six IA–58 Pucara aircraft to the islands, and the Naval Air Wing assigned four Macchi MB–339s. On the evening of that day, airmen stationed at the Patagonia-area bases saw on their television screens the extraordinary popular show of support by the Argentine people in the Plaza de Mayo. This complete, full, and pure state of euphoria permeated the population and, for the first time in many years, brought all of Argentina's citizenry together as one. The pilots blinked their eyes at this sight as their innermost feelings welled up. They, too, were in for the duration. They were bonded together by an emotional and close pledge to their people. They would not let them down.

The Airlift

The airlift, which had commenced operations at 0845 hours on April 2 with the landing at the Malvinas airstrip of the first C–130 Hercules carrying troops for that reduced garrison, saw its mission suddenly balloon into a much larger operation. A Malvinas military air base was quickly established in order to ensure basic services, both for support and for security, of the planes that would start coming in an unending stream as soon as the military junta decided to reinforce the troops on the islands.

Since the tarmac could barely accommodate one or two aircraft at the same time, it had to be enlarged in order to speed up unloading and turnaround time. As this was being hastily completed, the four-engine C–130s were being joined by FK–28s from the 1st Air Brigade and by Boeing 737 transports commandeered from the national airline, Aerolineas Argentinas, and backed up by Austral's fleet of BAC–111s, along with navy L–188As and FK–28s.

From April 2 through April 30, the airlift operated on a scale equal to similar efforts in recent history. For this area the volume was unprecedented. The figures tell the story: passenger traffic—total 7,989 (army, 6,712; navy, 414; air force, 863); cargo traffic (tons)—5,037.5 (army, 3665.8; navy, 200.1; air force, 1,171.6). Not only did cargo and troops have to be ferried to the islands, but the logistics on the mainland weighed in the balance. Whole units had to be moved from their peacetime bases to their staging areas. (A total of 49,165 personnel and 9,799.7 tons of material were mobilized throughout the duration of the war, and their movement required a total of 7,719.5 hours of flying time.) Whole army brigades had to be transported south. Several air bases and all their resources had to reach peak operational status as soon as possible, to handle the combat aircraft that would defend the islands. Radar equipment, guns, military vehicles, spare parts, ammunition, an endless list of supplies, and personnel were marshaled in a gargantuan effort to speed combat assets to the staging areas.

The British announcement of the naval blockade of the islands starting April 12 underscored the need for airlift capability and the magnitude of the task that lay ahead. If surface vessels could not get through, it would not be possible to move all necessary equipment to Puerto Argentino by means of the C–130 Hercules alone, no matter how great the will to try.

In modern warfare, logistics strategy is as important as strategies for the hostilities themselves. Battles are won by the courage, the fire, and the movements of combatants, along with the support of a logistics team. Without the latter, there can be no battle. The British were well aware of that. Their logistics effort could be rated as 50 times that of Argentina.

The Odyssey of the 3rd Infantry Brigade

Perhaps how Argentina attempted to prepare for battle with the United Kingdom could be best illustrated by the tale of the deployment of the 3rd Infantry Brigade, headquartered in Corrientes Province. In the early hours of the morning of April 2, its commanding officer, Brig. Gen. Omar Edgardo Parada, was headed from his quarters to his command post in the town of Curuzu-Cuatia when he was met by a city official who, brimming with excitement, asked him if he did not feel it would be proper to break out the flags and decorate the town in celebration of the great event. It was only then that Brigadier General Parada learned that Malvinas had been reclaimed.

This brigade commander did not have much time to concern himself with bedecking the city with flags or even to celebrate the event; he soon received official orders to prepare his brigade for transfer to the south, and one of his units, the 3rd Artillery Group, to be sent to the theater of operations on the Malvinas. At this juncture most of the draftees of the contingent born in 1962 had completed their service and had been mustered out, and the 1963 contingent had just been sworn in. He immediately went about the task of rounding up all the ''veterans,'' which he was able to achieve in large measure by sending messengers in all directions. Thus the all-too-recently demobilized conscripts from Corrientes, from the Chaco, from Misiones, from all over the country were once again herded front and center, many of them scrambling aboard trains laden with the brigade's regulars on their southbound trek. As they rumbled across the Colorado River, the 3rd Brigade had not mustered its full strength, but it had already accomplished its primary mission: a dragnet had brought in able-bodied men along the coast of Patagonia. While this was going on, it received a new assignment: reinforce the 9th Brigade in Santa Cruz Province. Before this latest mission was accomplished, it was burdened with yet a third: ship out to the Malvinas Islands.

Unit by unit, the brigade trekked along the dusty Patagonian roads to its staging area in Puerto Deseado, where it would board a ship for transport to its final destination. At that time, out of its eight main regiments, three were still at their peacetime bases, one was in the islands, one was at San Julian, one was in the city of Sarmiento, and two were on the move. They had begun their movements almost 20 days before, and they were still crisscrossing the country. Their odyssey was not to end soon; the ship, in the face of the British submarine threat, was ordered to remain in port. Unable to make the voyage by surface vessel, the men had to travel overland to Comodoro Rivadavia, where they boarded transports and were airlifted to the islands. At long last, between April 26 and 28, they struggled aboard the lumbering Hercules, taking with them what little equipment both their hurried departure and the space limitations of the aircraft allowed them to bear into battle. Behind them were the long days of marching, their heavy weapons, their vehicles, their field kitchens, their ordnance, their gear . . . not to mention their home provinces and their loved ones.

And so these brave men went to war against the cream of the British Army and Royal Marines. They soon made their stand at Goose Green, where they were bloodied by the 2nd Airborne Battalion, on which they inflicted heavy casualties, including its regimental commander, Lt. Col. Herbert Jones. Other young Argentines such as these would later bear the brunt of the enemy offensive against Puerto Argentino, where they had bivouacked for weeks in the worst possible conditions men in the field could bear, all while fighting an enemy more fearsome than the British themselves: the breakdown of morale brought on by the struggle against the merciless dampness, cold, winds, rain, and privations of every sort, under conditions worse even than those endured by the ground troops who wallowed in the muddy trenches of northern Europe during World War I.

The Blockade

Two important events occurred on April 7:

1. As General Menendez was assuming the military governorship of the islands, Britain announced the establishment of a naval exclusion zone radiating 200 nautical miles from the islands. Any Argentine naval vessel or auxiliary craft found operating within that zone would be deemed hostile and subject to attack by British forces.

2. The military junta, in keeping with its original plans, deactivated the Malvinas theater of operations and created in its place the South Atlantic theater of operations with a 200-nautical-mile jurisdiction from the mainland and around the southern islands (Malvinas, Georgias, and Sandwich). Its mission was to mount the defense of the reclaimed territories. By April 8, the 5th Marine Battalion had 600 men in position on the islands. There were units deployed on the approaches to the airstrip, at Fox Bay, and at Goose Green.

On April 11, the 10th Infantry Brigade began landing at the Malvinas military air base, under the command of Brig. Gen. Oscar Luis Jofre. The suspected presence of British submarines in the operations area seriously restricted Argentine naval movement. The following day, the transport *Cordoba*, which had been scheduled to weigh anchor at Puerto Deseado with a valuable military shipment for the Malvinas, performed an improper docking maneuver, scraped the wharf, and incurred sufficient damage to keep it from sailing. In its holds languished some 2,000 tons of army supplies (air defense weapons systems and ordnance) and air force equipment (aluminum landing mats for the airstrip).

The first success in outfoxing the British blockade fell to two Argentine Coast Guard cutters, GC–82 *Islas Malvinas* and GC–83 *Rio Iguazu*, which, fueled by courage and professional zeal above and beyond the call, successfully made the crossing to Stanley Bay, where they made landfall in the early hours of April 13. These vessels later proved vital in action, for, although they were scantily armed with one 12.7mm machine gun each—no match for the firepower of their adversaries—they faced the battle of the seas alone, in the absence of any Argentine Navy vessels.

These were not the only successful blockade runners. The merchant marine proved its mettle by skirting the enemy on April 20 as the ELMA company motor launch *Formosa* chugged into Stanley Bay, and on April 25 another ELMA vessel, the *Rio Carcarana*, entered Puerto Argentino on what proved to be a one-way voyage.

Last, but by no means least, the Bridas tugboat *Yehuin*, out of Ushuaia, made landfall in the islands at 1920 hours on May 1. Sent assist docking operations

Figure 1
The South Atlantic Conflict Chains of Command

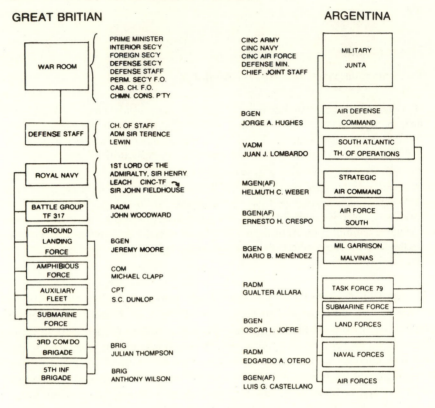

GREAT BRITIAN   ARGENTINA

at Puerto Argentino, it made port on the very day that hostilities broke out in earnest.

The Argentine Plan

Once the strategic decision had been made to reinforce the Malvinas garrison, the military junta decided to establish various operational commands in order to beef up the defense of both the islands and the mainland (see Fig. 1). Thus was established the South Atlantic Theater of Operations (SATO) command. It had the heaviest responsibility, for under it was the Malvinas military garrison, whose task it was to consolidate positions and keep the islands from falling back into British hands. Vice-Adm. Juan Jose Lombardo, chief of naval operations, was appointed SATO commander.

At the same time, the Strategic Air Command (SAC) was established. Its mission was conceived as being more defensive in nature, since Great Britain's military reaction had yet to be recognized in all of its might. Air Force Maj. Gen. Helmuth Conrado Weber, who had been air operations commander, was appointed to head SAC. SAC in turn established Air Force South, which would be entrusted with the implementation of tactical missions, using the Air Force's available inventory of attack aircraft, which would be provided to Air Force South on an as-needed basis. Mirage-V, A4-B, A4-C, IA–58, and MK–62 aircraft, as well as auxiliary and picket KC–130 and Boeing 707 aircraft, were the first-line planes.

Air defense of the mainland would be the responsibility of Air Command Defense Zone South. It would use the Mirage-III, the air defense radar network and antiaircraft weapons and ordnance.

SATO would have both Malvinas Military Garrison and the high seas fleet under its command, as well as the submarine force. The garrison would be commanded by Brig. Gen. Mario Benjamin Menendez, who established a joint command that included the three main components, one for each service, of which the most significant would be the land forces, which would have three infantry brigades assigned to it.

Air Force South established its command post in the city of Comodoro Rivadavia and assigned its attack aircraft, parceling them out among the main airstrips and bases throughout Patagonia. This is where the senior commands were established to face the main British threat, which loomed ever larger as the task force, 50 vessels strong, passed Ascension Island on 16 May, while other units steamed to rendezvous with it in the South Atlantic.

As the carriers *Hermes* and *Invincible* headed south along the coast of France, they sent up their Sea Harriers, with full battle gear, to simulate air-to-air combat with Mirage jets provided by the French government, just for practice. This same government had, in better days, supplied the Argentine Air Force with its fleet of Mirages, and the analysis of performance and behavior of both types of aircraft in simulated combat would be crucial for the British flyers to wrest control of the airspace, and thus superiority in the skies, from Argentina.

Argentina's pilots were not similarly blessed. The prospect of combat for an untested Argentine Air Force was a tremendous challenge, especially if one weighs in the balance the fact that not only would this be its first test of fire, but also that it was not specifically trained to this end, nor were the weapons systems available nor its pilots' training adequate for the type and characteristics of the battle that was about to be fought. Practice runs were made against a Class 42 destroyer of the Argentine Navy with equipment similar to that of the Royal Navy, in order to observe the performance of a modern guided-missile frigate under air attack. Few conclusive results were achieved from this trial: indications were that by following attack procedures that had thus far been the norm, survival rates for a formation were under 25 percent, with a 90 percent chance of being shot down by the ship's antiaircraft defenses.

As if this disadvantage were not enough, the 400 NM of water from the nearest mainland airstrips to the Malvinas constituted a formidable obstacle for Argentine fighters. This would reduce the over-target time for Mirage-V Dagger aircraft to two or three minutes, and the Mirage-III could barely make the islands without setting down, because of its short fuel range. None of these weapons platforms was fitted for midair refueling, which would have vastly increased both their ranges and their payloads. The Skyhawks (air force A4-B and C, and naval air A–4Q) must depend on in-flight refueling in order to have any chance of reaching the target, delivering their ordnance, and returning to base. The bottleneck was the availability of only two aircraft fitted for air-to-air refueling operations. In addition, the whole operation would have to be conducted in an emergency mode, for the slightest malfunction in the fuel transfer system or the aircraft itself would mean, in the best of cases, aborting the mission. The worst-case scenario foresaw pilots having to eject over the ocean as their aircraft ran out of fuel short of the closest available bases.

The Super Etendard-Exocet weapons platform and system recently acquired by the Argentine Navy was still being delivered. They had yet to be made fully operational, and with half of the order sitting on the docks at Marseilles under an embargo order, there was no way to get them delivered and operational. Therefore, 7 of the 12 aircraft purchased from France would be delivered only after the end of the hostilities, and five Exocet A/M 39 (air-surface) were available, if they could be made ready in time for action.

That being the situation, Argentina's chief advantage lay in operating with a land-based force. To make a long story short, the most important thing for establishing air superiority in a theater of operations is the ordnance that can be delivered to the military targets. This is in direct correlation with the time the delivery vehicles can remain over the target, which in turn depends on the number of available aircraft, their range, and the number of sorties they can fly in a day, multiplied by their bomb loads.

Task force carrier-borne aircraft would enjoy a significant advantage: the short distance from their base (the light carriers) to the target zone. By keeping these platforms on station at 90 to 120 NM miles off the islands, both the Sea Harriers and the Harriers would be able to fly a greater number of daily sorties and could remain over the target for a substantially longer time: from 20 to 30 minutes per sortie. As a measure to gauge the task force's ability to achieve air superiority, one should figure about 3,000 minutes' total, without taking into account the possibility of their flying night missions.

By applying a similar formula to measure the Argentine Air Force's prospects, one must figure that our own planes would spend most of their flying time going to and from the target area, and that the maximum over-the-target-area time could not be expected to exceed 150 minutes. This is a mathematical disadvantage that, although the result of calculations on paper, is nevertheless tangible and real.

However, power relations cannot be explained by figures alone if one does not weigh in the tactical situation. Attacking, for example, is not the same as defending. The attacker chooses the time, the place, and the best means to be effective. The defender, on the other hand, when not cognizant of the enemy's estimated time of attack, must ever be on guard; in air terms, this can become both exhausting and expensive in the absence of proper early-warning alert systems. This would be the task force's greatest weakness. Light carriers do not have the space to land and fly the early-warning craft that would give them the edge against incursions of enemy aircraft and enable them to fend off their attacks. This deficiency would spell the doom of numerous Royal Navy surface vessels.

Argentina's fighter pilots knew, in April 1982, that they were at a vital cross-roads in the history of their air force and of their own lives: there was an unofficial assumption that our modest air arm could muster at least two full missions with its available aircraft. Half the force would go down during the first attack, and half the remainder during the second. And that would be it; there would be no way to mount a third. But if during one of those two attacks they were able to send so much as a single British warship to the bottom, their reward would be well earned. This was by no means an exaggerated or fatalistic calculation; there was simply nothing on the books, no yardstick against which to compare the naval air engagement about to take place over our waters, and theory pointed to this foreseeable outcome. The truth of the matter was that the backbone of our air weapons system, the Skyhawk, was vintage 1962. These aircraft had seen 20 years of service, and they would be facing off with a fleet whose most venerable unit was youthful compared with our Falcons. The cream of the British fleet had been built in the past five years. They boasted the very latest in naval air technology.

Therefore, with due regard for their own limitations and a healthy respect for the oncoming enemy, but imbued with a boundless sense of duty and unwavering resolve, Argentina's airmen proudly polished their venerable warbirds, for this would be their finest hour.

Collision Course

While Secretary Haig pursued his shuttle diplomacy, the RAF was making ready ten of its Vulcan bombers for conventional bombing raids. About the same time, the *Canberra*, with 2,000 troops aboard, was putting into Sierra Leone for provisioning. On April 20, a Victor reconnaissance aircraft flew over South Georgia on a picture-taking mission. A day later, an Argentine Air Force Boeing 707 picked up the task force as it sailed into the IATRA security zone and split in two: the British plan called for retaking Grytviken first.

The government of Chile, meanwhile, shaken by Argentina's troop movements, ordered its own troop movements in the southern part of the country as a preventive measure. This unsettled Argentine military circles.

On April 22, the Argentine government formally proclaimed, through decree no. 757, the renaming of Port Stanley, as the capital of the Malvinas, as Puerto Argentino. That same day, Army Commander-in-Chief General Galtieri paid a visit to the Malvinas Islands. On his return, he ordered the reassignment of the 3rd Infantry Brigade and the 4th Artillery Group. General Galtieri's decision created additional problems, since it involved not only an extra burden for the airlift but also laid additional logistical requirements on the forces already on station in the islands: rations, ordnance, fuel, and bullets would have to be shared by the defenders. It also signified a fresh deployment and reshuffling of the forces already defending the islands, at a time when they were short on supplies necessary for properly establishing their positions.

Meanwhile, the task force had divided up and an advance force had set course for the South Georgias, where the submarine Onyx was already on the prowl. The Argentine Air Force's improvised reconnaissance aircraft, converted Boeing 707–320Cs, attempted to keep a sharp eye on these movements, but they would not get off scot free: at first contact south of Ascension on April 21, one of our Boeings was intercepted by a Sea Harrier flying from the fleet at 19°40′S, 20°37′W. It showed its weapons, dropped its wings, and allowed the cumbersome four-engine jet to make an early and undamaged withdrawal.

On April 23 the container cargo vessel Atlantic Conveyor left England with a valuable cargo for the South Atlantic. Its holds were laden with, among other things, a complete squadron of Wessex helicopters as well as three heavy Chinooks, along with spare parts and every imaginable type of gear for the forces in the war zone. A 15 by 25 meter landing platform had been fitted above decks to allow Sea Harrier operations.

On the following day, the first British casualty of the war was recorded. An HC–4 Sea King from Squadron 846 went into the sea during night exercises off the carrier Hermes and a crew member was lost. About the same time, the second wave of warships was ready to weigh anchor at Ascension to join the first wave, which was already steaming within the IATRA security zone. Also on April 24, reconnaissance sorties began to be flown by Nimrod aircraft attempting to pinpoint the location of units of the Argentine fleet.

The Argentine Air Force spotter planes continued to track the British fleet. A second encounter occurred on April 24 between a Boeing 707 and a Sea Harrier at about 33°S/28°W. At 1253 hours, the spotters picked up the two enemy light carriers and eight escort vessels, making 13 knots on a course to the Malvinas Islands.

THE BRITISH RETAKE THE SOUTH GEORGIA ISLANDS

Great Britain had decided to recapture the South Georgia Islands first, in order to make political points on the home front and thus give backbone to the decision to dispatch the fleet. For Argentina's forces, holding on to the South Georgias represented an almost impossible task. Far removed from any mainland support base, no air cover could be made available, and they would be easy prey for an enemy that could isolate them with naval forces. To reinforce the islands or to offer stiff resistance would not make much sense or be tactically necessary. A reduced garrison was maintained on the main island to distract the enemy and force it to divide its assets.

British air reconnaissance was quickly able to determine the total absence of Argentine naval units in the waters around South Georgia, but could not pinpoint the position or the size of land forces. This is why they took no chances. They detached a flotilla made up of the destroyer HMS *Antrim*, the frigate HMS *Plymouth*, the tanker RFA *Tidespring*, and the HMS *Endurance*. The latter, which had, as of April 3, kept its distance from its usual haunts in order to preclude any chance meeting with Argentine naval craft, joined the flotilla in mid-April about 1,000 miles north of the South Georgias and thus made a cautious approach while seeking to complete the tactical intelligence necessary for properly carrying out the mission they had been assigned. On April 24 the Class 22 frigate HMS *Brilliant* joined the group. An addition to the units already named, the submarine HMS *Conqueror*, moved into the area to patrol the waters surrounding the Georgias in order to ascertain the presence or absence of Argentine ships. In their absence the way lay wide open.

British landing forces consisted of 180 specialists attached to the Marine Corps, the Special Air Service (SAS) and the Special Boat Service (SBS) carried aboard the *Endurance* and the *Tidespring*. The British began the operation, code-named Paraquat, with a helicopter landing on the Fortune Glacier, since they had to send specially trained personnel to sound out Argentine positions prior to launching a frontal attack against their positions. The glacier was not the ideal place for such a task, but they decided to go ahead, despite being advised not to. Following a failed attempt to drop the men on the frozen and barren surface of the glacier, they were successfully landed, along with their heavy equipment, in what should have proven to be an impossible mission. Winds of up to 100 mph took the men by surprise as they attempted to go about their tasks. With wind chill factors up to–88°F, the patrols soon found themselves in a desperate situation.

The pilot of the Wessex 5 helicopter sent in to the rescue suffered a phenomenon known as whiteout (loss of visibility due to excess luminosity and suspended snowflakes) as he arrived on the glacier. Unable to find his bearings, he crashed on the icy waste and added his crew to those in distress. A second Wessex 5 fared no better, and it too was strewn over Fortune's icescape. At long last, in a fresh attempt by a Wessex 3, the 17 men were rescued in a daring maneuver. Overloading his helicopter dangerously past tolerances, the pilot, Lt. Ian Stanley, succeeded in landing them on the *Antrim*, where they were promptly sent to sick bay with incipient frostbite. Stanley was decorated for his bravery.

At this point the British, who had yet to make contact with the enemy, had lost two helicopters and gained their first hero. These losses were zealously kept from the British public, whose criticism might serve to weaken the prime minister's resolve. This was only the first of many such instances. But the misfortunes of those entrusted with wresting back the South Georgias in the name of the British Crown had yet to end. An SBS group, transported by helicopter to a valley on South Georgia, had to be evacuated because movement proved impossible in the area. At the same time, 5 inflatable dinghies with 15 SAS men attempted to reach the island's barren beaches. The outboard engines on two failed, and in the black of night the winds blew them out to sea. Only by chance were they picked by a helicopter the following day. Three dinghies made land, but they were slashed to shreds on the rocks and jagged ice along the shore.

On April 24, the British command of Operation Parakeet continued to be beset with unpleasant news. The presence of the *Submarine Santa Fe* in the area had been confirmed, and one of the frigates had been overflown by an Argentine Air Force C–130. On April 25, with the objective of attacking British shipping in the vicinity of the South Georgia Islands, Air Force South gave its approval to a plan of attack to be carried out by a squadron equipped with the only available long-range bomber aircraft in the air force: the Canberra MK–62. Considering the distance from the nearest airstrip to South Georgia Island, navigation had to be precise, for to make the 2,500-mile round trip, every drop of fuel had to be nursed.

At a few minutes past noon, the formation lifted off and immediately set a heading for the distant chain of islands. Their only chance of success was to catch the enemy out in the open, for Cumberland Bay was surrounded by steep mountains. Surprise was equally vital, for they would be easy targets for the ships' antiaircraft defenses. As they approached the islands, the Canberra formation was advised by a C–130 that weather conditions were unfavorable and that the fleet was completely inside the bay. Mission aborted! The flight returned to base with their bomb loads, having been unable to take the initiative in the opening action and support Grytviken's defenders. There would be no chance for a second try. The garrison soon surrendered to British forces.

At this point luck began to turn decidedly toward the British side. As mentioned in Chapter 3, the defenders of the island consisted of two small companies of marines: 40 men under Lieutenant Luna at Grytviken, 14 under Lieutenant Astiz at Port Leith, and Davidoff's 39 civilian workmen. This small garrison was being reinforced by the ARA *Santa Fe*, a submarine completely obsolete for the purpose of modern warfare. The *Santa Fe* had reached Grytviken in the early morning of April 25, having made most of the crossing on the surface. Its batteries had outlived their useful life cycle, and would hold only a minute charge.

As if these limitations were not enough, the submarine was restricted in the use of its weapons. Considering that surprise is paramount for the use of a submarine's primary weapon—the torpedo—it is understandable that the *Santa Fe'* skipper was anything but happy with his lot. The stormy seas through which the battered old hull had sailed had damaged the stabilizer, but it had nevertheless been able to evade detection by the British ships and had entered Cumberland Bay. It unloaded some supplies needed by the defenders and, before dawn, at 0630 hours, as it got under way for the return voyage, a Wessex off the destroyer *Antrim* picked it up on radar. Helicopters from the *Plymouth*, the *Brilliant*, and the polar vessel *Endurance* joined the fight. Seriously damaged and unable to make headway, it was put out of action. The venerable *Santa Fe*, mortally wounded by depth charges and other British ordnance, was grounded and abandoned by her crew, which could do nothing to save it. On land, they made for Grytviken. The British had chalked up their first victory.

Heartened by this sudden turn of luck, the British mounted the final assault on Grytviken. With most of their land forces aboard the *Tidespring*—which was still 200 miles out to sea—all available combatants were marshaled together. Some British authors put it at 75 marines; others, at 120. There was a noted tendency among British sources to decrease their own numbers and increase those of the opponents. This was the first such instance. While the Argentine positions were raked by naval fire, these men were landed on the bluffs above Grytviken at 1445 hours, then marched overland to the empty town. As they approached the area, the defenders raised the white flag of surrender. It was 1715 hours.

While the Grytviken garrison had laid down its arms, Lieutenant Astiz's small company was still at Port Leith. On the morning of April 26, Astiz ordered the civilian work force to head for Grytviken on foot. This they did, and upon arrival they surrendered to British authorities. That same morning, the destroyer *Antrim* sailed into Stromness Bay and accepted the surrender of Lieutenant Astiz's small band, who offered no further resistance. Called upon to make the surrender formal aboard the frigate *Plymouth*, he did so, stating that he had faced vastly superior numbers.

On April 27 a somewhat confusing incident occurred. An Argentine petty officer was fired upon by a nervous British sentry as he wrestled with the flood tank valves aboard the *Santa Fe*, obeying British orders to attempt to move the vessel from its position. The noise frightened the marine guard on duty, who opened fire on the defenseless Argentine crewman, causing his death. He was buried at Grytviken with full military honors.

So ended Argentina's attempt to reclaim South Georgia Island. In Admiral Woodward's words, South Georgia had been but a taste of what awaited his troops. The "main event" was still to come, as the fight for Malvinas themselves drew near. His words were quite prophetic, although not in the way he meant, for surely the magnitude of the losses about to be incurred by both sides had never crossed his mind.

THE DEFENDERS DIG IN ON MALVINAS

On April 25, the British proclaimed an exclusive air defense zone around the Falklands, with the objective of tightening a noose to strangle all resupply to the troops who were digging in on the islands. The airlift continued its task unfettered by this technicality. The United Kingdom continued to move personnel and materiel to Wideawake on Ascension, by means of four requisitioned jumbo jets and RAF aircraft. Also on April 25, radar operators at Puerto Argentino felt the first thrill of action as seven blips appeared on their scopes . . . bogeys 30 miles east of the islands. Course . . . incoming! The enemy was closing in for the attack.

On April 27, and with all haste in the face of the imminent arrival of the task force, General Menendez, who had been taken by surprise by the arrival of the 3rd Infantry Brigade, proceeded to deploy these troops to their battle posts: the 12th Infantry Regiment was helicoptered to Darwin; the 8th, to Puerto Mitre on Grand Malvina (West Falkland).

In London, the British government announced the landing of special forces in the Falklands, and the RAF wound up the training of the air crews for the modified Vulcan, performing practice bomb runs on target ranges on the Isle of Man and Cape Wrath, and sharpening their in-flight refueling and low-level navigation skills, thus putting the finishing touches on Operation Blackbuck, which called for the destruction of the landing strip at Puerto Argentino.

On April 28, the British Defense Ministry announced the establishment of a total exclusion zone for both air and maritime traffic within 200 miles of the islands. The next day, five Avro Vulcan long-range bombers set down at Wideawake, on what would be the first leg of Operation Blackbuck.

The Argentine Army suffered its first casualties on April 29 when a helicopter went down outside Comodoro Rivadavia, killing all aboard. The Argentine Navy established a naval air station at Elephant Bay on Pebble Island, northwest of the northern entrance to San Carlos Strait (Falkland Sound). Meanwhile, the doomed diplomatic efforts at a negotiated settlement were swiftly followed by the hasty military preparations of both sides. The British retaking of the South Georgias further whetted Prime Minister Thatcher's war lust as she made it known that this latest event would in no way deter the British from their main objective, retaking the Malvinas by force.

The Argentine planning staff's worst-case scenario, as remote as it had appeared at the outset, had become a reality: Great Britain would use all the power at its command to recapture the islands. Governor Menendez had reason for concern: the bulk of the officers and men in the field, scattered throughout the theater of operations, personnel for whom he was responsible, were no match for an armed confrontation of this scope. Many still nursed the illusion that their mission in the islands was to occupy, not to hold under fire. Diplomacy had failed utterly and time had run out.

General Menendez issued an excessively rigid outline for tactical defense, based on the supposition that the enemy would attempt to come ashore in the vicinity of Puerto Argentino. His men were thus frozen into position facing the sea, for it was felt that there was where the danger lay.

Battle Stations

When the Argentine armed forces were fully deployed for the defense of the Malvinas, the roster stood as follows:

At Puerto Argentino—27 primary and secondary ground units; 2 coast guard cutters, 1 freighter, 4 small craft, and 1 naval air squadron; the Malvinas military air base; 1 surveillance radar; and 1 air force information and control center.

At Darwin-Goose Green—1 reinforced infantry regiment, antiaircraft batteries, and the Condor military air base (1 squadron of Pucara aircraft).

On Gran Malvina (West Falkland)—1 infantry regiment and 1 company of engineers at Fox Bay; 1 reinforced infantry regiment at Port Howard; and the Calderon naval air station (1 squadron of Mentor aircraft) at Sea Elephant Bay.

The full complement of officers and men deployed on the Malvinas totaled 12,193. The rest of the Argentine Army remained at its peacetime bases. The 4th Airborne Brigade was put on standby as a strategic military reserve, in case it should be needed.

Deployment of the High Seas Fleet

Argentina's naval assets were organized for war as a task force under code number 79. They were placed under the command of Rear Adm. Gualter Oscar Allara. Task Force (TF) 79's assigned mission was to harass the enemy, either by wearing them down or by taking advantage of favorable opportunities to launch attacks against their units. The plan of operation further called for Argentine naval vessels to remain outside the exclusion zone and to refrain from utilizing their armament without prior authorization, since favorable results were still hoped for from the diplomatic initiatives that were being played out up to May 1.

The task force was divided into three task groups that positioned themselves in such a way as to constitute enough of a threat to the British task force that it could be obliged to split up. The Argentine fleet went on maneuvers off the coast in order to give the crews time to train. From April 16 to 26, it operated as three task groups: the first headed by the light carrier 25 de Mayo and the Corvette Division; the second was made up of the Destroyer Division; and the third brought up the rear with a venerable cruiser, the *General Belgrano*.

As war became imminent, the three task groups were redistributed as follows: TF 79.1, the *25 de Mayo* and four destroyers; TF 79.3, the *General Belgrano* and two destroyers; TF 79.4, three corvettes. Three support tankers were assigned to this complement. On April 30, the three groups were on station at the following locations: TF 79.1, east of Puerto Deseado; TF 79.3 north of Staten Island; TF 79.4, east of Comodoro Rivadavia.

The submarine service had in commission two World War II Guppy Class boats, as well as two modern Class 209 units, recently acquired from Germany.

Naval aviation deployed its newly delivered Super Etendard aircraft to the Rio Grande naval air station in Tierra del Fuego while maintaining the naval air group aboard the *25 de Mayo*, the backbone of which were A4-Qs, Trackers, and helicopters.

In addition there were auxiliary vessels for support tasks in transport, search and rescue, surveillance, medical services, and patrol.

It was a modest force indeed to face off with such a naval colossus as the British task force and its nuclear submarines. A tense state of alert reigned aboard all Argentine vessels. The looming British fleet clearly underscored London's willingness to resort to the use of force.

THE GENESIS OF FUERZA AEREA SUR (FAS)

Air Force South (FAS) originated on April 5, 1982, when SAC organized the means with which the air force would take part in the conflict. Air Force South would be commanded by Brig. Gen. Ernesto Horacio Crespo, chief of the 4th Air Brigade, based at Mendoza. Brigadier General Crespo was an old-line professional air force officer. On April 1, he received orders to report to the Condor (HQ) Building. He had no clue as to what was in the offing. He and his operations chief, Commodore Jose A. Julia, traveled to Buenos Aires, both somewhat excited over the prospect of something outside the usual routine. When the mission was laid out before him and he had received a situation briefing, Brigadier General Crespo was faced with the immediate prospect that the armed forces were about to be put in harm's way, that the consequences were dire, and that the air force would bear the brunt of the battle, if it came to war. The FAS command was based at Comodoro Rivadavia, while the staging areas for its units were the bases and airstrips along the coast of southern Argentina, strung from Trelew to the southernmost tip of the continent.

An early analysis of his mission indicated to Brigadier General Crespo that his objective was to serve as a deterrent in the Southern Cone area while a solution to the Malvinas dilemma was hammered out within the framework of the international community. As he leaned over the situation table with his closest, most trusted staff officers, he realized that the British response could be quite far from the expectations of Argentina's top military brass, and that the British could be fully expected to fight to retake those islands. His task was both pressing and thankless. He was faced with organizing, at very short notice, a combat-ready air arm to take on an enemy that outclassed him in both means and technology, and in a theater of operations that was alien to an air force that had neither the means nor the training for over-sea combat operations. He requested, and was granted, first choice in the selection of available assets—both personnel and materiel—to put together FAS.

Crespo appointed as his second in command Brig. Gen. Roberto Fernando Camblor. He had 30 days in which to evaluate the enemy's capability; train pilots in the fine points of naval air warfare; carry out operational testing; adapt weapons systems to the forthcoming task; acknowledge his own limitations— which were far from few—and seek ways to obviate them; study the operational potential of his attack aircraft, which, due to the location of the islands at such a distance from the mainland, could just barely make it to the target; familiarize pilots with the problems inherent in sea operations; and reconnoiter the islands in practice runs. He deployed his assets among the coastal bases in Patagonia as follows:

—The Canberra bomber squadron to Trelew

—C–130, fighter-bomber, search-and-rescue, and diversionary squadrons to Comodoro Rivadavia

—Two A4-C and Dagger attack squadrons to San Julian

—One Pucara attack squadron to Santa Cruz for coastal operations, and as replacements for those stationed on the islands.

—Two A4-B squadrons to Rio Gallegos

—One Dagger squadron to Rio Grande.

FAS deployed in this manner some 73 attack aircraft through the southern coastal bases and airfields, in addition to the eight Pucara stationed in the islands under the control of the commander of the islands' military garrison. The remaining air force assets were to remain at their peacetime bases, to be brought to the front as needed.

The commander of FAS had an increasingly difficult horizontal relationship with other commanders because the scope of his operation overlapped SATO and went out as far as the Malvinas military garrison, the command of which was not subordinate to him. In accordance with the organization lines drawn by the military junta when they established the operational commands, SAC—and FAS, which was subordinate to it—was a specific command. Brigadier General Crespo's area of responsibility was outside this organization. He had been given a mission—which was his alone—and the means with which to implement it. He informed his superiors of the immediate future prospects and told them that if war came, his men would fight to the finish, no matter what the danger or the losses.

On April 30, at sunset, his men, who came from all over the air force, were in a state of tense alert. Their hour of trial was upon them.

"STAR WARS"

Space vehicles, those ingenious products of man's inventiveness that had already come to play such a spectacular role in our contemporary world, came to be regarded by our staffs in the ensuing events as one of the basic sources of information and military communications in any theater of operations. The LANDSAT 3 mapping satellite, as well as the NOAA 8 and the GOES weather satellites, were in operational orbit. Both the British and the Argentines could tap them for information as they passed over the South Atlantic. But except for weather-related data, the possibility of gaining intelligence as to the position of ships at sea was limited to the pinpointing of small dots on photos of the ocean surface taken when there was no cloud cover. Conclusive data were not really available from that source.

The United States provided the United Kingdom with signals picked up by the NATO 3 communications satellite, which is linked to Fleet Satellite Communications. NATO 3 could pick up radio transmissions, which, once recorded on tape, were sent to London. Thus Great Britain had access to certain intelligence on Argentine communications in the theater of operations with an eight-hour delay until, shortly after May 1, it was possible to relay these transmissions directly to a ground station in Great Britain. This system also provided a direct, instant communications link between the war zone and the task force command at Northwood (U.K.), which served greatly to magnify, if only psychologically, the assistance received from the United States.

The Soviet Union had its satellite network buzzing with activity during the conflict. Eighteen satellites made a clean sweep of the South Atlantic/South Pacific region. They sped above the Earth at an altitude no lower than 80 miles and completed an orbit every 90 minutes. Their useful life was less than 30 days because they skimmed the upper atmosphere and disintegrated as they reentered heavier air. In addition to these assets, which were quickly sent up during the hostilities, the Soviet Union kept its fishing fleet and its submarines on station, rounding out an extraordinary observation and intelligence network. The opportunity to observe one of its most formidable NATO adversaries in action, as well as to check out the latest in Western military hardware and the effectiveness of their own satellite, electronics, and communications capabilities, could not be allowed to slip by. Argentina received no assistance from Moscow that would have enabled it to narrow the technological gap on the battlefield. On the other hand, Great Britain used every guise, through psychological action and trumped-up propaganda, to induce the Western world to let it use their satellite eyes.

On April 30, Secretary of State Alexander Haig announced the final breakdown of the talks. Argentina delivered a note to the United Nations stating that it would use its right to legitimate self-defense if attacked. Shortly thereafter, President Reagan announced his support of the British cause in this conflict, followed immediately by a full embargo on weapons exports and loans to Argentina. At the same time, Chile's armed forces were completing a deployment in the southern zone of that country equal to or greater than the one ordered in 1978 when the two republics had been on the brink of war over the Beagle Channel issue.

The cards in the grand game of politics were now on the table. With these latest events, Mrs. Thatcher was no longer holding aces; she was holding a royal flush. This most improbable of wars was about to break out, and nobody had done enough, had done all possible, to head it off. And nobody, at least in the West, would benefit from it.

On April 30, in the darkest of southern nights, a Vulcan bomber, serial number XM–607, from RAF Squadron 44, rolled down the runway at Wideawake, on

Ascension Island, and lifted off on the first leg of its long run to Puerto Argentino, where it would drop a load of 21 1,000-pound bombs over the air base. This was the United Kingdom's response to a nation that, on reclaiming what was rightfully its own, had not spilled a drop of its adversary's blood.

5

The Battle of May 1

We found, in the hard school of war, that without air superiority, there can be no exercise of naval power.
Air Marshal Lord Tedder, second in command, Allied forces, Europe

OPERATION BLACK BUCK

The benumbed defenders at Puerto Argentino were jolted by the detonation of the first bomb. Other bursts followed in ominous succession. Ironically, that first bomb, out of the 21 dropped by the Vulcan bomber commanded by 1st Lt. Martin Withers of the RAF, as well as the Sea Harriers flying from the task force, was the only one to damage the runway throughout the 45-day conflict. Thus did Great Britain strike the first blow, at 0440 hours in that chilly autumn predawn, in its quest to regain its lost colony. While the damage was minimal, the show was spectacular.

The crews manning Argentine air defense batteries had been relieved a scant 40 minutes earlier. The operator of the Skyguard battery, with its 35mm Oerlikon cannon, was taken by surprise as the bomber appeared on his scope. Was this a British attack? The noise of the Vulcan thundered in his ears almost at the same time he heard the first bombs explode. This was no drill, it was the real thing.

Following that first attack, damage assessment revealed, a 65-foot crater about halfway down the runway. The useful width of the strip was reduced at that point to about 60 feet, more than enough to allow continued operation of both the C–130 Hercules Argentine Air Force transports and the smaller aircraft flying airlift. The landing field remained fully operational. There was light damage to the terminal facilities: one fuel tank and one warehouse destroyed. Argentina's forces also recorded their first casualties in the battle for the Malvinas. Further,

Map 2
The Battle of May 1

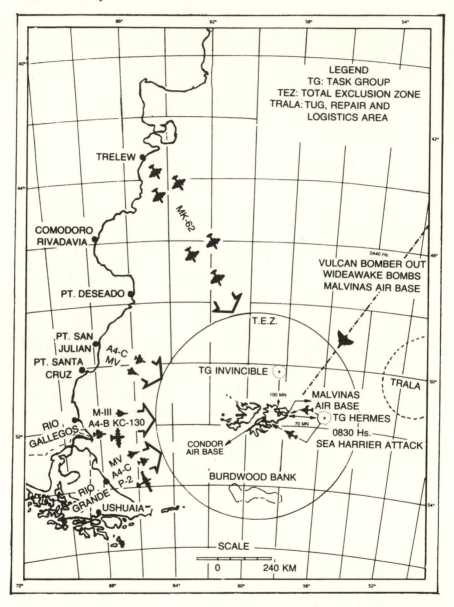

LEGEND
TG: TASK GROUP
TEZ: TOTAL EXCLUSION ZONE
TRALA: TUG, REPAIR AND
LOGISTICS AREA

TRELEW

MK-62

COMODORO
RIVADAVIA

0440 Hs

VULCAN BOMBER OUT
WIDEAWAKE BOMBS
MALVINAS AIR BASE

PT. DESEADO

T.E.Z.

PT. SAN
JULIAN   A4-C
PT. SANTA   MV
CRUZ

TG INVINCIBLE

TRALA

M-III
RIO   100 MN
GALLEGOS   A4-B KC-130

MALVINAS
AIR BASE
TG HERMES
0830 Hs.
SEA HARRIER ATTACK

70 MN

CONDOR
AIR BASE

MV
A4-C
P-2

RIO
GRANDE
USHUAIA

BURDWOOD BANK

SCALE

0   240 KM

two bombs with time-delay fuses exploded at 0629 hours. Of the 21-bomb salvo dropped by the Vulcan, 4 came to rest in the peat bogs and failed to detonate. At 0740 hours, a Sea Harrier flew a high-altitude reconnaissance mission over the landing field to survey the damage. A short time later, the BBC announced that the RAF had wiped out the airstrip at Puerto Argentino.

Sixteen hours after it left, the *Vulcan* bomber set down at Wideawake. Its return leg had not been entirely uneventful. It almost missed its rendezvous with a Victor tanker, and during refueling operations the boom disengaged, spewing jet fuel over Lieutenant Withers' windshield, blurring his vision for a few seconds. Black Buck had returned safely, leaving analysts wondering about its usefulness: the flight had been successfully completed, but had it truly accomplished its mission, in spite of the risks involved and the psychological effects it brought?

AIR DEFENSES AT MALVINAS MILITARY AIR BASE

Although joint action was not one of the Argentine armed forces' greater virtues, such was not the case with the air defense brigades, where the three services joined hands and linked up, with the meager assets at hand, a magnificent network of antiaircraft batteries equipped with artillery and missiles. This array would put the skill and courage of Britain's flyers to the test.

The British plan consisted basically of Operation Black Buck: a Vulcan bombing mission followed by further bombing raids by the Sea Harriers. Having thus "paralyzed" his opponent, Admiral Woodward would offer General Menendez the opportunity to surrender, and perhaps everything would come off much as it had on South Georgia, where he had encountered only token resistance from the defenders.

If the same were to occur on the Malvinas, the task force would have carried out its mission with no major problems in a minimum time frame. Then the ships' crews and the expeditionary force could quickly return home, and the Royal Navy would have written yet another glorious chapter in the history of its exploits in defense of the interests of empire. Were Argentina to put up stiff resistance, then the air raids would continue, followed by naval bombardment. Advance information on Argentina's armed forces had been sketchy and fell far short of recognizing any real threat in the event of hostilities. Special precautions had, however, been taken in the face of a potential submarine threat. After all, Argentina did have two modern German-made submarines, along with two Guppy Class boats nearing retirement. British intelligence did not, moreover, acknowledge any appreciable threat from the Argentine Air Force, whose outdated inventory, added to the distance from the theater of operations, would render its capability for effective operations practically nil.

During the night of April 30, the British divided their naval arsenal—17 warships—into two task groups that would position themselves on station, one north of Soledad (East Falkland) Island, about 70 NM from Puerto Argentino, with the carrier *Invincible* as its flagship, while the remainder would lie 50 NM east of the islands, with the carrier *Hermes*. Since the *Hermes* carried the greater complement of Sea Harrier aircraft, it was decided that its squadrons would launch attacks and raids against Argentine installations while aircraft flying off the *Invincible* would fly air-to-air defense with its Combat Air Patrol (CAP) teams, usually consisting of two aircraft each. The location of each carrier was determined in accordance with a rational tactical layout geared to the missions flown by their aircraft. The *Invincible*, better equipped, should lie astride the most probable routes of any Argentine intruders, although its station was further from the islands. This took into account the range of the Sea Harriers, which, because of the lightness of their payloads, could fly further, either to pursue Argentine aircraft or to provide cover in the islands, and be able to return to their ship. The *Hermes*, on the other hand, was stationed only 50 miles off the islands and further east, so that it lay at a minimum distance from the targets (the Malvinas and Condor air bases at Puerto Argentino and Darwin), and therefore allowed a greater load of armament and ordnance—at the expense of fuel—while still keeping the ship at a safe distance from the Argentine Air Force's land bases, thereby achieving a compromise between maximum security and their mission as a carrier-borne naval air fighting arm.

In the briefing room aboard the *Hermes*, Squadron Leader Lieutenant Commander Andy Auld passed the word to his men. This would be the first test of fire for all of them. The good news was that the Vulcan had encountered no anti-aircraft defenses, and that the weather was right for carrying out the operation: partially cloudy skies, good visibility, and light winds. Twelve aircraft would fly the mission: nine would attack Puerto Argentino, and three would head for Darwin.

If the Vulcan's run had had any effect, it was to put both the inhabitants and the defenders at Puerto Argentino on their toes. Having overcome their initial surprise, they sized up the damage and cared for the casualties incurred during the raid. Communications linking the mainland and the islands began to crackle with excitement. The commander of FAS at Comodoro Rivadavia ordered the attack aircraft based along the coast made ready for action, while the commander of SATO, Vice-Admiral Lombardo, flashed Task Force 79 to stand by for a possible engagement with the British task force. At 0800 hours, General Menendez decided to cancel transfer of the 3rd Infantry Brigade to Gran Malvina (West Falkland) Island, in order to reposition the units around Puerto Argentino. About the same time, he received a message from Admiral Woodward, who offered him helicopter transport to the *Hermes* in order to formalize the surrender of his troops. Even before General Menendez was able to draft a fitting response, the answer had come from the ranks in terms that left no doubt in the British task force commander's mind that Argentina was determined to fight for the islands. With some misgivings, the British admiral ordered the previously laid plans into operation.

By 0825 hours, defending radar was tracking incoming intruders. An intense

Map 3
The Battle of May 1: The Attack against Malvinas Air Base

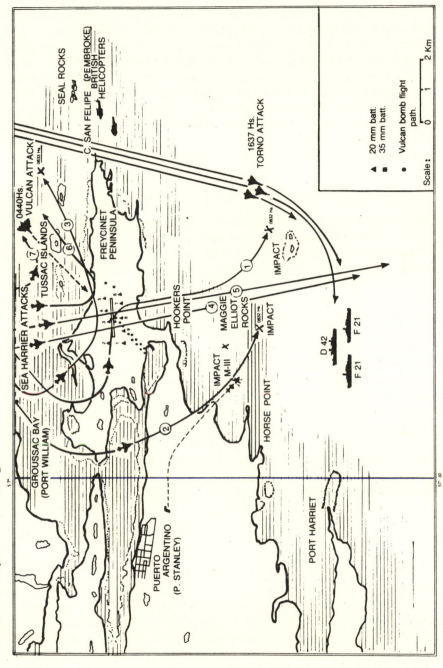

battle ensued between the attacking aircraft and the air defenses, which this time were at the ready to repel the invader. Nine Sea Harriers roared in at extremely low altitude and dropped their 1,000-pound bomb loads in passes of two or three aircraft each, while the air defense crews manned their guns, adjusting their range under fire for the first time. The attack came at the airstrip from the north, raking it with bombs, rockets, and 30mm cannon fire. The planes came in at an ideal altitude and angle for the ground gunners, who exacted a terrible toll: two Sea Harriers plunged landward in flames, struck by 20mm cannon fire. Four others took many hits as they withdrew toward their mother ship, trailing black plumes of smoke. One of them went into the water beyond radar range, and a fourth was knocked out of the sky by a Marine Tigercat battery.

CONDOR MILITARY AIR BASE UNDER ATTACK

From its inception, the Condor military air base lacked the essential elements for the effective organization of an operational unit. This unit was to be equipped with Pucara aircraft deployed to the islands, but the impossibility of basing them at Puerto Argentino, which would surely become the main objective of the enemy, and the almost total lack of landing strips in the islands, forced us to make do with the precarious facilities at Darwin, which was no more than an oddly shaped pasture some 1,500 feet long and 300 wide, with a noticeable low area in the center. Some facilities were improvised, but the area lacked shelter, fuel storage facilities, ammunition dumps, camouflage, barracks, and services. This conflict obliged us to make do without vital support that would have been essential for any weapons system save the Pucaras, which had been designed to operate from improvised and unimproved facilities. Nevertheless, hardships at this wretched place were overwhelming, especially when the runway became nonoperational following the all-too-frequent rains at that time of year, which turned the whole area into a quagmire. The hapless defenders of Condor would receive their baptism of fire on May 1.

As the Vulcan B–2 bomber made its run, the Pucara aircraft, which had been sitting in the open and would have been easy prey to enemy fire, were ordered moved to Calderon naval air station at Sea Elephant Bay on Pebble Island, northwest of the northern approach to Falkland Sound. This was another jerry-rigged facility, but the only one available aside from the two already mentioned. Only two aircraft were able to evacuate. A third caught its nose gear in a pothole and blocked the others, which remained on the ground like sitting ducks. It was 0730 hours.

The attack took the base by surprise while crews attempted to remove the crippled aircraft. One of the planes, registry A–527, took a direct hit as its ground crew and gunnery technicians were assisting its pilot, Lieutenant Daniel Antonio D. Jukic, to prepare it for action. As a result of the explosion that rocked the area, Jukic and seven NCOs were killed and nine others seriously wounded.

Air defenses at Condor were sketchier than at Puerto Argentino. Six Rheinmetal 20mm cannons equipped with ELTA radar and a two-barrel Oerlikon 35mm battery with a Skyguard tracking system were available to the defenders. The gunners had been ordered on alert, but an unfortunate coincidence hampered their effectiveness. They had been warned that the Pucara squadron was being removed from the base, and that as of 0825 hours, they should be on guard to avoid firing on their own aircraft. At that same time a flight of Sea Harriers screamed in from the northwest, at treetop altitude and high speed. When the gunners gained their wits and realized they were not friendly planes, it was too late. Thousand-pound bombs were bursting all around them, and took their toll among the defending forces. One aircraft dropped MK–17 ordnance and two "Beluga" bombs. (The "Beluga" bomb is a fragmentation device that spews grenades on detonation. These, in turn, burst, releasing thousands of steel shards. They are especially effective against personnel.)

This was a bitter pill for the air base. Not only had an aircraft and its pilot been lost, but casualties had been inflicted on the ground crews, six of whom had been mechanics and armaments specialists and would be difficult to replace. The fuel dump had gone up in flames. This would prove critical, for fuel was in short supply due to the British blockade. Further, one of the Pucaras removed to Calderon snapped its nose gear on landing because of the wretched condition of the airstrip.

FACTS VERSUS FICTION

Their mission complete, the intruding aircraft left Puerto Argentino and Darwin behind in a hasty retreat to the *Hermes*. According to British sources, the only damage sustained was a fin nicked by a 20mm shell. All British accounts describe Commander Auld's euphoria and excitement as he was debriefed on the *Hermes*. In the face of withering antiaircraft fire, he had been able to accomplish the mission without losses. He further reported that two 1,000-pound bombs had detonated on the runway, a statement at odds with the facts. The defenders at Puerto Argentino smiled in grim satisfaction. The air defense batteries' opening performance was in every way promising, and the losses sustained by the enemy were significant. A warm sense of security came over the men as they savored the fact that the enemy had not gotten off scot-free.

One of the greatest obstacles in researching hostile action is making information gained from both sides stand up to the test of reality. The dissemination of unconfirmed or irresponsible reports, as well as the work of agencies specializing in psychological action and operational intelligence, distort reality to unseemly extremes. But the information given here is the facts as they were known at the time of writing: the air defense batteries confirmed their four kills, plus two aircraft damaged; the British have asserted they suffered no losses. Air defense radar and crews of the third battery, who followed the action closely on their screens, were able to track every move of the attacking aircraft, and on-site verification has determined that four planes did not return to the *Hermes*.

Another noteworthy fact in regard to these events is that this low-altitude Sea Harrier attack against facilities at the Malvinas air base was the last of the war. The British did not use these aircraft against Puerto Argentino's air defenses again.

THE AIR FORCE RECEIVES ITS BAPTISM OF FIRE

The commander of FAS and his staff had devoted long and tense hours to prepare for those fateful events that became reality on May 1: facing off with an adversary that was vastly superior in both technology and means, in a theater whose nature was alien to the men of the air force. This was a typically naval theater of operations where aviation should have played a secondary rather than a direct role in the action.

The main operational military problem faced by FAS was the survivability of its assets: How does one go about attacking a modern guided-missile frigate with any chance for the attacking aircraft to return to base? U.S., Israeli, NATO, and Warsaw Pact sources, as well as our own navy flyers, were pumped for information. World War II dive-bombing techniques also were studied. None of these consultations revealed any sure-fire solutions to the problem at hand. Everything seemed to point toward the practical invulnerability of the guided-missile frigate, a feeling shared by the world's main navies, which can afford to maintain and operate such vessels.

Also, about mid-April, air force aircraft made practice attack runs against one of our navy's Class 42 guided-missile destroyers, with mixed, or at least unclear, results. Our own naval personnel concluded, to the consternation of our flyers, that practically every attacking aircraft had been "shot down." Air force observers did not entirely share that finding, for they had noted that an aircraft bearing in at full throttle, skimming the whitecaps, could achieve enough surprise to forestall the on-board warning systems, thus not giving the ship's defenders enough time to get their weapons into firing position for an effective defense before the attacker had released his ordnance. The only glimmer of hope for overcoming this problem lay in using an untested system and working out the techniques along the way. There would be no drills; the test would be conducted under combat conditions. But the heaviest burden of all was the responsibility shouldered by those who would make the decision to send their men to what seemed a certain doom, and fathomless was the courage of those who flew those missions: the combat crews.

It was under these circumstances that the air force prepared to make its stand. It did so, convinced that every means at its command, made available by the nation for the defense of the heritage that had been wrested away in 1833, should be put to use. Every man saw his duty laid before him, and was prepared, unflinchingly, to give his all. It should also be underscored that patriotic pride in realizing they were about to take part in a quest to regain what was rightfully theirs and make their land whole, as it had been at its inception in 1810, went far beyond any thoughts about the existing political institutions in their country at the time.

FAS scrambled its first combat formation at Rio Gallegos at 0644 hours. Its two Mirage-III aircraft, armed for air-to-air combat, were over Puerto Argentino at 0730 hours. All too soon—scant minutes, because of fuel constrictions—they winged their way back to their mainland base without having made contact with the enemy. The second formation of Mirage-V Dagger aircraft, code-named Toro (Bull), configured for aerial combat, left their base at Rio Grande at 0745 hours to intercept enemy aircraft. They were armed with two missiles each, and cannon. As they came in at 22,000 feet over the islands, ground control alerted Toro that a flight of Sea Harriers on combat air patrol was vectoring in with the obvious purpose of intercepting the Argentine fighters. The British planes closed with the Daggers, passing each other at 18,000 feet and initiating a sort of merry-go-round as each side circled in an attempt to get behind its opposite number. The Toros' limited fuel supplies obliged them to break contact just as a Sea Harrier fired a missile that missed its mark. Unable to catch up with the Mirage formation, which enjoyed superior speed and operating ceilings, the Harriers broke contact, thus ending this first, and bloodless, air engagement. It was abundantly clear that fuel constrictions would be the Achilles' heel of the Argentine squadrons, and the British wasted no time in getting the message. Their tactic would be easy. They would simply bide their time as the foe came into the theater of operations, wait a few minutes, and then close for the kill at a time when the Argentines could no longer engage in air-to-air combat for lack of fuel, and always at low altitude.

Also leaving Rio Gallegos at 0843 hours was one of the KC–130 tankers, code-named Perro (Dog). Throughout the hostilities, it would have the most delicate of tasks, that of refueling the Air Force Skyhawks (A4-B and C) in flight. The KC–130s were soon to ensure in-flight refueling for the Navy's A4-Q and Super Etendard craft, for these planes did not possess the range required to reach their targets in the islands without this service being available. Since the air force had only two tankers in its inventory, it was impossible to plan massive attacks with numerous concurrent sorties. The KC–130 was followed in carefully calculated sequence by the Topos (Moles) (A4-Bs), the Osos (Bears) (A4-Cs), and the Pampas (A4-Cs), all armed with bombs and cannon to attack naval targets. This meant they could not engage in aerial combat, because their heavy loads of ordnance would render them unable to face off with an interceptor. About the same time, the Tablones (Planks), Limones (Lemons; two Mirage-IIIs), and the Focos (Focuses; two Mirage-Vs) left their bases in Patagonia. Their mission was to disperse and confuse British efforts in a diversionary action to keep the interceptors at a distance from the main thrust of the attack, which was to be carried out through low-altitude penetration to the targets. This tactic paid handsome dividends to the FAS attackers throughout the conflict, for instead of ensuring a direct cover to the intruders, they served as pickets for detecting and intercepting the enemy.

The Limones, coming in over the islands at high altitude were alerted by ground control that two Sea Harriers were closing fast, but at a lower level. They passed under the Mirage-IIIs, and in a blink the British aircraft gave a demonstration of their superior maneuverability, for, as if by magic, as they passed the oncoming line of Daggers, they fanned out and reversed course, coming in on the tails of the intruders. But here was where the radar operators at Puerto Argentino showed their stuff, for they were able to warn Limones of this maneuver, which allowed them to get to a safe distance and altitude from their pursuers, once their real mission, which had been to distract the British from the main thrust of the attack, had been accomplished. Their superior speed and operating ceiling were the aces up their sleeves.

While all of this was unfolding in the skies over the islands, ground personnel were keeping a sharp eye on developments, for they were in awe of the impending and fearsome British landing. At 0925 hours, command headquarters of FAS received news that a ship was approaching Annunciation Bay and Argentine lookouts at an emplacement at Fitz Roy reported four helicopters approaching the beach, which led the men to believe an airborne landing by chopper was imminent in that area.

At 0945 hours, Sea Harrier aircraft off the *Hermes* were spotted approaching Puerto Argentino. They turned back short of their targets, however, no doubt mindful of the thrashing they had taken earlier at the hands of the islands' air defenses. At 0950 hours, ground control reported incoming blips due north of the islands, probably the Sea Harriers from the *Invincible* on their way to intercept Topos. At that same time, the naval commander of the Malvinas, Rear Admiral Otero, confirmed a Tigercat victory, at 0830 hours, over a Sea Harrier. At 0955 hours, ground control at Puerto Argentino reported blips on its radarscopes at 110 degrees (ESE), revealing the approach of helicopters. This was followed in quick succession by confirmation of more incoming choppers, as our radarscopes lit up with around 50 bogeys.

Under total "condition red" (state of alert denoting imminent enemy air attack), the defenders at Puerto Argentino braced for what appeared to be the expected British assault wave: chopper landings along the southern shore of the Freycinet Peninsula and the approach of several warships in Annunciation Bay, north of Port William. But at 1000 hours, our own formations of aircraft neared Puerto Argentino. Could it have been the coming together of intent, intuition, and just plain luck that they swooped in at the exact scheduled time of the British landing and assault? Almost simultaneously, a British wireless was intercepted, ordering the chopper formation to withdraw "due to unexpected unfavorable situation." Possibly the British were deterred from their planned landings by our planes. Had they gone ahead as scheduled, the task force landing group might well have sustained serious casualties. It may also well be that the number of incoming Argentine aircraft may have surpassed the *Invincible'* CAPs, which would have seriously curtailed its prospects of intercepting and putting all the Argentine aircraft massing over the islands at that time out of action.

Around 1200 hours, as FAS was scrambling two more flights, the Ciclones (Cyclones; two Mirage-Vs) and the Pingos (Fast Horses; two A4-Cs), the British situation appeared undefined. Puerto Argentino radar reported numerous Sea Harrier sorties returning to the carrier before reaching the islands and without making contact with the enemy. Intelligence sources confirmed the kills during the 0830 attack, while "red alerts" followed in quick succession at every hint of another British assault wave. Around 1248 hours, the enemy fleet was estimated to be divided into two main task groups, one of them lying less than 30 NM off Puerto Argentino at 020° (NNE) with a formation of four ships, while the second, approaching from 145° (SE), with five vessels, was a scant 12 miles away. The British CAPs remained at least 15 miles from the airstrip. Admiral Woodward's forces gave the appearance of being somewhat off balance.

The enemy was apparently marshaling its forces for a second helicopter landing, after having fallen back and regrouped following the failed first attempt. This assumption was soon confirmed when the lookout posts began reporting the presence of three ships and a carrier approaching Annunciation Bay from an east-northeast heading, with heavy chopper activity. It was surprising that during their first try, the British did not risk their ships' coming close to the Freycinet Peninsula to soften up our positions with naval gunfire. Perhaps they were not sure of the range of our coastal artillery. In any case, they took no chances, remained well out of the estimated range of our defenses, and sent aircraft to do the job—to the obvious distaste of the pilots of the task force, who sometimes turned back prior to reaching their objectives.

But at 1425 hours, three ships stationed themselves nine miles ESE of the Malvinas military air base and initiated a naval bombardment, guided by a helicopter that hovered at an appropriate spot to enable the ship's guns to get within range. Shortly thereafter, another helicopter landed within sight of the 3rd Battery's gunners, but just far enough out of range to avoid being repelled. By 1500 hours, there remained little doubt as to the British plan. Five smaller vessels made an approach from the east, 13 miles off the coast. They were of a type similar to the Fearless landing system launches, and they were covered by helicopters. These ships came into the clear view of land-based spotters and served to underscore the enemy's design, for the choppers were seen to unload troops (which were later withdrawn).

Air Force South scrambled several more squadrons to repel the British task force's second landing attempt. The Pampas (two A4-Cs for cover and dispersion) took off for their run at 1523 hours, followed by the Dardos (Darts; two Mirage-Vs assigned to the same task), while at Trelew, three Canberra MK–62 bombers sortied on a bombing mission against naval targets. At 1535 hours, a KC–130 took to the air to stand by for in-flight refueling of the A4-Bs and A4-Cs. Four A4-C Lanas (Wools) for antiship warfare, as well as two Mirage-V Fierros (Irons), for cover, also sortied.

These were followed in quick succession by the Tornos (Windlasses; three Mirage-Vs for antiship warfare) at 1545 hours, the Fortines (Fortresses; two

Mirage-Vs for cover) at 1550 hours, the Buitres (Vultures; two Mirage-IIIs for cover) at 1553 hours, and at 1555 hours the Rubio (Blond; one Mirage-V out of two slated initially; its pilot would not be held back in spite of the fact that he would have to fly the mission alone and that his not going was justified, for his companion had been grounded by mechanical problems). A second formation of MK–62 bombers sortied at 1605 hours, along with the Truenos (Thunderclaps; four A4-Bs for antiship warfare), which scrambled at 1617 hours.

Practically every available combat aircraft that could fly had been marshaled and was winging its way to its objective. Many would never return home, but the British forces were made to pay a heavy price.

Air Force South Spills its First Blood

At 1540 hours Rear Admiral Otero confirmed to SATO that a " . . . landing by helicopter in the northern sector of the islands, supported by logistics vessels or the carrier is in progress. The ships are positioned on a radius between 010° and 145° off Puerto Argentino and stationed at 90, 40, and 10 nautical miles. Sea Harriers are providing cover for helicopter landings.''

The enemy had stationed three CAPs from the *Invincible*, one in the airspace south of Puerto Argentino and two north of Soledad (East Falkland) Island, as the waves of Argentine warplanes approached their target areas at low altitude or strung themselves out without dropping down to meet possible enemy interceptors. They reached their target areas at 1620 hours and, in successive waves, the Tornos, Dardos, Buitres, Fortines, and El Rubio fanned out to cover their assignments. Some were to divert the CAPs upstairs, while others skimmed over the water to sneak in unnoticed. With one eye on the fuel gauge, the instruments, the leader, and possible "bandits," they had the narrowest of time frames in which to stay over the target, complete their missions, and survive . . . or die trying.

At 1630 hours, the two Mirage-IIIs of the Dardo squad tangled with two Sea Harriers northeast of Puerto Argentino. The opposing aircraft faced off in a classical scissors maneuver, and as they closed, they went into a steep climb, attempting to get on each other's tail. The greater maneuverability of the British plane allowed one pilot, First Lieutenant Paul Barton, to execute a sudden deceleration and position himself behind and just below an Argentine Mirage, an ideal launching point for the deadly state-of-the-art AIM–9L Sidewinder missile that found its mark before Argentine pilot, First Lieutenant Perona, was fully aware of what was happening: he felt a strong jolt, followed by violent shaking and loss of control. Thinking he had collided with the Sea Harrier, he ejected over Pebble Island, where he was picked up later.

Squadron Leader Capt. Gustavo Garcia Cuerva encountered Lt. Cmdr. Robert Thomas's Sea Harrier.

Both had launched their missiles from too far away or from unfavorable positions, all to no avail. But engaging in a dogfight had cost the Argentine pilot precious fuel that would otherwise have seen him safely back to base. There was no way out. He could have headed his doomed plane toward an unpopulated area, radioed his position, and pulled the ejection lever. Search-and-rescue choppers would have done the rest, and he would soon have rejoined his unit. But every flyer reacts differently to a given situation. Captain Garcia knew he was flying a fully operational aircraft of which his unit had dire need. He thought of his plane—not of himself—as he radioed Malvinas tower for emergency landing instructions. The landing strip had come under bombardment, and there was no time to coordinate with Argentine air defense. He was ordered to eject. Garcia Cuerva's voice crackled over the airwaves: '' . . . bringing this aircraft in, in one piece. Clear me with air defense, I'm coming in.'' Jettisoning his ordnance and external tanks, he banked gracefully in. Caught on final approach in the cross fire of his own antiaircraft guns, his plane careened past the runway and crashed into the sea near Maggie Elliot Rocks, off the Freycinet Peninsula. It was 1638 hours.

Almost simultaneously, the lone Rubio was caught in a deadly game, with the deck stacked in the opponents' favor. First Lieutenant Ardiles in his Mirage-V found himself face to face with two British CAP Sea Harriers. As they closed, the Harriers broke in opposite directions. First Lieutenant Bertie Penfold jockeyed his plane into firing position. His lethal missile disintegrated his opposite number over Bougainville Island. The pilot had been unable to eject.

On the ground, control picked up Ardiles' dying gasp even as his voice was blotted from the frequency, his blip disappearing before the horrified eyes of the dumbfounded operators, who watched helplessly as the curtain rang down on this act in the grand drama of warfare.

According to poets and philosophers, man is doomed both to greatness and to oblivion. Here he had been ennobled by both the sacrifice and the selflessness of these brave flyers, who had honored their names, their service, and their heritage. Many others, whose resolve it was to fly high like the eagles, rather than cower like barnyard fowl, were to follow in their flight paths.

Torno Squadron to the Attack

As things turned out, the supreme sacrifice offered up by Garcia Cuerva and Ardiles proved not to have been in vain: both had accomplished their mission to the fullest, for while they were engaged in combat in the skies over the islands, a squadron of three Mirage-V aircraft commanded by Capt. Norberto Dimeglio, had dropped down from their cruising altitude 115 NM from Puerto Argentino and were skimming undetected over the whitecaps in search of their targets: three enemy vessels had been reported entering Annunciation Bay. The Tornos were unaware that they were about to write a chapter in the history of naval air warfare. As they passed the north coast of the islands, Dimeglio streaked over the entrance to San Carlos Straits and kept his nose on his target. Visibility was six miles, and he was flying low, under a 500-to–1000-foot cloud cover, over calm seas. As he came in over Cape Corrientes, he banked to starboard and bore south toward his targets. He was deeply disappointed to discover that they were not at their reported positions.

He normally would have returned to base, having carried out his mission. Dimeglio certainly had no fuel to waste, but a glance at his fuel gauges told him he could chance a couple of minutes more before turning back. He continued south, and as he passed Port William, he spotted, a little further on, what he was looking for. The three warships were there, firing their guns on Puerto Argentino. Without a moment's hesitation, Dimeglio assigned a ship to each of his squadron, and they screamed in on their run to the targets. The three Tornos flashed past the hovering helicopter that was directing the ships' fire. It happened so fast the chopper pilot probably did not spot them, for he remained on station and continued to direct the naval bombardment. The ships also seemed unaware of the impending attack. There were three vessels: a Class 42 destroyer and two Class 21 frigates. Captain Dimeglio and his no. 2 man, Lieutenant Aguirre, zeroed in on the destroyer, unaware that they were aiming for the same target. Number 3, First Lieutenant Roman, had singled out one of the smaller ships. It was about 1637 hours.

Target selection is in fact a figure of speech, since when flying 600 mph at wave level, there is not much that can be done to change course. As they came into range, the three pilots pressed their firing mechanisms. Surprise was complete. Not a single ship reacted, or, by the time they did, Daggers 1 and 2 had dropped their deadly loads: two 500-pound parachute delayed bombs each. Likewise no. 3, which met a light spray of antiaircraft fire but rode to the target without mishap, raking the frigate with cannon fire as it streaked over.

Captain Dimeglio figured his ordnance had overshot the target because his wingman was unable to confirm hits. Lieutenant Aguirre was equally unable to confirm his own hits because his aircraft had passed directly over the target and visibility was blocked. Both had made their runs at the stern of the ship. But as no. 3 flew over his target, he noted, just ahead and to the left, a large orange fireball followed by a dense blanket of black smoke. Number 2's bombs had struck home and detonated. The destroyer was ablaze in the water, and the frigates had sustained lesser damage.

The first postwar naval-air engagement had just taken place. The Tornos made a hasty withdrawal, having been warned by ground control that two Sea Harriers were closing in on them from 20 miles out and were homing for the kill. At the same time, the Buitres, which had been flying cover 70 miles from that location, were obliged to turn back for lack of fuel. The British CAP followed, chasing them for 80 miles before disengaging. The Fortines, who were still in the area, flying two Mirage-Vs, were directed to intercept the Sea Harriers. As they came into view, the British planes withdrew northward and headed toward their carriers, fully aware that this time their position was unfavorable. The Buitres and Fortines headed back to the mainland without further incident.

The Canberra Squadron Does Its Bit

The MK–62 Canberra bomber can carry up to 10,000 pounds of ordnance in its bays, which, along with its extended range, gives it considerable leeway in action. For this reason it operated out of Almirante Zar base at Trelew, in order not to overburden the more southerly bases that serviced the shorter-range aircraft. The Canberra had seen 20 years of service in the Argentine Air Force, and neither its speed nor its equipment made it the ideal platform for the difficult task that lay before it: attacking the British fleet.

Heavily laden with 1,000-pound bombs with iron casings, the units of the first squadron lumbered down the runway at 1533 hours and set their bearings for Puerto Argentino. Their mission, as well as that of the squadron that would follow within minutes, was to bombard the British vessels in the vicinity of Annunication Bay. The first formation reached cruising altitude and set out for its target area. As they passed along the Gulf of San Jorge, they spotted a group of Argentine Navy ships and decided to drop down, in spite of their distance from the target. About then, they entered the total exclusion zone, without realizing that their heading was taking them straight down on the task group headed by the *Invincible* (one carrier, one Class 42 destroyer, and two or three frigates).

When the carrier's radar picked up this formation coming in on its rear flank, something not reckoned with, the group was barely able to swing its defenses around to meet the MK–62s. A nearby guided-missile frigate fired off its Sea Dart missiles. The Canberras realized their situation as missiles streaked past and one struck the leading edge of the starboard wing of the lead aircraft. Its skipper had already turned about as the CAP zeroed in for the attack. He felt the impact, followed by a strong shudder. He restrained his navigator, who was on the verge of bailing out, for he still had control response, and was attempting to turn toward Puerto Argentino, where he could make an emergency landing. But as he completed his turn, coming in low over the water, his eyes bulged in surprise: there before him loomed the outline of what could only be an aircraft carrier. He was also able to determine the presence, blocking his path to that majestic vessel, of two airborne objects. Planes or helicopters, it was hard to say, but he came to the quick conclusion that his best bet was to execute a fast turn and put as much distance as possible between his crippled Canberra and the enemy. He made away at the top speed his engines and his damaged airfoil would allow, while the rest of the squadron ran interference with the pursuing Sea Harriers. He set down at his home base without further mishap at 1857 hours.

The second formation of Canberras was not so lucky. This time the carrier was on full alert, and the interceptors claimed one bomber, which was abandoned at 49°30'S/59°35'W. Two parachutes were seen blossoming over the icy South Atlantic waters at 1704 hours. Neither flyer was ever located. The other two

Canberras returned to Trelew without further incident. It was truly a bad day for the MK–62 squadron, since none had come close to accomplishing its mission. They had had the worst of luck at the very beginning of the engagement, for they had stumbled across the main carrier task group entrusted with the air defense of the British fleet. In a word, they had wandered into the lion's den.

But a point had been made: the highly rated electronic and missile defense grid surrounding a powerful modern war fleet was not invulnerable, and those Argentine flyers would not be the only ones to lay eyes on a British carrier during the hostilities.

Action on Land

The lion's share of land operations on May 1 fell to the 25th Infantry Regiment deployed on the Freycinet Peninsula to cover the Malvinas military air base, regarded as one of the enemy's prime objectives. First British air operations, and then the naval bombardment, held the troops of the regiment pinned down during most of the day, except those troops assigned to observation posts around the regiment's defense perimeter.

The observation posts on San Luis Peninsula were also under total alert, since their location allowed them to follow every move the British naval units made to the northwest of the airstrip, and they were on the lookout for the feared landings that did not come that day (nor did they come at that location, because of the defenses that had been massed at Puerto Argentino). At 1816 hours, 81mm mortar fire opened against British units being helicoptered into Bird Island, action that was reinforced at 1830 hours by the guns of the 3rd Artillery Group, which would come to play a major role, especially during the final actions in the conflict.

The naval bombardment went on into the night. It had no real effect on the 25th Regiment, which was well dug into its positions. At 2105 hours, one of the surveillance radar sets sustained light damage that was quickly repaired. The apparent objective of the British bombardment was to knock out the air defenses around the Malvinas military air base. They made copious use of artillery antipersonnel grenades (which explode about five feet off the ground), but the defenders sustained no casualties.

It was, however, an uncomfortable position for the 3rd Artillery, since the British guns were firing from a position that lay beyond the range of their own pieces, the largest of which were the 105mm Otto Melara guns. The 155mm Sofma howitzers, with a range of 15 miles, had not been moved to the islands. Had the Sofmas been available, enemy vessels would have had to station themselves further out, rendering their 4.5-inch guns useless against the superior range of the 155mm. This was to prove a major weakness for the Argentine side throughout hostilities.

CONFIRMATIONS

Making "confirmations" was one of the most thankless tasks that befell air force staff officers, who spent sleepless nights trying to clear up uncertainties, racing against the clock in search of trustworthy answers in time to order up the next flight. Each pilot was fully debriefed following each mission, the better to gather all the pertinent data that would enable the planning of follow-up missions to go forth while keeping constant tabs on the tactical situation as it developed.

All this intelligence had to include losses sustained by the enemy. This required exceedingly careful analysis, in order to avoid distorting reality. This is why all kills, as well as "possibles" and damage reports, had to be subject to confirmation from other sources, usually other units or formations, before being chalked up as certain. This was made more difficult because the very nature of the tactics used by our aircraft when they made their runs against British targets made it hard for our pilots to verify their hits and the effect of their weapons against the enemy, which obliged the staff of Air Force South to devote much time to detailed analysis. It was often possible for the members at the rear of a formation to confirm whether the lead aircraft, or its wingman, had scored a hit, but under normal circumstances, the very fact that a warhead had impacted on a vessel was not automatically assumed to have caused harm, for the ordnance had to detonate. Ordinarily such explosions were not visible to the attacking crews because the time-delay fuses installed on the bombs kept them from bursting until some seconds after impact.

Air Force South limited confirmation, in the absence of sources of intelligence or reconnaissance means for evaluating the results of our action, to the results of the in-depth analysis of reported damage or kills, since news reports collected and released to the public by the media—including official sources—on the battle of May 1 were all too often at great variance with the facts, and even entered the realm of fantasy, such as the reported attack of a Pucara against the carrier *Hermes*.

The South Georgia experience, where unfounded reports were widespread and took hold of public opinion, was repeated to some extent on May 1, but, having learned its lesson, Air Force South was exceedingly conservative in passing on any information it had not verified and that came from numerous sources, for it was indeed possible that the enemy was spreading false rumors for psychological purposes. As for the number of Sea Harriers actually shot down on May 1, so many reports came in that it became practically impossible to make an assured confirmation of some of these enemy losses. The fact that the downing of an aircraft in combat is often reported by several parties belonging to different units or forces, and that confusion can set in as to whether they are reporting on the same or on different aircraft, in the absence of hard data as to time and place of occurrence, should be kept in mind.

Furthermore, since the air attacks sustained by Puerto Argentino on May 1 were aimed at the landing strip and base facilities, and these are situated on a peninsula surrounded by water on the north, south, and east, all downed aircraft went into the sea, which denied the defenders any chance of physically verifying the kills. Moreover, the British launched their offensive from directions that enabled their flyers, in the event they were hit by our air defenses, to eject over the water, which made the job of the task force rescue service very easy. Had they ejected over land, their task would have been almost impossible.

Operational commands and their staffs received and confirmed the following reports:

1. 0825 hours, GADA 601: landing strip attacked by Sea Harrier aircraft; one aircraft shot down, falling in the sea; another hit, withdrawing with damage
2. 0830 hours, 3rd Battery: landing strip under attack by ten aircraft; artillery brings down two or three Sea Harriers
3. 0950 hours, Malvinas garrison command: one Sea Harrier brought down by Tigercat missile
4. 1138 hours, joint staff: military commander, Malvinas, reported one Sea Harrier shot down
5. 0950 hours, Air Force South: two aircraft confirmed kills, two probables
6. 1122 hours, Air Force South: confirms three British aircraft downed during 0830 offensive.

ACTION AGAINST NAVAL TARGETS

According to an eyewitness account, the Torno Squadron attack occurred at 1630 hours, 37NM south of the Freycinet Peninsula. At 1626 hours, the task force fleet detachment had moved up to bombard the Malvinas air base. According to British sources, this task group was comprised of the cruiser *Glamorgan*, and the frigates *Arrow* and *Alacrity*. (Lieutenant Tinker relates the British version of this action, in his *Letters*, which may serve to prove the task force intelligence censored his mail. According to our sources, the *Glamorgan* at that time was precisely 90 miles east of the Freycinet Peninsula, the scene of the action.) At about 1630 hours, these ships came under attack by Captain Dimeglio's squadron of three Mirage-Vs. As a result of this action, two ships sustained light damage and another sustained heavy damage. Following the attack, these ships withdrew out to sea on a southeast heading. One became enveloped in flames that were clearly visible to hundreds of persons in the area.

Statements of Witnesses

Unlike other actions that took place during the hostilities, there were numerous witnesses to this event, among whom were the following:

1. Captain Dimeglio, Torno Squadron leader: "I assigned a ship to each of us. I came in on the stern of one, identification unknown. I released two bombs. They did not impact. It was no. 2's bombs that hit the target."

2. Lieutenant Aguirre Faget, no. 2: "I attacked a ship at the stern. I did not see the lead man's bombs impact, but I fired my cannon and dropped my ordnance lengthwise over the ship. They must have gone through the deck, but I was unable to see the impact."

3. 1st Lt. Cesar F. Roman, no. 3: "Number 2 came in at a certain angle and raked them with cannon fire. I released my bombs only. As I pulled out, I saw a terrific explosion over the water, just ahead of me, with black smoke first, followed immediately by intense flames, and then by heavy white smoke."

4. Maj. Alberto Catala, staff aide to General Menendez's joint command at Puerto Argentino: "There were three ships, and although they were far out, one appeared larger, with its array of antennas, and two smaller ones. The ship that was hit had a large, squared-rigged antenna."

5. 1st Lt. Eduardo A. Gonzalez, advanced tactical air control observer at Sapper Hill. His statement bears great weight because of his privileged observation post: "We were with navy Lt. Cionchi, of the 5th Marines, at the position when we saw the Daggers attack the ships, which appeared to be two frigates and a destroyer. One could see the line of fire, and as the aircraft pulled up, white smoke was billowing from the foredecks. A fiery glare was visible that evening for at least 45 minutes in that direction.

6. Navy Lt. Rodolfo O. Cionchi observed the attack along with Lieutenant Gonzalez: "The attack and the explosion were both perfectly visible from our observation post." Asked what type of vessel, he stated: "A Class 42 frigate, sir." Asked if he was sure, he replied: "How could I not recognize it? I know them perfectly because we have the same class ships" (the ARA *Hercules* and the *Santisima Trinidad*).

7. Lt. Jorge Reyes, antiaircraft battery chief at Malvinas air base: "It was the first ship attacked by nos. 1 and 2 that sustained the explosion. Following the attack, we could see thick smoke as a frigate drew alongside to render assistance. The vessels then moved away at high speed, while the third, which had sustained damage, made very slow headway."

8. Maj. Hugo A. Maiorano, commander antiaircraft artillery, Malvinas air base: "I saw an explosion aboard a frigate, with black smoke, followed by white smoke. At night a glow was visible from that direction. At about 1830 hours, there was a flash. Then the glow disappeared."

9. Capt. Pablo Marcos Carballo (*Trueno* squadron leader): "I came in over the south of Freycinet Peninsula, for I was planning my return leg across the north sector of the islands, when I saw a ship completely covered with smoke, to the extent it was impossible to identify it . . ." (sighting shortly following the attack).

10. Perhaps the best eyewitness account of the event was given by the M–1 air observer network post located on Mount Low, four miles north of Puerto Argentino, since, although somewhat removed from the action, the elevation enabled the observers (S. M. Ocampo and his assistant, Biasotto) to witness not only the attack itself but also the ensuing events, considering that the overview of the area broadened their sight range to the horizon. They submitted a detailed report of how one of the ships began to release billows of smoke as it moved slowly through the water, while the others made much quicker headway on a southerly course. Between 1830 and 1900 hours, loud detonations were heard and the horizon lit up

brightly, making them think that a naval engagement was in progress. Later, between 2200 and 2300 hours, they could still hear explosions, albeit more faintly, and see a glow, just barely visible, "like small lightning flashes." There can be little doubt that these two spotters had witnessed the British destroyer's final moments, when the fire reached the fuel bunkers and the magazines loaded with Sea Dart missiles.

Conclusions Regarding This Action

1. There is ample evidence that a British ship was hit by the Torno Squadron and sustained extensive damage and fire aboard.

2. There is ample evidence that, of the three vessels engaged in the naval bombardment of Puerto Argentino, the heavily damaged ship was a destroyer, in view of its antenna configuration. It was also the largest of the three vessels on station there.

3. According to British sources, the task group carrying out this operation was comprised of the HMS *Glamorgan* (County Class cruiser) and the Class 21 frigates *Arrow* and *Alacrity*.

4. Official British sources confirmed, following the end of the hostilities, that the Class 42 frigate lost in action was the HMS *Coventry*, sunk by the detonation of three 500 pound bombs dropped by A4-B aircraft on May 25. The numerous eyewitness accounts of the events described here have been ascribed to error, for the smoke seen has been alleged to be "exhaust gases of the ship's Olympus turbines."

British Sources

There were no official or news reports issued by the British that gave credence to the fact that any task force vessel had sustained serious damage. The following statements have been obtained:

British Defense Ministry communiqué (1230 GMT, May 2, 1982):
In the late afternoon [of May 1] Task Force units stationed within the TEZ bombarded Stanley Airport to reinforce the effects of the bombardment and to hamper repairs.
In the evening, the Argentines launched an attack against the Task Force. One Canberra was brought down by a Sea Harrier. Another sustained severe damage. The attack was not effective.
Only one ship sustained damage, which was superficial. The frigate continued its operational tasks. There was one casualty, Seaman Ian Britell, who was wounded. His injuries are superficial and he is ambulatory.
There are no further reported contacts as of this date. In the past 24 hours, no aircraft or helicopters have been reported lost.

The last statement is factual, considering that aircraft were shot down at 0830 hours on May 1 and this communiqué was released at 1230 GMT (0930 Buenos Aires time) on May 2.
Remaining media or book references to this event give similar descriptions.

Britain had been forced by the results of the battle of May 1 to mask the facts deliberately, but at that time we Argentines were unaware of this.

DEBRIEFING THE FIRST DAY OF COMBAT

Argentine Staffs

Debriefing the first day of combat action for Argentina's armed forces following 100 years of peace, during which not a shot had been fired in anger against any foreign power, brought about painstaking evaluations within the operational commands and the joint staff, in the light of the day's events and of their not always precise interpretation.

From a political and military strategic standpoint, it was obvious that Great Britain had set about gaining its political objectives through the violent use of the task force's offensive assets, with the purpose of obtaining a swift victory and forcing the Republic of Argentina to give up its goal of reclaiming the Malvinas Islands. The taking of Puerto Argentino was the top military and political prize, for Great Britain could not incur the risk of getting tied down in a drawn-out struggle, not only for considerations of weather, for the hard southern winter was at hand, but also for domestic and foreign political considerations.

At the close of the first day of hostilities, our forces had limited themselves to defending against air attacks—through antiaircraft artillery—and against naval bombardment—using Air Force South assets to launch attacks against enemy warships. Two conclusions can be drawn from these actions: that intended enemy landings had been repelled, and that the task force had withdrawn further out, thus demonstrating that it was not entirely immune.

From the strategic operational standpoint, actions carried out by British forces seemed to be tailored to the objectives of interdiction, harassment, and implementation of the naval blockade, the attempted helicopter landings having been repelled. This translated into significant naval air losses for the task force, due to the shooting down of the Harriers and the decrease in its naval power due to Argentine air attacks against its assets. The withdrawal of British task groups further out to sea were in all probability in response to a perceived need to keep them out of range of our aircraft, regroup, and await reinforcements.

The staff of Air Force South, at Comodoro Rivadavia, followed the air force in its first test of fire. It was exceedingly difficult to remain impartial as actions were analyzed, for our men were sacrificing their lives—giving their final measure—and some of our priceless aircraft—for they were at that time irreplaceable—had been put out of action. The unbalanced way in which these means had been sent into battle betrayed the emotions that may have blurred the vision of those who drew plans and made decisions, and in whom those who carried out the orders placed deep and serene confidence.

Given the scope and perspective of the day's events, it was difficult to gauge the extent of the successes achieved against the British expeditionary force.

Furthermore, we had no insight into the British plan, what the next move would be. We could not fathom whether the task force's removal further out to sea was a tactical withdrawal or the result of our frustrating its attempts to establish a beachhead. There was no sure count of enemy aircraft losses or the extent of damages sustained in combat.

What was certain, though, was that the enemy fleet had disappeared from the radar scopes at Puerto Argentino and had moved further east; that the most feared event of all, the landings, had not taken place; that the air defenses had proven their effectiveness, having destroyed or damaged several Sea Harrier aircraft; and that our own planes had been able to hit home with their less complex warheads. State of the art they were not, but they had earned the respect of the men who manned the British task force.

Air Force South also gained great satisfaction from the fact that, thanks to the willingness and resolve of our flyers who carried the battle to the enemy, so many of the scheduled missions had been able to achieve their objectives. The cloud of uncertainty that had at first shrouded the prospects of successfully attacking guided-missile frigates gave way to the conviction that they were not invulnerable and that they could therefore carry on the fight with a measure of dignity and a decent prospect of inflicting damage on the enemy.

This first day of combat also demonstrated some flaws that would have to be reckoned with throughout the hostilities. The most marked disadvantage was the exceedingly short over-target time our flyers had available to them by virtue of their fuel constrictions. There was also the availability to the enemy of what would prove to be the star performer in the war for the skies: the AIM 9L Sidewinder missile, which can be fired from any position, an advantage not enjoyed by Argentina's Magic, Matra, or Shafir weapons, which were primitive compared with the Sidewinder. The advantage lay, therefore, not so much in the sophistication of the platform (the Sea Harrier) as in the technology gap, as well as in Air Force South's Mirage aircraft, which lacked the range to get to the scene of the action, let down, engage, and return to base.

Air Superiority

Having thus outlined the first day's action, the definition of air superiority over the battlefield—the key to success or failure in modern warfare—must be established.

The Argentine Air Force's conception of air superiority is as follows: "A situation in a given time and space where the use and exploitation of airspace is feasible at an acceptable cost, in which enemy utilization and interference against our operations is negligible and of low magnitude. It is general when it encompasses a whole theater of operations, and is local when it is limited to a restricted area."

The definition of the U.S. joint chiefs of staff is this: "Degree of domination exercised by one force over another in aerial battle which enables one to carry

out land, naval and air operations at a given time and place without significant
interference from the opposing forces.''

Some Argentine authors have stated that the enemy had total air superiority.
This is not in keeping with these definitions, for had this been so, none of our
aircraft would have inflicted any significant damage on the enemy. The facts
tell us otherwise. In spite of the final victory having gone to the British, the
very heavy losses they sustained during the hostilities were incurred through the
action of Argentina's air arm. Any statement to the contrary would belittle the
efforts of those who carried the fight to a formidable foe, in spite of the unfavorable odds that were stacked against them from the very outset and that
remained so throughout the conflict. In fact, except in localized areas, or for
short periods of time, neither opponent was really able to establish air superiority
over the other. Not only was this our own finest feat of arms, it was the single
biggest drawback for the task force.

Admiral Woodward's Staff

May 1 is certain to have gone down as an unforgettable day for the commander
of the British task force. Everything had led him to believe that Argentine
resistance would be, as had been the case on South Georgia, more of a token
act than a military stand, and that the defenders would fold at the very sight of
the British fleet as it hove into view.

The Vulcan bombing run had reportedly put Stanley Airport (Malvinas air
base) out of action. The mass media had put on a flashy show both to Great
Britain and to the world. Britain's resolve and infallibility, personified by her
prime minister, the "Iron Lady" out to prove of what mettle she was made,
had been demonstrated. For the British government, the sending of the fleet
appeared to have been justified by its actions, thus neutralizing any objections
raised by the opposition within Parliament or among the public. Further reports
indicated Argentine losses in aircraft; one British frigate sustaining light damage
and a single, equally light casualty; and all Sea Harriers safely returned to their
carriers.

As Admiral Woodward gathered with his closest advisers to evaluate the first
day of hostilities, they encountered a series of surprises for which no contingency
plans had been drawn up. First and foremost, they had met a formidable air
defense array at Puerto Argentino that had cost the task force upward of 20
percent of its available aircraft. Such a loss rate would be unsustainable in future
operations, for there would be insufficient air cover for the fleet as well as for
the planned landing on a beach in the vicinity of Puerto Argentino. Second,
hostile air action had unleashed a lethal blow against one of his ships and damaged
another, which revealed a flaw that might well compromise the whole operation:
it signified that the ships were vulnerable, that the enemy was capable of foiling
air defenses and carrying the offensive to the task force as it approached the
islands—despite the distance separating them from their bases. The surprise was

as much operational as it was technical, for the British had not figured that, for example, a Mirage-V aircraft, with an additional 1,700-liter fuel tank under its belly, could fly that far afield, thus breaking with all previous forecasts relating to the design performances of this type of aircraft and what it was capable of in action. The need to bomb mainland Argentine bases, the only effective way of neutralizing this unexpected air threat, dawned on the British. Political problems (U.S. pressure) would, however, stay their hand.

General Menendez's response had underscored the land forces' determination to resist, and, to top things off, an Argentine submarine had managed to infiltrate one of the task groups, had fired its torpedoes—which proved to be duds—and had evaded British antisubmarine action.

Therefore, the operational picture was radically different from the one imagined by political circles in London and in staff evaluations—so much so that the British task force commander felt that his duties would be expanded beyond all expectations. This war would be no walkover; it would be lengthy; and it would be costly in both human and material terms. Admiral Woodward was a rational and thoughtful human being. He fully grasped the fact that this change of events could temper the decisions of the government in London. He was deeply convinced that these islands were not worth the heavy cost of reclaiming them.

He discussed the issue with his commanders, then ordered the task groups to retire to a safe distance from the islands. Naval bombardment would thereafter be preferably at night, since the Argentine Air Force operated under daylight conditions. Sea Harrier attack sorties over Puerto Argentino would be suspended. A lengthy list of messages for headquarters at Northwood would be forthcoming. This whole situation had to be rethought.

If Argentina's high command had been in a position to eavesdrop on these deliberations, they would have become convinced that the battle of May 1 had been a great victory for their own men of arms. But by the same token, it would further stiffen the resolve of the United Kingdom and its linchpin ally, the United States. The very survival of Mrs. Thatcher's Conservative government rode on the outcome of the South Atlantic conflict, for it could not overcome a military fiasco. Therefore, victory had to be complete, whatever the cost. Argentina's leadership should have taken this into account at the inception of the conflict, for they should have been well aware that nothing is more fearsome than a trapped lion and that, once the fleet was under way, Mrs. Thatcher's options were locked in.

6

The Sinking of the Cruiser ARA *General Belgrano*

There are six things the Lord hates, yes, seven are an abomination to him: Haughty eyes, a lying tongue, hands that shed innocent blood; A heart that plots wicked schemes, feet that run swiftly to evil, the false witness who utters lies, and he who sows discord among brothers.

Proverbs 6:16–19

THE BATTLE ON THE SEAS

The first combat skirmishes occurred for the task force as early as the second fortnight of April. As the fleet steamed south of Ascension, the sonar gear on some of the British warships began picking up the telltale pings of what might be Argentine submarines in the area. There were none. What the delicate underwater sensing devices were tracking were whales, or schools of other cetaceans, which read like submarines. How many of these noble mammals lost their lives to British depth charges can only be surmised, but the pursuit of hostilities did nothing to ensure the continued flourishing of their species.

Although Argentina's submarines never saw action, they nevertheless cost the British fleet an inordinate amount of consternation and efforts. As they sailed south from Ascension, the fleet felt compelled to move in special antisubmarine formations and to employ early warning helicopter-borne detection systems, as well as other preemptive strategies that consumed time, effort, and resources, in order to ward off possible Argentine submarine attacks. It would have been unconscionable had NATO's leading antisubmarine force, and the free world's second largest navy, lost a warship to the action of a submersible from a "third-rate country."

British edginess was shared on the Malvinas. One night, an outlying observation post reported what appeared to be a landing of frogmen, moving inland
in single file. The spotters were instructed to order them to halt, and if they kept
coming, to open fire. There ensued a heavy and sustained discharge of gunfire
against the presumed intruders. It was not returned. The following morning, on
reconnoitering, the bullet-riddled forms of several lifeless king penguins were
found.

The Argentine Navy's three task groups lay arrayed outside the exclusion
zone. Since the British would have to enter the zone in order to launch their
attack against the Malvinas garrison, there was little likelihood of any direct
naval engagement between the opposing forces, with the possible exception of
submarines. At that stage, though, neither opponent could ascertain the intent
or the movement of the other. These circumstances notwithstanding, our fleet
was positioned in accordance with its assigned mission: it was to hold positions
aimed at tilting the odds in its favor should the opportunity arise. There was to
be no direct engagement, for such, given the superiority of the British, could
prove deadly. The objective was to await a target of opportunity, to inflict
damage.

It should also be pointed out that, in addition to the opposing fleets, Polish
and Soviet fishing vessels were operating in the vicinity of the exclusion zone.
They went peacefully about their business of tending to their nets along the
continental shelf, but it can be safely assumed they were following the action
with hawk eyes. Three British submarines were operating in the exclusion zone
on May 1: the *Conqueror*, the *Spartan*, and the *Splendid*. Surely the Soviets,
who must have had a sophisticated network of submarines, trawlers, and satellites
tracking the area, were out to glean any information they could get in order to
evaluate British capabilities in action.

Back in Puerto Argentino, several transports were in various stages of unloading at the pier. Conditions were hazardous, as operations were pursued under
continuous bombardment that day, in a state of constant red alert. During the
day, the three Argentine task groups moved about, seeking to station themselves
at positions that had been predetermined as a means of harrying the task force
and possibly compelling it to split up its assets.

Task Group (TG) 79.1 (light carrier *25 de Mayo* and the 2nd Destroyer Arm)
went on station about 270 NM east of San Jorge Gulf; TG–79.4 (Destroyer
Escorts Arm) was assigned to the northeast quadrant of the station (see Map 4),
for they were the lightest of the group; and, to round it out, TG–79.3, with the
General Belgrano, steamed east-southeast of its station area, and at 2200 hours
lay about 260 NM south of Soledad (East Falkland) Island.

While both the position and the layout of the British warships represented an
unknown factor for Vice-Admiral Lombardo, the same was true for Rear Admiral
Woodward's central plan. His number-one priority was to locate and sink the
25 de Mayo; his ace in the hole was the task force's submarine group. Fortunately
for Rear Admiral Allara, his flagship escaped detection at this time. The second

Map 4
Naval Engagements, May 1–4

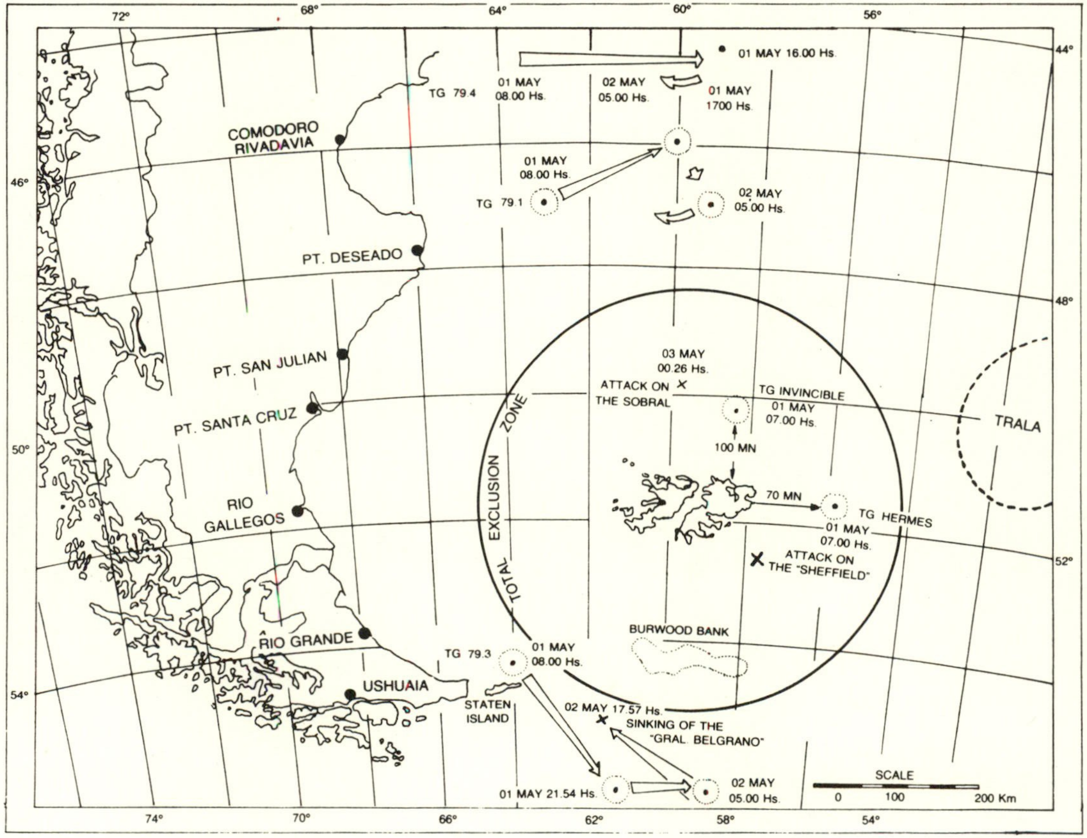
72°
68°
64°
60°
56°
44°
46°
48°
50°
52°
54°
74°
70°
66°
62°
58°
54°
01 MAY 16.00 Hs.
TG 79.4
01 MAY
08.00 Hs.
02 MAY
05.00 Hs.
01 MAY
1700 Hs.
COMODORO
RIVADAVIA
01 MAY
08.00 Hs.
TG 79.1
02 MAY
05.00 Hs.
PT. DESEADO
PT. SAN JULIAN
PT. SANTA CRUZ
RIO
GALLEGOS
RIO GRANDE
USHUAIA
STATEN
ISLAND
TOTAL EXCLUSION ZONE
03 MAY
00.26 Hs.
ATTACK ON
THE SOBRAL
TG INVINCIBLE
01 MAY
07.00 Hs.
100 MN
70 MN
TG HERMES
01 MAY
07.00 Hs.
ATTACK ON
THE "SHEFFIELD"
TRALA
BURWOOD BANK
TG 79.3
01 MAY
08.00 Hs.
02 MAY 17.57 Hs.
SINKING OF THE
"GRAL. BELGRANO"
01 MAY 21.54 Hs.
02 MAY
05.00 Hs.
SCALE
0
100
200 Km

largest vessel in Argentina's naval fleet would not be so fortunate: the cruiser *General Belgrano* had been sighted by the submarine HMS *Conqueror*. This deadly and silent undersea killer stalked the venerable cruiser as it radioed its position and awaited further orders.

During the afternoon, as the air-sea battle raged over the islands, Vice-Admiral Lombardo's staff, headquartered in Puerto Belgrano, was beginning to get a clearer picture of the British plan and the layout of the enemy task groups. Reports trickling into his operations situation room seemed to indicate an imminent British landing on the outskirts of Puerto Argentino, but the signals were unclear and at times appeared contradictory. In the heat of battle, each contender's decisions are influenced and altered by the reaction each action brings. Such was the case of the intended helicopter-borne landing on the north shore of Freycinet Peninsula, which was warded off by the sudden appearance of aircraft from Argentina's Air Force South. It can be surmised that the loss of a number of Sea Harriers during the first wave—brought down by antiaircraft fire over Malvinas air base—as well as the damage sustained by British ships in the wake of the Torno Squadron attack, compelled the British admiral to shelve any notion he may have entertained of checkmating further hostilities that day.

Meanwhile, in the islands, as it became obvious that the enemy had targeted Puerto Argentino for the main thrust of its attack, it was decided to remove the ships lying at anchor in Stanley Bay as a preventive measure, to shield them from attack by the Sea Harriers. This had its drawbacks, for the area surrounding the bay, the town, the port, and the outskirts of Puerto Argentino boasted the best defenses. Removing these vessels might put them at greater risk, for the alternative sites had no defenses other than the natural cover provided by steep-sided coves and inlets, which alone would not foil keen British observers, who were being aided and abetted by the local population.

The ships anchored at the Malvinas naval mooring were the ARA *Bahia Buen Suceso*, the ARA *Isla de los Estados*, the ELMA *Formosa*, the ELMA *Rio Carcarana*, and the requisitioned *Forrest* and *Monsunen*, which were intended for interisland transport, as well as the *Isla de los Estados*. The tugboat BRIDAS *Yehuin*, out of Ushuaia, put in that day to assist in docking operations.

The *Bahia Buen Suceso*, having brought in a large shipment of vital supplies for the islands' defenders, was tied up at the naval station and being used as makeshift quarters. It was removed to Port Fox, where, having been attacked and damaged by enemy aircraft, it was abandoned by its crew.

The *Formosa* completed unloading on May 1 and sailed that afternoon at 1500 hours to undertake the hazardous return passage to the mainland. The transport had to thread its way through enemy-infested waters along the southern route from the islands. It barely missed being overtaken by the British fleet rounding the south coast of Freycinet Bay to initiate the naval bombardment of the airstrip, but as it was making full steam south of Fitz Roy Bay, it was pinpointed by *Trueno 1*, the squadron leader of one of our own A4-B groups, who, unaware that one of our ships could be steaming in those waters, strafed it with 20mm cannon fire, inflicting light damage. It also released a bomb that landed in the hold without detonating. In the heat of battle, there had been no time for coordination. The *Formosa* was the only Argentine vessel to make it back to mainland.

The *Isla de los Estados* also played a vital role in the island campaign. It made possible the distribution of material that was overflowing the limited dock facilities at Puerto Argentino by shuttling back and forth between there, Fox Bay, Port Howard, and Darwin. It sailed mostly within the confines of San Carlos Straits, on whose bottom it found its last resting place a few days later.

The *Rio Carcarana* had run the British gauntlet on April 26 with a shipment mainly of rations for the troops. Before complete unloading of its cargo, which included aluminum matting for widening the airstrip, it was removed to a protected cove to spare it the British bombardment during May 1 at Puerto Argentino. It was its last run.

These few ships were all that were available to General Menendez to meet his forces' needs for naval transport. By this time, the military junta had decided against risking further surface transport, which made his garrison's survival all the more precarious, for its needs overwhelmed the airlift's capacity for shipping vital supplies, and there were pitifully few helicopters in the islands to deliver them where needed.

Task Force 79: Orders To Attack

By midafternoon, all reports indicated that the situation forecast in the high seas fleet's plan of operations was about to materialize. This led to the commander of SATO to grant TF–79 full freedom to carry out its mission. About that time, a message was received confirming the presence, north of Puerto Argentino, of a British task group, thereby tipping TF–79 off to the presence of the carrier *Invincible* and its escort, even before the British were able to locate the carrier *25 de Mayo* and her task group. For Rear Admiral Allara, the moment that every commander is trained for was at hand: giving the orders committing his men to battle. The time was 1600 hours.

Given the distance separating his own task force from the prospective enemy naval targets, Allara maneuvered his flagship, the *25 de Mayo*, closer to the edge of the exclusion zone, in order to position his carrier-borne A4-Qs for the attack. His aircraft were severely handicapped by the load factors imposed by the distance to the target area and prevailing winds (over 250 NM separated the two task forces, and the wind rarely exceeded five knots).

For an A4-Q to operate with a full combat load, the wind factor had to be above 20 knots. In a light wind, only the carrier itself could provide the speed boost necessary to make up the shortfall. This in turn made the mission unfeasible or unacceptable, in light of the distance the A4-Qs had to travel to reach their targets. To make a bad situation worse, the area was at the center of a high-pressure zone, which rendered the wind factor almost nil, to the further detriment of the aircraft's load and range. By 1730 hours, the attack had become unfeasible. The aircraft were not equipped for night operations, and it was almost sundown; the whole mission had to be scrubbed. Admiral Allara issued the order to postpone until dawn the next day.

In the meantime, the submarine ARA *San Luis*, lurking inside the exclusion zone in the murky waters north of the islands, made contact with enemy vessels. The *San Luis* fired its torpedoes, which, to the frustration of both skipper and hard-working crew, zoomed past their mark. (Recent unconfirmed reports from British sources have it that a torpedo did in fact pierce the hull of the *Exeter* without detonating, which would explain its leaving the theater of operations during May for repairs.) Due to the haste with which the military junta had ordered the occupation of the islands, the submarine had not had time to debug its weapons systems. British antisubmarine teams immediately turned about and swung into action against the bold intruder, and for the next 24 hours or more, the submarine and its crew lived through an ordeal similar to those experienced by their World War II counterparts. But to the great annoyance of the British task force, the Argentine submarine was able to wriggle its way through the dragnet and shake itself free from its pursuers undamaged, thereby writing a noteworthy chapter in our navy's campaign at sea. Given the formidable dimensions of our opponent, this was a crucial lesson both for Britain and for NATO. If an Argentine submarine had managed to penetrate the fearsome defenses of the powerful Royal Navy, had managed to fire off its "fish," and, to top it off, had succeeded in giving its pursuers the slip, undamaged, the Lord only knows what the outcome might be in an engagement between NATO and Warsaw Pact forces, since the awesome submarine arsenal of the Soviet Union is acknowledged.

Task Force 79: Order to Withdraw

The notion prevailed among the Argentine naval high command, in spite of U.S. efforts to convince them otherwise, that the enemy had available to it U.S. satellite data pinpointing Argentine ships' positions. If this were true, and an effective enemy psychological campaign would lead our high command to take the possibility seriously, then the surface units of our high seas fleet were useless, for they would be sitting ducks for the faster British nuclear submarines.

At 1937 hours, Malvinas reported the approach from a 155° heading (SSE) of three vessels, which came within 14.5 NM at 1943 hours. By 2039 hours, General Menendez's staff had evaluated the enemy's intent as being a helicopter-borne landing southeast of the airstrip, with the objective of securing it. At 2055 hours, in the midst of heavy naval gunfire, helicopters lifted off the ships at distances from 5 to 12 miles. But, at 2350 hours, the ships backed away and the landing was scrubbed. Darkness fell over the islands, and the defenders breathed easy for the first time that day. Shortly after midnight on May 1, the commander of SATO completed his evaluation, and since it appeared that Admiral Woodward would not attempt a landing, he ordered the commander of TF–79 to set aside any plan to attack, since his ships would be in serious danger if the enemy were not lying at anchor.

Confirmation was received about 0500 hours on May 2 that British reconnaissance aircraft attached to the *Invincible*'s task group had pinpointed TF–79.1 and were beginning to stalk its every move. This intelligence would prove vital to Admiral Woodward, for although the submarine HMS *Conqueror* had already established the position of TF–79.3, along with the *General Belgrano*, this would not suffice to give a broad picture of the situation and reveal the probable intent of the commander of SATO. It should be noted that Admiral Woodward's staff had rated Argentina's capability of launching a massive, all-out attack, using its air and naval assets to the fullest, as an extreme threat. Therefore, the reported position of the *25 de Mayo*, which could seemingly launch its aircraft in a deadly blow against the task force while it was in the midst of a landing operation, was cause for deep concern.

Although Vice-Admiral Lombardo was unaware whether the *General Belgrano*'s task group was being tracked by the *Conqueror*, it was obvious that the enemy fleet was not lying in close formation and that the task group headed by the *25 de Mayo* had been spotted. Sensing imminent danger for his own vessels, he issued the order for them to withdraw to shallow waters at about 0500 hours. The carrier put into its slip at Puerto Belgrano, where it lay moored for the remainder of the hostilities.

The *General Belgrano*'s Last Mission

The venerable Brooklyn Class cruiser *General Belgrano* had been commissioned into the U.S. Navy in 1939 as the USS *Phoenix*. It was among the surviving vessels following the Japanese attack on Pearl Harbor on December 7, 1941. Shortly thereafter, as a unit in the fleet commanded by Admiral Oldendorff, it took part in the battle of Leyte Gulf against the Japanese Navy in the Straits of Surigao. In 1943 it transported U.S. Secretary of State Cordell Hull to the Casablanca Conference. It was sold to the Argentine Navy in 1951. It was the last ship of its class still in active commission, which made its loss all the sadder.

On April 30, Task Group 79.3, comprised of the cruiser and the destroyers ARA *Bouchard* and *Piedrabuena*, was lying north of Staten Island, awaiting orders for deployment to the operations zone. Upon receiving its orders, it steamed on an east-southeast heading. TF–79's sailing orders specified its mission as "to wear down, neutralize, or destroy enemy units, if a favorable opportunity presented itself." The operational concept enjoined the force from entering the exclusion zone and from firing its weapons without prior clearance.

The task groups steaming from the north were to present a collateral threat that would compel the enemy to split up its forces. Following this game plan, TF–79.3's mission was to maintain surveillance over the southern approach to the theater of operations, including possible interception or neutralization of enemy units. This was to be interpreted as attacks against logistics vessels or isolated, damaged units, without in any way committing the task group to taking part in an action against the enemy task group. It should follow logically that Argentina's high naval command, fully aware of Britain's superiority in submarines, could reasonably be expected to refrain from sending its high seas fleet into a futile frontal attack against the task force, which would result in a predictable holocaust.

At 1254 hours, the *General Belgrano* was steaming on an easterly heading at 56°30'S/61°15'W, leaving behind it the safety of the inlets around Staten Island, with the shallows of the Burwood Bank (a broad expanse of shallow waters covering a rise in the seafloor south of the main islands) to port. The British submarine HMS *Conqueror* was patrolling the waters west of the islands; it was relieved by another submersible, the *Splendid*, and was assigned a quadrant further south. This is where it picked up the *General Belgrano* and the two destroyers. According to the *Conqueror*'s log, made public at a later date, this occurred on April 30. For the remainder of that day, and during the early hours of the next, the *General Belgrano*, escorted by the destroyers *Piedrabuena* and *Bouchard*, entered deep waters, which increased its risk of exposure to enemy submarine action, even though it remained at a safe distance from the exclusion zone.

Foreign analysts have pointed out that the *General Belgrano*, armed with a formidable arsenal of artillery superior to that carried by any unit in the British task force, would have been an exceedingly difficult threat to neutralize had it been anchored in Stanley Bay, since at that location—aside from being sheltered from submarine attack—the enemy would have been able to proceed to the attack only at considerable, if not unacceptable, risk, in view of the proximity of the town and the antiaircraft batteries. Even if it had been grounded, it could have been employed as an effective gunnery emplacement, because of the shallow depths at the site. The Argentine fleet staff did not share the view.

At 0630 hours on May 2, at the time Task Group 79.3 received its orders to return to its previously assigned area, it lay 280 NM south of Darwin, several hours from any potential combat zone that could have constituted a real threat to the ships of the British task force. This was not lost on enemy intelligence, which admits that it was transmitted enciphered, with key words, and was immediately interpreted by both British task groups, which swung around on a heading toward the mainland. The order to return was also picked up by U.S. Navy intelligence sources.

Meanwhile, the *Conqueror* trailed at a safe distance and closely tracked the headway being made by the Argentine vessels, waiting for them to sail over the line into the exclusion zone. The *General Belgrano* and the destroyers set a course of approximately 280° heading, making for the shallowest waters in their immediate area that did not lie within the exclusion zone. The jittery crew began to rest easy as they steamed away from the war zone. They had reached safer waters, or so they thought. None aboard harbored so much as an inkling that the British would break the rules of engagement they themselves had so diligently laid out, that they would renege on the very essence of those great virtues of chivalry and fair play for which they had always been held in high esteem. Those Argentine sailors were unaware that there were reasons for sinking their ship that went far beyond the tactical exigencies of the moment.

The *Conqueror*, which kept open its communication line to its headquarters at Northwood, England, kept close tabs on the Argentine convoy as it steamed slowly away from the operations area, making a speed of 14 knots. At 1557 on the fateful afternoon, as it became obvious that Task Group 79.3 would not be crossing into the exclusion zone, and was making obvious headway on an opposite course, Commander Wreford Brown, skipper of the *Conqueror*, contacted Northwood to give them this update and request further instructions. The decision came straight from the war room, presided over by Mrs. Thatcher: Shoot to sink! Commander Wreford Brown was aghast. His disbelief was such that he had the order repeated three times, until there could be no mistaking the will of his superiors. The *General Belgrano* was not just to be damaged; it was not just to be put out of action; it was to be *sunk*. As the cruiser steamed at 55°24′S/ 61°32′W, The skipper turned about and positioned his ship at a range of 1,400 yards opposite the escorts and fired a salvo of two MK–8 torpedoes. The ''fish'' zoomed true to their mark and smashed into the port side of the venerable old cruiser, which shuddered under the deadly impacts and began to settle into the sea. Thus was consummated the most merciless, and apparently most unconscionable, act of the war.

THE BRITISH ISSUE CONFLICTING ACCOUNTS

The rationale for the sinking of the *General Belgrano*, at a time and place of the British government's choosing, has yet to be satisfactorily clarified. This state of affairs may persist for many years, since Great Britain has placed the matter of the South Atlantic conflict under wraps as a ''military secret.'' For the record, and in order to shed some light on the truth, a truth that is not now, nor ever shall be, a source of humiliation for Argentina, the author has deemed it both proper and necessary to bring into focus some contradictions into which the British government has fallen with regard to this event. The British authorities, in their attempts to rationalize the motives behind the sinking, have offered a series of conflicting accounts, some of which are as flawed as they are divorced from reality. These inaccuracies are alarming in the face of an act of such grave consequences, an act that took the lives of 323 men while endangering those of another 674 crew members who had the good fortune to rescued. The main contradictions recorded as of this writing are presented below.

Conflicting Account Number 1

What were Britain's political and military objectives in regard to the Falkland Islands?

The dispatching of the task force appears to have been a military response aimed at compelling Buenos Aires to accept the terms of Resolution 502. Adm. Sir John Fieldhouse stated as much to the London press at the time, describing the objective as being to "achieve Argentine withdrawal in accordance with Resolution 502." Furthermore, the British government, perhaps bowing to international pressure and the British Labour Party, outlined its military policy as being a minimum use of force under strict political control, in order to achieve the diplomatic goal sought.

This affirmation is in keeping with two events that appear to bear it out. The first occurred at the time Admiral Woodward requested instructions on how to handle Argentine reconnaissance aircraft as they repeatedly sighted the task force while it sailed its southerly course. Should they be shot down? The war room had responded that since they were unarmed aircraft flying outside the exclusion zone, they should be left alone. The second occurred when a British submarine spotted an Argentine vessel laying mines in the approaches to Puerto Argentino. Should it be torpedoed? The answer was again negative, based on the fact that at the time, no hostilities had begun, and that unnecessary casualties should be avoided.

During the action on May 2, Argentina's armed forces had gone to great lengths to ensure that the enemy sustained no casualties. Their action on May 1 had also been defensive in nature, for they fired only when fired upon; first during aerial bombardment, then during naval bombardment. According to British sources, a single casualty was sustained on May 1, a minor chest wound (Seaman Ian Britell, of Teighnmouth, Devon, crew member of the *Arrow*, during the Torno Squadron's action).

How do these facts and events tie in with the decision to sink the *General Belgrano?*

Conflicting Account Number 2

It has been well established that the Argentine vessel was attacked 39 NM from the maritime exclusion zone established by Great Britain, as it was steaming toward the sheltered waters of the Argentine continental shelf. The British government had proclaimed the maritime exclusion zone on April 9, effective April 12 at 0700 hours, with the purpose of establishing an effective naval blockade around the islands and enabling their means of offense to have the necessary leeway to use their weapons whenever deemed appropriate for accomplishing their mission. This action also served warning on ships of all flags that this was a war zone, in order to avoid liability in case the ships of other nations came in harm's way within that zone.

The 200 NM radius established for the exclusion amply covered the area deemed necessary for reclaiming the islands by military means. No military operations had been foreseen outside this perimeter—and none occurred—as the location of the task force task groups demonstrated. It follows, then, that the rationale for such a decision was not dictated by the military situation. Something must have occurred between April 30 and May 2 that compelled the British political powers that were to take a step that was condemned around the world and that took a heavy political toll.

Here it should be underscored that the official British report of the attack stated that "the action took place at the very limit of the TEZ, just outside of it." This is patently false. Furthermore, the exclusion zone proclamation specified in no uncertain terms that "any vessel or aircraft . . . found within the zone . . . would be deemed hostile and subject to attack" Shortly after the sinking, on May 7, Great Britain broadened the war zone to include everything up to 12 NM off the coast of Argentina. In other words, in order to ensure it would not again be caught off-bounds, it extended the playing field right up to our territorial waters.

This serves to underscore the fact that the motives behind the sinking of the Argentine cruiser lie deeply concealed somewhere within the 30-hour time frame immediately preceding the sinking—during which the *General Belgrano* was spotted by the *Conqueror*—and also the ensuing few hours in which the negotiations undertaken at the initiative of the president of Peru were hanging in the balance. Something must have occurred during that period that was of sufficient magnitude to warrant risking the political and diplomatic support of the United States, the EEC, and the U.N. Security Council.

Neither the British government nor Parliament has thus far presented—either to the world or to their own people—a plausible explanation for their overwhelming urge to commit such an act.

Conflicting Account Number 3

"The *General Belgrano* was sunk because it posed a threat to the task force" (statements made by both the defense secretary and the chief of the Defense Staff to the British Parliament). Proud as our seamen may have been upon learning of the alleged rationale for the sinking of one of their warships, a pride that would have been more than justified had the circumstances warranted it, the fact remains that the doomed cruiser met its fate at the hands of its stalker at a distance of over 350 NM from the task group closest to the British task force, and like the vessels in TG–79.1 and 79.4 and its escorts, the *Piedrabuena* and the *Bouchard*, had received orders to reverse course several hours earlier. The heading of every unit in Argentine Task Force 79 could have left no doubt whatsoever as to their intended destinations. This was noted by the British intelligence services and by the captain of the Conqueror, as well as the spotter planes flying reconnaissance off the *Invincible*, which had picked up TG–79.1.

The "risk factor" the British appeared eager to avoid, given the position of the Argentine warship at the time of its sinking, was that it might approach neither the exclusion zone nor any task force vessel, therefore fast obviating any justifiable excuse for sinking it in a more favorable position. Let the record then speak for itself: At 1556 hours, TG–79.4 was making 14 knots on a 280° heading, straight for the sheltered waters of Staten Island, skirting the southwest demarcation line of the exclusion zone at a distance of 39 NM, in compliance with orders from above. Not a single British surface vessel was to be found anywhere west of the Malvinas Islands, and the units attached to the *Hermes* task group were lying 350 NM from the cruiser's position, and 120 NM east of Stanley. By no stretch of the imagination could the *General Belgrano* have posed any sort of a threat to the British task force.

Conflicting Account Number 4

"Concerned with the possibility of losing contact with the *General Belgrano* were she to seek refuge in the shallows of the Burwood Bank, the commander of the task force requested and was granted a variance in the rules of engagement enabling him to torpedo her outside the exclusion zone" (Admiral Woodward to MPs).

As has already been pointed out, TG–79.3 had never intended to head for the shallows, not only because that area lies entirely within the exclusion zone, but also because this was not in accordance with orders. On the contrary, the *General Belgrano* was sailing over 50 miles west of the shallows and steaming on a westerly heading at the time of its sinking.

It is all the more surprising that Admiral Woodward would have uttered such a statement, for it is flawed in naval tactical terms and also is out of line. Not only was the British submarine force not in his chain of command, but it answered directly to headquarters in Northwood, which issued its orders.

Furthermore, the shallows of the Burwood Bank could in no way have served as a haven for TG–79.3 since they lay within relatively easy range of British air attackers, but beyond the range of the cruiser's antiaircraft defenses and those of the Argentine destroyers. Also, they would have come close to one of the task force's task groups, comprised of a carrier and numerous escorts, with greatly superior firepower. As for the shallows, if the elevation of the seafloor on the bank was somewhat of a hindrance to the maneuverability of British nuclear submarines, such was not true of conventional subs; thus this could in no way cancel out the danger posed by nuclear or conventional undersea platforms. (The *Conqueror* draws 55 feet of water fully submerged, its radar is equipped for shallow-water operations, and the average depth of the Burwood Bank area as a whole is around 500 feet.)

Conflicting Account Number 5

Statement of Defense Secretary John Nott before the House of Commons

This powerfully armed surface group [the cruiser and the two destroyers] were near the total exclusion zone and were closing in on our task force, which lay some hours away. We knew the cruiser had substantial firepower, that it mounted 18-inch guns with a 13-mile range as well as Sea Cat antiaircraft missiles. Along with the destroyer escorts, which we believe to have been equipped with Exocet antiship missiles, with a range of better than 20 miles, the threat to the task force was such that the commander thereof could have only ignored them at great risk.

The term "powerfully," as used by the secretary, can be but a euphemism unworthy of further discussion if one compares the power of the two task forces that could, in theory, have faced off. The cruiser *General Belgrano* and the destroyers *Bouchard* and *Piedrabuena* were vessels that were reaching the outer limits of their useful service lives, and the longest-range weapons available to them were Exocet surface-to-surface M–38 missiles (25 miles) mounted on the destroyers, which were not attacked. At a distance of 350 NM from the task group closest to the task force, and lacking local air or submarine superiority, they would have been hard put indeed to attempt any approach to the carrier *Hermes* and its numerous modern escort vessels, also equipped with Exocet missiles, not to mention other state-of-the-art weaponry.

Let the record again show that the *General Belgrano* and its escorts were not heading in the direction of any task force vessels. Quite to the contrary, they were steaming away from them and had left the demarcation line of the exclusion zone safely behind them. When it became obvious to the *Conqueror* that the *General Belgrano* did not intend to cross into the exclusion zone, it passed this information on to headquarters, which in turn issued the fateful order: "Shoot to sink!"

Conflicting Account Number 6

"The *General Belgrano* was preparing to execute a pincer movement against the fleet along with the carrier *25 de Mayo*" (statement by Sir Terence Lewin, chief, defense staff).

The intentions of the Argentine high seas fleet had been clearly established in its plan of operations. At no time had there been any plan to enter the exclusion zone, since its mission was to maintain surveillance on the southerly approaches to the theater of operations, to serve as a deterrent within the regional framework, and, if the opportunity presented itself, to neutralize any isolated enemy units. This could clearly be seen due by its distance from the exclusion zone, for its course should have been the key to its mission.

Had the cruiser been sent to the bottom during the battle of May 1, it could, in fact, have been deemed a threat to the task force, for in that time frame Argentina's intentions were a question mark. The presence of TG–79.3 south of the operations zone was in keeping with the idea of compelling the task force to split up in the face of a potential attack from the north by the task group headed by the carrier *25 de Mayo*, had the enemy been found at anchor. Such an attack did not take place, and the three task groups received orders to withdraw to the shallow waters off the mainland. But, as of 0500 hours on May 2, at the time TF–79 was ordered to turn about, there is no way that, by any stretch of the imagination, the *General Belgrano* could have been construed to pose a threat to any British vessel, much less to have been involved in a pincer operation.

The real motive for the sinking must lie deep in some mysterious event that either occurred or was to occur within a 30-hour time frame just prior to, or just after, the action. It is to be surmised that had such an event been made public, it might have caused Great Britain—or, more precisely, its Conservative government—damage of inestimable proportions.

Conflicting Account Number 7

"On May 2, the *Conqueror* located the *General Belgrano*" (Admiral Sir John Fieldhouse, commander in chief of the fleet, and Sir John Nott, British defense secretary).

In spite of the high office held by both individuals cited above, it was the British themselves who disclosed the true date on which the *Conqueror* first located and starting tracking the Argentine cruiser. Commander Wreford Brown's own words, which were widely reported throughout the British Isles, were as follows: "The cruiser was being escorted by two destroyers. We made visual contact with her at noon on May first. We tracked her over 30 hours. We passed on the word that we had made this contact. We trailed several miles behind her. We had orders to attack only in the event she were to enter the exclusion zone." He added that he received the order from his command at Northwood changing the rules of engagement and ordering the sinking on May 2.

These statements have been corroborated both by the media and by the *Conqueror*. Therefore there can remain no doubt as to the date and time at which the cruiser was sighted. In spite of all this, the decision to sink was made that same morning, prior to noon. The orders specified that the engagement was to be initiated at such time as TG–79.3 entered the exclusion zone or began moving away from it. This happened a few hours later, at 1557 hours Buenos Aires time (1857 hours GMT).

All these events would seem to indicate that the potential success of the negotiations had little—or no—influence on the British War Cabinet's decision. Several hours had elapsed, in which a change of orders could have been issued, between the time the order was given and the time it was carried out by the *Conqueror*—if one wishes to suppose that the prospects for achieving a peaceful solution were still being held out. The only other possible objective was the purposeful torpedoing of the efforts to seek peace.

Was the sinking of a ship with 1,093 souls aboard necessary to achieve this latter aim?

The British government has yet to throw light on the quibbling of its representatives when their utterances were falsehoods—rather than errors—since they were already aware of the truth. In consonance with logical reasoning, it appears that there has been an attempt to veil the fact that the *Belgrano* was pinpointed at least 30 hours prior to its demise, although statements would lead one to believe that the sinking order was given almost at the same time the *Belgrano* was located. The purpose is to circumvent a question to which there was no answer: Why was it not sunk sooner?

Conflicting Account Number 8

Once the sinking of the *General Belgrano* became public knowledge in Britain, on May 4 and 5, 1982, Parliament, the media, and the British public were convinced that the action had taken place in accordance with rules of engagement previously laid down. The defense secretary emphasized that "decision to fire off the torpedoes was clearly the submarine commander's decision."

Even without prior knowledge of Commander Brown's later statements, such an affirmation had a hollow ring, since hostile action of this scope could have been undertaken by the ship's commander without precise orders to that effect only under the direst of circumstances, for he would otherwise be setting himself up for a swift appearance before a court-martial. The professionalism, training, and knowledge of those who command nuclear submarines is certainly not left to chance by the nations that operate them, for were that to be so, the whole planet could quickly be engulfed in a worldwide conflagration.

On July 5, Cmdr Christopher Wreford Brown flew the Jolly Roger pirate emblem from his mast as he sailed his nuclear submarine into his home port at Faslane, Scotland. This was indeed a sad postscript to an event that was played out with the cards stacked in his favor against a much weaker foe, an action that doomed the hapless crew members of the *General Belgrano* to a watery grave, in an undeclared war, in an area that his own government had supposedly agreed was off limits to hostile action, and through which the Argentine naval units were steaming, lulled into a false sense of security. Once the ship's company was again on terra firma, the media bored in relentlessly to ascertain who had issued the order to torpedo the *General Belgrano*. Commander Brown gave a clear and straightforward answer that was the truth. Eric MacKenzie of the daily *The Scotsman* wrote, following his interview: "The decision to attack was made by the General Staff of the Navy and communicated to the commander of the submarine."

But surely not even the commander in Chief of the Royal Navy could shoulder the responsibility single-handedly. The decision came straight from the war room with Mrs. Thatcher at the helm. The October 5, 1982, edition of the Canadian daily *The Guardian* published the following statement under the byline of its war correspondent, David Fairhall: "The decision for the *Conqueror* to sink the *Belgrano* was made by the Prime Minister and her limited war council, with her most trusted advisors, who were at lunch at Chequers on May 2nd. "On that fateful morning, as on many other occasions when momentous decisions were made, the reduced War Council, headed by Mrs. Thatcher and attended by Defense Secretary John Nott and Cecil Parkinson, Conservative Party head, was meeting at Chequers—an official residence used by the prime minister on weekends—when Admiral Fieldhouse came into the room with the latest bulletins received through his general headquarters at Northwood. By this time, the *General Belgrano* had received its orders to change course, and the information that the naval commander had to share so precipitously with the prime minister and her entourage was that the Argentine ships had turned about and were steering a course toward the mainland.

About that same time, Secretary Haig had discussed the latest peace initiative proposed by Peru over lunch with his colleague Sir Francis Pym in Washington. The latter contacted Mrs. Thatcher to bring her up to date on the good progress these talks were making; but the prime minister had a different set of priorities that day, and the possibility of achieving peace and sparing hundreds of victims did not fit into her plans.

The return of the *Conqueror* to its base at the conclusion of hostilities, and the statements given by the crew members, satiated, at least for the time being, the appetite of the media; but by then—it was July 5—the *General Belgrano* had been lying on the bottom, a war memorial to her entombed crew, for 64 days. The euphoria of the victory had numbed the British public to any thought of who might have been the architect of that criminal order, for Mrs. Thatcher's government was enjoying an all-time level of popularity. She felt under no obligation to offer explanations, and when they were requested, the curtain of "military secrecy" was promptly rolled down.

CONCLUSIONS AS TO THE RATIONALE BEHIND THE SINKING OF THE *GENERAL BELGRANO*

In accordance with the evidence set forth in this chapter, the following proven facts with regard to this event may be established:

1. Great Britain's original military policy called for retaking the islands with the least possible use of force, under strict political control.

2. At the time of the sinking, the Argentine armed forces had purposely restricted themselves to not inflicting casualties on the enemy and to playing a defensive role against British attacks on May 1.

3. The original exclusion zone was freely established by Great Britain. It covered an area deemed ample enough to carry out military operations. The *Belgrano* was sunk 39 NM outside the zone while steaming away from the battle area.

4. TG–79.3 posed no threat whatsoever to the British task force when it was fired upon, since it was steaming, along with the remainder of the fleet, toward territorial waters and was 350 NM from the closest British task group.

5. Argentina's plans did not call for the execution of a pincer movement. The plan had been to launch carrier-based aircraft on an offensive that had to be scrubbed.

6. The submarine *Conqueror* had located TG–79.3 on April 30, at 1630 hours Buenos Aires time, according to recent reports.

7. The decision to sink the cruiser was made by the reduced War Council, presided over by the prime minister, prior to 1200 hours London time.

8. The decision of Argentina's naval high command to withdraw the fleet to shallow waters was made at 0500 hours Buenos Aires time (0800 hours GMT) on May 2, prior to the sinking of the cruiser.

9. At the time of the decision, and during the ensuing hours prior to the sinking, peace talks were under way that raised hopes for a cessation of hostilities.

10. British authorities have repeatedly resorted to falsehoods in their attempts to convince both Parliament and the public that the *Belgrano* was sent to the bottom under circumstances that were at odds with the facts.

11. British intelligence had intercepted the Argentine fleet's radio traffic and thus was aware that the vessels were sailing toward the mainland.

12. This decision cost Great Britain a high political price, for the whole world recoiled in horror at the news.

13. The British government has put the whole South Atlantic conflict episode under tight wraps, classifying the event as a "military secret."

Following logical reasoning, the following conclusions may be drawn:

1. The *General Belgrano* was not torpedoed for military reasons.

2. The immediate consequence of the cruiser's sinking was the breakdown of talks that had been going on through the good offices of the president of Peru.

3. The military response to this act was that Argentine aircraft went on an offensive in which any British vessel was fair game. This only served to escalate the conflict to unforeseen heights, not provided for in the plans of either side, and had the net result of inflicting heavy casualties on both sides.

4. Mrs. Thatcher's government apparently was prepared to accept the high political risk inherent in such an action. It can be safely assumed that the cost must have been less than it would have been had the cruiser not been sunk. The reasons behind this are unknown and are zealously cloaked in secrecy by the British government.

THE PRESIDENT OF PERU TAKES THE INITIATIVE

The British offensive against the defenders on the Malvinas Islands, as well as the position assumed by the United States, had profound worldwide repercussions, but they hit an especially raw nerve in Latin America. In Argentina, the media as a whole presented lengthy accounts of the previous day's events, with bold headlines. President Galtieri had addressed the nation shortly before midnight. His strongly worded message stated:

... no other way was left open to us to recover our inalienable sovereignty than to act as we did, and we have put the world on notice. The vast majority of the American peoples have sent us a clear and open message. They are our brothers, they are with us. Such was the position of those who have always believed, freely and without reservations, that our hemisphere has its plan and its destiny, and that our colonial past was dead and buried and had returned to the dust and consigned to the back seat of history . . . .

These words whipped popular support to a frenzy, and as the effect snowballed, it was quite impossible to expect any measure of cool-headedness to prevail among either the governed or those who govern.

At the United Nations, Argentine ambassador Eduardo Roca presented his case before the Security Council. He charged Great Britain with "ignoring the will of the United Nations to guide the parties to the dispute toward a peaceful solution of the issue, and violating Resolution 502." In turn, the British Defense Ministry stated publicly that "it had been necessary to initiate such action in the face of Argentina's refusal to implement paragraph 2 of Resolution 502, approved following her invasion of British territory. This action was carried out in the exercise of the United Kingdom's immanent right to self-defense, acknowledged by Article 51 of the the U.N. Charter."

The U.S. media gave these events very broad coverage, but their objectivity fell far short of what should have been expected from the opinion-forming organs of the greatest of Western democracies. Secretary of Defense Caspar Weinberger's tactless harshness in his response to questions about the extent of assistance to be provided to Great Britain—"any type of logistical or military assistance that may be required"—was surprising. His country, after all, had offered to play the role of peacemaker, had unilaterally declared the failure of its initiative, and then had gone against the decision of IATRA, of which the United States is a signatory. This, in turn, deeply compromised the future credibility in Latin America of such a "peacemaker."

RELATIONS BETWEEN BUENOS AIRES AND WASHINGTON

Secretary Haig's actions and the position assumed by the State Department gave rise to a reaction within Argentina'a military government that may well have represented the all-time low point in the history of bilateral relations between our two countries. The text of the protest note addressed by Dr. Nicanor Costa Mendez to Secretary of State Alexander Haig on May 2, 1982, excerpts of which follow, illustrate this state of affairs all too well:

Mr. Secretary of State:

Until a few short hours ago, the U.S. had acted as a friend to both parties, helping them to seek a negotiated, fair and honorable settlement. Now, having alleged the breakdown of its initiatives, the U.S. has . . . openly sided with one of the parties and is imposing sanctions unacceptable to us with the obvious intent of breaking down our resolve, of forcing upon us solutions which are more in keeping with the very special aims the United States Government entertains in regard to this issue.

The Secretary of State has laid the blame for the failure of the talks at Argentina's doorstep, underscoring our unwillingness to compromise. As for British stubbornness and their aggressive posture, not a word is said. The Secretary appears indifferent to the fact that the United Kingdom is marshaling, at the very moment of his own statement, its naval and air forces in final preparation for an attack on my country; quite to the contrary, the Secretary of State appears to feel that it is fair to contribute to such an aggression by providing British forces with whatever material assistance they may require. This, indeed, constitutes a strange way of cooperating to head off the escalation of the conflict.

Argentina did not reject proposals put forth by the Government of the United States. The Secretary of State acknowledged himself during an interview we held that no demand was being made that we accept them in their entirety, and that we were free to make our comments.

This U.S. stance comes at a time when the Foreign Ministers of the Americas, met together within the framework of the Inter-American Treaty for Reciprocal Assistance, are backing Argentina's statements and calling for a cessation of hostilities. It is therefore surprising that the Secretary of State should make reference to Hemispheric solidarity as one of the basic considerations guiding his conduct, when in the face of the facts his position is one of manifested disregard.

The people of Argentina will neither understand nor soon forget that at one of the most critical junctures of their history, in stark contrast to the expressions of solidarity pouring in from the corners of the Hemisphere, the United States have preferred to cast their lot with an extra-continental power and be a party to its aggressive designs.

In London, the media gave evidence of the worldwide repercussions brought about by the British offensive. The tremendous psychological pressure exerted by Mrs. Thatcher's government was manifest at every turn throughout the conflict. The broadest coverage was given to the "destruction" of the airstrip at Stanley, the U.S. support enjoyed by the British in this conflict—on which Mrs. Thatcher capitalized heavily from a political standpoint, for there would be no replay of the Suez crisis this time—and the fact that British forces had sustained no losses!

In Parliament, meanwhile, all was not praise and glory. The attack split the Labourites into two factions: those who supported and agreed with the prime minister's policy, and those who espoused the opposite viewpoint. Judith Hart, head of the Social Democratic Party, voiced her condemnation of the attack as a clear violation of Resolution 502, while M. P. Tony Benn added that the Cabinet was censoring the press, the BBC, and the ITN in order to keep the British people in the dark as to which policy was being followed—a statement that, among the many aired that day, was the one right on target.

In turn, Dennis Healey, Labour Party spokesman for the Foreign Office, warned that although he supported the government's decision, the crisis could not be resolved by military means alone—which would not prove to be true. But the war propaganda machine set in motion by the Conservative government would soon see to that, for all news coming in from the South Atlantic became subject to an iron-fisted central clearinghouse that would make the British correspondents into mere spectators stripped of their skill to reflect upon the realities of warfare and share their views through their releases. They were powerless to compete with the "newsworthiness" of official British Defense Ministry communiqués.

The U.S. decision to support the United Kingdom was equally editorialized by the British press, which stated:

Reagan's decision, which is a first in the history of the U.S., to support Europe against America, gives rise to both hopes and pitfalls. Reagan has jeopardized the essence of the Monroe Doctrine and, in so doing, the very foundation of U.S. leadership in the Hemisphere. Friday [April 30, when the United States cast its lot with the British] was as much a field day for Cuba as it was for Great Britain. The Soviet Union had been just waiting for this convergence of traditional nationalistic outrage and anti-U.S. sentiment. (*The Observer* [London], May 2, 1982).

A Washington correspondent reported that, U.S. sanctions against Argentina notwithstanding, "Great Britain could expect just about any type of military assistance it might ask for. A State Department official had stated that British requests had thus far been moderate, but that President Reagan's inclination was to look favorably upon all British requests, unless they fundamentally jeopardized our long term relationship." (*The Observer* [London], May 2, 1982).

In Washington, the meeting between Alexander Haig and British Foreign Secretary Francis Pym received the widest of publicity. This meeting dealt with U.S. military assistance to Great Britain. This in turn dovetailed with the announcement that U.S. Secretary of the Navy John Lehman would travel to London to consider British requests for military assistance.

This analysis of media reports of the events of May 1 boiled down to the following conclusions:

1. The British government was withholding the truth for political-military considerations, which revealed weakness on either or both fronts, since hard facts were being concealed.

2. The international press, but especially the European and U.S. media, trumpeted the British version of the news at the expense of Argentina's, the news sources of the latter lacking credibility in their eyes.

3. The U.S. press did not keep public opinion objectively informed, but slanted its reports to benefit the British cause.

Argentine arms had achieved a significant battlefield victory on May 1, but it was painfully obvious that the rest of the world either did not know this or would not believe it. Great Britain was winning its losing battle through lies and deceit.

THE WASHINGTON-LIMA-BUENOS AIRES CONNECTION TAKES SHAPE

As April came to an end, Secretary Haig still had not lost hope of playing a major role in settling the issue that was seriously affecting his nation's foreign policy in two vital ways: relations with his number-one European ally, Great Britain, and with Latin America, in his own backyard—in other words, his strategic-political interests in the Old World, on the one hand, and his own hemisphere, on the other. This situation, in which the United Kingdom had become the turning point for any acceptable settlement, led the State Department—taking advantage of the forthcoming Washington visit of Foreign Secretary Pym, who was arriving from London to outline the military assistance his country would be needing—to pull out all the stops in its quest for a negotiated way out of the conflict. In coordination with the government of Peru, a proposal was worked out that would be broached to the Argentine government by emissaries from Lima and to which the British foreign secretary would be hard put to object in light of the exceedingly sensitive mission with which he had been entrusted. Secretary Haig lost no time in activating his contact with Lima in order to implement this initiative.

In the final hours of May 1, Peru's foreign minister telephoned his counterpart in Buenos Aires to inquire as to the outcome of that day's action in the Malvinas Islands, and also to sound out Argentina's amenability to possible negotiations. At 0130 hours on May 2, President Belaunde Terry of Peru called General Galtieri to pass on a proposal set forth by Secretary Haig, who had betrayed noticeable concern over the steadfastness of the British stance and the need for a timely settlement. President Galtieri indicated Argentina's willingness to talk, saying that, having waited for 150 years, "What were one or two more?"

The peace proposal submitted over the telephone by the president of Peru read as follows:

—Immediate cessation of hostilities

—Mutual and simultaneous withdrawal of forces

—Presence of third parties not linked to the parties to the dispute for the purpose of establishing a temporary government in the islands

—Both governments to acknowledge the existence of points of disagreement over the status of the islands

—Both governments to acknowledge that the viewpoints and the interests of the local population must be weighed in the balance in order to achieve a final settlement of the issue

—The contact group to play an immediate role in the negotiations to implement such an agreement would be Brazil, Peru, the Federal Republic of Germany, and the United States

—The above group of countries would pledge to achieve a final settlement prior to April 30, 1983.

Secretary Haig would be meeting with Francis Pym at noon (1000 hours, Washington time) on May 2. He would sound out the British foreign secretary while President Belaunde Terry did the same with Buenos Aires. On the morning of May 2, while the Casa Rosada was pouring over the U.S.-Peru proposal, a second call came through from President Belaunde Terry. Dr. Costa Mendez took the call. The main point raised by the president of Peru dealt with point 5 of the proposal. He stated that he had received a call from the U.S. ambassador to Lima proposing that the term "viewpoints" be changed to "wishes." The British had apparently brought pressure to bear on Washington to seek the introduction of such an amendment, knowing full well that this was an insurmountable stumbling block for Argentina (thus laying bare the British intention to cause this latest proposal to fall flat). The Argentine foreign minister pointed out that the word "wishes" was not acceptable, but that he would agree to consider replacing that with "the viewpoints regarding the interests" as well as the discussion of other issues.

The fact that headway was again being made in the talks can be gleaned from the transcript of the conversation between the president of Peru and the foreign minister of Argentina:

Belaunde Terry: Tell me, Mr. Minister, the wording of the seven points, is it generally acceptable to you?

Costa Mendez: Yes, sir; just as long it is made perfectly clear that the local administration will not be returned . . . .

This stance was confirmed in a conversation held that morning between Dr. Costa Mendez and the chairman of the Council of Ministers of Peru, Dr. Manuel Ulloa Elias, to whom he gave full assurance of Argentina's interest in this proposal, and its willingness to resort to other international bodies should this initiative fail.

To give in on the term "wishes" (of the local population) not only was contrary to U.N. Resolution 2065 but also was tantamount to giving a blank check, with the consequence of having to do the unbridled bidding of 1,800 islanders.

It must be borne in mind that at this stage of the game, these telephone conversations were held on open, unsecured commercial satellite links, and most assuredly must have been subject to interception by both Washington and London.

At noon, it was obvious that as a result of these talks, the Republic of Argentina was prepared to sign an agreement. At 1450 hours, one hour and seven minutes before the sinking of the *Belgrano*, President Galtieri and President Belaunde Terry held yet another telephone conference, the basic points of which could only raise every hope for the prospects of the proposal. Argentina would send notification of its confirmation that very night, following a meeting of the military junta, which—as the top decision-making body of state—had to adopt the measure. In Lima, preparations were being made for a ceremony to mark the formal cessation of hostilities, for an agreement appeared imminent.

The issue was discussed by the Foreign Ministry and the Special Working Group on the afternoon of May 2. The consensus was for accepting the proposal. But as these meetings were being held in Buenos Aires, a sinister shadow was looming ever larger over the *General Belgrano* in the frigid waters of the South Atlantic. An order from London would seal its doom. The first report of the attack, which was confirmed shortly thereafter, came in at 1845 hours.

The news of the sinking of the venerable cruiser turned Argentine officialdom upside down. It was not only inexplicable, in light of the scant military threat it posed to a flotilla such as the British task force, but also senseless. Would Britain go so low as to disregard the rules of engagement it had laid out in its self-established war zone? What sort of enemy were the armed forces of Argentina up against? Could such an unspeakable act truly have been committed by a Western power against a decidedly weaker adversary from its own bloc? What had been the true aim of the nuclear submarine's weapons? Had they been intended to pierce the flanks of a ship steaming away from the action, or had they been intended to torpedo the efforts aimed at achieving a negotiated settlement? Could Mrs. Thatcher's government possibly have been a party to such an act of political-military skulduggery?

The military committee met at 1900 hours to ponder the results of the analysis worked up by the agencies and officials concerned. As the meeting broke up at about midnight, a consensus had been reached that in spite of the sinking of the *Belgrano*, the proposal should not be shelved, and that President Belaunde Terry should be so informed. In fact, the commander in chief of the air force was the strongest proponent that Argentina advise the president of Peru that, with the exception of some very minor amendments, Argentina stood ready to agree to the terms of the proposal.

General Galtieri telephoned President Belaunde Terry at about 0300 hours on May 3. Although he outlined what had transpired during the latest meetings, his words did not clearly indicate that, in spite of everything, Argentina was not closing the door on the U.S.-Peruvian proposal. The President of Argentina couched his position in the following terms: "While we are reconsidering the wording of some aspects of the seven points, the news about the cruiser *General Belgrano* has caused the study of such reasoning to be set aside and has become the central focus, which is psychologically and politically transcendental, even beyond military considerations, in the eyes of the Argentine public.'' The president of Peru understood President Galtieri's words to mean that the sinking of the *Belgrano* signified that the talks were being broken off. He mentioned in passing that following his latest contact with Secretary Haig, he had felt that the secretary of state was overcome by a great sense of frustration, for he had sized up Mr. Pym as being a gentleman who had not the slightest interest in achieving peace, and was in fact inclined to see the British war effort through to the finish, as the only way to settle the issue.

The final telephone exchange between the two presidents took place on May 5. Peru's president outlined some aspects of Secretary Haig's proposal in the hopes of keeping alive the initiative he had undertaken in a brotherly gesture to help seek a peaceful resolution of the conflict. But as of that date, Argentina had decided to pursue these talks within the framework of the United Nations, and President Belaunde Terry was so informed.

CONCLUSION

The sinking of the cruiser *General Belgrano* is not only the most controversial and shady event of the war; it was an ignominious act perpetrated by the government of a Western and Christian nation—an act that, thanks to a monolithic propaganda machine and the manipulation of the mass media, was shrunk to insignificance and voided of all consequences beyond those that are well known. This can be deemed no less than a war crime, for the *Belgrano* had violated no territorial space and was sailing, unwarned, on a course away from the zone of operations. It is a crime for which no one has yet been made answerable.

Following the cessation of hostilities, both governments empaneled boards of inquiry to ascertain the facts. Great Britain published the Franks Report, while Argentina issued its report through its Commission for Weighing Responsibility in the South Atlantic Conflict. But, while the Franks Report was aimed at holding the British government harmless from any liability, Argentine justice went about its investigation in an entirely different manner, and delved deeply and objectively into the roles played by all authorities involved.

The Republic of Argentina went to war with Great Britain under a de facto government that had not been put in office by popular election, but it has made a full and clean breast of its shortcomings. Not so Great Britain, for it sailed to a brutal and frontal war with Argentina, with the blessing of a democratically empowered government, which therefore bears a broader civic mandate.

The British government is burdened with a debt, both to the world and to its own people, who profess and believe in a set of values that are the very essence of Western civilization. These people were given a distorted view of the actual events of the war, and their sense of national pride was subliminally taken advantage of, to the point that they were led to believe in the justice of election to further terms of office for the Conservatives. Such would most assuredly not have been the case had there been no recourse to such exploitation.

We Argentines, on the other hand, have been compelled to do penance for our sins, for we are not blameless, neither in this regard nor in the area of human rights. We are indeed deeply sorry for our misdeeds. The 368 seamen who went down with the *General Belgrano* were human beings, and the reason for their demise has yet to be brought to light. The burden of blame, as well as the opprobrium of the Western world, rests on the shoulders of Mrs. Thatcher's government. There is obvious justification for withholding the facts while hostilities are in progress; but to persist in maintaining the veil of secrecy once they have ceased, reveals intent to withhold the truth, not from the enemy of the moment but from friend and foe alike, from the United Kingdom itself, even from its own allies.

Perhaps the time has come for citizens at large, as well as the kin of the men of the *Belgrano*, to raise such a cry as to be heard in Trafalgar Square, where righteous Britons might join in and make Argentina's grief their own.

Let no one forget: There remains a debt to be cleared!

7

The Sinking of the Destroyer HMS *Sheffield*

Our hope and our faith lie in the final judgment of history.
                    Carlos Colcerniani (Argentine journalist), 1983.

THE PHOENIX SQUADRON

From the day hostilities opened May 1, through the final engagement, one air unit remained unsung. It was the Phoenix Squadron, comprised of Lear jets and similar aircraft belonging both to the air force and to private Argentine firms that made them available. It was not a regular air force unit; rather, it was organized for whatever combat contingency might arise, in accordance with the ingenuity of the planning staffs.

The Phoenix Squadron's most important, and most risky, mission was diversionary. Using civilian aircraft, it simulated formations of A–4 or Mirage attack aircraft with radar signatures similar to those of a squadron closing for a run against an enemy. The enemy, on picking up the approaching aircraft on radar, was compelled to take immediate defensive action, such as scrambling its carrier-borne aircraft or shifting the position of those ships most likely to be targeted. This caused the expenditure of considerable time and effort that proved to be futile. Once penetration of the enemy's airspace and radar nets had been achieved, the diversionary squadron would reverse course and head for home. This tactic was executed numerous times, under both day and night conditions, throughout the hostilities.

It was like playing with fire. The British, who learned of this now legendary squadron only following the cessation of hostilities, admitted to both their surprise and the innumerable headaches that these tactics caused them.

THE ACTION ON MAY 2

In the wake of the intense engagements of May 1, there were no contacts on May 2 save for the sinking of the *General Belgrano*. Sightings of British task group units indicated that, as of 1200 hours, a large number of ships were on station east of the islands, in an area beyond the exclusion zone that the British had designated as their TRALA (tug, repair, and logistics area). At 1130 hours, the presence of a task group comprised of a carrier and six escorts was confirmed on a 1200 heading out of Puerto Argentino, at a distance of less than 60 NM. Farther from this group and to the west, the echo of a ship could be picked up 90 miles south of Puerto Argentino. Could this be the abandoned hull of the destroyer that had been attacked the previous day by the Mirage-V squadron, or was it an early-warning radar picket positioned to sound the alarm should an incoming air attack against this task group be detected?

At 1500 hours, an Argentine Navy cutter, the *Sobral*, advised that it was initiating a search-and-rescue operation, within the exclusion zone, for the crew of the Canberra aircraft shot down the previous day. It had been assigned to that duty by the commander of SATO.

At 1514 hours, a Sea Harrier approached Puerto Argentino at high altitude but turned back without attacking.

At 1630 hours, the first news bulletins reporting the torpedoing of the *General Belgrano* were received.

At 2000 hours, following confirmation of the sinking of the cruiser, SATO ordered two destroyers to proceed to search-and-rescue operations. They were soon joined by the cutter ARA *Gurruchaga* and the polar vessel ARA *Bahia Paraiso*.

At 2020 hours, Malvinas military air base confirmed that both the runway and the tarmac were operational following repair and cleanup, and verified that no further time-delay bombs had been located.

At 2130 hours, SAC received confirmation from Malvinas that no contacts with the enemy had been reported. Its task groups had been moved east, outside the range of Puerto Argentino's radar. Only two ships were patrolling 20 miles north of San Carlos: the HMS *Coventry* and a modern Class 21 frigate, operating as a radar picket on the task force's northeast flank. It was this ship that picked up the *Sobral* as it crossed into the exclusion zone.

At 2345 hours, in what was one of its last messages, the *Sobral* advised that it had been overflown by a British helicopter.

The cutter *Sobral*, a small auxiliary craft assigned to search-and-rescue operations, was ordered to conduct a search for the crew members of the Argentine Air Force Canberra B–110 who had been seen parachuting into the sea. It crossed into the exclusion zone and reached the Canberra's last known position at 1500 hours on May 2. At 2345 hours, it was spotted by a British helicopter. By this time, the sinking of the *Belgrano* had been confirmed, prompting the commander of SATO to order the *Sobral*'s return just after midnight on May 2. It proved to be too late: at 0026 hours, Sea Lynx helicopters flying off the *Coventry* and the *Glasgow* returned to the scene and opened fire with Sea Skua missiles, while the *Sobral* tried to defend itself with meager 40mm anti-aircraft cannon. By 0050 hours, contact with the vessel was broken and it was given up for lost. The plucky little ship had taken a direct hit to the bridge, costing the lives of eight men, including the skipper.

Battered as it was, with its company of dead and wounded, its communications gear shot up, and its navigational aids knocked out, the *Sobral* slowly began limping back to Puerto Deseado. It was spotted on May 5 by one of our helicopters as it wallowed in the water, just barely making headway, at 1400 hours. It made Puerto Deseado under its own power a few hours later. Although it fell short of fulfilling its mission—so well spelled out in the motto of the rescue service, "That Others May Live"—because of enemy action, its record stands out as a shining example of teamwork and sacrifice.

This was only the first time the British turned their wrath on Argentine search-and-rescue units.

THE ACTION ON MAY 3

As on the previous day, engagements on May 3 were by and large limited to isolated skirmishes. For Argentina, all eyes and hopes were pinned on the search-and-rescue operations surrounding the survivors of the *General Belgrano*. At 1040 hours, SATO announced the sighting of three lifeboats by the destroyer *Piedrabuena*. The search went on with the *Bouchard* and the *Gurruchaga*, as well as naval aircraft. At 1340 hours, 15 boats overloaded with haggard crew members were located. As further finds were made, the breadth of the tragedy and the anguish of loved ones were somewhat allayed. When rescue operations were complete, 368 Argentine sailors of a ship's company of 1,042 officers and men had found their final resting place in the depths of our southern seas.

Meanwhile, bad weather kept all aircraft at the Darwin and Sea Elephant Bay airstrips grounded. Air force spotter aircraft continued to comb the vast ocean reaches in search of British naval units or clues to their intentions. At 1321 hours, a C–130 reported sighting a logistics vessel with two other ships about 50 NM south of Cape San Felipe (Pembroke). At this news, Air Force South scrambled several squadrons. Their mission was to attack naval targets and provide cover or execute diversionary tactics. The enemy apparently was keeping a safe distance from the island coasts, for the Argentine aircraft returned to base empty-handed. This may well have something to do with the radar echo picked up the day before by the scanners at Puerto Argentino.

Shortly after noon, a member of a squadron of Macchi MB–339 naval aircraft based at Puerto Argentino crashed short of the runway as he was returning from patrol. His aircraft was demolished and he was killed.

Enemy air activity was limited to a few CAPS (Sea Harriers flying in pairs), which approached Puerto Argentino at high altitude.

In the meantime, Condor air base had cleared the damage sustained during the attack on May 1. The wounded were removed to Puerto Argentino for treatment and evacuation, and the dead were buried in temporary graves by the Darwin race track.

At 2248 hours, the enemy, having backed away from daylight attacks, directed a naval bombardment against Puerto Argentino.

As these events were unfolding in the South Atlantic, the Defense Ministry in London, upon receiving Admiral Woodward's report of the first day's combat activities, took a series of sweeping steps to respond to the urgency of the situation at the front. The ocean liner *Queen Elizabeth II*, as well as the container ship *Atlantic Causeway* and two "roll on, roll off"–type freighters, were quickly requisitioned to strengthen the logistics loop through Ascension Island. This brought the number of vessels assigned to this operation to 75. At the same time, the 5th Infantry Brigade was ordered mobilized and made ready, while the remaining available Sea Harrier and Harrier GR–3 aircraft, as well as other military assets, were undergoing modification and being prepared for action.

Specialized offices at the Pentagon were taken aback at the volume of British calls for supplies, the scope of which went far beyond reasonable expectations regarding certain of these requests (for instance, the recently built KC–10 tanker, not yet commissioned in the U.S. Air Force, was requested). High on their list of priorities was the need for intelligence on the armed forces of Argentina, especially the air force, for British intelligence services had totally neglected this vitally needed data. U.S. Secretary of Defense Caspar Weinberger and U.S. Navy Secretary John Lehman saw to it that these requests were expedited with all haste.

MAIN ENGAGEMENTS ON MAY 4

The Vulcan bomber XM–607 was dispatched yet again by the RAF on another grueling marathon, in a second attempt to put the airstrip at Puerto Argentino out of action. The mission itself was uneventful, but the results were even more dismal than the first time.

At 0540 hours, this "early bird" came in low over the beleaguered airfield. As it passed over the long strip of asphalt, it released its load of ordnance: 21 1,000-pound bombs. The string of craters spattered across the landscape was not even close, for the nearest bombs detonated over 60 yards off the west end of the runway. The raid's main effect was to put the 25th Infantry Regiment on full alert.

Admiral Woodward had calculated that all aerial activity in the islands must be smothered if serious casualties were not to be sustained during the landing. With this objective in mind, in addition to the futile flight of the Vulcan, he laid plans for another raid on the facilities at Darwin, where intelligence sources had confirmed the presence of a squadron of Pucara aircraft, which could pose a threat both to his infantry and to his helicopters, for this aircraft was ideally suited for antihelicopter warfare. He was encouraged by the fact that during the action on May 1, there had been no sign of antiaircraft defense activity at that location.

Following this reasoning, Woodward ordered the *Hermes* and its escorts to a station southeast of Puerto Argentino, from which was dispatched a flight of three Sea Harriers to take out the improvised air facilities located on the Darwin isthmus. The May 1 raid had seriously damaged the Pucara squadron. There was a single ground crew, and the inventory of spare parts and most of the available fuel had been blown up. It was a lopsided balance indeed with which to face such a formidable foe, but the air defenses were intact and the men, whose morale ran high, were spoiling for a rematch. They had a single-minded aim: return the "courtesy" to the enemy. On that morning of May 4, they would get their chance.

Moments before 0840 hours, ground control and information at Puerto Argentino flashed the warning to Condor base that bandits were headed on a course for Darwin. The intruders appeared over the Choiseul Channel and were zeroed in on by air defense. The lead Sea Harrier took a direct hit from the Oerlikon 35mm batteries before reaching its target. Flames shot from aft of the cockpit and the plane was blown to bits just short of the base. Its pilot, Lt. John W. Taylor, died instantly. His wingman was able to release his Beluga fragmentation bombs, but he was riddled with cannon fire from the 200mm batteries. Going into its death spin, the Harrier trailed a dense plume of black smoke as it disappeared behind the hills and went into the sea a few miles to the south, where British helicopters made an all-out effort to rescue the pilot. The third pilot, dazed by the fate of his two mates, hastily released a 650-pound parachute fragmentation bomb that failed to detonate, and beat a retreat to the safety of the carrier.

Damage assessment following the raid revealed light shrapnel from the second attacker's fragmentation bombs imbedded in the airfoil of a Pucara aircraft. With this action, Condor base had seen the worst of the British air offensive, for in spite of repeated subsequent raids, this was the last time damage control had anything worthwhile to report.

Meanwhile, the British task force's naval air arm could scratch two more aircraft from its available assets. Added to the losses sustained during May 1, they represented a disproportionate drain on its means. If these statistics were to be projected over time, the task force would be stripped of air cover in two weeks.

For Argentine Forces on that day, the sweetest was yet to come.

THE TABLES TURNED

A new destroyer came on line: the *Sheffield*, the first of a new class of light destroyers designed to fill the needs of modern fleets. Its multiple operational role is built around the latest generation of missile systems. Its air defenses are the Sea Dart weapons system, one 4.5-inch Vickers naval gun, and two *Oerlikon*

20mm cannons. These systems are tied into a computerized firing control device. There is also radar detection and tracking gear. In the antisubmarine configuration, these vessels are equipped with state-of-the-art sonar devices and carry MK–2 helicopters armed with torpedoes and guided missiles. Its twin 50,000 gas turbines allow it to reach maximum speed in minimum time. This class of warship, developed by British naval engineering, was the pride of the Royal Navy and has enjoyed wide acceptance on world markets. Argentina had been among the first to commission them in its navy, having acquired two: ARA *Hercules* and ARA *Santisima Trinidad*.

Built at the Vickers shipyards in Lancashire, and following the example of others of its general configuration, the *Sheffield*'s armor had been sacrificed for other factors deemed more vital to modern naval warfare, such as maneuverability, versatility, additional space in which to house sophisticated weapons systems, and a broad electronics capability. Historically, the name *Sheffield* was not new to the Royal Navy. The name had belonged to a World War II Town Class cruiser that had played a vital role in tracking down the German battleship *Bismarck*. It gained fame as a lucky ship, for the *Royal Ark*, a British aircraft carrier that took part in the same engagement, confused it with the enemy vessel and attacked with a wave of torpedo bombers equipped with weapons tipped with a new magnetic fuse. Most of the torpedoes exploded on contact with the water, and the original *Sheffield* was able to evade the rest. This error laid bare the problem of these faulty "fish," which, once refitted with conventional fuses, quickly spelled the doom of the *Bismarck*.

But in this month of May, 41 years later, the *Sheffield*'s namesake fell short of matching its predecessor's feats. This time, its lucky number did not come up. The later *Sheffield* had been commissioned into the Royal Navy in 1975 and, as a touch of irony, had been skippered by Admiral Woodward. It was on maneuvers in the Mediterranean on April 2, as part of a task group assigned to NATO's Spring Train exercises. The crew had been advised that the following day, the ship would return to port in time for the Easter holiday. The skipper, Capt. James Salt, had to tell his men that, due to orders from Northwood, their next port of call would not be Portsmouth but the gloomy waters of the South Atlantic, date of return unknown.

The *Sheffield* arrived on station in the South Atlantic with the first task force contingent, and as numerous photographs attest, the Class 21 frigate *Arrow* was steaming alongside and went to its assistance as the doomed ship was engulfed in flames.

Super Etendard to the Attack

The Super Etendard-Exocet weapons system was being fitted to Argentine naval aircraft even as the events at Port Leith were unfolding and the Malvinas were taken. Five units had been delivered at the time France clamped an embargo on exports of military equipment to Argentina, stranding most of the remaining aircraft and missiles, which had been procured through a binding contract with Dassault-Breguet, maker of the aircraft, and Aerospatiale, maker of the missile, on the docks at Marseilles.

Argentine technicians worked miracles in jerry-rigging what had been delivered of the system in order to come up with something that was both operational and trouble-free. There was no way to test it under real conditions, and there was no way that performance could be assured because of the hasty and somewhat unorthodox manner in which it was pressed into service in the Malvinas theater of operations. The 2nd Naval Air Fighter and Attack Squadron, comprised of Super Etendard aircraft, had been deployed to the Rio Grande Naval Air Station. From there, on May 4, it underwent its test of fire.

An unidentified echo had been picked up in the southeast quadrant off Puerto Argentino on May 2. On May 3, as a C–130 was attempting to run the British blockade with a shipment of supplies for Puerto Argentino, it made visual contact with three British naval units some 60 miles south of Cape Pembroke. At great risk, it executed a 180° turn at very low altitude, at a distance of about 5 NM, in order to confirm the sighting.

The crew members of the C–130 believed they had spotted an assault vessel escorted by two frigates, the latter vessels following at some distance (from the perspective of the spotters). The three vessels were stopped in the water, making no headway at all. What were they up to? There was no way to ascertain their intention, but the assumed presence of an assault vessel was interpreted by the staff of Air Force South as a probable enemy intent to push ahead with a landing. We now have reliable information indicating that such was not the British plan. The very fact that the C–130 did not come under attack reveals that the ships were not fitted with Sea Dart missiles, whose range would have allowed them to do a swift job on the aircraft. This in turn leads to the conclusion that there were no Class 42 destroyers or cruisers such as the *Glamorgan* or the *Antrim* in that area, for all of these are fitted with that missile system. The three vessels were in fact the support vessel *Fort Austin*, a Class 21 or 12 frigate as an escort, and probably the hull of a damaged ship that the other two were attempting to assist or take under tow. That same day, Puerto Argentino-based radar and spotter aircraft had detected naval activity in that area. They noted the presence of one large echo and two medium ones, with a third medium echo somewhat further out, north of these positions. These signals tended to indicate a vessel the size of a carrier (large echo), along with two or three Class 42 or similar vessels (medium echoes).

This was all that was needed for the 2nd Naval Air Squadron to scramble a flight of two Super Etendard aircraft, equipped with one AM–39 each. The aircraft lifted off at 0944 hours and set a course to the target area, where the presence of three vessels had been confirmed: One large ship and two mediums, position 52° 34'S/57°40'W, with another medium ship not far off. (See Map 4.)

The weather that morning was generally bad throughout the area. But while unfavorable weather conditions made life hard on the C–130s attempting to resupply Puerto Argentino, they were ideal for the Super Etendards. After being refueled in flight by a KC–130 tanker, they slipped below a dense cloud cover and broke out over choppy seas with limited visibility due to scattered squalls. This would make it difficult for the enemy to spot them.

The lead aircraft, piloted by Lt. Cmdr. Augusto Bedacarratz, with wingman Lt. Armando Mayora, dropped down to water level and skimmed over the whitecaps, heading straight at the enemy vessels. As they screamed past the rocks off the Beauchene Islands, the lead aircraft fired its Exocet at a large target that had been locked in by the sensitive missile platform system, turning the missile into a "smart" bomb homing in on its target. It was 1104 hours. On seeing this, the wingman fired his missile in turn, and both aircraft, having launched their weapons from a distance of about 25 NM from the British ships, made their escape.

What became of the Exocets? In theory, if the missiles were locked in on the larger target, it would be almost impossible for any technical error to make them veer off and lock in on another target. Suppose, now, that the second Exocet was not fully programmed to home in on the larger target. It could have selected another target, or gone wild and spent itself in the sea. The fact is, these missiles cannot be influenced by any external factors until they are about 6 NM from the target. At 12 seconds from impact, the on-board radar kicks in and focuses the target, in order to compute and correct last-minute deviations, and make necessary corrections to home it straight in on the target. Only then can they be subject to interference such as chaff, which could act as a fake target and divert them from their course.

The Exocet missile is tipped with a high-precision detonation system. The fuse causes detonation of the explosive charge on impact with the target. A hole about 10 feet in diameter can be made in the hull of a ship. If such a hole does not cause the vessel to sink, it most certainly can put it out of action. This was demonstrated in a test carried out prior to May 4 in which a practice run was made against a target vessel, since no Exocet missile had ever been fired under real combat conditions.

The presence of the light carrier *Hermes* in the area has been fully documented, not only by radar contacts made by P–2 aircraft and by the Sea Harrier raids against Darwin that day, which assisted in estimating the position of the carrier, but also by the flight plans found on Lieutenant Taylor's body, which pinpointed the exact location of his home ship. "We are surprised," said a naval expert at navy headquarters in Buenos Aires, "because they acknowledged the loss so quickly, for our target had been a carrier, not a destroyer."

Aboard the *Sheffield*

On May 4, the *Sheffield*'s crew had already endured five straight months of sea duty. From the balmy Mediterranean to the bone-chilling South Atlantic, the morale of the 288-man ship's company was being tested to the limit. They had sailed into the war zone with the first task group of surface vessels under the command of Admiral Woodward, ready for whatever the conflict might bring. The group was comprised of three Class 42 destroyers—the *Sheffield*, the *Coventry*, and the *Glasgow*—and two Class 22 frigates: the *Brilliant* and the *Broadsword*. The latter two were the only units fitted with guided missile air defense weapons systems effective against low-flying aircraft, the latest Sea Wolf missiles. The remaining defenses rested on the shoulders of the gunners manning 20mm and 40mm antiaircraft emplacements housed aboard both the frigates and the destroyers. Time, experience, and the progress of technology would prove these weapons obsolete.

The Sea Dart missile system mounted aboard Class 42 vessels is designed for high-altitude air defense, and it is not very effective against incoming aircraft at water level. During the deployment to the Mediterranean on maneuvers, Captain Salt's crew had their confidence boosted by the fact that one of their Sea Darts had disintegrated a drone aircraft flying at supersonic speeds at an altitude of 51,000 feet.

According to available accounts, the *Sheffield* had just relieved the *Coventry* on radar picket duty south of Puerto Argentino. At 1100 hours that day, the crew was conducting exercises at the second level of alert. The radar gear was switched off, ostensibly to reduce interference with communications in progress, via satellite, with London. The British later confirmed that the Super Etendard's shadow had been picked up in the ship's operations room. The watch officer on duty on the bridge, looking west, spotted smoke a second before issuing a missile warning. Five seconds later, the ship was mortally wounded by that missile, which exploded on impact in compartment 2, near the engine room, ripping a hole in the starboard side.

The ship was engulfed in a sheet of flame. Its superstructure, built of lightweight materials to give it improved stability, turned white-hot and began to melt. Its engines were on dead stop, and its communications and steering gear were almost completely out of commission. The explosion split the hull in two sections between which no communication was possible. The fire control network was inoperative, and many of the men, surrounded by thick, black smoke that began to spread throughout the ship, suffered smoke inhalation.

Confusion spread to the remainder of the task group. Communications with the *Sheffield* had been cut off, and a column of smoke was seen rising from its position. Whether it had been hit by an Argentine submarine or the smoke was due to an accident was a matter of conjecture. The *Hermes*, on station 30 miles to the east, ordered the frigates *Arrow* and *Yarmouth* to render immediate assistance to the ship in distress, dispatched a helicopter in the direction of the thick, billowing smoke to ascertain what had happened, and ordered the *Glasgow* to take over the *Sheffield*'s duties. The confusion worsened as the *Yarmouth* reported it had been narrowly missed by a missile, and both frigates reported sighting torpedo trails in their area. The *Glasgow* launched its Sea Lynx helicopter, which fired MK–46 antisubmarine torpedoes; they promptly headed for the only radar shadows in the area . . . those of their own two vessels, for there were no Argentine submarines there.

A short time later, the Sea Lynx put down on the flight deck of the *Hermes*, delivering the operations and air warfare officers of the *Sheffield*, who gave Admiral Woodward a full briefing. Meanwhile, Captain Salt continued directing the desperate fight to save his ship. The *Arrow* came alongside to render assistance, but there was not much it could do. Nearby, the *Yarmouth* again picked up underwater echoes and immediately proceeded to launch depth charges, which further increased the fearful possibility that the whole fleet had come under attack by the Argentine Navy. Faced with this grim prospect, the increasingly unbearable heat being given off by the ship's structure, and the advance of the flames toward the magazine housing the Sea Dart system, the impeding massive explosion of which loomed ever higher, Captain Salt issued the order to abandon ship. It was 1600 hours (1900 hours GMT).

The abandoned hull drifted dead in the water for three days, then was reboarded by its captain in the hopes of keeping it afloat and getting it to South Georgia for repairs. On May 10, as it was being towed through heavy seas by the *Yarmouth*, it capsized and sank. It was originally reported that it had been scuttled by its crew with explosive charges placed in the hull, possibly in a last-ditch effort to deny any such sinking by Argentina.

A tortuous tale indeed, to explain a basic happening. The above data were the facts as they were made public by British sources. What was not reported that same day, May 4, and at the same time as the attack against the *Sheffield*, is that accredited news correspondents aboard the *Hermes* heard a loud explosion and felt the ship's structure shudder. They had been below decks and could see nothing, but upon inquiring as to the nature and source of that loud report, they were told that a Sea Harrier had experienced a mishap on the flight deck. A likely story indeed, for no such mishap appears in any action report, and none has ever been corroborated. The journalists were hastily transferred to the *Invincible* and did not return to the *Hermes* for the remainder of the conflict. (This admission was made by British reporter John Witheroe to a Uruguayan colleague.)

Mrs. Thatcher was the first to receive the news of the *Sheffield*. It fell to Defense Secretary Nott to break the news to Parliament, which, gathered in emergency session, listened in mute bewilderment. The announcement was made the very afternoon of the happening. Thus the myth of the "invulnerable armada" came tumbling down with a resounding crash, bringing with it the shattered illusion that the naval expeditionary force to the South Atlantic would return, flags flapping, following the successful outcome of its quest, with nary a scratch.

A thunderous uproar ensued in the House of Commons as it was swept with wave upon wave of questions for which no answers could be found. The opposition, led by the Labourites, demanded that the government put an immediate end to this action, since it had been agreed that sending the fleet was only a means to exert pressure, and had in no way been an endorsement of acts such as the sinking of the *General Belgrano*, which had only served to escalate the conflict and bring about the loss of the *Sheffield*. The government was also called upon to reopen the talks within the framework of the United Nations.

Foreign Secretary Pym, who apparently had done his homework and was prepared for such an onslaught, responded that any potential peaceful settlement was tied to two prerequisites: withdrawal of Argentine troops and no preconditions regarding sovereignty. As for the specific demand that the issue be bound over to the United Nations, he stated: "Options are being kept open for a possible mediating role for the U.N., but Great Britain has neither been approached by that organization for the purpose of intervening in the Falkland crisis, nor indeed was such her desire at this time." This last affirmation is patently untrue, since Secretary Pym had received, as had the Argentine delegate, an offer of negotiation through the secretary general of the United Nations, in Washington on the night of May 2.

The British public was being kept up to date. A television broadcast detailing the circumstances surrounding the sinking of the *General Belgrano* was in progress when it was interrupted for a special news bulletin on the *Sheffield*. The hot gush of popular enthusiasm was turned to a cold drip at the news from the front. From that moment on, the heady euphoria of self-righteous indignation that had buoyed the public as they saw the task force off at the piers gave way to gnawing anguish and dread over the fate of those who had sailed away so bravely. Now, more than ever, was the time to seek a negotiated settlement to this dispute.

The *General Belgrano* was barely settling to the bottom as the governments of France and West Germany voiced their concern over the escalation of the hostilities, and policymakers within the foreign ministries of every EEC member met in Brussels to discuss the possible lifting of sanctions against the government of Argentina. Ireland, Japan, and the nonaligned countries, as well as the OAS and the Warsaw Pact nations, joined the gathering cry of reprobation swelling against the British action. In the European Community, early expressions of solidarity gave way to consternation and even condemnation of Great Britain, which ran the risk of finding itself standing alone. Only the United States remained steadfast at its side, as Secretary Haig decried the Argentine government's "lack of flexibility."

It was perfectly obvious at this stage of the game that each side, having suffered the loss of a capital ship and human lives, had to end this futile holocaust, which would only become bloodier and costlier if allowed to continue. But Mrs. Thatcher gave short shrift to the feelings of her people, the stance of the opposition, the wishes of her allies, and the dictates of sane judgment, not to mention the dead and crippled men who would be the bitter aftermath of such a conflict. She had plans afoot to cover her government in glory.

GNAWING SUSPICIONS

The two members of the Super Etendard flight were faced with a frenzy of questions upon their return. Their comrades and superiors alike could not get enough. They confirmed their launching of two missiles locked in on a large target. They thought the lead plane's missile might have done the job. The ground crew who had jerry-rigged the Exocet system was ecstatic. They had done it! The news would not be long in coming. At 1740 hours Buenos Aires time, the teletypes at the Telam news service sprang to life and clattered out "urgent" cable 222/T.I.87:

Britain acknowledges loss: One destroyer sunk

London, May 4, 1982 (Telam)—The British Defense Ministry acknowledged today the sinking of the destroyer *Sheffield*, 3,500 tons . . . .

The cable went on to report heavy losses of life.

Meanwhile in the United States, "ABC Evening News" was on the air, confirming this event for U.S. viewers to see and hear. It was 1620 hours EDT, 1820 hours Buenos Aires time.

Shortly after 1700 hours, a British message was intercepted: "Mercury cannot fly." Was this a reference to the task force?

At 1830 hours Buenos Aires time, a second Telam cable came in over the wires. No. 231/T.I.94, with the heading "British Concern," read as follows:

London, May 4, 1982 (Telam)—"For the first time, the British Defense Ministry has acknowledged the loss of men and materiel in the South Atlantic Conflict," a Venezuelan diplomat said here today.

It is this diplomat's feeling that such a change of attitude may signify that Margaret Thatcher is attempting to prepare British public opinion, in order then to acknowledge further loss of life, and that the aircraft carrier *Hermes* may be seriously damaged or sunk.

It would appear that this Venezuelan diplomat had sensed something that Argentines already knew for a fact: British reports were not trustworthy; they twisted the facts or withheld them altogether.

For the time being, the day's events could give rise to every sort of speculation with regard to damage sustained by the task force. Perhaps this second Telam cable would prove unfounded in the light of confirmed facts; nevertheless, during those times suspicion and distrust got the best of Argentine or Latin American critics and analysts. Who, or what, was Mercury?

The First Uncertainty

The first doubt regarding the contents of Telam's cable received at 1720 hours arose from a hard fact: the British had effectively acknowledged sustaining losses for the first time. The same cable also mentioned the loss of "two" aircraft, but further cable traffic mentioned only one plane. This could, of course, be in keeping with the need for British forces to disguise their true losses, for each aircraft shot down translated into a 5 percent decrease in the task force's available air strength at that time. They thus restricted their reports to those, such as Lieutenant Taylor's Sea Harrier, that had gone down over land.

Following this line of reasoning, it is not entirely clear why the British would acknowledge lethal damage sustained by their capital ships, especially considering that Argentina had no means of confirming the success or failure of its attacks except through such information as the British Defense Ministry chose to make public. Confirmation of damage sustained by the *Sheffield* was a tip-off to the fact that the Exocet missile system had been successfully fitted and employed. Three of these warheads were still on inventory, and the world market was being scoured for more. Had the British kept this intelligence under wraps, the effectiveness of the system would have remained shrouded in uncertainty, and might have undermined Argentine confidence enough to preclude its further use. By making such information available, British intelligence had committed a grievous error.

The Second Uncertainty

The speed with which confirmation of damages sustained by the ship was made gives immediate rise to further suspicion. When Secretary Nott reported the sinking of the *Sheffield* to Parliament, the crew was still battling the flames in an attempt to save the ship, which foundered only six days later, according to British sources. Why the rush? Another question unanswered.

The Third Uncertainty

The fact that it was the *Sheffield*—again according to British sources—that took the Exocet amidships, and not the target that had been intended, has given rise to no end of controversy and puzzlement at the uppermost echelons of the Argentine Navy. For openers, news reports affirming that the carrier *Hermes* lay 30 miles east of the *Sheffield's* position do not track with Argentine detection data that enabled the targeting of the Super Etendards on their mission, nor even with our tracking data moments before the missiles were launched.

Furthermore, it is a known fact that British news correspondents encountered myriad hurdles in their reporting duties, for every shred of information they were able to glean was scrutinized by Defense Ministry experts, to such an extent that the news agencies that had dispatched them to the South Atlantic found it more convenient to parrot the official line than to run the piecemeal reports that managed to filter from their war correspondents through the maze of censorship.

Also noteworthy is a report filed by a correspondent aboard the *Hermes*, who stated: ''I watched as the sailors abandoned the destroyer *Sheffield*, which was ablaze following a missile hit during an Argentine air attack. I was on the deck of the *Hermes* when the attack was carried out, within the TEZ.'' (United Press, May 5, 1982). Surely a professional newsman would not make the mistake of reporting the details of a blazing ship being abandoned in the descriptive terms used, when it was supposedly 30 miles away. Either someone did his writing for him, or the *Hermes* was not where the British claimed it was.

The broad conclusion to be drawn from the scrutiny of the circumstances and aims surrounding the release of information by the enemy is that such news accounts were less than accurate due to the censorship to which they were subjected. And the official reports, which have maintained this claim to the date of this writing, were even less so.

The Fourth Uncertainty

According to official British sources, the missile launched by the Super Etendard lead aircraft did not detonate. The fire aboard ship was caused by unburned rocket fuel, which spread upon impact. Gases released by flammable materials in the ship's structure were so toxic that the air became unbreathable, which explains most of the 87 casualties, of which 21 were deaths. According to the crew, however, there was in fact an explosion, which created the hole in the side of the ship that is visible in just about every photograph taken shortly following impact. As for the veracity of either account, there can only be conjecture; but since both are from British sources, it can be concluded that probably neither is accurate.

Now, assuming the Exocet detonated, it would have wrought greater damage in the *Sheffield's* hull than is shown in the photographs of the ship, yet had its explosive charge not gone off, there would be no reason for exhibiting the breach in the starboard side, which gives every indication of having been caused by an explosion from within.

It is therefore somewhat incomprehensible, given the facts, that 21 crew members lost their lives and another 66 were wounded if no explosion occurred aboard the ship. Flames spread at a given rate, and a properly trained crew is able to take protective measures to secure themselves against the effects of fire. The stated number of casualties can be attributed to the effects of a sudden explosion aboard ship that does not give time to those within its lethal radius to seek shelter.

The Fifth Uncertainty

According to Hastings and Jenkins, on May 4 "The weather was calm that morning, and visibility unusually good." This statement is at odds with our own findings. The weather report from Puerto Argentino was as follows: "Winds from the west, 10 knots, cloudy skies, 1.6 mile visibility, mist, low ceiling: 275 feet, pressure 1017.5 mb." For the sake of argument, the *Sheffield* lay over 50 miles off Puerto Argentino at the time of the attack, and weather conditions may vary over such a distance. Such, however, was not the case in this instance, for the weather conditions were the same throughout the area of the islands and the exclusion zone because a high-pressure system was holding over the islands, with a warm front coming in from the north. This translates into a uniform weather report sufficiently broad to blanket the whole area.

If this does not constitute fair evidence, the best reports can be had from eyewitnesses, the pilots of the Super Etendards. They have gone on record as follows:

That morning, unfavorable weather was to prove the ally of the Super Etendards. Visibility was limited (less than 3/5 of a mile) throughout the islands, beginning 150 miles east of Rio Grande, with squalls and thick banks of fog . . . . We entered the thick cloud cover, and when we came out from under, we were flying low over the sea, a dark sea with whitecaps in sharp contrast to the blackness of the water. The weather downstairs was definitely bad.

The clinching argument was a description of conditions at 1104 hours, the moment the Exocets were launched: "As we banked to turn back, we almost skimmed the water with our right wing tips. Before completing our turn, we were swallowed up in a squall. Visibility dropped to nothing. We couldn't see up, but we could make out the choppy surface of water as the sea rushed by under our bellies" (Villarino, p. 130). It thus can be inferred that the three references to the prevailing weather conditions in the launch area are in complete agreement with the weather report for May 4, 1982. This is a proven fact, which has finally been acknowledged by British sources (Burden et al., p. 35).

Furthermore, all photographs taken immediately following the attack show the *Sheffield* ablaze on calm seas with good visibility. Wind speed over the ocean can be figured within one or two knots in relation to the movement of the surface of the sea by using the Beaufort scale. At that time, and following that method, wind speed was four knots. Therefore, the following conclusions, as obvious as they are clear and valid, may be drawn:

—At the time of the attack on the *Sheffield*, the prevailing conditions were light winds and good visibility.

—These were not the weather conditions prevailing on May 4, 1982, when the British Defense Ministry announced the attack on the *Sheffield*.

It follows that the British have concealed the true date on which the destroyer was attacked. The question remains: Why?

It should be pointed out that part of this is conjecture and could prove untrue. But what is undeniable is that the British government has resorted to repeated distortions in the reporting of these events, and therein lies the crucial test. Can full faith be placed in such a source of information? It is entirely within the rules of the game for adversaries locked in mortal combat to conceal, disguise, or otherwise veil certain information as the conflict unfolds, for intelligence can be vital to the final outcome. But the fact that one side, the British government, should continue to stand such a zealous guard over the true facts so long after their occurrence strains the bounds of credibility. This makes the unmasking of the truth all the more a challenge.

For the record, events following May 4 revealed decreased British carrier activity. Rumors were aired in the press to the effect that the *Hermes* was under tow on a course for Curacao, for repairs—so much so that workers at that location issued a statement denying any such thing. Our own reconnaissance spotted a carrier surrounded by six escort and support vessels on May 10. The group was making slow headway east, about 300 miles from Puerto Argentino, thus rekindling spirited argument as to the true resting place of the Exocets launched on May 4.

This author is not alone in raising doubts as to the accuracy of events reported in this chapter. Restive journalists, with their natural inquisitiveness, attempted on various occasions and under diverse guises to throw some light on these events and uncover the true facts. As early as May 25, 1982, while the war was still on, Argentine media were speculating that the *Hermes* might have sustained damage, based on the limited availability of British aircraft within the operations zone, and the fact that those aircraft always appeared from, and returned to, the same seaward location. The speed with which the British government acknowledged the sinking of the *Sheffield* was equally suspicious, to the extent that one could infer that the ship may have in fact fallen prey to the attack of May 1, and the *Hermes* took the hit on May 4.

A Telam release published June 5, 1983, underscored the close link between the attack on the *General Belgràno* and the sinking of the British destroyer, which would have been caused on May 1 by a 500-pound bomb from the Dagger attack on that date, followed by a detailed report on news items gathered in Great Britain on this event, as well as technical details that should be taken into account in order to underwrite such a theory. It concluded by pointing the finger of blame at Mrs. Thatcher and ended thus: "Our hope and our faith lie in the final judgment of history."

THE CLINCHING HYPOTHESIS

Picking up on the concern expressed by a Venezuelan diplomat in London shortly following the British announcement on the *Sheffield*, and adding to those raised in the Argentine press during May 1982, and especially in several national papers on June 5, 1983, one could be led to theorize that the ship hit by the Torno squadron attack on May 1 was the *Sheffield*. Let us assume this as a hypothesis, a supposition presumed to be factual but not based on sure evidence, to serve as a starting point for a logical process of reasoning.

Had the sinking of the *Sheffield* and the loss of several Sea Harriers to air defense fire at Puerto Argentino during that first engagement on May 1 between British forces and the armed forces of Argentina been made public in London at that time, what consequences might have ensued? Mrs. Thatcher, who had dispatched the fleet in the absence of a full consensus within Parliament and against the wishes of various groups, most assuredly would have lost the confidence of that body, a situation that would have compelled her to resign. It therefore can be logically inferred that the truth was disguised in order to preclude such an outcome, thus buying time to inflict a similar loss on Argentina so as to present a more evenly balanced scenario to public opinion, both at home and abroad. Seen from this perspective, one can catch a glimmer of the true motive underlying the decision to sink the *General Belgrano*. Turning back to Chapter 6 and factoring this argument into the eight conflicting accounts, we find the following.

Conflict Number 1

Considering that the aim of the United Kingdom was to achieve the withdrawal of Argentina's troops in compliance with Resolution 502, which was then being negotiated through the good offices of the president of Peru, the only interpretation one can give to the British decision to sink the *General Belgrano* is that they found themselves compelled to do so because they had already sustained the loss of a ship, either sunk or severely damaged; were Argentina to have accepted the conditions proposed at that juncture, with the ensuing cease-fire, the score card would read very badly for the task force and would be up there for all to see.

Conflict Number 2

The torpedoing of the *General Belgrano* outside the exclusion zone can be rationalized only by the sinking of the *Sheffield* on May 1. The political cost of the former was far more palatable than the consequences of the latter, which, had it come to the knowledge of the British public, might well have spelled the downfall of Mrs. Thatcher's Conservative government.

Conflict Number 3

Defense Secretary Nott's affirmation to Parliament that the *General Belgrano* "was sunk because it posed a threat to the task force" was nothing more than a subterfuge, an excuse that we know to be unfounded, concocted as a plausible explanation for making public an act that had no justification, and to conceal the unavowable truth.

Conflict Number 4

As for Admiral Woodward's explanation that the *General Belgrano* was approaching the shallows of the Burwood Bank, where the *Conqueror* would be unable to pursue it, there is no technical foundation for such an argument, even should one consider that the Argentine task group was heading in that direction—which is not factual, and the British know it.

Conflict Number 5

Secretary Nott's statement to Parliament in which he affirmed that task group 79.1 was "dangerous" and that it was "closing" on task force units, was no more than an attempt to explain the unexplainable on the basis of falsehoods in his zeal to conceal the truth.

Conflict Number 6

The statement above applies here as well. The *General Belgrano* may have posed a relative threat on the previous day, until it received the order to reverse course. It had not been subject to an attack because it was sailing outside the exclusion zone and the *Sheffield* had yet to meet its fate. Following the latter event, the *Conqueror* began stalking it in the hope it would enter the exclusion zone. When the *Belgrano* reversed course, the order to sink was issued before it sailed further away, taking with it the chance to even the score.

Conflict Number 7

In their attempt to distort reality, both Defense Secretary Nott and Fleet Commander Sir John Fieldhouse were at odds with the truth when they affirmed that the *General Belgrano* was sighted only on May 2, therefore avoiding any possible association between this sinking and the damage sustained by the task force on the previous day.

Conflict Number 8

The affirmation that the decision to attack the *General Belgrano* was Commander Wreford Brown's alone is yet another example of the irresponsibility and the hedging of those officials involved in seeking a way out. It did serve the purpose, in that time frame, of keeping those who pried too closely within the War Cabinet at bay, for the truth was be revealed only two months later, upon the return of the *Conqueror* to its base in Scotland, with the war won and Mrs. Thatcher's power base fully secured.

In sum, the eight conflicting accounts outlined in Chapter 6 come into sharp focus when analyzed in this light. Morality aside, they are logical and in keeping with the British resolve not to publicize battle tales that might have been the undoing of the government.

THE *SHEFFIELD* AND THE BELAUNDE TERRY INITIATIVE

Some of the ins and outs of the Peruvian president's generous but unsuccessful initiative, at the behest of the White House, to achieve a negotiated settlement to the conflict have been outlined in Chapter 6. It is entirely within the realm of possibility that Secretary Pym journeyed to Washington on May 1 without knowledge of the outcome of the Torno squadron's mission, for he had a very urgent one of his own, the thrust of which was to secure U.S. military assistance, since Britain's war efforts would be seriously hampered from the very first engagement if the Pentagon did not do its bit. In exchange for U.S. help, Secretary Haig would attempt to extract some concessions from his counterpart that would achieve an agreement acceptable to both parties. Pym's instructions were to give in only on whatever would not jeopardize forthcoming U.S. military assistance, nor be at odds with Britain's preestablished conditions for talks: compliance with Resolution 502 and a return to the status quo prior to April 2.

As the British foreign secretary was winging his way across the North Atlantic to the United States, the *Conqueror* lurked in the South Atlantic waters, lying in wait for the *General Belgrano* to cross the line into the exclusion zone in order to dispatch her to the bottom. Following the demise of the *Sheffield*, headquarters at Northwood was eagerly awaiting the right chance to sink a capital vessel of the Argentine Navy. The *General Belgrano* became the only prey to heave into view, since the whereabouts of the task group surrounding the *25 de Mayo* had not yet been pinpointed. Since the British had only three nuclear submarines on the prowl in the area, they had been unable to patrol the full zone effectively in order to locate the Argentine task force, with the exception of the waters within the exclusion zone. This is the main reason they were unaware of how Vice-Admiral Lombardo had deployed his assets.

It should also be pointed out that neither the political nor the military authorities in Argentina had a full grasp of the whole picture of the events of May 1 as they unfolded, since news from the front was sketchy, confusing, and sometimes overrated with regard to some of the facts. The conjecture was that one vessel had sustained heavy damage and that two or three aircraft had been brought down that day, as is borne out in official joint staff reports.

In the early morning of May 2, President Belaunde Terry forwarded an eight-point proposal to General Galtieri that was scrutinized that morning at the Casa Rosada even as the *General Belgrano* was being shadowed by the *Conqueror*. Had Argentina agreed to the proposal, Britain would have been hard put to reject it. Such a rejection in the face of U.S. pressure to accept, and the political price of losing U.S. military support were Britain to persist, as well as the even higher domestic cost of accepting in the light of its unfavorable position at the conclusion of the first day of hostilities, put Britain in a no-win situation. The British government rose to the occasion by finding a clever compromise that entailed stalling the talks, and British diplomats were so instructed. So it was that the

U.S. ambassador to Lima advised President Belaunde Terry that Great Britain desired to change the word "viewpoints" in point 5 of the agreement to "wishes." This was conveyed by telephone to Argentina's foreign minister by President Belaunde Terry, who knew full well that such an amendment would be unacceptable to Argentina.

Officials in Buenos Aires continued to weigh their decision. About noon, they came out of their huddle with what appeared, with minor amendments, to be a positive answer, as is revealed by the Galtieri-Belaunde telephone exchange that took place at 1450 hours.

But about that same time, at Chequers, the War Council was faced with a clear-cut decision: if they dallied, Argentina would accept the proposal and the *General Belgrano* would have reversed course, away from the exclusion zone. The Admiral Sir John Fieldhouse bolted out of the meeting and headed straight for Northwood, whence the order to the *Conqueror* to sink the *Belgrano* would soon be issued. The order was quickly carried out. It was 1557 hours Buenos Aires time (1857 GMT).

It was an operation worthy of Macchiavelli. The Royal Navy avenged its tarnished honor, the British government was assured the necessary support to remain in power without being found out, Argentina would reject the proposal, and the United States would remain steadfast at the side of its European ally. Mrs. Thatcher had a blank check to seek a military victory, settling the conflict by force of arms—a conflict now bound to escalate.

There remained, however, one gnawing problem: how to "cover" for the *Sheffield*.

THE FIVE BIG QUESTIONS

Doubts have been aired as to the circumstances surrounding the announcement of the sinking of the *Sheffield*, all of them arising from British reports, both official and unofficial, that are not in line with the facts as they are known in regard to this most crucial of engagements for retaking the southern islands.

First Big Question

The confirmation—and this was a first—of damage sustained by the task force, without Argentina's forces having been able to get their own verification, serves a double purpose: to conceal a vitally important piece of intelligence—that one of the aircraft carriers had sustained a hit by an Exocet—and to use this attack as a piece cover story for the *Sheffield* by saying that the latter had been sunk on May 4, thereby disguising the date of the attack and the true motive behind the sinking of the *General Belgrano*.

Second Big Question

Britain's swift acknowledgment that one of its task force vessels had been sunk by an Argentine attack served the need stated above to "cover" for this loss; otherwise Britain would have had to manufacture an accident to justify the loss of the vessel.

Third Big Question

At least one of the two Exocet missiles launched by the Super Etendard Escadrille hit the carrier, which had been detected and confirmed to be in that area. This would clarify the technical problem involved in explaining how both missiles could have been diverted from their true target; the attack took the British forces absolutely by surprise, since they had no idea that the system could have been made operational by the Argentine technicians and, therefore, had not provided for any countermeasures, such as scattering chaff across the path of the missiles.

Fourth Big Question

The effect of the weapons that damaged the *Sheffield*, if one is to believe the photographic evidence, does not match the type of damage normally sustained by a ship's hull upon impact of an Exocet missile. The bombs released by the Torno squadron were BRP 250s (parachute delayed 500-pound bombs) with a fuse set to go off after a minimum three-second flight. This means that the minimum altitude for releasing these bombs is 150 feet, an extremely perilous altitude for the Daggers. This would explain why the bombs dropped by two of the squadron's aircraft did not detonate. The flight path of no. 2, however, who had to execute a maneuver rendering him more vulnerable to attack from the destroyer, allowed him to drop his ordnance from the proper altitude. This was the explosion seen by no. 3 as he completed his pass over the frigate *Arrow*, which he had strafed with his cannon. It was this same explosion, followed by fire, that was witnessed by the whole of Puerto Argentino. This is what the British have doggedly tried to conceal or deny in the face of hundreds of eye-witness accounts.

It was the detonation of the BRP 250 that started the fire aboard the British destroyer and spelled its doom.

Fifth Big Question

The prevailing weather conditions on May 1 and 4 can be submitted as the most convincing evidence of the true date of the attack on the *Sheffield*. We already know the proven weather conditions prevailing in the area on May 4.

Prevailing conditions on May 1 are given below. They are in complete consonance with the pictures taken of the destroyer shortly after the attack.

1. Weather conditions prevailing May 1 from 1200 to 1700 hours at Puerto Argentino and vicinity: Winds from the Southeast at 5 knots; partly cloudy skies (2 to 4/8 cloud cover), ceiling 650 to 1,000 feet, visibility over 4 miles.

2. This report describes a general high-pressure system just off the islands, with partly cloudy skies, low-hanging clouds, and variable light winds from the southeast. The afternoon's satellite photos showed strong stratocumulus formations and good visibility.

Eyewitness accounts of weather conditions prevailing in the area were given by pilots who flew missions on that date, at approximately the time of the attack:

1. 1620 hours—Captain Carballo, flying the A4-B that observed the ship completely surrounded by billowing smoke shortly before arrival on the scene: "I took my plane down over a calm and gray sea" (Carballo, p. 28).

2. 1600 hours—First Lieutenant Roman, member of Torno squadron shortly before the attack: "We came in over a calm and gray sea, as close to the water as we could" (ibid., p. 25).

Finally, and as closing argument to this discussion, it should be pointed out that the surface of the sea is the best yardstick for measuring wind velocity. According to the Beaufort scale, whitecaps first appear when the wind speed reaches eight knots. A glance at the published photographs will reveal the absence of whitecaps, which means a wind speed of under eight knots, as well as the clear visibility of over four miles. These were the conditions prevailing in the area on May 1, not May 4, 1982.

This chapter mentions several ship sightings, and visual, southeast of Puerto Argentino. It becomes obvious, then, that the radar readings of May 2, 90 miles to the south, were those of the hull of the *Sheffield*, abandoned by its crew. The visual sighting was by the crew of a C–130. They spotted a support ship, escorted by a frigate, that had returned to the wreck to get it under tow.

THE MORALITY OF HUMAN ACTION

In wrapping up this chapter, the writer reminds the reader that the presentation of an argument is not, in and of itself, a full verdict of what is truth. It serves only to tie up loose ends and to shed some light on events and circumstances that otherwise have no rationale.

It is now up to honorable Britons to delve deeply into the true reasons underlying the sinking of the *General Belgrano* and present such evidence as does exist—if they have the freedom, and the necessary inclination and forthrightness, to do so. This is as it should be, not so much in recoil at an unnecessary war act as to enable us to go on believing in the set of values that have been the hallmark of our culture. The civilization we have all created should not serve as a safe haven from whence powerful countries may subject weaker or defenseless peoples to their every whim and bidding.

"Acts of men shall be either good or evil, perfect or imperfect, in accordance with whether they are what they should be; in other words, if they become a reflection of God's boundless perfection, and if they tend to bring men closer to him" (St. Thomas Aquinas). Therefore, things shall be neither good nor evil in accordance with man's intelligence to judge them so. The judgment of reason, which is the immediate ground for the morality of human behavior, measures the evil or the good of an act by the degree to which it is appropriate from the standpoint of the aim of such an act, and of the circumstances surrounding it. When an action is wrong, neither the end to be gained, nor the intent, nor the will can make it right.

We have the act in itself (the sinking of a ship), as well as the end to be gained (keep the British government in power and torpedo a peace initiative), and the circumstance surrounding it (an attack outside the exclusion zone in an undeclared war). We find ourselves face to face with an example of the extreme perversity of mankind.

8

Holding Out for Reinforcements and Solutions

Fairness is not the issue here. What we seek is to destroy and root
out any obstacle standing in the way of our governing, and nothing
more!

Hermann Goering, 1944

INITIATIVES OF THE U.N. SECRETARY GENERAL

The secretary general of the United Nations, Dr. Javier Perez de Cuellar, had
proposed as early as May 2, by means of a memorandum addressed to the
delegations of Argentina and the United Kingdom, an alternative to the negotiations being pursued through the good offices of Peruvian president Belaunde
Terry. On May 4, the military junta decided to accept this offer, and the Argentine
government made known its willingness to negotiate an immediate cease-fire as
a primary—but not exclusive—element of such an initiative. The official answer
was conveyed to Dr. Perez de Cuellar on May 5. His initiative was welcomed,
and arrangements had been made for the Argentine deputy secretary for foreign
affairs, Dr. Ros, to take over the negotiations within the United Nations. Argentina's position, as British unwillingness to seek a fair negotiated solution to
the conflict became increasingly obvious, began to gain sympathy within the
international community, most notably in Latin America and among the nonaligned nations. It could safely be said that at that juncture, most of the countries
sitting on the Security Council might have adopted a resolution in Argentina's
favor. However, this change of heart came too late, for Great Britain would use
its veto to block any attempt to achieve peace through any means other than
those it had chosen from the very moment it decided to resort to the discretionary
use of force.

Mr. Pym, in consonance with his government's policy, stated his belief that
no diplomatic headway could be made until the Argentines withdrew from the

islands. This could be achieved as Britain brought increased military pressure to bear on Argentina. His government had requested no such intercession by the United Nations, nor was it desired at this time.

In the meantime, the Irish Republic's U.N. representative made it known that since the events unfolding in the South Atlantic were converging to open warfare, his country stood ready to request an emergency session of the Security Council aimed at defusing the conflict. He would, however, withhold his call for an immediate meeting in order to permit the secretary general to pursue his initiative.

In London, U.S. Secretary of the Navy John Lehman met with British Armed Forces Secretary Peter Blake in order to discuss U.S. assistance to the United Kingdom. With support such as this, the British government could hardly be expected to lean toward a cease-fire or a negotiated settlement, in spite of the escalation of hostilities on the military front. Here the burden of responsibility borne by the U.S. government gains increasing weight, for had the United States seen fit to tone down the support so freely offered the British, London might well have found it to its advantage to adopt a more conciliatory stance. Washington's position was framed in an Associated Press wire datelined Brussels, which reported that U.S. Secretary of Defense Caspar Weinberger had justified the British attack on the *General Belgrano* as a "response" to Argentine "acts of aggression." The smooth meshing of the U.S.-British alliance became as painfully obvious as the Argentine military junta's overestimation of the relationship they thought they enjoyed with the administration in Washington.

At this stage of the game, the following basic circumstances surrounding the management of the crisis could be discerned:

1. From the military standpoint, two capital war ships had been sunk. The toll in human lives was a portent of the casualties to come.

2. Within the Security Council, the tally was slowly shifting in Argentina's favor: China and the Soviet Union gave indications that they would be inclined to veto any resolution favorable to Great Britain, while Spain, Poland, and Ireland—along with Panama— appeared willing to back a cease-fire. They would probably have been joined by Jordan, Togo, Uganda, and Zaire. With that, Argentina would have had the votes it needed to support its position.

3. Within the General Assembly the nations of Latin America, almost as a block, as well as Eastern Europe and the nonaligned countries, were weighing in on Argentina's side. There were a few exceptions, such as Chile, Guyana, France, and Japan, which would abstain for reasons of their own.

4. Great Britain and the United States stood alone against a negotiated solution not under the conditions the United Kingdom chose to impose.

In a nutshell, practically the whole concert of nations had rallied round Argentina and its claim, but their weight was not enough to bend the warrior will of the United Kingdom.

ACTION ON MAY 5

In Washington, the U.S. Congress adopted Resolution 441, which called for "the immediate withdrawal of Argentine troops from the Islands" and offered unrestricted assistance to Great Britain to force the Argentine government to do its bidding. In the meantime, the first glimmer of concern for the future of U.S. relations with Latin America began to arise within some U.S. political circles. Nevertheless, no publicity was given to Argentina's position, nor to the background of its claim to sovereignty, in spite of the surging swell of unanimity rolling in from throughout Latin America.

Meanwhile, in the theater of operations, Admiral Woodward took stock of the meager results achieved by his forces during the engagements of May 4, and limited his planning to future strategy and regrouping his forces, while seeking to harass Argentine forces and maintain an effective naval and air blockade around the islands. With the demonstrated vulnerability of his Sea Harriers to the islands' air defenses, as well as that of his warships to air attacks launched from the mainland, his best option was to await the arrival of reinforcements, for to embark on a full-scale landing with the means at hand could prove exceedingly unhealthy for his amphibious forces.

Weather conditions that day were foul. Air Force South was forced to scrub a C–130 flight into Puerto Argentino and to ground all attack aircraft. At 0430 hours, radar at Puerto Argentino picked up unusual enemy helicopter activity to the southeast. Five choppers were apparently engaged in search operations in an area about 35 to 54 NM out, probably to rescue the pilot of the Sea Harrier brought down the previous day by the antiaircraft batteries at Condor military air base. The activity continued through 1108 hours, at which time a helicopter was observed hovering over a ship. Whether they found the man alive has never been told. We hope so. To survive in those cold seas is a feat worthy of our respect. British CAPs flew over the area, fearful that our Pucaras might attempt to interfere with the search-and-rescue operations. That would not be Argentina's way of fighting a war. Let the record show, for all to see, that at no time did our forces ever attack or otherwise interfere with the enemy when he was engaged in any such humanitarian pursuit, our not having been granted the same courtesy notwithstanding.

Later that day, an enemy aircraft carrier was estimated to be lying 100 NM southeast of Puerto Argentino. British flight activity, as well as our own, was strictly limited on that date. Neither side made any attack sorties.

About noon, SAC headquarters received and evaluated a report indicating that the *Hermes* had sustained damage that had rendered its aircraft elevator inoperative, thus severely limiting its operational capability, for the planes could not be lifted to the flight deck. It thus appeared that as of 1258 hours, *Hermes* had been moved back east of the exclusion zone, and two ships were deployed for radar picket duty north of the Jason Islands. These were probably Class 22 or

42 destroyers, which were to ensure a double shield against high- and low-level air attack, following the lessons learned on the previous days.

A few minutes later, a SAC Boeing 707 on a long-distance scouting patrol sighted an enemy fleet steaming 1380 NM east of Mar del Plata—the middle of the South Atlantic—making 14 knots on a course for the operations zone. At its center was a major vessel (either a large freighter or an ocean liner), escorted by two frigates. Admiral Woodward's reinforcements were plying their way southward.

ACTION ON MAY 6

News reports for the activities of May 5 could be summed up as follows:

Germany has called for a cease-fire in the conflict. The Labour Minister has stated that it is inconceivable that a war be fought over the Falklands.

European solidarity with London hangs on Great Britain's respect for international law.

Reporter Ian Davidson: Falklands, The Time to be Generous. Were military victory possible, there would ensue a requirement for a defensive capability we would be unable to achieve. We should therefore acknowledge that a straight military victory is a second unfavourable option, the first being defeat at the hands of the Argentines. (*The Times* [London])

Falklands: Military Escalation of Growing Concern to Great Britain's Allies. Great Britain's early offensives had re-created in the British press the myth of the Invincible Fleet, ringing with statements by Nott, who went so far as to quote Admiral Nelson. But the Argentine response has brought this castle of cards crumbling down. (*Journal de Genève* [Geneva])

It is alarming indeed that the EEC has become a group which resorts to trade sanctions in order to achieve political or diplomatic aims, or to support the war effort of one of its members, said a Third World diplomat . . . . (*Financial Times* [London])

Meanwhile, in the United States, the media continued to air a slanted version of events that bewailed Argentina's rejection of the Peruvian president's proposal as being intractable while Great Britain was putting forth its best efforts to accept it, when the fact was that Buenos Aires had already accepted Perez de Cuellar's initiative. In the Security Council, the British delegate resorted to dilatory tactics regarding Ireland's call for a meeting to deal with the South Atlantic crisis, revealing a malicious attitude that subtly underscored London's refusal to seek a negotiated solution to the conflict.

In the operations zone, both the weather conditions and the tactical situation remained unchanged. Staff members aboard the task force flagship were wrestling with the military operational question raised by the specter of Argentina's new-found prowess with the Exocet A/M 39 missile. Although in their best estimates Argentina only had three more in its inventory, it was impossible to be entirely certain. By the same token, plans for a helicopter landing near Puerto Argentino had been shelved, and to spearhead the operation upon the arrival of the requested reinforcements, the location of a new beachhead had to be thought out. This was a matter of grave import, and would keep Admiral Woodward's staff gainfully employed for long, grueling hours. The news from the home front was, however, encouraging: a container ship, the *Atlantic Conveyor*, had weighed anchor that day at Ascension, laden with eight Sea Harrier and three Harrier aircraft that had landed at Wideawake on May 3 following record-breaking nonstop flights for this type of plane. These reinforcements were part of the recently mustered Squadron 809. They had been refueled in flight, not once but several times. Following the unexpected toll of the first days' engagements, Admiral Woodward anxiously awaited the arrival of reinforcements for his air assets, without which any attempted landing would be futile.

The Argentine staff groups pondered the very real possibility that their Rio Grande air base might come under enemy attack, for that was the home of the naval air wing's Super Etendards as well as the air force's Dagger attack bombers. Nonessential aircraft were removed inland for shelter, bases secured, patrols beefed up, blackout procedures tested, and the civilian population gently made aware of the fact that their homeland, which had been at peace with the world for over a century, might suddenly become the front line.

Radar at Puerto Argentino reported limited enemy aircraft sorties that day. Between the hours of 0700 and 1800, only eight CAPs were sighted, most of them at different times, and they approached no closer than 29 NM. The carrier, in all probability the *Invincible*, was estimated to be 92 NM due east, and a submarine was spotted in Annunciation Bay.

That same morning, two transports carrying military items, including desperately needed aircraft spare parts, landed in Buenos Aires on flights from two South American nations. At noon, a C–130 transport, registration TC–65, lifted off from Comodoro Rivadavia and, foiling the British blockade for the first time since the opening of hostilities, landed at Malvinas air base with a cargo of vital military supplies and equipment, as well as mail for the defenders. These flights were made with great care, in order to achieve surprise with each penetration and evade British radar. Cunning was the only defense available to such cumbersome aircraft, since their size would make them sitting ducks for any enemy interceptor that happened to lock in on them. TC–65 took off on its return flight at 1835 hours, on what proved to be one of many shuttle flights the venerable old "Herkies" would make, right up to the final day of the war. They flew without mishap, for in spite of their size, never once did they come into the range of an enemy radarscope, nor into the cross hairs of a prowling enemy fighter.

At 1700 hours, an Argentine F–27 on sea patrol sighted an enemy submarine 150 NM southeast of the coast of Bahia Blanca, at the entrance to Argentina's main naval installations. This caused no small turmoil at navy headquarters aboard ships. The presence of submersibles had not gone unnoticed by TG 79.1, which had sighted one in its vicinity. This served to reinforce our impression that the British were determined to keep a sharp eye up and down Argentina's coastline.

For the first time, the chief of staff of Air Force South, Brig. Gen. Roberto Camblor, broached the possibility of mounting the Exocet M/M 38 missile system around Puerto Argentino with Navy liaison officers. The missiles could serve as a deterrent against British ships bombarding from offshore locations.

That same day, there was a British report of a midair collision between two Sea Harriers shortly after takeoff from the carrier, with the loss of both pilots and aircraft. There appears to be no record of such an accident. Was this another British bluff to cover for two of the losses sustained on May 1? Such a theory seems to dovetail with the events recorded on May 1. The pilot of one of the planes (aircraft no. 2 brought down by the Tigercat) must assuredly have been killed instantly. The other fatality could be surmised as the pilot of aircraft no. 1, which impacted violently on the water.

EVENTS OF MAY 7

While the U.N. secretary general went about making overtures to both governments in an effort to lay the groundwork for a meeting of the minds, Great Britain extended the exclusion zone to 12 miles off the coast of Argentina, up to its territorial waters. This policy, apparently aimed at throwing hurdles in the path of any possible negotiation through the implementation of aggressive measures, was in consonance with stances already assumed:

—On April 12, while Secretary Haig was still in Buenos Aires conducting talks, Britain established the first maritime exclusion zone.

—On April 16, while Secretary Haig was on his second visit to Buenos Aires, Britain informed the Argentine government, through the Swiss embassy in Buenos Aires, that any vessel or aircraft—civilian, commercial or military—found in the exclusion zone would be deemed hostile and subject to attack. On that same date, the British fleet weighed anchor at Ascension and steamed south.

—On April 25, just as the Haig initiative was reaching its crucial juncture, the Grytviken garrison came under attack, and the total exclusion zone was declared established.

—On May 2, the *General Belgrano* was sent to the bottom at the very moment Argentina was preparing to accept a peace agreement.

All of this was carried out under the guise of Article 51 of the U.N. Charter, which provides for self-defense. War operations on May 7 were practically nil. Almost no enemy aircraft movement was observed. Our own most significant movements were those of three C–130 transports that shuttled in and out of Malvinas air base without incident at 1215, 1410, and 1540 hours, ferrying weapons, ammunition, rations, clothing, spare parts, field gear, and general cargo on the outgoing leg, and 13 wounded on the return.

At 0750 hours, Task Group 79.1, including the carrier *25 de Mayo*, was at the mouth of the Rio Negro, making perilous headway in the face of the enemy submarine threat, searching for safe haven in the shallow waters off Puerto Belgrano. By noon, the position of the enemy task groups was estimated to be due east of the islands, and a convoy of about ten vessels, some of considerable size, was sighted northeast, steaming on a direct heading toward the exclusion zone. At 1930 hours, the Argentine submarine ARA *San Luis* made contact with enemy vessels north of Soledad (East Falkland Island). It was unable to launch torpedoes successfully.

Meanwhile, the Argentine joint staff estimated that the enemy task force would abstain, at least for the time being, from conducting offensive operations or attempting a helicopter landing. This was in light of heavy losses sustained by their air assets, plus their having to await the arrival of reinforcements that would enable them to implement other action in order to achieve their objectives.

EVENTS OF MAY 8

Diplomatic ground zero was centered in the U.N. Security Council, where volleys of verbal artillery were followed by blizzards of notes, which, like bomb clusters, sought to blanket their targets with rationalizations and justifications, each side bolstering its position. Of course these skirmishes did not take the same toll of casualties as those recorded on the battlefield, but the hopes of those who were actually fighting were pinned on the diplomatic joust, for its success or failure would determine whether or when the hostilities would end and whether they would make it back home.

But when one of the parties is doggedly determined not to talk and is stiffened by the support of one of the superpowers or the indifference of others, the complex and costly international mechanism intended to preserve peace is found wanting. It was crystal clear the Great Britain intended to have its way by military means, but it was also aware that world public opinion might thwart that design. The political price that it would entail would be too high. So it orchestrated an intense campaign to convince the world that the intractable party to this dispute was in fact Argentina. This campaign of psychological warfare, which found willing allies in the U.S. media, can be traced to Alexander Haig, who, in his own words, had pointed the finger of blame at Argentina for the failure of the negotiations. The London press eagerly took up the cry:

British actions in the Islands crisis have enjoyed the full support of NATO. Members of the Alliance may receive requests to facilitate deployments beyond the support area of vital interests for all. This is interpreted as being the providing of facilities for the resupply and replacement of forces as well as the ensured right of overflight. (*Financial Times*)

Pym spent the day yesterday [May 7] marshalling world public opinion on Great Britain's side, . . . while laying the blame on Argentina for the failure to reach a peaceful settlement.

Haig has underscored the United States' favorable response to British requests for military support. Haig has expended considerable efforts to play down American reluctance to take a hard line against Argentina, and has gone out of his way to persuade the Common Market countries to maintain the steps taken against the Galtieri Government. (*The Guardian*)

The passage "persuade . . . Government" brings to light the true role played by Secretary Haig, the man to whom Argentina had entrusted the negotiations at the very outset of the conflict, the mediator on whom all of Latin America pinned its hopes for a fair and equitable settlement of the dispute, the man who ended up undermining the future of hemispheric relations and discrediting his country's policies toward Latin America.

But while the U.S. embargo and the application of sanctions by the EEC were tightening the economic and political noose on Argentina, the nations of Latin America and the regional organizations limited themselves to oratorical breast-beating and loud wails that came to naught. A single Peruvian labor union, the airport and dock workers, stood up to be counted. Their boycott of British aircraft and ships, which they refused to service, shone as a light in the darkness. A small consolation indeed for a whole continent, which, in order to live its destiny with dignity, may well need the solidarity of all of those who share it.

Perez de Cuellar launched his initiative under gathering clouds: the U.S. Department of State took a very dim view of this U.N. undertaking, and the animosity of the secretary bode it further ill. A spokesman for this worthy agency labeled Perez de Cuellar's ideas "amateurish" and the role of the United Nations "characteristically destructive." The U.N. secretary general was headed for a very bumpy ride indeed.

Meanwhile, in the South Atlantic, a vital decision for the conflict was made on May 8. The British War Council, gathered at Chequers, decided to order the landing force, then anchored at Ascension, to the operations zone. This involved an extremely complex commitment, for once it had been sent south, such a force could not—for political reasons—be brought home empty-handed. And by the same token, the establishment of a beachhead "after the failure of the Royal Navy's attempt to gain air superiority before the arrival of the amphibious force, the government and service chiefs [had] committed themselves to an even greater gamble, that of sending in the landing force regardless" (Hastings and Jenkins, p. 317).

The risks entailed by a decision of this magnitude gave rise to no end of argument and debate between secretaries Pym and Nott, who, in the long run, appeared reconciled to going through with it. The defense secretary was a strong advocate of maintaining the blockade, for the risks of a landing were overwhelming, as were the logistical requirements for backing it up, even were final victory to be theirs. The foreign secretary was mindful of Sir Anthony Eden's experience at Suez, and he carefully weighed the consequences of an eventual internationalization of the conflict. But in decisions of a political and strategic scope, it is the interplay of personalities that tilts the balance. The prime minister made this crucial decision. Although the landing site had yet to be pinpointed, the convoy was expected to come in sight of the Falklands following a ten-day voyage, which meant that the operation could be expected to come anytime after May 18.

About the same time, the Air Force South headquarters had drawn up its own estimate of the probable British landing site. At the top of a list of possible sites were the north shore of San Carlos Strait and Fitz Roy. The bays and surrounding areas had been checked out in April as likely sites for airstrips to support deployments.

The weather continued to be bad that day. Flight activity was limited to two C–130 sorties to keep the island supplied.

ACTION ON MAY 9

As a portent of the difficult road that lay ahead of the U.N. secretary general, the British fired the opening shots that day with an intense naval bombardment of Puerto Argentino, which caused the sinking of an Argentine-flag trawler, the *Narwal*. Both actions were denounced to the United Nations by Argentine Ambassador Roca, who passed on to the Security Council the verbatim account of the attack on the *Narwal* as reported by the joint staff in its communiqué no. 34. Following this attack "British aircraft strafed the lifeboats being lowered by the trawler. It was reported that only one of these remained afloat, with 25 survivors and one fatality. This latest act bears witness once again to the inhumanity and disregard for international law shown by the British Task Force, which engages in conducting attacks against defenseless craft and even survivors in lifeboats."

This "peaceful" act by means of which Great Britain saluted Perez de Cuellar's initiative was part and parcel of a modus operandi that was not unfamiliar to Argentine diplomacy. Alerted to the true intent of such an unjustified action, Foreign Minister Costa Mendez issued his first response: that very morning, he instructed his deputy, Ambassador Ros, who was in New York, to make it absolutely clear that "Argentina continues to negotiate." That same day, Costa Mendez appeared on "Face the Nation" with the aim of softening the image of Argentine intractability that the British were spreading abroad. He stated that at no time had Argentina demanded acknowledgment of sovereignty as a precondition for negotiating, while allowing that the dispute was definitely centered on the issue of sovereignty over the islands. But while Argentina was attempting to lay the groundwork for serious talks, Great Britain was rousing public opinion in order to convince it that a military showdown was the only way left open:

The Cabinet has accepted the idea that the only realistic way to achieve a solution to the crisis will be to force the surrender of the Argentine garrison, with or without casualties to either side. (*Sunday Times* [London])

Argentina concedes to initiate dialogue with Perez de Cuellar on the basis of a plan which does not call for advance acknowledgement of claim to sovereignty over Islands. Such a concession is not viewed as particularly useful. British concessions seen as broader.

Following a press conference with Captain Hector Bonzo of the cruiser *General Belgrano*, observers in Buenos Aires have begun speculation that this vessel . . . was ordered out for the express purpose of being sunk so as to create sensation both in Argentina and abroad. (*Daily Telegraph* [London])

As one can see, the psychological action pursued by certain of the London media knew no bounds, since now not only was Argentina to blame for the breakdown of the talks, it also had purposely orchestrated the sinking of the *General Belgrano*.

However, some of the British media were right on target:

A stiff upper lip has not been the mainstay of the Latin American character, unless the whole population of Buenos Aires has fallen into a state of shock. The reaction to events in the South Atlantic has been incredibly restrained and calm. What occurred following the sinking of the *General Belgrano* was not an outpouring of hatred or outrage, nor did they jump for joy at the sinking of the *Sheffield*. The largest share of hostile sentiment was directed against the United States, for having openly taken sides with the British. (*Sunday Times* [London])

This war is viewed by Argentines as a continuation of the wars for independence and provides immigrants with an opportunity to relieve the experiences of the Nation's forefathers. On the other hand, the English people have all become Falklanders, when in reality they had long forgotten this handful of Islanders to whom even the right to reside in Great Britain had been denied.

Sir Henderson has described aid received from the United States as "determined, generous, and unabashed." Furthermore, Secretary Haig, working behind the scenes had been of decisive assistance to Great Britain when he gave her European allies, whose support had been flagging, assurances that it was Argentina that was raising obstacles to the negotiations. (*Observer* [London])

The British daily gave renewed testimonial to the secretary of state's "Americanist" conscience. But very possibly the most interesting piece of information regarding the nagging problem of British news sources was to be gleaned from the pages of the *Observer*:

Problems between British journalists and authorities. The British press is concerned over the fact that the Ministry releases scant information . . . while restricting and perhaps even suppressing reports coming in from correspondents covering the Intervention Force. Anger is growing particularly over the lack of photographs and television footage. The Defence Ministry has approved two very strict rules with regards to information:

1—No information detrimental to the Intervention Force shall be released.

2—Nothing shall be published without first being scrutinized, re-examined, and ascertained as to its veracity.

Reports filed by correspondents must first go through the Defence Ministry and from there on to the press. The most recent photographs of the *Hermes* are three weeks old.

So in fact, British media were forbidden to publish any news dealing with the following:

—Speculation as to future fleet movements

—Operations plans

—Readiness, operational capability, movements, and deployment of units

—Details regarding military tactics or techniques

—Logistics details

—Intelligence regarding Argentine forces

—Equipment capabilities and flaws

—Communications.

It is obvious here that the British press's usual professional skill in getting at the truth was completely stymied. The cloak would not be lifted even long after the conflict was over.

On May 9, Admiral Woodward decided to implement a new tactic involving a D–42/F–22 (class 42 destroyer, Class 22 frigate) that, in accordance with prior calculations, was deemed fail-safe because of the Sea Dart missiles of the former and the Sea Wolf weapons of the latter. The airspace surrounding the ships would be under an umbrella against low-flying and high-flying aircraft. Furthermore, faulty intelligence had been received to the effect that General Menendez had established his command post at the Moody Brook barracks, formerly the home of the British marines stationed on the islands. Taking advantage of poor weather conditions that kept Argentine aircraft grounded, Admiral Woodward moved his vessels forward in the early hours of the morning to open a naval bombardment against this target.

Following is an account of events, according to British sources:*

Early that morning, the British ships detected an incoming Hercules transport [D–42 *Coventry* and F–22 *Broadsword*], one of the nightly shuttle into Stanley which so dismayed the naval staff seeking to tighten the blockade. [False: No C–130 sortied that morning.] It was escorted by two Skyhawks. [False: No Hercules received any fighter escort throughout the conflict.] At maximum range, 38 miles, *Coventry* fired her Sea Dart. The missiles missed the Hercules, but one exploded beneath the two Skyhawks. At first the British believed they had missed the targets altogether. Then they saw the Skyhawks disappear from the radar screen. [False: No Skyhawk flew that morning.] The pilots almost certainly ejected. Shortly afterwards, *Coventry* again fired Sea Dart at a radar contact 13 miles

*This account should not so much be attributed to the authors, Hastings and Jenkins, as to the source, the British Defense Ministry.

distant. There was a vivid orange explosion as a Puma helicopter blew up. For the first time in the missile age, the Royal Navy had fired salvos in anger. (Hastings and Jenkins, p. 158)

And now for the real story.

The staff of Air Force South had determined that, in order to wrest air superiority from the enemy, two advance radar picket ships, whose mission it was to watch for the approach of Argentine aircraft, attack them, and sound the warning for the British carrier-based CAPs, had to be put out of action.

At 0040 hours on May 9, enemy ships were reported to have initiated a heavy naval bombardment against Argentine positions. A flight of two Lear jets sortied at 0106 hours and arrived over Malvinas air base at 0236 hours. At this point the ships ceased their bombardment and pulled back, and the British sortied a CAP from their carrier. Having achieved their objective, the Lears returned to base. At 0645 hours, a second flight of Lears took off on a similar mission. As they approached Malvinas, 80 NM out, ground control warned them of a CAP zeroing in to intercept. The Lears skillfully guided by ground radar, foiled the incoming Sea Harriers and returned to base without mishap.

The next mission was flown by a single aircraft. Since it was delayed by weather conditions, the next sortie overtook it, and both flights headed in with the same objective as before. The no. 2 man of the second flight saw a flash as he was flying north of Soledad (East Falkland) Island. He warned his lead man as the flash came at them. The two Lears broke off at 90° angles, and watched two sleek missiles flash past in horizontal flight, without quite realizing their point of origin. They felt a muffled explosion in their wake. They dropped low and returned to base without mishap, unaware that the British had chalked them up as two Skyhawks, supposedly brought down by the *Coventry*'s salvo.

The solo aircraft came into the Malvinas control area at 1145 hours, five minutes later, from a 300° (west-northwest) bearing. He was 50 miles from Puerto Argentino. Unaware of what was happening around him, he received orders from ground control to execute a right turn. Control urged him to keep tightening the radius of his turn. As a Sea Dart buzzed his tail section, he realized ground control had just saved his life. He dropped low and returned to base. These crews already had their war stories to tell, if they could survive what was yet to come.

Meanwhile, at 0905 hours, the Argentine trawler *Narwal* radioed a distress signal. It was sailing south of Puerto Argentino at 52°45′S/58°02′W when it came under attack by an enemy aircraft. This trawler, while going about its daily routine, also kept a discreet but sharp eye on events around it. A Sea Harrier from Squadron 800, piloted by Lt. Cmdr. David Morgan, received orders to proceed to the attack. At 0940 hours, the trawler radioed that it was foundering, that it had wounded aboard, and that the company of 25 would attempt to board two small black boats with orange coverings, and an orange dinghy. Another message was received at 1048 hours reporting that the lifeboats were under attack by a Sea Harrier and were sinking. The survivors dived into the water and hauled the wounded aboard the one remaining craft. One of the wounded succumbed to his injuries.

Shortly afterward, British helicopters picked up these survivors, who had been eyewitnesses to yet another inexplicable occurrence in this conflict: Lifeboats with survivors, including wounded, of an armed attack on a defenseless commercial vessel had fallen prey to the weapons of war. Whether those responsible acted on their own or on orders from above, and whether the British conducted any inquiry into this act, remains a mystery. Most mystifying of all is this incongruous interpretation by Britain of what constitutes the right to self-defense.

But the drama that unfolded as the trawler was ripped by a hail of bullets did not end there. As the distress call was picked up by Puerto Argentino, a rescue mission was sent out to render assistance to the survivors. General Menendez ordered an army Puma helicopter into the area. With unswerving devotion to duty, and at great risk to themselves, the crew undertook what proved to be their final mission, for they were the ones who fell prey to the *Coventry*'s salvo.

Meanwhile, at staff headquarters in Comodoro Rivadavia, following the successful completion of the Phoenix Squadron's mission, the decision was handed down to Air Force South to mount an attack on the Class 42 destroyers on station northwest and southwest of Puerto Argentino. The weather remained unfavorable, but the latest reports indicated some breaks to the east of the islands; no reliable data were available for the west sector. By noon, the exact position of the British warships had been confirmed, with an additional two vessels detected southwest of Puerto Argentino. In a few minutes, Air Force South scrambled 18 sorties. Their mission: get those ships.

Air Force South was dogged by bad luck that day. The weather closed. As the rain became torrential and visibility dropped to zero—so bad that they could not hold formation behind the lead man—the squadrons reluctantly turned back, one by one. When Air Force South realized that it was down to two isolated teams flying toward the target area, it ordered their return. One section didn't get the message and flew on. Fate, and devotion above and beyond the call of duty, would emblazon forever the names of the two pilots, Lts. Jorge R. Farias and Jorge E. Casco, in the hearts of their countrymen.

Following the end of the hostilities, the British came across the shattered remains of two aircraft on a remote, deserted island. They had attempted a crash landing on South Jason Island.

ACTION ON MAY 10

The *Narwal* incident was aired in the Security Council. Argentina's protest note was quickly followed by the British retort (note S/15063), seeking to justify the attack as having been the exercise of the "immanent right to self defense . . . therefore, our aircraft released a small bomb alongside the ship and fired a short machine-gun burst." There had been 14 casualties among the crew of 25—

1 killed, 1 serious injury, and 12 minor injuries—all due to "one small bomb" and a "short . . . burst."

In London, *The Guardian* was calling attention to increasing pressure being brought to bear by the EEC countries on Great Britain to achieve a negotiated settlement to the conflict:

The German Development Ministry fears that the military confrontations may give rise, among the Latin American peoples, to resentment against the industrialized world.

The majority of the French people believe that their Government should withhold further support to the U.K. in the event of a threat which could involve France in a broader conflict, according to a poll published yesterday.

British Landing Plans

During the early days of May, reinforcements for the task force had been flowing in almost continuously, to the relief of the commander and his staff. By this time, in addition to the first wave of warships and auxiliaries already in the area, 2 amphibious assault vessels, 5 logistics landing vessels, 11 support vessels, and 8 transports were on their way to the theater of operations or already on station. A further wave of urgently requested reinforcements was on its way. This flotilla included the following:

—The destroyers *Bristol* and *Coventry*

—The frigates *Active, Ambuscade, Antelope, Avenger, Argonaut, Penelope, Minerva*, and *Andromeda*

—The submarines *Courageous, Valiant*, and *Onix*.

Yet to arrive were the *Queen Elizabeth II* and 22 other ships to support the British war effort.

On April 29, General Moore had flown to Ascension to confer with Brigadier Thompson and Commodore Clapp as to the selection of a landing site. Following consideration of 19 possible areas, the final selection was reduced to three:

1. Magellan Inlet, north of Annunciation Bay, at the extreme northeast of Soledad (East Falkland) Island

2. San Carlos Bay, on Falkland Sound but at a distance from the capital of the islands and far enough to establish the beachhead in the face of counterattack thrusts from Puerto Argentino or Darwin-Goose Green, the two main garrisons on the island

3. Annunciation Bay, north of Puerto Argentino.

Inexplicably, they failed to consider a location that would have been ideal for a landing area and the establishment of a beachhead: Teal Inlet, on the north shore of the island and halfway between San Carlos and Puerto Argentino.

On May 10, as the British convoys steamed south, an important gathering of Royal Navy, Royal Marine, and Royal Army top commanders and senior officers was held aboard the *Fearless*. The briefing was presented by Brig. Julian Thompson, commander, 3rd Commando Brigade. The subject was establishment of a beachhead on the Falklands. The first and third options were set aside as too dangerous, in a view of the proximity of General Menendez's garrison and the fact that these natural harbors offered little in the way of safety or cover. San Carlos was selected as a compromise. It had flaws, but it also had its advantages. The main shortcomings were the long distance to Stanley and the proximity (15 miles) to the Argentine garrison at Darwin Isthmus, from whence an attack could be launched.

Huddled with his advisers aboard the *Fearless*, Brigadier Thompson announced to the men gathered in the wardroom that although they had yet to fix the final time for D-Day, sometime on or after May 19, the first wave to go ashore would be the two paratroop battalions, along with the 40th and 45th Commando Battalions, while the 42nd would be held back on the *Canberra* in reserve. The place would be San Carlos.

The audience was electrified to learn that the *QE 2* was to take the landing force close in to the beachhead. It would sail from Southampton on May 12. The beachhead would be secured in 48 hours.

The Day's Operations

The tactical situation reported on the islands on May 10 remained fairly unchanged from the day before. Shrouded in miserable weather, the enemy warships lay off the coast and renewed their fire against the garrison, which had no means of responding other than the aircraft from Air Force South, which remained grounded.

Far-flung scouts spotted the logistics landing vessels sailing into the exclusion zone. The *Uganda* was also sighted steaming south, along with a group of ships far outside the zone. A carrier surrounded by support ships appeared to be in some sort of distress. This assumption is backed by the fact that air activity following the May 4 attack on Condor appeared to be greatly reduced, and that hostile fire and other enemy activity against coastal defenses were being effected by ships that were obliged to come dangerously close to Puerto Argentino for their naval bombardment to be effective.

The *Sheffield*, which had been under tow by the *Yarmouth* near the southeast border of the exclusion zone, was formally given up for lost.

The single most significant enemy movement that day was that of the Class 21 frigate *Alacrity*, which had been ordered into San Carlos Bay on patrol, to check for possible mine fields and, more specifically, to reconnoiter the bay, where the landing was scheduled. In view of the risks involved in this assignment, the *Alacrity* had to operate alone. Fortunately for the crew, it encountered no hostile units, except the 1,900-ton, light freighter ARA *Isla de los Estados*, moving cargo, including fuel, from Port King to Port Howard. As it was sailing 10 NM off the latter, and passing Shag Cove, it took a direct hit from the *Alacrity*, sustaining heavy damage. The shot hit the fuel bunkers, which went up in a ball of flame. It was 2235 hours. Eighteen crew were killed or missing; the ship quickly foundered and was abandoned by the survivors.

That evening, as the British ships left the strait north of East Falkland, the *Alacrity* was sighted and attacked by the Argentine submarine *San Luis*, which fired its torpedoes—once again unsuccessfully.

ACTION ON MAY 11

In Buenos Aires, a poll revealed that 98 percent of the population favored Argentina's decision to reclaim the islands by military means, an increase of 10 percentage points over the previous sampling. This could be attributed not only to the United Kingdom's acts of war and cruelty, but also to the unabashed support from the United States, whose un-American dealings had become the object of revulsion, not only in Argentina but throughout Latin America.

During a meeting of the military junta, this state of affairs was taken under consideration. Perez de Cuellar, realizing that his initiative was being stonewalled not only by the British but also by the U.S. State Department, had become resigned to not sharing in any future agreement. He was further disenchanted by Argentina's decision to reject the Peruvian-U.S. offer and to pursue the negotiations within the framework of the United Nations. This latest attempt at mediation came too late, however. Secretary of State Haig had also had his chance, but he let the opportunity slip through his fingers when he cast his nation's lot with the British. He, too, had caved in to British diplomatic pressure following the failure of his own initiative, regardless of cause, effect, or the rights of those for whom he had attempted to mediate. The Reagan administration, in an effort to improve both its image and its relationship with Argentina, sent General Vernon Walters, an expert at handling sensitive situations, to hold council with the members of the junta. The commanders in chief viewed with interest the possibility that this special envoy might bear a new proposal from the White House, which would imply new hope for restarting the negotiations. General Walters brought no such proposal. His mission was to convince the military junta that the United States was not providing the British with satellite intelligence, at a time when national sensitivity had been wounded to the quick by the assistance being rendered so freely by the United States to the United Kingdom, with the public blessing of Secretary of Defense Caspar Weinberger.

We know now that the White House envoy spoke the truth to the members of the junta, but at that point in the conflict, whether his words were true or not was irrelevant. The fact remains that U.S. aid granted to a colonial power was openly and solely responsible for ensuring the continued viability of the British fleet's operations, for without this vital assistance, there would have been no task force operating in the South Atlantic. Secretary of the Navy John F. Lehman later acknowledged in a statement made in London, "Britain would have withdrawn from the Falklands if the United States had cut off the aid" (UPI, May 30, 1988).

On May 11, what would prove to be Britain's final position on Dr. Perez de Cuellar's initiative was made known. No previous U.N. resolutions would be taken into account, which meant that instead of progress, a reverse course was being taken, at Argentina's expense.

The London media were beginning to question some of their government's affirmations and to suspect the political slant of their nation's diplomacy:

The Government has tightened up its campaign against the "lack of patriotism" of the media, which, for the sake of truth, have tried to fill the gaps in information imposed by Defense Ministry censorship and red tape, by using alternative news sources, mainly from Argentina, but also from the U.S.

It was pointed out that, while it was displeasing to some circles, a group of dissident M.P.s had underscored the fact that each time a crucial phase of the negotiations was being undertaken, it could be predicted that the Task Force would receive orders to carry out some military action . . . this appears tailor-made to torpedo the talks . . . .

This situation is further illustrated by the verbatim release in the London media of details made known by the Peruvian Foreign Ministry on the proposals forwarded by Belaunde Terry. The cold facts reveal that Argentine "intractability" as charged by the British is nothing but a myth. (*La Nacion*, May 11, 1982, from its London correspondent)

But probably the best witness to the truth of these news reports is a most illuminating bit of information made public that same day in London by the International Institute for Strategic Studies:

. . . due to the great accumulation of entries to the debit side of this morbid conflict, Mrs. Thatcher's Government in reality is not desirous of a negotiated settlement, rather, the ironclad intent is to pursue the objective of the military conquest of the Falklands.

The main operation carried out on May 11 and 12 was detailed to an SAS group whose mission it was to gather intelligence on Calderon naval air station on Pebble Island, because of its strategic location at the entrance to San Carlos Strait, the gateway to be secured if British forces were to establish their beachhead in San Carlos Bay.

A British helicopter fitted for operating in total darkness landed eight members of the SBS on the east coast of West Falkland Island. It was a cold, cloudy, windy day. They remained in hiding for most of the day in order to elude discovery, awaiting the right time to launch the rubber boats they had brought with them. Two of these were later found by Argentine patrols, alerting them to the British presence.

General Menendez ordered beefed-up land patrols throughout the sector, and initiated planning for the deployment of a combat team to San Carlos Bay area in anticipation of an enemy incursion. Its code name was Guemes. The British commandos bided their time. At the right moment, under cover of darkness, they rowed silently over to Calderon, where they spent May 13 reconnoitering the area's defenses.

On the morning of May 11, the submarine *San Luis* was withdrawn from the operation zone after its failed attempt to attack British warships. While this weapons platform was no match for the nature of this conflict, its presence, as well as its skill at foiling the task force's antisubmarine defenses, was a cause of great concern to Admiral Woodward.

Task force air activity followed a fresh tactic. The Sea Harriers attempted a high-altitude bombing of the facilities at Malvinas air base. Although their altitude put them beyond the reach of Argentine air defenses, it also deprived them of their capability for precision targeting. Their bombs scattered harmlessly about the countryside, detonating far from any objective worthy of note.

Meanwhile, the first Nimrod, modified for in-flight refueling, left Wideawake on an antisubmarine probe. Air Force South flew some probes of its own. The *Uganda* was again sighted. It proved to be the most closely plotted ship in the task force, for it was a hospital ship and was not to be attacked, even though intelligence had been available at the time of its sailing that there were troops aboard.

At staff headquarters, Brig. Gen. Ernesto Horacio Crespo and his advisers busied themselves with the planning of attack operations against enemy ships, any of which could have been executed had the time and conditions been right. On the next day, the time would be right. Air Force South would fly its second naval air engagement of the war. Casualties on both sides would mount.

ACTION OF MAY 12

In the various capitals swept up in the conflict, diplomatic maneuvering continued unabated, but the talks remained stalemated. In London, the BBC took an independent tack from the government line and presented a somewhat more objective report of the unfolding conflict while other media, egged on by the Conservatives, branded such reports as "treacherous, odious, and subversive." From a more neutral standpoint, Geneva's *La Suisse* editorialized thus:

The Malvinas conflict, regardless of its genesis, will have disastrous consequences for the western world if it is prolonged. European States that supported Britain at the outset are now scurrying to modify their stance. Spain puts Hispano-American solidarity first, Denmark wishes for a peaceful settlement, Germany and France wish to avoid appearing as automatic supporters of the UK.

As for the US, they have given full backing to the British cause. This has dealt a cruel blow to Latin American relations, for that alliance has suffered grievously. Reagan's statement that Argentina's claim has "some legitimacy" comes too late. This Western division plays into the hands of the USSR.

Great Britain is prepared to extend the war regardless of the consequences. As it escalates, it deepens the split in the Western world and weakens European defenses.

Would it not have been better to make an accommodation for Argentina's takeover of the Falkland Islands, contrary as it may be to law, than to create a serious threat to Western unity?

Fortunately for the West, the Argentine military government proved to possess one cardinal virtue. It did not give in to the temptation of alliances that could have been had for the asking, for, although they might have tipped the outcome in Argentina's favor, they would nevertheless have seriously endangered world peace and the way of life of a nation that professes to be both Western and Christian. It preferred to stand alone against an alliance of nations of similar thinking, but with a slightly different concept of the meaning of those words. Argentina and the nations of Latin America began to take stock of the nature of the world around them as a result of this conflict. The fact that the enemies of our Western and Christian civilization began to appear more palatable and our so-called friends less so began to take shape.

And Mrs. Thatcher, deaf and blind to these realities, continued undaunted in the pursuit of her goal.

The *Queen Elizabeth II* sailed from Southampton on May 12. Its decks would not feel the tread of monied pleasure seekers on a luxurious cruise this voyage, but the boots of the British Army's 5th Infantry Brigade. The pier became a sea of waving white handkerchiefs, bidding adieu to 3,000 men as they set sail on their southerly quest. To the surprise of many an experienced warrior, the 5th Brigade had in its numbers the 2nd Battalion of Scots Guards and the 1st Battalion of Welsh Guards, both outfits more accustomed to the ruffles and flourishes of ceremonial reviews than to the rigors of a hostile terrain, ungodly weather, and the fight that lay ahead.

Day broke over the Malvinas with strong winds but with visibility enough for the fighters to sortie. As early as 0530 hours, the British vessels positioned themselves offshore to commence the naval bombardment anew. The first salvos rang out at 1132 hours. The time was right for Air Force South to launch its attack.

The Guemes combat team moved out for San Carlos Bay that morning. It was comprised of 120 men of Company C, 25th Infantry Regiment, under the command of 1st Lt. Carlos D. Esteban. They were backed by a support group from the 12th Infantry Regiment.

At 1335 hours, a Sea Harrier was sighted flying high over the Puerto Argentino airstrip on an obvious reconnaissance mission, and on another long-distance probe over the South Atlantic, an Argentine Boeing 707 and a Nimrod 2P crossed paths. The two aircraft looked each other over as they passed high above the ocean, unable to take action because both were unarmed. The RAF fitted its aircraft with air-to-air Sidewinders, but no further chance encounters of this sort occurred.

Meanwhile, with incoming British shells crashing about them, Malvinas military garrison called Air Force South for air support against the British fleet lying offshore. The attack was approved. Two formations, Oro (Gold) and Cuña (Wedge), with four aircraft each, were scrambled. Each plane carried a 1,000 pound bomb known as a "bomb-ball." It was an iron-sheathed bomb nicknamed for its weight and power as well as for its ballistic profile. The Cuñas streaked off at 1230 hours, rendezvoused with the tanker for a fill-up, and made a beeline for the target area. They were followed by the Oros, which sortied at 1252 hours, refueled in flight, and headed for the battle zone. As the Cuñas came in sight of the islands, they dropped down to sea level, skimming over the water, shooting past Darwin over Choiseul Sound, where they encountered fog banks that reduced their visibility. The low altitude at which they were flying created the additional problem of salt buildup on their canopies. Then, off to their right, the ships suddenly rose into view, stationed about 1,000 feet apart. At 1408 hours, as the Cuñas came within five miles of their naval targets, the effect of antiaircraft artillery over the water became clearly visible. The *Brilliant* fired its Sea Wolf missiles for the first time in anger, and two Skyhawks plunged seaward in a trail of flame just short of the target. The third A4-B went down as it tried to clear the area, and the fourth dropped its bomb as it streaked over the ship and pulled out. The bomb fell short of its mark. Number 4 made the return flight alone, its salt-caked canopy reducing the pilot's visibility to practically zero. He was talked in for a blind landing and barely escaped cracking up.

At 1418 hours, it was the Oros' turn to attack. They had the disadvantage that the ships were now on combat alert and may have moved from their original positions, which would make the final bomb run more difficult. Three aircraft closed on the *Brilliant*, whose Sea Wolf missile system had been expended during the first wave. The three bombs ricocheted along the surface of the water and bounced harmlessly over the superstructure. But *Oro* No. 3's bomb found its mark. Zeroing in on the *Glasgow*, it impacted right at the waterline. The bomb did not burst, but its momentum ripped a hole clear through the ship, from side to side. Exiting the opposite side, it detonated in the water. The MK–17 has awesome explosive power, enough to have sealed the doom of the *Glasgow* had it gone off amidships.* But the gaping hole it left, through which one could see the sea, caused the *Glasgow* to ship so much water that it had to be withdrawn from the war zone and sent home to England, limping at barely six knots.

To Admiral Woodward's great consternation, a third task force Class 42 destroyer had been put out of action. He was down to a single unit of this type, the *Broadsword*, which escaped unharmed.

The four members of the Oro Squadron had come through the attack without a scratch. Elatedly, they confirmed their victory. But fate dealt a cruel blow to the plane that had delivered the scoring shot against the British destroyer. Due to the limited visibility caused by the salt buildup on his canopy, Oro 3 wandered

---

*A spirited discussion ensued among Argentine air and naval headquarters officers; the former affirmed that it was an "underwater bomb," while the latter insisted it had to be a "flying torpedo."

into restricted airspace over Darwin, and before the local air defense crew realized he was friendly, their 35mm batteries had dropped him from the sky. The remaining three squadron members returned safely to base, landing blind because of their salt-clouded canopies.

This first A4-B attack gave rise to detailed analysis. It had been a noteworthy achievement, yet there remained some bugs to be ironed out. There was no time to be wasted. Air Force South was strengthened in its contention that the guided-missile frigates were indeed vulnerable; and although the cost of doing them in could be exceedingly high, it was within the realm of feasibility. Crucial to the success of such an intrepid undertaking was the unshakable, boundless willing-ness and devotion of the pilots, who, flying aircraft a good 20 years older than their targets, had proven the feasibility of inflicting substantial damage to the latter. In spite of the staggering loss rate sustained by their own numbers, they stood ready to have at it again and again, for this, they felt, was their bounden duty.

9

On Toward the
Beachhead

Res non verba

(Actions, not words)

ACTION ON MAY 13

The Military Committee met that day, to discuss the general situation in light of the latest events. Dr. Costa Mendez was present. A visit to the United States by Brazil's president, Joao Figueiredo, held out hope for Argentina. President Figueiredo would be laying out for President Reagan the broad picture of where Latin America stood in regard to the conflict, and would elicit a U.S. promise to spare no efforts to ward off any possible British attack against the South American mainland.

The British media reported that the Class 22 frigates *Broadsword* and *Brilliant* had sustained heavy damage during the previous day's action. Hope was expressed that Air Force South would pursue its strategy of low-altitude attacks, where the Sea Wolf missile system had had an auspicious test under battle conditions. By the same token, high-altitude attacks were to be avoided, for 80 percent of the Class 42 destroyers fitted with the Sea Dart missile system against high-flying aircraft had been put out of action. This revealed a weakness that had not been reckoned with by British staff planners, who would have been all the more convinced of the need to avoid this situation had they been aware that Sea Dart was not even remotely as effective as its manufacturer—or trial launchings—would have had them believe.

During those days of trial for both men and their deadly machines, on the proving ground for modern weapons systems that the South Atlantic had become, this reality became Air Force South's little secret. Not reckoned in this concept, however, is the success Argentine pilots had with the battle-proven weapon they employed successfully in combat against an array of the most sophisticated naval electronic gear known to man: the bomb-ball.

In pursuing his initiative, Dr. Perez de Cuellar underscored the fact that the British had not made the slightest response to the main points being negotiated, and noted that the talks were being mired down by dilatory tactics. By the same token, international press reports were beginning, on May 13, to lean more toward Argentina's side than they had at the outset. But the political machinery had already been set in motion, and British resolve would, for all intents and purposes, continue unremittingly on its established course.

. . . in short, the first mistake in the Falklands was the failure of British politicians to find their way out of an untenable position by political means, before it was too late. (Anthony Lewis, *New York Times*)

Great Britain was elated with her early successes; then came Argentina's first great moral victory [the sinking of the *Belgrano*], followed by her first naval victory [the sinking of the *Sheffield*]. (*The Economist* [London])

May 13 had been selected for a third bombing raid against the airfield at Puerto Argentino. Again the Vulcan, registry XM–607, left Wideawake on its appointed round. Unfavorable winds en route, which would have raised its fuel consumption beyond the margin of safety, caused the mission to be scrubbed. The British fleet did not draw closer to Puerto Argentino for a naval bombardment that day. Task force action was limited to electronic jamming, and even the Sea Harriers kept their distance from the islands. Possibly the single most noteworthy tactical move that day was the delivery to the islands of a 155mm Sofma gun, airlifted in by a C–130. As the artillery piece was being unloaded, between 1630 and 1700 hours, Argentine gunners hurriedly moved the weapon into place near Eliza Cove and Look Out Rocks. Then all they had to do was wait for the British ships to draw nearer for the next round of naval bombardment.

ACTION ON MAY 14

It was assumed both in Buenos Aires and in diplomatic circles at the United Nations that Great Britain was preparing a broad-scale military operation. Any British response to Perez de Cuellar's initiative was expected to be unacceptable to Argentina, all the more to justify sending the landing force in to the attack. This assumption was right on target. It is now known that the British task force was prepared to land in San Carlos Bay as early as May 18, D-Day having been postponed to the early hours of May 21 because of unfavorable weather conditions.

British action on April 14, unveiled a new task force tactic. The Sea Harriers came in at very high altitude, beyond the range of the deadly air defenses. As they approached the target area, they went into a steep climb. As the aircraft were almost vertical, they released their 500-pound bombs, which vectored up and out, and arched, into a fall. This tactic had been practiced for dropping nuclear warheads, since the formidable effect of such weapons made precision targeting unnecessary, and the maneuver allowed the aircraft to outrun the blast wave. But the British conventional bombs simply scattered harmlessly, hitting at best an occasional target of opportunity. The defenders were undismayed. All they wanted was for the attackers to come down a little closer. This bombing technique, known as "LAB" or the "catapult," was executed by the Sea Harriers at 0720 and 0730 hours, and again at 1141, 1220, 1530, and 1720 hours. No casualties were recorded.

Argentine long-distance patrol flights confirmed previous sightings of a cluster of ships about 1,000 miles due east of Puerto Deseado, and a light carrier was operating northwest of the islands within a 040° to 070° radius, from 60 to 95 NM out. The third wave of reinforcements for the task force was also spotted 1,200 NM east of Rio de Janeiro. It was comprised of a tanker, two Class 21 frigates, two Class 42 destroyers, and a Leander Class frigate.

The best morale lift of the day for the defenders was the sight of British ships drawing closer to the coastline to initiate their nightly naval bombardment. They were right on schedule, at 2330 hours. The Sofma gun was ready and waiting. As one of the ships came within ten NM, the gun roared. The ship had a quick change of heart. With every bit of speed it could coax from its turbines, it reversed course and made for safety.

ACTION ON MAY 15

May 15 can be established as the turning point of the moderation process undergone by the Argentine diplomatic position, for Argentina backed off from its demand for recognition of sovereignty as a precondition for negotiations and accepted Dr. Perez de Cuellar's suggestion of not going into the talks with preconceived notions. The secretary general's initiatives came to a dead halt, however, because both British ambassadors in the United States, Mr. Parsons to the United Nations and Mr. Henderson to the United States, had been called home to London for consultations and would not return before May 17. This sudden trip was more in tune with the forthcoming landing at San Carlos than with the ongoing peace talks in New York.

Prospects for an early meeting of the Security Council were dimmed by the fact that Great Britain would be forced into wielding its veto in order to preclude being targeted with an unfavorable resolution. Such are the mechanics of an international tribunal of this type, where one of the judges is also party to the litigation before the court.

Even the most detached and experienced observers of such international quid pro quos had slim hope that London could be expected to scrub the landing or recall the fleet without some decisive achievement on the battlefront. In the United Kingdom, the tone of the statements issued by the defense secretary was a clear indication that public opinion was being prepared for the acceptance of the military option as the only way of settling the matter, the peace talks being doomed to failure. *The Guardian*, however, stated:

Argentina has made several genuine concessions: she has agreed to withdraw her troops and haul down the flag as long as the peace plan is carried out and temporary U.N. administration of the Islands is accepted while their future status is discussed with Great Britain. But paramount is that she has agreed not to impose recognition of sovereignty as a pre-condition. Great Britain should then make a concession with regard to the role of the Islanders.

Meanwhile, continental Europe was reverberating with the echoes of a mini scandal involving a paper released by the French Foreign Ministry—which would not be denied by France's foreign minister—stating that an internal Foreign Ministry memo reflected Paris' growing disillusionment with British management of the crisis and the "ingrained and instinctive British contempt for the Latins," and complained bitterly of the "weakness, shortcomings and obvious pretentiousness of Great Britain before and during the crisis." The Paris daily Le Figaro went even further:

Comments attributed to [French Foreign] Minister Cheysson may well point toward the existence of sufficient old imperial hardhandedness and instinctive contempt for any proposal offered by Latin peoples. The Foreign Office's technocratic reaction to unsuitable information, as well as its obvious wish that common people, or not so common politicians not meddle in their sophisticated thinking. . . .

It was obvious that the British attitude was stirring up some visceral feelings among staid European societies, but France's socialist government would see Mrs. Thatcher's conservative government faithfully through thick and thin. Arms embargoes and other sanctions would remain firmly in place against a nation of Latin heritage, for vested interests in modern international societies would have more weight and worth than sentiment, people, and the political bent of the governments that lead them. All of this came about 24 hours prior to the deadline the Common Market had established for lifting the collective sanctions imposed against Argentina.

At 0418 hours, HMS *Glamorgan* initiated a heavy naval bombardment against the positions around the small airfield located on Sea Elephant Bay, where Argentine aircraft had been positioned, and now were bogged down. The small garrison, which had spent those days in precarious living conditions due both to the soggy weather and to the remoteness of the area, was taken by surprise by the intensity of the shelling.

Two Sea King helicopters carrying 45 men from D Squad, 22nd SAS Regiment, landed on a spot marked by the eight members of the advance team that had scouted the area and, reinforced by units from the 148th Naval Artillery Battery, proceeded to a spirited attack against the aircraft lashed down there. Wielding grenades, rockets, and clubs, interspersed with bursts of automatic arms fire, they crippled five Pucaras, four Mentor T34-Cs, and one Sky Van. They fell back under heavy artillery cover as the defenders, who, on seeing the onslaught and perceiving the objective as being to take the airfield, detonated explosive charges that made the field useless, bathed the intruders in a shower of mud, and caused two casualties. The British party was picked up by helicopter and returned to their ship, a short distance offshore, without mishap. At 0546 hours, the operation was complete. The invaders left behind several 40mm and 61mm mortars, 66mm NK portable rockets, 7.62mm MAGs, 7.62mm portable weapons, 40mm hand grenades, and plastic explosives. They also left more damage to Argentine defenses than the combined action of all British ships and aircraft over the previous fortnight.

The destruction of these aircraft left the way open for the landing of the amphibious forces, planned for a few days later. What the enemy did not know was that the combat team Guemes, 120 men strong, had secured their positions on the high ground around San Carlos Bay, across San Carlos Strait.

The task force staff took stock of the Argentine Air Force's capability and willingness to pursue the offensive. They figured that following the most recent action against the destroyer *Glasgow* and the frigate *Broadsword*, the British pilots might switch tactics. During their opening attack, on May 1, the Daggers had managed to get away unscathed; but on May 12, Sea Wolf missiles had exacted a frightful toll against the first squadron of Skyhawks: two aircraft out of four shot down. Furthermore, they had yet to neutralize an enemy capability considered deadly: the Exocet A/S 39 weapons system. Countermeasures such as scattering chaff in their paths had been implemented. This entailed considerable effort, for in order to defend each ship, several helicopters had to remain on picket along the probable path of any incoming missiles, a mission that was exhausting for both men and machines. Although the British had no way of knowing this, luck would again be their lady, for Argentina's entire inventory of Exocet A/S 39 missiles numbered only three.

May 15 also marked the return of the task force's aerial activity to pre-May 4 levels. Again the British CAPs spent the better part of the day patrolling high over Puerto Argentino—some to the northwest, others to the south—while attack aircraft sortied systematically on bombing runs that kept the area shaking from the explosions. The bombing was anything but precision, but use of time-delay fuses as an antipersonnel device kept the men on their toes for hours following each raid. To make things more devilish, the Beluga bombs were employed during this action.

In spite of the turmoil and upheaval that day, three C–130s shuttled into the airport, laden with vital shipments, at 2016, 2130, and 2305 hours. Two B–200s managed to run the blockade that day, and made the return leg to Rio Grande without mishap, as did the Hercules. A Navy MB–339 also got through, and remained in the islands to back up the local fleet.

At 1045 hours, a Sea Harrier executed an attack against Sea Elephant Bay, in case the commandos had missed something. In the meantime, Air Force South beefed up the islands' inventory of aircraft, moving four Pucaras from Santa Cruz. They arrived without incident and went into the flight line to replace those lost during the earlier attack.

One of the C–130s brought a second Sofma 155mm artillery piece. It was set in place 500 yards south of Sapper Hill.

Following an investigation, General Menendez decided against evacuating the naval air station, which had come under attack. His decision proved providential, for in the hard fight yet to come, many an ejected Argentine pilot would owe his life to search-and-rescue units operating out of that base.

For analysts in Argentina's War Council, the outcome of the day's activities was not encouraging. In addition to the successful attack mounted by British commando units against the base at Calderon, the talks in the political field were stalemated; in the strategic field, British resolve to impose the military option appeared to stiffen; and in the tactical field, both carriers were again in full operation off the coast of the islands. The one that had appeared to be sidelined for ten days was obviously back in action.

ACTION ON MAY 16

The British War Council met on the evening of April 15 under the leadership of the prime minister. The next day, Defense Secretary Nott issued the following statements in regard to the conflict:

1. The British government will soon come to a decision in order to settle the Falkland Islands crisis. Basic issues in the U.N. secretary general's initiative remained unresolved.

2. The government's objective is to reestablish British administration in the islands. A posteriori a period of maximum military alert will be imposed.

3. Once the United Kingdom's sovereignty is reestablished, a long-term solution will be negotiated with countries in that area, but no possibility for transfer of sovereignty to Argentina is foreseen.

4. The prospect for bombing the Argentine mainland persists, although this would constitute a major escalation.

5. Great Britain does not feel it will lose Europe's support, even if it reclaims the islands by force of arms.

6. The government has available a broad array of military options, ranging from blockade up to and including invasion. In the event of the latter, every attempt will be made to secure the objective with the smallest possible number of casualties, although this by itself should not be deemed an obstacle to such action.

The Observer (London) made the following outline of the situation:

Both parties, as well as Mr. Perez de Cuellar, insist that the negotiations have run up against insurmountable obstacles. Britain's negotiating position has stiffened in the face of the attitude taken by the House of Commons and by public opinion, and because military forces are poised to settle the issue far from the negotiating table.

But the distance separating the two parties has closed to the point that it would be unthinkable to break off the talks or force the issue by escalating the struggle. To do so would cost not only precious lives, but also the support of a large part of the world, including some of our closest allies. These are the voices Mrs. Thatcher should give ear to, not the siren songs from the right.

Mrs. Thatcher appears to have turned the Nation's eyes more towards the battlefield than the negotiating table.

Through mid-May, task force staff officers were not particularly happy with the performance and results achieved by the British fleet. The loss of three Class 42 vessels, as well as the damage sustained by other mainstays of the fleet, opened their eyes to a reality on which they had not counted. The loss of six Sea Harrier aircraft to the precision fire of Argentine air defenses had seriously hampered the effectiveness of these scarce and hard-to-replace assets. Five helicopters also had gone down in combat operations.

Since there appeared to be no chance of any naval engagements, the task force was limited to its routine nightly coastal bombardments, firing salvo after salvo without knowing what they were firing at nor how effective they were. The ever-looming danger of an enemy air attack compelled extreme security measures aboard all vessels.

On April 16, the naval air attack group aboard the carrier *Hermes* was ordered out on a reconnaissance mission over San Carlos Strait. They attacked targets of opportunity, coming in low over the 8th Infantry Regiment's positions at Fox Bay at 0430 hours. As they pulled up, they left behind four wounded Kelpers and extensive damage to civilian facilities. Argentine military targets were barely scratched.

Following a reconnaissance overflight in the vicinity of San Carlos and Darwin, aircraft proceeded at 1000 hours to attack unarmed shipping. The ELMA *Rio Carcarana* and the ARA *Bahia Buen Suceso* were hit at 1315 and 1435 hours, respectively, as they lay at anchor in Port King and Fox Bay. Following the attack, the *Rio Carcarana* was abandoned, in flames, by its crew. The other vessel sustained light damage.

British CAPs flew a series of significant sorties. Their main objective continued to be the perimeter of the airport, which had cost them so dearly on May 1. They used fragmentation bombs that explode a few feet off the ground. The effect on personnel can be devastating, so much so that the use of such weapons had been forbidden by the U.N. Disarmament Commission. At 1430 hours, during one such attack, two aircraft made a low penetration from the lighthouse at Cape Pembroke, at an altitude that left them wide open to the withering fire of the 35mm antiaircraft batteries. The lead plane dropped its bombs and executed a tight turn, followed by the wingman, who mistakenly fired one of his missiles. The missile homed on the lead plane, which maneuvered wildly to shake off its pursuer, to the jeers of the onlooking Argentines. During a later attack, a Sea Harrier was raked by antiaircraft cannon fire. His own forces, and shortly thereafter an official British communique, confirmed one aircraft damaged. Naval bombardment resumed that night, incoming shells softening up the Malvinas airfield perimeter between 2125 and 2240 hours. This time the *Sofma* artillery rang out. Their resounding claps thundered out over the water, and the enemy beat a hasty retreat—to the delight of the defenders, who cheered as the British ships churned the ocean into foam on a reverse course to safety from the range of the 155mm guns.

At 1420 hours that afternoon the *Queen Elizabeth II* dropped anchor off the coast of Mauritania. Relieved of the duty of shadowing the Argentine Navy, British submarines drew close to the coastline of Patagonia in order to report any outgoing aircraft heading toward the task force. At nightfall on May 16, one of them dropped off three rubber boats carrying frogmen, whose objective was to sabotage aircraft and base facilities at Rio Grande. Under cover of darkness, and shrouded in thick fog, they were taken by surprise by the Argentine destroyer ARA *Bouchard*, which had been patrolling the area. The intruders withdrew under heavy naval fire, until their blips were no longer visible on radar.

ACTION ON MAY 17

Ambassador Parsons returned to New York. On his arrival from London, he answered reporter's questions about Argentina's concession on the issue of sovereignty, stating that it was not of any significance. A short time later, he delivered to Dr. Perez de Cuellar a document outlining Britain's position regarding the dispute, with a final statement indicating that the basic terms were unalterable and nonnegotiable. The basic points stated that the agreement covered only the Falkland Islands, that two advisory councils with a single Argentine representative should be maintained in the islands, and that the 1971 communications agreement would be renewed following withdrawal of Argentine forces. It also called for the British fleet to remain on station at a distance of 150 miles. The paper was delivered to Ambassador Ros at 1545 hours New York time. The British demanded an answer by the following day.

In the meantime, Mrs. Thatcher's public position was becoming ever stiffer. The sense of her statements could be summed up as follows:

1. The British government had made every possible concession.
2. Aggression, as an example to future generations, should not be allowed to emerge triumphant.
3. There was no division within the Cabinet; rather, interest was concentrated on keeping British loss of life in the South Atlantic to a minimum.
4. It was unacceptable that Argentina aspire to solutions that prejudged the outcome.
5. The United Kingdom did not stand to lose the support of the international community.

At the same time, representatives of the EEC countries met and decided to extend sanctions imposed against Argentina for another seven days. This fell considerably short of Great Britain's wishes. This lack of enthusiasm on the part of the members of the Brussels Club should not be construed as a political decision. What Great Britain's partners were really seeking was further concessions in the area of farm prices, which means they were less concerned about the events unfolding in the South Atlantic than about the advantages to be gained by their EEC partner.

In Buenos Aires, the British proposal was given careful consideration that very day. It was concluded that:

1. The South Georgia and South Sandwich Islands were not covered.

2. For practical purposes, the Malvinas would again come under British administration.

3. No previous U.N. resolutions were mentioned. Article 73 of the U.N. Charter was quoted, which involved bringing into question the issue of nonautonomous territories. This was unacceptable for Argentina.

4. No prejudgment had been inferred as far as future sovereignty was concerned.

5. The interim agreement did not provide for a stated expiration date.

On the following day, having thoroughly studied the issue, the Argentine government forwarded to the secretary general a text outlining Argentina's position, which was deemed flexible. It did not modify the British document, which had been issued as definitive. The document was delivered to the British delegation at 2235 hours.

Intense consultations were held on April 19 as the secretary general attempted to reconcile each party's positions. But Britain felt that it had gone to the limit in its response to Argentina's proposal of April 18, since most of the 11 points had been deemed unacceptable. Great Britain, moreover, felt that the negotiations were closed. So much so that the British proposal became an ultimatum, for nonacceptance meant war.

Thus British diplomacy had achieved rationalization for the forthcoming landing at San Carlos. It had successfully concealed Britain's intractable stance and made Argentina appear unyielding, while buying the time needed to mount Operation Corporate. Britain would steer the course it had set on April 4: to expel Argentina from the islands and reestablish British rule there.

As for hostile action on April 17, a naval bombardment against Port Harriet was initiated at 0019 hours, and an enemy helicopter dropping flares around Fitz Roy was repelled. At 0825 hours, a flight of Sea Harriers approached Freycinet Peninsula from the east and released two bombs. One landed in an uninhabited area, and the other splashed into the sea. At 1433 hours, a Navy F–28 flew into Malvinas, followed at 1558 and 1730 hours by two C–130 shuttle flights, shadowed at a distance by prowling CAPs. The *Pucaras* flew some reconnaissance flights, and long-range probes flew from the mainland. In the meantime, Artillery Group 3 put the finishing touches on the new 155mm battery emplacement at Lookout Rocks.

ACTION ON MAY 18

The Argentine government mulled the possibility of resorting to the U.N. General Assembly if no solution were forthcoming in a reasonable period of time. The foreign minister met with political leaders to keep them abreast of events and to sound out possible options as they were being broached to the military government. There was now an agreed position on the controversial issue of Argentine sovereignty over the islands. But as the military junta went over the British proposals again, they realized a fact that had already begun to dawn: the government they represented had painted itself into a corner. There was no way out; no doors, no windows through which to flee the dogged determination of the British Conservative government, which had seized upon this conflict as a windfall opportunity to consolidate its domestic position and to blind British public opinion to other issues that had beset Mrs. Thatcher prior to April 2, to the extent that the outcome of the forthcoming British elections had been in doubt.

In light of this discouraging political setting, the words of columnist C. Monnier gain currency:

The Falklands dispute, as well as infighting within the Common Market, serve to underscore certain persistent British characteristics. Following her entry into the EEC, Great Britain came to realize that some "investments" outweighed their returns. She did not stop short of blackmail to bring about a change in the bylaws, even to the point of threatening withdrawal from the group and carefully obstructing its functioning. In her community relations, Great Britain appeals to pragmatism, . . . while presenting herself, in the Falklands conflict, as the defender of the principle that it is unacceptable to modify the international order of things by means of violence. (*La Suisse* [Geneva], May 18)

The landing and the establishing of a beachhead at San Carlos Bay was to be called Operation Sutton. The plan was laid before the War Council by the British chiefs of staff on May 18. Each service chief outlined the chances and risks of the operation, which was later the object of a briefing for the full Cabinet. There was no doubt by this time that the operation would go ahead regardless of the status of the talks and the disappointment felt by the Royal Navy for having failed to win the air war. The issue of air supremacy had been a thorny one for Admiral Woodward, who had had his share of disagreements with Brigadier Thompson, who in turn had expressed deep concern over the fact that the task force had been unable to achieve air superiority by mid-May.* Never once had he been officially told that the Royal Navy's pledge of air superiority over the

---

*The first agreement made by the commanders at Ascension called for carrying out the operation under an umbrella of complete air superiority. Admiral Woodward had affirmed at the time that this was the Royal Navy's show, and not that of the commander of land forces. He had made light of the concern that it might not be achieved.

beachhead could not be fulfilled. Brigadier Thompson became obsessed with the issue: "I don't care what happens to your ships," he stated, "... I am going in to win the war." The success or failure of Great Britain's designs rested on his shoulders alone. He knew there would be no second chance.

The disputes arising among the top brass of the task force and of the land forces could be traced to a decision made by the War Council on May 8. It had been decided, for reasons more political than military, to go ahead with the task force even though it could not count on air supremacy, for they could not scrub the whole operation and bring the expeditionary force home empty-handed. Obviously, these statesmen preferred to bring their armed forces home with their hands full, albeit with the blood of several hundred men as the cost. Arguments within the staffs became so heated that several of their members contacted their superiors in London and asked them to visit Ascension.

The commander of the SBS Squadron was bitterly upset by the task force commander's decision to sail for the South Atlantic, leaving him and his staff behind at Ascension on board the *Fearless* while his men were being shipped out with part of their equipment still on the runway at Wideawake. They had been told the Harriers would stand between them and the mainland. The Amphibious Force task group rendezvoused with the *Hermes* on the high seas. Step by step, three days from D-Day, the task force was preparing for the final push that would spell success or failure of the mission for which they had been deployed to the South Atlantic.

Meanwhile, in the Malvinas theater of operations, a lull fell over the area. Malvinas base sustained several Sea Harrier raids. A third U.S. tanker was deployed to Ascension to ensure the vital flow of fuel to the ships and planes of the task force. One Sea King helicopter was lost to mechanical failure but its crew was picked up. At 1615 hours, a C–130 made the shuttle run into Malvinas during a lull in CAP activity. At Port Howard, the 5th Infantry Regiment skirmished with an enemy patrol. Pucaras on reconnaissance in the area provided air cover. Under cover of darkness, task force ships tried to move up for their nightly bombardment, but were repelled by the Sofma guns, and on the mainland, three C–130s were being made ready for a paradrop resupply run.

ACTION ON MAY 19

In New York, Secretary General Perez de Cuellar was faced with a fait accompli. As he stared at Britain's final proposal, which he knew would be unacceptable to Argentina, he realized that his initiative was at an end. The Argentine government submitted a document to the secretary general that was not so much a response to what amounted to a British ultimatum as it was a position statement. The U.N. top officer's final efforts only served to underscore the fact that Great Britain regarded the negotiations as closed.

Incoming cable traffic on April 19 reported U.S. aid to Great Britain and served to enhance the shameful conduct of Secretary of State Haig toward a country that had placed its trust in its big brother to the north, who in turn had incited the European NATO allies to condemn Argentina roundly in the international community. The *Journal de Genève* told the sad tale:

Peering out over the Guns in London and Buenos Aires

Talks on Malvinas within the framework of the U.N. have been suspended for 24 hours in order to allow Argentina to study the British proposal.

The British War Council has sized up the readiness of their forces, the weather conditions, and other decisive elements weighing into the order to proceed with the attack. The meeting was held in a crisis atmosphere. In Luxembourg, Alexander Haig and Joseph Luns [NATO secretary general] issued a statement declaring the full support of Britain's allies, even at the expense of worsening the state of affairs with Argentina. The 15 NATO foreign ministers reaffirmed their total backing of London and their condemnation of Argentina's act of aggression. This success was tempered, however, by the fact that only seven of the EEC member nations decided to extend their economic sanctions against Argentina.

In the islands, May was a month of dwindling rations for units in the field, especially those manning remote outposts. The lack of helicopters for ferrying food and supplies, added to the absence of safe means of interisland surface shipping, caused these outlying units to endure conditions of real hardship, so much so that headquarters had to resort to dropping supplies from C–130 aircraft. At 1614 hours that day, the beleaguered garrison saw eight tons of rations and supplies parachute from a Hercules sortie that had managed to elude marauding Sea Harrier flights and enemy ships lurking offshore, thus alleviating what had become a critical shortage.

In other news that day, the discovery of what appeared to have been an intentionally torched Sea King helicopter in neighboring Chile made headlines. The chopper had British markings, registry ZA 290, and appeared to have made an uneventful landing, following which its crew burned and abandoned it. No trace of the latter was found. This Sea King seemed to be part of an airborne commando operation flown from a nearby vessel and aimed at infiltrating operatives into Argentine territory. The apparent mission was surveillance and possible sabotage of Argentina's southern air bases, as well as to serve as an early warning system whenever warplanes sortied. The commandos were unable to fulfill their mission. They lost their bearings as they trekked overland, and eventually were evacuated from Chile.

The biggest news event of the day was the British announcement of the loss of a Sea King helicopter at sea, with all hands: 22 SAS commandos and two crew members. This accident, apparently caused by engine failure due to an albatross having been sucked into the intake scoop, was the worst to befall the SAS Squadron since 1945. The men who perished in this incident had taken part in the retaking of South Georgia and the successful assault at Sea Elephant Bay. British sources made no mention of the failed commando attempt on May

16 nor the casualties sustained by that unit, which leads one to surmise another "accident" as a cover for the casualties sustained during the *Bouchard*'s preemptive attack.

Further news was similar to that of previous days. Naval gunfire occurred at 0150 hours against the coast of Choiseul Sound, where no troops nor guns were in place. There were isolated Sea Harrier raids on the airstrip, and at 1620 hours, two Sea Harriers jettisoned their bombs into the sea. The blockade was foiled once again by a C–130, which shuttled into Malvinas at 1315 hours, followed by a Navy F–28, which landed at the base at 1610 hours.

The British Defense Ministry acknowledged the loss of two Wessex and one Sea King helicopters. The usual evening call by British gunboats was repulsed by the Sofmas at 2230 hours, which wrapped up the day's activities.

ACTION ON MAY 20

Argentina's last-ditch efforts at diplomacy proved, as could be expected, totally barren. Mrs. Thatcher charged that Argentina had rejected all of her peace offerings, and therefore all proposals were off. Nothing was left on the table to negotiate. The British media, "misinformed" by their own services, broadcast flawed reports regarding the state of the talks, thereby concealing a terrible truth.

This sounded the death knell of the military junta's policy of "occupy to negotiate," established prior to April 2. This aim was totally overwhelmed by the policy of "no negotiation but retake militarily," imposed from the very outset by the British government. A cruel design indeed, for Great Britain, with its winning diplomacy and its allies, could have achieved a renewal of the talks that could have stretched out, for all purposes, indefinitely, as they had prior to April 2, and thus avoided sending so many young Britons and Argentines to their deaths on the battlefield. In this, the United States shares a heavy burden of guilt.

In the waning hours of April 20, Dr. Perez de Cuellar notified the Security Council that his initiative had come to naught. At that time, the British joint task force was steaming inside the exclusion zone on a direct heading for the north mouth of San Carlos Strait (Falkland Sound), in its bid to establish a beachhead on the Falkland Islands.

On May 19, Sir John Fieldhouse, commander in chief of the British fleet, had radioed Admiral Woodward the code word that was the green light to proceed with the attack, on the date and at the hour of his choosing. The commander of the task force felt the burden of responsibility weigh heavy on his shoulders. It was his meteorologists' call. The weather and time had to be right. Conditions should be just bad enough to keep the Argentine Air Force on the ground, but good enough to allow his own helicopters to operate. The weathermen warned that there was no such thing as a sure thing, for there was always a 30 percent chance that conditions could undergo a sudden change.

Another decision that was Woodward's alone was the time of the landing.

Brig. Julian Thompson wanted to make landfall at the appointed spot early in the evening, in order to ensure as many hours as possible of darkness to secure the beachhead before being discovered and attacked by the Argentine Air Force. But Commodore Michael Clapp, commander of the amphibious forces, wanted to make the crossing to San Carlos Strait under cover of darkness for as long as possible, in order to lessen the chances of his ships being sighted and attacked prior to the landing. A compromise was reached. H-hour would be 0130 on April 21, a decision that would insulate Admiral Woodward if he had to rationalize a failure.

Having overcome these two problems, Admiral Woodward mulled over the great unknown factor that had so long been at issue during the planning phase of Operation Sutton: How would enemy aviation respond, and what was the extent of the damage they could inflict upon the amphibious force? He disagreed with Brigadier Thompson and other members of his staff over the potential offensive capability of Argentina's air forces. He trusted in his ships' ability to fend off any such attacks, were they to come. On the final approach to the beachhead at San Carlos, the amphibious force would sail in tight formation to achieve maximum cover from the defense shield provided by the two available Class 22 frigates fitted with the Sea Wolf system. He was further aware of the liability of what had come to be called the Great White Whale, a nickname for the Canberra, which stuck out like a sore thumb among the warships that surrounded it. A single successful attack against this ocean liner, or against one of the light carriers, would doom any favorable outcome for the British expeditionary force. Once he had reached San Carlos Bay, he would slip his fleet into the inlet. There the combined vessels would constitute a formidable challenge to any enemy attempt to attack such a well-defended target, and would be sheltered from the Exocet threat, as well as from Argentina's submarine fleet, which was effective only in open water.

Woodward also gave great weight to the advice of a veteran U.S. combat pilot, Col. James MacManaway, U.S. M. C., who, having been consulted prior to the initiation of hostilities, had asserted that Argentina's air assets were vastly inferior to the Sea Harriers, whose chances for success, even if the adversary's aging fleet of poorly equipped Skyhawks and Mirages were doubled, were seen by him to be excellent. In MacManaway's estimation, the Skyhawk was a 1954 vintage design, outmoded, 110 mph slower than the more maneuverable Harrier; and the Mirage-III and Mirage-V, although faster—even supersonic—could not make use of this extra speed, for to achieve it, the afterburner had to be used. Doing so greatly increases fuel consumption, which in turn shortens the range, a crucial factor in the Malvinas conflict, where distance from base to target and back figured vitally in the balance.

Regarding the Argentine Air Force's prospects of an attack against the British fleet, MacManaway felt the only effective option would be to mount a mass offensive, using all assets simultaneously. Aircraft that made it through the ring of Sea Harriers would be brought down by missiles fired from ships lying on the outer perimeter. Any aircraft foiling this line of defense had a remote chance of coming within attack range of a ship only if it was not taken out by antiaircraft fire.

MacManaway was also of the opinion that to put one of the British carriers out of action would require mounting a mass attack, in which as many as 50 aircraft could be lost, an almost unacceptable kill rate. The colonel's military experience, added to the fact that the U.S. Marine Corps flies the Sea Harrier, weighed mightily in the balance, to the extent that the phrase coined to describe the problem was that the British had hawks, while the Argentines had blackbirds, a statement soon picked up on by British Defense Secretary John Nott.

Admiral Woodward was confident that his losses might amount to one or two ships, at the most. The fleet, which was lying to the northeast, was reprovisioned, and the Amphibious Force was ordered into the exclusion zone on a heading toward Puerto Argentino. Once in sight of the islands, they were to change to a westerly course, and head for San Carlos Strait.

Two C–130 aircraft succeeded in running the blockade. As they approached for landing, they encountered strong crosswinds that forced one to turn away. As this flight, code-named Acuario, did so, it was picked up by the British, who swiftly sent up two CAPs in hot pursuit. Having aborted its landing attempt, the lumbering Hercules set out on the return flight to the mainland. Its only defense against the pursuing CAPs was to drop down to sea level and make its escape to the west. After it had disappeared from British radar, it executed a 90° turn right, on a northerly heading, while the CAPs kept up their search to the west. They returned empty-handed to their carrier, while the C–130 again set a course for the mainland. The other C–130 dropped 9.5 tons of supplies and rations over Fox Bay for the troops manning the outpost, in what would be the final airdrop of the war. The operation was carried out uneventfully in spite of strong winds prevailing in the area.

About that time, and for the first time in the theater of operations, GR–3 Harriers, freshly transferred from the vertical takeoff or landing (VTOL) platform rigged on the *Atlantic Conveyor*, sortied from the *Hermes* into the combat zone.

By midnight, the Amphibious Force had succeeded, against all odds, in evading discovery by the Argentines. This was the most critical juncture of the penetration, for the Argentine Air Force could have inflicted a terrible toll on ships laden with men and materiel, had they been detected. Our navy headquarters had not, however, reckoned that San Carlos Bay was a proper location for a serious landing attempt, mainly because of its limited size. Argentine scout aircraft also failed to spot this powerful landing force approaching the coastline. When they finally did so, it was too late.

THE POLITICAL ARENA: MAY 21–27

The U.N. Security Council: *Verba, non res*

The task force hit the beach at San Carlos Bay on May 21. The public was kept abreast of the news by communiqués released by the Argentine Joint Staff that were also forwarded to the U.N. Security Council. Until that time, Argentina had entrusted negotiations to the U.N. secretary general. Great Britain had broken off further talks within that organization, but not before setting aside Dr. Perez de Cuellar's appeal to refrain from resorting to acts of war during his initiative. It was plain that Great Britain had resorted to dilatory diplomatic tactics. It had left both the secretary general and a new proposal by President Belaunde Terry dated May 20—which Argentina had accepted—unanswered, while pursuing a propaganda campaign that Buenos Aires was to blame for the breakdown of the talks.

As British troops were preparing to go ashore at San Carlos, cable traffic at the Foreign Ministry indicated that U.S. ambassador to the United Nations Jeane Kirkpatrick had intervened, appealing to Argentina to accept Dr. Perez de Cuellar's proposal, now backed up by President Belaunde Terry's second proposal, with minor amendments to the original wording. "If you say yes, you come out in any event as the net gainers in the conflict,"said Mrs. Kirkpatrick to the Argentine delegation. This appeal was sadly misdirected, for it was not Argentina that was turning a deaf ear to the offers, but Great Britain.

The Security Council held a meeting on the morning of May 21, during which it was apprised of the failure of the secretary general's initiative. This meeting came at a very bad time for Great Britain—which was seeking to secure a beachhead—and for the United States, since the public debates would lay bare the latter's opposition to Argentina. Later in the day there was an informal meeting of that body that began at 2:30 P. M. with a briefing by the secretary general outlining his failed initiative, followed by statements by Dr. Ros and other speakers. Foreign Minister Costa Mendez was on his way to New York to attend the meeting the following day.

European concern could be summed up in a news item published in *La Suisse*:

London Makes Europe Dance to the Tune of Its Flute.

On entry to the EEC in 1973, Great Britain became a party to the Treaty of Rome. She subsequently became aware that by sharing in the various Common Market systems, she was giving more than she was getting back. She sought to amend her status. She did not hesitate to resort to blackmail (We are prepared to pull out of the Common market) and to systematic obstructionism (her current rejection of farm prices negotiated in Brussels until . . . her request for "accommodation" has been accepted).

In other words, Great Britain has made light of the very basis of any juridical order, the principle of *pacta sunt servanda*: that a deal is a deal. (If this principle is rejected, we might as well return to the law of the jungle, where the rules are written by the strongest in keeping with their own best interests at a given moment.)

Great Britain has argued in her defense that when the terms of an agreement become impossible for one of the parties to fulfill, such an agreement must be amended: such is British pragmatism.

In the Falklands dispute, on the other hand, Great Britain has based her whole case on the defense of a different principle, whereby it is unacceptable to resort to violence to modify the international order. This is where British pragmatism comes up short, by giving to steel-handed toughness.

In the first example, England is asking the Continent to "be flexible"; in the second instance, she is calling on it to "be firm, please." Such contradictory attitudes have a single common benchmark that both identifies and rationalizes them: British interest. Or, at least, what Mrs. Thatcher perceives as the British interest.

It can be seen here that Britain has relinquished none of her insular habits. She establishes what her interest is, and, by whatever means at hand, attempts not only to bend everyone else to her will, but to say that she is right in the bargain. Certainly, continental Europeans are no babes in the woods, and are surely sometimes prone to rethink their positions. Not so, superb and egocentric England.

British selfishness leaves continental Europe somewhat at the mercy of British whim. Therefore, in the case of the Falklands, continental Europe found herself having to accept jeopardizing her future relationship with Latin America by proclaiming [illegal] sanctions against Argentina, all while taking up the slack, on very short notice; for the Royal Navy, in the performance of Atlantic defense duties normally ascribed to it, had suddenly gone A.W.O.L. [absent without leave].

The Americans lost no time in sending this message to Europe:

1. The Falklands dispute shows that you have interests to uphold beyond Europe and the United States.

2. The time has come to extend formally the boundaries of NATO to allow European military forces to carry out security operations throughout the world.

As one can see, England—impossible though that may seem—has compelled continental Europe to embark upon a voyage with her to faraway seas. May Heaven help us to gain our sea legs.

While the delegates from the nations within the Security Council outdid each other with flourishes of eloquence, Britain remained steadfastly entrenched in its ironfisted determination not to talk. The representatives of Spain, Uruguay, Mexico, New Zealand, Venezuela, the Soviet Union, Canada, Cuba, the United States, and Bolivia, followed by France, Nicaragua, Poland, Colombia, Honduras, Peru, and Panama, lined up at the podium in turn. The attack against Great Britain in some of the statements was so stinging that its delegate exercised his right to reply. The tempest of rhetoric grew stronger as the list of speakers lengthened; but no mere words could abate this storm, for if the United Kingdom had harbored no will to achieve a negotiated settlement to this issue, it would be even less so inclined at the very moment it was securing a beachhead.

The Argentine Foreign Ministry began to consider the possibility of seeking relief under the Rio Treaty. It was May 23. This was particularly disturbing to the United States, for it could only wreak further havoc with the conciliatory stance Washington was so anxious to assume vis-à-vis the Latin American community, which had been wounded to the quick by the U.S. pro-British posture in the conflict. Statements made by Secretary of State Haig on "Face the Nation" about that time did nothing to allay the malaise. He held that the United States would stand by the policy made public on April 30, in which it had stated that the use of force made no sense and could not be justified. The United States, according to Haig, supported the United Kingdom militarily, short of sending troops. Argentina had affirmed that it was receiving no assistance from the Soviet Union, and he had no reason to doubt its word. Argentina was, however, receiving aid from other Latin nations, although it was very low key. Secretary Haig went on to say that the United States had issued a warning to the Soviet Union not to make this crisis into an East-West confrontation. He further added that the United States had no interest in new Security Council resolutions, since 502 contained all the elements needed to deal with the problem. He stopped short, however, of casting any light on why he failed to apply, in his own backyard, a policy similar to that followed in the 1956 Suez crisis, in which the United States had nipped in the bud a Franco-British expedition aimed at gaining control of that strategic waterway, demanding the withdrawal of European and Israeli troops from Egypt, thus precluding a broader conflict and earning the trust of the Arab world.

At the same time, the U.S. and British press were touting the flow of supplies flooding into Ascension from the United States by both surface and air transport, for transshipment to the task force. Three tanker loads of fuel, satellite weather information, KC–135 aircraft—to replace British Victors that had been deployed to the South Atlantic—were being sent to Great Britain, along with additional AIM–9/L Sidewinder missiles to replenish its dwindling arsenal. Facilities at Charleston, South Carolina, were being made available to the British to overhaul and refit their tankers for service with the task force.

To make things worse, the London media spread all this good news, enhancing the facts with lengthy British "wish lists," regardless of whether all the goods would actually be delivered. This British reaction to the U.S. contribution to its war effort had a strong political effect. It was a media blitz, but in all the turmoil the British lost view of the fact that they were seriously undermining their ally's future relationship with the denizens of its own backyard.

In London, The *Sunday Times* sounded a cry in the darkness: " . . . maintain the Islands will entail a military, administrative, and financial effort all out of proportion to Great Britain's needs and interests. There is no British interest linked to these Islands." The London daily erred only by omitting the word "legitimate" from that last statement, for it is well known that the government had every intention of milking the crisis to the benefit of the governing party, since this was the all-powerful piston rod that cranked the drive wheels down the track onto which it had inexorably switched itself.

At the United Nations, the flood of words continued to crest. The Soviet Union charged Britain with completely abandoning the talks. Panama, Venezuela, and Nicaragua made pointed reference to the arbitrariness of EEC sanctions against Argentina. Argentina denounced arbitrary EEC sanctions, the British military onslaught, and the British threat to include the Rio de la Plata in the exclusion zone, which was a source of deep concern to Uruguay, and had elicited an immediate response from the Soviet Union. Uruguay recognized Argentina's sovereign rights over the southern island chains. Brazil submitted its own peace proposal to both parties. Surinam supported Argentina's claim.

China wrapped up its presentation with the following reflection:

The government and the people of China have always strongly supported the struggle of Third World Nations to safeguard their sovereignty and territorial integrity. The Argentine people's national aspiration to safeguard their sovereign right is understandable.

It is our sense that the Security Council should uphold the recent findings of the Non-Aligned Nations Bureau of Coordination and the OAS meeting of consultation of foreign ministers, and support Argentina's claim to sovereignty over the Falkland Islands.

On May 24, the EEC again resolved to extend the deadline for economic sanctions against Argentina, which had already been extended that month.

Argentina's Foreign Minister made a formal statement for the record, clearly expressing a reality that should not be forgotten:

At the same time the British have renewed their military offensive against Malvinas Islands, the European Community has renewed its political support of the aggressor.

By deciding to extend indefinitely their embargo against exports to Argentina, the European Community has reaffirmed a conduct that is an open violation of the U.N. Charter and GATT. This time, they have acted at the very moment that the Security Council, a body that is empowered by the U.N. Charter to impose sanctions, was met . . . to consider the conflict.

The vested interests of the North have prevailed over the political deportment of the Community. The appeals of the American nations within the framework of the Rio Treaty, and those of Latin America and other developing nations on numerous occasions and in numerous settings, have fallen on deaf ears.

The government of Argentina deplores that, far from contributing to the cause of peace, the conduct of the European Community has had the practical effect of encouraging military aggression. We feel that such an attitude on the part of the European Community has caused serious damage to North-South relations, and are of the sense that the interests of the developing nations have been jeopardized.

It had become obvious that the old Latin adage *Res, non verba,* was being properly applied by some, and backward by others.

Resolution 505 of the Security Council

On May 25, as Pope John Paul II made known his wish to visit Buenos Aires, the first arguments were being submitted to the Security Council, which had opened discussions at 1030 hours, New York time. Foreign Minister Costa Mendez took that opportunity to make a presentation summing up Argentina's position and case. The following day, Resolution 505, based on a draft submitted by Ireland, and seconded by Guyana, Togo, Jordan, Uganda, and Zaire, was adopted. The Argentine delegate expressed his gratitude for the efforts toward peace being made within the framework of that body. He was followed by the representatives from the United Kingdom, Spain, Ecuador, and Colombia.

For all practical purposes, the resolution was of little or no significance: It served more as an acknowledgment of the secretary general's efforts, and the expression of the wish for compliance with Resolution 502 and the achievement of peace in the area. It concluded with the hope that the secretary general would pursue his peace initiatives. For a body entrusted with such a heavy responsibility, it was as unimpeachable as it was insignificant.

May 25 being Argentina's National Day, the Casa Rosada received a stream of greetings and congratulatory messages from numerous countries. One of them stood out, so surprising was its wording. From President Reagan, on behalf of the United States, came the following:

The people of the United States join me in expressing to you and to the people of Argentina our warm and sincere congratulations on your national holiday. Never has it been more important to reaffirm the common interests and values which link Argentina and the United States, and to reiterate our pledge of cooperation in this hemisphere and throughout the world.

It was painfully plain that this was a canned message, one that could be sent to any country in the world. All one had to do was fill in the blanks: name of country, date of holiday. It was also plain that the Washington bureaucracy was not geared to interpret the facts of life as they were being lived at that time by both countries. Somebody neglected to edit the computer-generated message. That is the problem with computers. Anything not programmed into its memory banks, such as a war, is passed over as if nothing had happened, and business goes on as usual.

Whatever the reason for that glitch, President Galtieri could in no way have let such a golden opportunity slip through his hands. The next day, the following message went out to President Reagan:

Mr. President: If our government and our people are at a loss to understand the totally unexpected position of the United States in taking up Britain's side in her conflict with Argentina, today, upon receiving your congratulatory message on the occasion of our May 25 celebration, our consternation is boundless.

Your affirmation that "Never has it been more important to reaffirm the common interests and values which link Argentina and the United States, and to reiterate our pledge of cooperation in this hemisphere and throughout the world" is completely at odds with your government's current position, and is therefore incomprehensible under the circumstances.

In another vein, cable traffic on May 26 noted the arrival in Singapore of the New Zealand frigate *Canterbury*, on the first leg of a voyage to the South Atlantic to do its bit for the United Kingdom. In view of the course of the conflict, was this really necessary? Here was a completely gratuitous act of aggression by a sovereign nation that Argentina had in no way harmed. Rather, both countries had brought about a first, by establishing air service linking them, the thrust of which had been to break the traditional isolation in which both out-of-the-way nations had been bound. This had opened up bright prospects for further links between Oceania and the Southern Cone area of South America. This regrettable decision proved to be as unique—no other country followed suit—as it was irrelevant militarily and senseless politically.

Meanwhile, in New York, Dr. Perez de Cuellar picked up his renewed mandate from the Security Council and pursued it vigorously. As for achieving any meeting of the minds between the parties to the dispute, his effort would again prove futile, for nothing had really changed. What could possibly lead to the belief that Great Britain might back away from its obstinate design?

In Buenos Aires, the City Council bowed to popular demand and issued an ordinance changing the name of Britannia Square to Argentine Air Force Square, in tribute to the latter's performance, and in sad recognition of the state of affairs with the former.

In London, the press gave prominent coverage to a U.S. State Department release: "The Reagan Administration appears confident today that British forces in the Islands would achieve a quick victory over the Argentines. Mr. Haig expressed the hope that Great Britain, having been vigorous in battle, would be magnanimous in victory" (*The Guardian*, May 25).

Rio Treaty: *Verba, non Res*

In the face of repeated British actions tending to negate any possibility of negotiating a way out of the conflict, as evidenced by London's refusal to support the secretary general's initiatives, Argentine diplomacy sought desperately for some avenue that would open the way to talks. The focus was on the provision of Resolution 502 dealing with cessation of hostilities. In seeking leverage to bring the United States and Great Britain to accept a cease-fire, Argentina turned to the area countries, where sympathy for its position had been the strongest. In earlier contacts with the member nations of the Organ of Consultation, Argentina had underscored its intention to achieve a vigorous condemnation of Britain's aggression while seeking the lifting of U.S. sanctions.

The meeting of the Rio Treaty countries was set for May 27. On that date, the British forces that had landed at San Carlos were already spearheading a drive to retake Darwin-Goose Green, and the Washington and London media were giving ample coverage to the flow of U.S. military supplies to Great Britain.

The twentieth meeting of consultation of the Inter-American Treaty for Reciprocal Assistance (Rio Treaty) was a storm of controversy in which the forces that moved the sovereign decisions of the Latin American states were clearly discernible. The United States brought its full diplomatic pressure to bear throughout the hemisphere in an attempt either to block the meeting or to achieve a resolution that would show it in as favorable a light as possible before its hemispheric neighbors. The Latin American republics were torn between these pressures and their own needs, as well as their emotional empathy for Argentina's situation.

Foreign Minister Costa Mendez made an extensive presentation that focused on the righteousness of Argentina's cause, while Secretary of State Haig underscored the rejection of proposals offered by him, by President Belaunde Terry, and by the government in Buenos Aires. A succession of speakers took the floor during May 27 and part of May 28. Four draft resolutions took shape, and following intense discussions and negotiations both on and off the floor, the draft submitted by Argentina was adopted with minor changes. The unwavering support of numerous countries unwilling to bow to pressure from Washington was as remarkable as it was commendable.

The resolution condemned the "unjustified and disproportionate" attack carried out by the United Kingdom, as well as the establishment of a combat zone. The United Kingdom was called upon to cease its hostilities against Argentina. It further chastised the United Kingdom for obstructing the negotiations initiated by the U.N. secretary general. It urged the achievement of a peaceful settlement. It appealed to the governments of the United States, the EEC, and other states to lift the coercive measures applied against Argentina, and especially called upon the United States to cease its material assistance to the United Kingdom. It further encouraged all to lend "the assistance deemed appropriate by each" to Argentina.

The resolution, as drafted, gave the following perceptions:

1. That Argentina continued, almost without exception, to enjoy the support previously achieved within this group

2. That the provisions of Article 8 of the Rio Treaty, which were mandatory, were not implemented

3. That by and large, the document was nothing more than a statement: it expressed wishes, but fell short of adopting any type of effective measures or sanctions.

As far as the unfolding of military events in the conflict was concerned, the document's effect was null and void. That very day, May 29, the Darwin-Goose Green garrison surrendered to the British. The flow of military assistance continued unabated between the United States and Great Britain. The EEC upheld its sanctions against Argentina, and the Security Council pursued yet another barren course.

The resolution gave the Argentine government no additional negotiating leverage. Its elbow room was inversely proportional to the effort required for Great Britain to retake the islands, an effort that was entirely centered on the military.

10

The Battle of San Carlos

Never in the history of warfare since 1914 have flyers come face to face with such a terrifying convergence of lethal obstacles.
Pierre Clostermann, French World War II ace

In a world such as ours, where the rule of thumb is to demand but not to give, the shining example of these flyers, who gave their all, asking nothing in return, not so much as a pat on the back, is so moving as to blind the senses.
Jose Maria Carrascal, Spanish journalist

THE ENGAGEMENTS OF MAY 21

At 0250 hours, Combat Team Guemes spotted five vessels threading their way south through San Carlos strait. The naval gunfire that had been softening up the northern perimeter of San Luis Peninsula, added to increased air sorties and harassment of the area around Darwin, were telltale signs that the British were coming, that the landing was at hand.

SATO's outline plan dated April 12 did not pinpoint any specific prospective sites for establishing beachheads. This unknown factor was no small source of speculation at Malvinas garrison command headquarters. The commander had drawn up an evaluation that surmised that the enemy, faced with multiple choices, would not readily consider a penetration through San Carlos Strait, if only because, from a naval standpoint, a fleet's capability is linked to its ability to maneuver. This made San Carlos an unlikely candidate for a date with history.

But Admiral Woodward had the good fortune to include among his advisers Maj. Ewen Southby-Tailyour, who had some invaluable experience to share. He knew the coastal areas of the islands like the palm of his hand, for he had spent years sailing in and out and around them in a small sloop. Luck again was a British lady, for he knew the ships would encounter no major difficulty in negotiating the waters of Falkland Sound (San Carlos Strait) or, for that matter, the shallows of San Carlos Bay. Therefore this is where the landing force aimed its thrust. The light carriers were left out of harm's way to the east of the islands, escorted by two warships: the destroyer *Glamorgan* and the frigate *Ambuscade*. The Class 42 destroyer HMS *Exeter* should also have joined this patrol, but apparently was out of commission.

The amphibious force was comprised of the transport *Canberra*, accompanied by the *Fearless* (with Commodore Clapp and his staff aboard), the *Intrepid*, the *Fort Austin*, the *Elk* (laden with 2,000 tons of ordnance), and the *Norland*. Among these were spread the members of the landing party and their equipment, which included eight antiaircraft Rapier missile batteries. These vessels sailed under the cover of the County Class destroyer *Antrim* (also designated a light cruiser), as well as the Class 22 frigates *Broadsword* and *Brilliant;* the Class 21 Frigates *Ardent, Antelope, Argonaut;* and the Rothesay Class *Plymouth* and *Yarmouth*. The last available Class 42 destroyer, *Coventry*, was deployed north of the strait, where it lay on station as a radar picket. The rest of the array included three of Admiral Woodward's four submarines, which lurked in Argentine territorial waters in order to sound the warning of any impending air sorties. The forth submarine roamed about the carrier group, adding to its defenses.

It was clear that the commander of Task Force 317 was incurring great risk to himself. One successful attack against his carriers would spell the doom of the task force. The sinking of any of his transports prior to the landings would mean the failure of the attempt, and discovery of the beachhead before it had been secured could lead to the massacre of his amphibious troops.

HITTING THE BEACHES AT SAN CARLOS

D-Day for the British Amphibious Force was a far cry indeed from those World War II films depicting troops going ashore on tropical palm-lined beaches. As H-hour approached, Brig. Julian Thompson strode about the *Fearless*, steadying his men, instilling confidence. It was the calm before the storm, motionless except for the inner stir of doubt that besets every commander as his most carefully laid plans are on the verge of being submitted to the trial by fire. The silence was shattered by a red alert, the warning of an imminent air raid. Calm was restored upon assurance by the experts, whose intelligence reports had been carefully drawn up, that the "Argies" couldn't fly at night. A false alarm.

After the marine battalion had been loaded aboard the four landing craft and all had been made ready for the final push to the beaches, a holding order came down. There had been an accident aboard the *Norland*, which carried the 2nd Airborne Battalion (the unit that was to spearhead the landings). When they finally set sail, the marines were swallowed up in the blackness of the night as they sought Blue Beach 2, as the landing point had been designated, and proceeded to go ashore at a location not precisely the one designated. Meanwhile,

Map 5
The British Landing on May 21

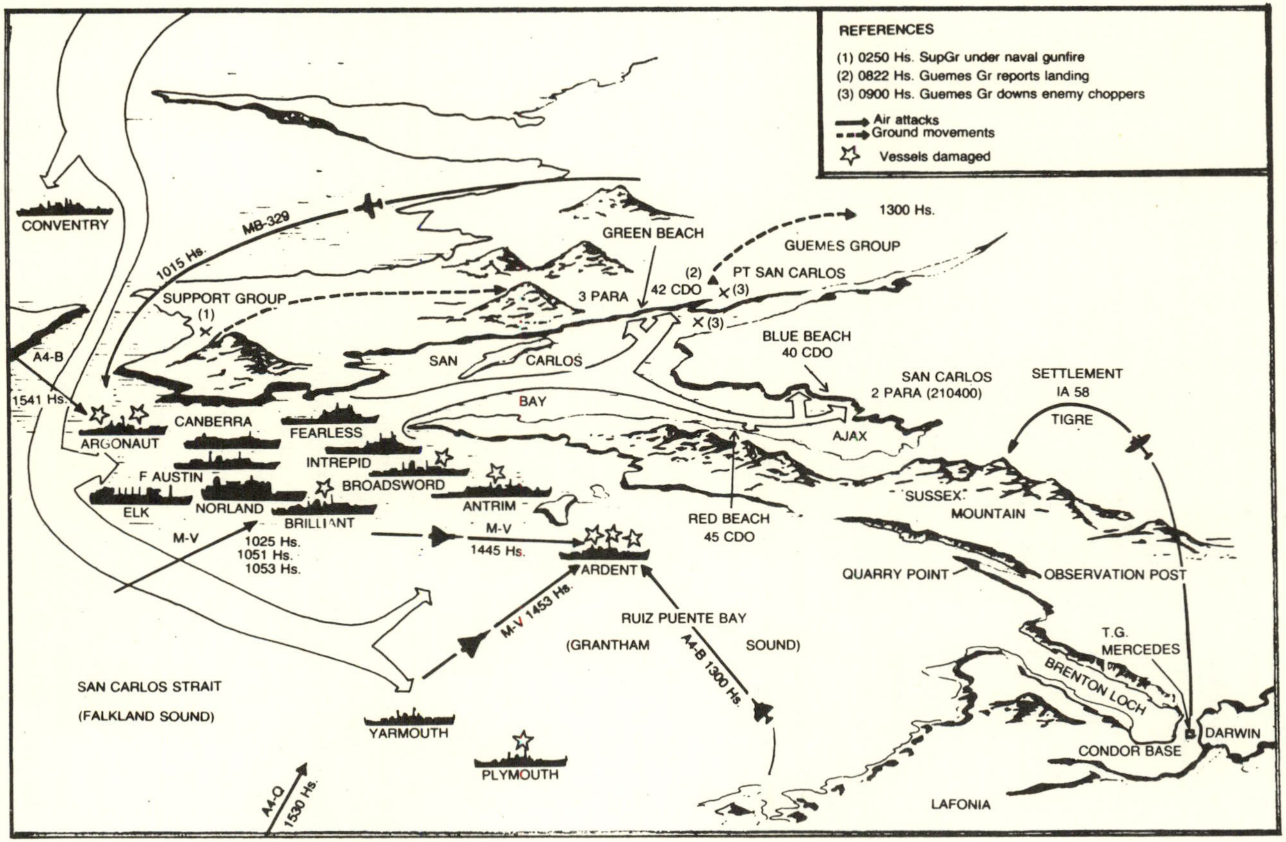

REFERENCES

(1) 0250 Hs. SupGr under naval gunfire
(2) 0822 Hs. Guemes Gr reports landing
(3) 0900 Hs. Guemes Gr downs enemy choppers

→ Air attacks
⇢ Ground movements
☆ Vessels damaged

Company A, 3rd Airborne Battalion, transported aboard the *Intrepid*, initiated its run in the landing craft. As they sailed blindly in the inky darkness, trying to get their bearings for a heading toward the shore, they took three times the time allotted them. As the units attempted to rendezvous, in total darkness and unfamiliar surroundings the lack of coordination was obvious. Daylight—and the total absence of resistance—returned the British landing party to a state of normalcy. The invasion of the Falkland Islands was under way.

The first men to hit the beach landed somewhat behind schedule (at 0400 hours), under the command of Lt. Col. Herbert Jones. The place was the south branch of San Carlos Bay. They were followed, a few minutes later, on the east beach of the bay, by the 40th Marine Commando Battalion, along with the scouting party of Squad B of the Blues and Royals, with their Scorpion and Scimitar armored vehicles.

With daylight came the red alerts as Argentine aircraft approached the area. The first run was made at 0930 hours by a Pucara aircraft, well respected by the British troops for its firepower. Meanwhile, helicopters assisted in the emplacement of the Rapier antiaircraft missile batteries, for the landing party's positions had to be secured against the forthcoming Argentine Air Force raids.

The units took up positions on the beach and on the flanks of the surrounding hills in order to cover an expected thrust by Argentine forces garrisoned at Darwin-Goose Green. Men from Company C, 40th Commando Battalion, ran the Union Jack up a mast near the area administrator's home, thus symbolizing the beginning of the retaking of the Falkland Islands. Across the east branch of the bay, men of the 45th Commando Battalion took up positions in the abandoned refrigeration plant on Ajax Bay. Thus had British forces successfully, and in a surprise action, consolidated the securing of their largest beachhead since World War II, in a place 8,000 miles from home.

But the last word had yet to be said. As wave upon wave of Air Force South aircraft screamed overhead, a nightmare stretched out of what seemed like interminable hours for the Amphibious Force, whose men, both on the beaches and huddled in the holds of the ships, along with their crews, prayed for their lives and awaited the moment they would join their comrades who had found safe haven in their bunkers on land. Through their action that day, Argentine pilots earned the deep respect of the British foe.

Combat Team Guemes enjoyed a ringside view of the most momentous events since April 2. They had deployed a support section to the mouth of the strait, with heavy weapons, while the command group and the rifle company had taken up positions at Port San Carlos. The support section, comprising an officer, 4 NCOs, and 15 men, was positioned on the Guemes promontory, elevation 767 feet, which looks down on the north mouth of the strait and the entrance to the bay. At 0130 hours, they spied the silhouettes of ships threading their way into the strait and opened fire with their recoilless guns. Naval fire forced them to silence their pieces, and their communications gear was knocked out. Running low on ammunition, they fell back to the east, in order to avoid encirclement by the British who had landed northeast of their position, submitting them to heavy fire and causing two casualties. In spite of this, they were able to disengage the enemy, thanks to both fire and movement, by 0500 hours. Following this, they started a long, hard march overland to Puerto Argentino, on short rations, while remaining under cover from the enemy. On June 11, they were captured by the British as they approached Puerto Argentino.

At first light on May 21, an Argentine spotter sighted the *Canberra* groping its way into San Carlos Bay, followed closely by three warships. Landing craft were being lowered from the *Canberra* amid a flurry of helicopter activity. At 0822 hours, the point man of that spotter squad, First Lieutenant Esteban, radioed the commander of Task Force Mercedes, at Goose Green, the news of the landing, which was passed on to the commander of Malvinas military garrison at Puerto Argentino. Following this, the spotters withdrew from Port San Carlos and fell back to previously established positions further east, where they came under heavy British mortar fire while a Sea King helicopter tried to cut them off from the rear. The squad opened fire on the chopper, which sustained damage and was obliged to withdraw. It was followed shortly by a Gazelle, which came in close for a rocket attack. On doing so, it came into range of the squad's automatic weapons fire. Damaged by withering fire, the helicopter dropped from the sky and went into San Carlos Bay with a resounding splash. It was quickly followed by a second Gazelle that made an equally unsuccessful attempt to put Esteban's men out of action. The automatic weapons on the ground exacted their toll, and the chopper careened toward the position of its foes, ripping into the ground in a hail of bullets. All three crew members were killed in action.

The squad held its position until 1300 hours, then proceeded to cover its withdrawal. Fighting effectively, and inflicting casualties on a numerically and tactically superior enemy, Combat Team Guemes (2 officers, 9 NCOs, and 31 men) was able to regroup and shake off its British pursuers. They were picked up by their own helicopters at Douglas Settlement on May 26.

The first reports filtering into General Menendez's staff headquarters on the penetration of several enemy vessels into San Carlos Bay were met with the natural skepticism of those who held that the British landing "could not occur there." It had to be some sort of diversionary tactic. But the truth finally sank in. The British were in fact securing their beachhead. The commander of SATO received the news at 1030 hours, local time. By that time, Air Force South was in the air, streaming toward its targets.

THE AIR FORCE RISES TO THE OCCASION

At 0636 hours, Air Force South had already positioned a KC–130 tanker at a rendezvous point for in-flight refueling of the Skyhawks while the latter feverishly prepared for action against the enemy. Weather reports indicated a low-pressure zone centered southwest of Tierra del Fuego, associated with a cold front holding along the Andes, which meant unfavorable conditions in that area but good operational conditions over the target area, though the latter were expected to deteriorate as the day went on.

At 1004 hours, an Aeromacchi MB–339 aircraft sortied from Puerto Argentino on reconnaissance, followed from Darwin-Goose Green by two flights of Pucaras. The MB–339 headed west along the north coast of the islands. As it flew over the hills north of San Carlos Bay, it spotted the landing force. The pilot, presented with a target of opportunity, took aim and fired his weapons, then made a fast escape east, landing uneventfully but ecstatically at Puerto Argentino, where he lost no time in enthusiastically sharing his experience with his comrades. He was especially in awe of the scope of the enemy Amphibious Force. The object of the MB–339's attention during the attack had been HMS *Argonaut*, which sustained three casualties and heavy damage to its 965 surveillance radar system.

The Darwin-Goose Green garrison had been the object, during the night, of a hostile action carried out by 32 SAS men whose mission it had been to simulate a battalion-sized landing south of that location. Relief was flown in from Condor air base, which sortied four IA–58 aircraft, code-named Tigre (Tiger). At first light, as the squadron was preparing for takeoff, a red alert was sounded as a vessel initiated a bombardment of facilities from out in Falkland Sound. It was the frigate *Ardent*, whose mission it was to harass Argentine troops and pick up the SAS group. Amid bursting shells, the lead aircraft succeeded in taking off and set a southerly heading to carry out the assigned mission. After an hour's flight, and having seen no trace of the enemy, he broadened his reconnaissance radius, gaining enough altitude to allow him to see past the hills into the Sound. And there was his target of opportunity: a British frigate. He had no way of knowing that the landing was in progress, and that as he approached San Carlos, an advance column of Company B, 2nd Airborne Battalion, was lying in ambush. As he passed over, they fired a U.S. Stinger missile that put a sudden end to his sortie. Dangling from his parachute, the pilot landed behind British lines and, following a harrowing escape through enemy-occupied territory and a 17-mile march overland, he returned to base at Darwin, on foot, at 1900 hours.

The other members of the Tigre formation had taken off shortly after their lead man, and proceeded to reconnoiter the San Carlos perimeter. As they came over the spot where the Stinger had been so successfully employed on the first try, its operator tried to make history of the three Pucaras, but his five shots went wild as the formation broke off in various directions. The squadron then took aim on a spot where British troops, apparently an SBS squad that had taken cover in a building, were calling ranges for naval gunfire. The three aircraft streaked over and raked the target with rockets, totally destroying it. But a Sea Harrier CAP had vectored onto the Argentine planes' path, and the chase was on.

Considering that the IA–58 does not carry armament for air-to-air combat, and that its speed is considerably slower, the only way out was to attempt an escape. There ensued a spectacular chase scene, with aircraft buzzing in and out and above and about the topographical features of the area, the Sea Harriers launching missiles as they went, while the Pucaras, thanks to their maneuverability, dodged up and down and over and around, all but one managing to make good their escape. The no. 3 man was brought down by the British 30mm Aden cannon. He ejected and was picked up by his own men. What the Sea Harrier pilots did not know was that three flights of Dagger aircraft were at that very moment gunning for enemy warships in Falkland Sound, entirely unmolested.

That same morning, a British CAP on patrol south of the straits got word of the existence of an Argentine helicopter landing and servicing facility. When they pulled up from the area, one Chinook, one Puma, and one army Huey were in flames, further hampering Argentine mobility, for these were the workhorses of the modern infantry.

The British also paid the price that day. A Harrier from RAF Squadron I was reconnoitering about Port Howard when it was hit by portable arms fire that shook the plane like a hailstorm. It went down over the northern peninsula beyond the harbor as its pilot, First Lieutenant Glover, ejected. He landed in the water with a partially opened parachute, but was safe. Wounded, he was rescued and taken prisoner by Argentine troops. It was 1000 hours. Unconfirmed reports indicated that a second Harrier had fallen prey to a Blow Pipe missile, fired by personnel from the 601 Commando Company in that same area. As the plane went into the waters of the straits, the pilot was not seen to eject. The time was 1520 hours. The RAF was thus feeling the sting of the loss of its scarce assets in combat, for these were not the only aircraft they lost in the course of their deployment to the South Atlantic.

Air Force South to the Attack

The succession of events during the coming hours and days proved to be the most gripping saga of the South Atlantic war, if not one of the most outstanding actions of recent military history. The commander of Air Force South, Brig. Gen. Ernesto H. Crespo, and his second in command, Brig. Gen. Roberto F. Camblor, grasped the immediate significance from the initial reports that something big was afoot in the waters of San Carlos Strait (Falkland Sound), and that, if the landings were on, the only way to forestall them was to send in the attack aircraft at once.

The first diversionary mission commenced at 0930 hours, and the first attack squadron, code-named Nandú (Ostrich) left the runway at 0944 hours. It comprised three Mirage-V Daggers. The mission: attack naval targets in San Carlos Strait. They were followed a minute later by the Perros (Dogs), backed up, at 0953 and 0955 hours, by the Zorros (Foxes) and the Leones (Lions), flying identical formations on a mission with a single objective. At 0956 and 1001 hours, two flights of Mirage-IIIs, configured for air-to-air combat, screamed off to fly cover. At this time, Navy A4-Qs joined Air Force South on the offensive: six Skyhawks, code-named Tábanos (Horseflies), left the runway at Rio Grande at 1018 hours.

In a scant few minutes, over 23 aircraft had been scrambled and were winging toward their target areas. Each Dagger was mounted with an MK–17 1,000-pound bomb, and the A4-Qs carried four MK–82 500-pound bombs each. At 1025 hours, the first of them appeared over the targets. The British CAPs were still on their merry chase over hill and dale behind the elusive Pucaras; thus, the first Argentine attack squadron came over the targets unopposed. The Nandú squadron reached its targets at almost the same time as the Perros. There were the ships arrayed before them across the bay: without trying to identify them, they closed for a daring attack. The targets were a light cruiser, the *Antrim*, and two frigates, the Class 22 *Broadsword* and a smaller vessel. Nandús screamed down at the ships as the latter launched their missiles. Number 2 sustained a missile hit, and the pilot ejected into the bay. He is still listed as missing. Number 1's bomb dropped short of its target, and no. 3's bomb overshot its mark. As they streaked over the ships, their 30mm cannons raked the decks and inflicted serious damage to one in the hangar area. The two aircraft made the return to base without mishap, leaving the *Broadsword* out of commission until nightfall, riddled with over 40 hits throughout the superstructure.

The Perros banked in for an attack on the *Antrim*, which brought all its heavy array of air defenses to bear. But for all its Sea Slug and Sea Cat missiles, its 4.5-inch guns, and its 20mm cannon, it was unable to sway the determined assailants. Its heavy hull was hit by two MK–17 bombs and a hail of cannon fire. Neither bomb detonated, but one smashed through the Sea Slug missile magazine, causing damage that left the ship defenseless. Damaged, it made slow headway in search of shelter within the bay.

At 1035 hours, the three-plane Zorro formation made its entrance on this dramatic stage. It proved to be the lucky day of the ship they chose to attack. As they closed on the *Brilliant*, their bomb releases jammed, but as they passed over, their 30mm cannons blazed away, leaving a gaping hole in the ship's operations room. The *Brilliant* succeeded in escaping major damage, but it sustained numerous casualties and light damage. It nevertheless had to be withdrawn from action, since, in a second wave, the attackers left its complex electronic systems a smoking shambles.

Two minutes later, two Mirage-Vs of the Leon formation made their appearance over San Carlos. They proceeded to attack two unidentified vessels, one a large frigate, with bombs and cannon fire. They watched in frustration as their bombs bounced harmlessly off the ships' hulls without detonating.

The Daggers returned safely to base, where, on debriefing, the pilots excitedly described their attack against a formation of frigates. When the film from the gun cameras mounted aforeships, which operate when the cannon is being fired, was shown, their surprise was boundless. There was the evidence they had crippled the light County Class cruiser *Antrim*, 6,200 tons of steel with a crew of 471 men. To the great consternation of the task force, one of its most formidable capital vessels had to be withdrawn from action for major repairs. During this first wave of attack aircraft, 11 Daggers had achieved penetration to their targets with the loss of only one to British antiaircraft fire. The books balanced favorably. In their wake, several ships lay in various states of disrepair.

Hawks versus Blackbirds

The second attack wave was comprised of A4-B and A4-C aircraft flying out of Santa Cruz and San Julian air force bases. The Skyhawks had an advantage over the Mirage-V Daggers in that they were fitted for in-flight refueling, which allowed them a broader operational range. By the same token, their missions required more careful planning, because the timing for their operations and refueling had to be just right. The KC–130s had to be placed strategically for the incoming and outgoing flights in order to provide the vital fuel for operating over the target area and returning safely to base. Since the Mirage-Vs could not be refueled in flight, their penetrations had to be more direct, which increased their vulnerability.

To intercept their attackers, the British sortied three Sea Harrier CAPs of two aircraft each, one over the north mouth of Falkland Sound, one over the the south mouth, and the third over West Falkland Island. All of them were well armed with the lethal AIM–9L Sidewinder missiles and 30mm cannon. They flew holding patterns for about 20 minutes, and then were relieved by their mates, in order to maintain an ongoing warning system for intercepting and shooting down intruding Argentine aircraft that, in successive waves, closed on the San Carlos area in their thrusts against the amphibious landing force's vessels. This arrangement was not always effective in preventing Argentine squadrons from releasing their bomb loads against their targets, and although the CAPs succeeded in sending a whole formation down in flames, they were unable to discourage the attacking pilots, who came at their targets again and again.

The Argentine aircraft cruised at very high altitude in order to save fuel. About 100 NM from their target areas, they dropped down to sea level, where, as they skimmed the waves, fuel consumption doubled but they were able to evade British radar and thus take British defenses by surprise either through the mouth of the straits or by threading their way through the hills of West Falkland, appearing suddenly over the channel that separates the two main landmasses to ferret out—in the few seconds available to them—their prey, unleash all the bombs and cannon fire they could muster, and then seek the best avenues of escape.

Due to the lack of pinpoint information regarding target location, Air Force South gave its squadron leaders ample initiative to select their prey once they were over the area. Another disadvantage was that radar facilities at Puerto Argentino were too far removed to be of use in vectoring the aircraft, which were, as a result, vulnerable to enemy CAPs. It was also a basic restriction in directing them toward their targets.

A decision that caused much questioning among British forces was the concentration of Argentine air power against naval vessels instead of against troops on the ground. This can be rationalized two ways:

1. The Argentines knew from experience that the soft, spongy Falklands peat bogs served as natural shock absorbers for the explosive force of air-launched ordnance. In order to take out a target that was dug in, every bomb had to be aimed so as to produce a direct hit, thus rendering this tactic completely impractical. The few casualties that could be inflicted against British ground troops versus the cost in downed Argentine aircraft, which would have been frightful, was a strong deterrent. On the other hand, the damaging or sinking of enemy shipping had an immediate and telling effect on beachhead operations.

2. To attack camouflaged ground targets, those targets have to be pinpointed by friendly forces, in order to direct the aircraft to them. The pilot of a modern attack aircraft cannot pinpoint a target unless it is quite large, for his plane flies at speeds of between 800 and 900 feet per second.

Furthermore, fuel constrictions were a crucial factor for attacking pilots, since they prevented them from performing zigzag maneuvers to evade would-be pursuers, making re-runs,* or selecting secondary targets. Once they had penetrated San Carlos Bay, they had to proceed posthaste to the first available target. As soon as an enemy vessel came into view, they pounced. They barely had time to determine the type of vessel they were attacking, so they could hardly afford the luxury of being choosy. Surviving the British air defenses was a feat in itself, eluding pursuing Sea Harriers a greater feat, and making it home on more than fumes was an act of heroism not achieved by all. To return from such a mission without mishap was, to put it bluntly, a contingency based on the bringing together of all the above-mentioned factors. Meticulous calculations, added to the extraordinary good luck of the flyers, must not be hindered by the slightest glitch.

It was a lopsided fight indeed. To come out alive, the Argentine planes first had to foil the CAPs that maintained tight surveillance over the area. They stayed low, for this had proved to be the best incoming tactic. Then they had to fly a gauntlet of concentrated enemy missile and cannon fire coming at them like a storm of hail from a massed array of ships. If they strayed over the opposite coast of the straits, over Soledad (East Falkland Island), a generous welcome from the automatic weapons and missiles of the landed infantry lay in wait. Not to be ignored were friendly areas whose airspace had been designated off limits, and to be shot down by friendly antiaircraft artillery had already proved to be a cruel twist of fate for their planes. And, to top things off, one had to be careful to avoid disturbing the Harriers, which, having been alerted to their presence,

---

*In an aircraft attack maneuver, a rerun is a repeat run over the target, if ammunition remains available. It is exceedingly dangerous to perform when attacking a naval target.

lay in wait for them as they returned to the mainland. These interceptors were well aware that the intruders carried no air-to-air missiles and that, in order to use their cannon, they had to be rid of their external loads (bombs, fuel pods), which could mean the sacrifice of their mission.

Add to all of this the handicap to these aircraft represented by the task force Sidewinders, which turned their pilot's jobs into child's play, for they knew their prey carried no air-to-air armament and that Argentine Mirage-IIIs, whether flying interception, diversion, or escort, could not join the melee for lack of fuel.

Alas, there was truth to the words of Defense Secretary John Nott. Modern British Harrier and Sea Harrier aircraft fought a battle heavily weighted in their favor, as hawks against blackbirds. In fairness, let it be said that this was due as much (if not more) to the circumstances of the engagement as to the skill of their pilots or the performance of their aircraft.

Penetrating the San Carlos area at the controls of a combat aircraft in those days of May was a feat of arms in itself. Coming back for more after having flown into hell and back on the first round, as the brave pilots of Air Force South did again and again, proved that theirs was a mettle far beyond the call of duty. If a chapter on heroism was written during those days, the story was theirs.

In Search of Targets

Eight A4-C aircraft headed out from San Julian air force base between 1117 and 1138 hours, code-named Pato (Duck) Flight. Four were forced to return to base, but the others rendezvoused with the KC–130 and, tanks topped off, arrived over the operations area at 1245 hours. There they penetrated West Falkland by threading through the Hornby Hills. About that time, but approaching from San Julian (Queen Charlotte) Bay to the southwest, came the Mulas (Mules) section, two A4-Bs, piloted by Captain Carballo and Second Lieutenant Carmona, who had left Santa Cruz at 1130 hours. This time the enemy was ready and waiting. As the Sea Harriers led by Group Cmdr. Andy Auld were about to engage the Mulas, they received word that four bandits were headed into San Carlos and, faced with what appeared to be the greater danger, they turned to intercept that formation. The four A4-Cs were still over West Falkland and had yet to reach the combat zone or launch their weapons when the Sea Harriers engaged in hot pursuit. Wingmen nos. 2 and 4 went down in flaming glory, hit by the deadly Sidewinders. The two remaining aircraft were able to make their escape and returned to base, but not before one observed a Sea Harrier crash at Independence (Mount Adams) Hill and explode on impact, due either to pilot error or to some mishap, since neither Argentine pilot had been in a position to go on the offensive. Official British reports made no mention of this incident, although they acknowledged shooting down one Argentine Skyhawk.

The Saga of the Frigate *Argonaut*

The third wave of Air Force South aircraft was comprised of assets from the bases at Rio Grande, San Julian, and Rio Gallegos. A squadron of Mirage-V Daggers, code-named *Cueca* (an Argentine dance) left base at 1355, and the navy A4-Qs again went into action with a six-aircraft squadron code-named Tábano, which took off at 1408 hours. They had a single mission: attack the enemy fleet at San Carlos. A flight of five A4-Bs, code-named Leo, along with a flight of Mirage-IIIs, lifted off from Rio Gallegos, the former to attack naval targets and the latter to fly cover. From San Julian came two formations of Mirage-Vs, code-named Ratón (Mouse) and Laucha (Small Mouse). Within minutes, 23 aircraft were headed for the combat zone, following the path of the first wave, and similarly armed. First over the target area were the Leos, which on arrival at San Carlos at 1437 hours, started combing the Sound from south to north in search of enemy ships.

The Class 21 frigate *Argonaut* was steaming into the mouth of the bay to relieve the light cruiser *Antrim*, which had sustained serious damage during the first wave. Its mission: protect the vital entrance to the beachhead. Suddenly, from the south, a wave of Skyhawks pounced upon it as the helm was spun hard to starboard, toward the shelter of a 600-foot bluff by the north entrance to San Carlos Bay. The gallant ship had already undergone a baptism of fire when it was raked by the cannon of an MB–339. In its second engagement that day, it fired its antiaircraft weapons against its assailants. The incoming fliers bored through the Sea Cat missiles and other projectiles bursting in air, and proceeded to attack with unshakable determination. They took aim and released their bombs. As the lead man—First Lieutenant Filipini—pulled up, he was so close to his target that his left fuel pod struck one of the ship's antennae, twisting it back as he executed a sharp climb to avoid hitting the solid wall of rock that lay dead ahead. None of the Leo Squadron was hit by enemy fire, and all returned safely to base.

HMS *Argonaut* was not so lucky. Two of the five 1,000- pound bombs released against it struck the hull, and the other three streaked over the superstructure, missing by inches, but drenching it in a shower of water and debris as they detonated in the bay. The bombs that found their mark failed to explode, but one came to rest in the boiler, which promptly blew up, filling the compartments with billows of live steam, while the second burrowed below the waterline to the fore, pierced a fuel bunker, and struck the Sea Cat magazine, causing three missiles to explode. Having lost his engines just as he was making full speed, the captain, who saw his vessel heading out of control, with water pouring into the bow and fire before the bridge, ordered the anchors dropped in a desperate attempt to arrest the forward momentum before it smashed into the bluff. All the while he was directing damage control as the spreading flames, and the heat propagated by the fire, started to melt the aluminum superstructure. This prompt action soon brought the fire under control, and with the assistance of helicopters, evacuation of the wounded was initiated as the *Plymouth* pulled alongside to render assistance and shield the *Argonaut* from further attack. At nightfall, it was towed well into San Carlos Bay, where the crew set feverishly about defusing the unexploded bombs, repairing the damage, and making ready the weapons systems to fend off further attackers. It took the crew nine days to make the *Argonaut* seaworthy enough to undertake the long voyage back to England. It was returned to active duty only after more than two years.

Eyewitnesses to the Agony of HMS *Ardent*

Observation post Roca (Rock) had been established atop an outcropping known as Punta Cantera (Quarry Point), behind Ruiz Puente Bay (Grantham Sound) by the air spotter network attached to Condor air base. In that lonely spot, 2nd Lt. Mario Eduardo Egurza and Pvt. Juan Domingo Coronel shared lookout duty over the northwest perimeter of the base. Their sole link with the rest of the Argentine force was their radio and a helicopter that made occasional supply drops. At first light on May 21 they had spied, among the wisps of mist rising from the placid waters of Falkland Sound, the silhouettes of two ships. At 0830 hours, they made out a Class 21 frigate heading slowly into Grantham Sound, which, upon approaching the coast, initiated a naval bombardment against Condor base. Two other vessels kept a constant vigil in the area: the *Plymouth* and the *Yarmouth*. Until noon a ship—which had yet to be identified as the frigate *Ardent*—moved toward the northernmost part of the bay. All of this was dutifully reported to the base by the observer team.

During this time, the Mula section had been freed from the interference of Sea Harriers, which had felt they had found better things to do elsewhere. It flew over Falkland Sound on an easterly heading and, skimming the whitecaps, sighted a ship at Port Egg, on the west coast of East Falkland. The lead man took aim but had difficulty in identifying his target and did not release his ordnance. His wingman's bomb hit what seemed to be a logistics vessel. The leader ordered his young wingman home, since he had dropped his bomb, but kept up the search toward the north, flying over Grantham Sound. Suddenly, there it was: an Amazon Class frigate lying north of the bay. Flying through a withering hail of antiaircraft ordnance, he took aim and released his MK–17.

At the same time, about 1300 hours, the two lone spotters on Quarry Point heard the faraway whine of a jet aircraft coming in through the straits. The dot grew into a single A4-B that streaked through the bay on a beeline for the British ship, passing between its masts. Seconds later an explosion rumbled cross the water as the MK–17 detonated. The frigate was rocked by explosions and shrouded in billowing black smoke as the Skyhawk made its escape westward, having taken note of his hit. The frigate became enveloped in a towering plume of smoke. At about 1400 hours, flames began to flicker about the damaged structure while the crew of the *Ardent* carried on a gallant struggle against the spreading fire and tended to the numerous casualties. But the ordeal was far from over. The third wave of Air Force South aircraft were just coming over the area. The four in Dagger Cueca formation were first, at 1445 hours. They wended their way through a valley in the Hornby Hills on West Falkland. Foul weather forced them down to within feet of the ground. They flew in file under the cloud cover until the leader discerned in the mountains a sort of window, a triangle formed by the sides of two hills and the cloud ceiling. They headed for that window. As they did so, the pilot bringing up the rear of the formation realized a column of pursuing Harriers had locked unto the formation. Trying to warn his comrades, he found his radio was dead. He was caught immediately thereafter by a Sidewinder and ejected, yards off the ground, as his plane splattered over the landscape. He was picked up, alive, the next day.

The rest of the planes, thinking their comrades had missed the window and crashed, headed over the straits in search of their prey. The first ship to appear in their sights lay to the north in Grantham Sound. It was the beleaguered *Ardent*. They went straight for the ship, 30mm cannons ablaze, dropping their MK–17s as they went. The leader's bomb fell ten yards short and pierced the bow at the waterline. Number 3's bomb also found its mark; and as he passed over the ship, he had to execute a sharp turn to avoid hitting a huge chunk of antenna that was cartwheeling over the vessel. The Cuecas gunned their craft for a fast escape, with a Sea Cat missile in hot pursuit of the lead man. The *Ardent*, for all its woes, was putting up a fight to the finish. Number 3 spotted the missile, executed a sharp right turn, and the missile kept on going straight. They returned to base without further mishap at 1528 hours. The *Ardent* was now afire amidships and experiencing steering problems. Watched by the men of the 45th Battalion, which had occupied the heights around the Sussex Hills, the ship started churning in circles.

At 1453 hours, it was the turn of the Laucha Daggers. It is possible that because of its position, which was clearly visible from afar, or because of the smoke, every squadron of attack aircraft that penetrated the bay spotted the the *Ardent* as its first target and made a beeline for it. The *Lauchas* made their pass, cannons ablaze and bombs dropping, while the no. 2 plane headed north to attack another ship that was not immediately identified (possibly the frigate *Alacrity*). At this point, there was a frenzy of Sea King helicopter activity in the area. Suspecting the presence of Argentine submarines, they carpeted the bay with depth charges as another frigate had made its way into these waters (presumably the *Yarmouth* or the *Plymouth*). Meanwhile, the Lauchas turned for base, leaving a trail of smoke over the Quarry Point spotters' heads as they went. They landed safely at 1545 hours.

Silence once again surrounded the awe-struck witnesses to these actions as the last whisper of the Mirage-V turbines died out in the distance. They would neither see nor hear further aircraft that day. But they were not alone. To the west of their position was the moving scene of a ship's crew fighting for their lives. At about 1600 hours, a frigate, HMS *Yarmouth*, drew alongside the stricken *Ardent* to render assistance. Search-and-rescue helicopters flew in and out on their missions of mercy while an expanding fleet of bobbing lifeboats floated about in a final salute to the courageous crew of HMS *Ardent*, of whom 24 had died and 30 had suffered wounds of varying degrees.

Lieutenant Egurza and Private Coronel soon noted that the vessel, now dead in the water, was slowly being carried out to the middle of the sound by the currents. As the sun went down, it drifted into the evening fog, and its position could be determined only from the glow of the flames that consumed it. At 0900 hours the following day, the burned-out hulk again came into view. Half an hour later, it went down by the stern in Falkland Sound. This gallant ship, which had sustained heavy damage during the first attack by a single aircraft, had scored no victories over its attackers. But its service to the British beachhead was no less valiant, for fate put it in harm's way not once but several times, as those attacking squadrons, had it not been for the *Ardent*, would have sought out other targets, with similar or perhaps more dire consequences for the British task force.

Ratones and Tábanas: A One-Way Trip

Ratón formation left San Julian at 1400 hours, and came in over West Falkland at 1458. There they were taken by surprise by the British Sea Harrier patrol lying in ambush at the north entrance to Falkland Sound, along the route they now knew to be the one followed by the Argentine attackers as they came in at low altitude. The Mirage-V Dagger has a larger heat source at the exhaust nozzle of its engine then does the Skyhawk, which is in proportion to its greater thrust. It also makes an ideal target for the Sidewinder missile, which homes in on heat given off by an aircraft's structure.

The Mirage-Vs caught sight of their assailants in time and, jettisoning their external loads, turned to face their foes with 30mm cannon. It was an uneven balance, because of the superior armament and maneuverability of the British contenders. But, in one of the aerial turns executed by the pilots in the course of their dog fight, a British plane presented its underbelly to Dagger No. 1 (Captain Donadile), which lost no time in pumping in a heavy stream of cannon fire. Apparently the British plane, its fuel tanks ruptured, went down in the sea short of its carrier. Nevertheless, the day went to his mates, for in the course of this action, all three Daggers were knocked out of the skies. Their pilots, who had succeeded in ejecting, were picked up a short time later.

The navy A4-Qs saw action for the second time during Air Force South's third wave. They came in over the south entrance to the strait at 1515 hours and headed north. As they sighted their target, a frigate, they were spotted by the British CAPs that lay in waiting at the southern entrance to the sound. They homed in on the Tábanos, knocking down the lead man with a Sidewinder missile. The pilot ejected as the British closed on his fellow Skyhawks, blazing cannon fire as they went. A second Skyhawk went into its death dive over the channel. Its pilot rode it down, while No. 3, having sustained lethal damage, was able to coax his craft as far as Puerto Argentino, where he executed a controlled ejection into the frigid waters of Stanley Bay. He was picked up, shivering but safe, a short while later.

These three A4-Qs were followed, 15 minutes later, by a second section of Tábanos. Coming in over the south entrance to the straits at 1530 hours, they followed the route of their downed fellows and came upon the frigate, which was making headway toward the west. As they streaked overhead, their bombs whistled toward the ship, raising huge columns of water as they detonated in the channel, fore and aft of the vessel, suspected to have been the *Alacrity*.

The fourth attack wave launched by Air Force South that day was comprised of two formations of A4-Cs and one of A4-Bs. They came in over the combat zone at 1702 and 1712 hours and fanned out in search of targets. None was to be found. The British, having realized the vulnerability of their vessels in the open waters of Falkland Sound, had marshaled their ships into protected areas around San Carlos Bay, where their Argentine pursuers could get at them only with the greatest of difficulty.

At 1054 hours, in the heat of battle, a C–130 attempted the routine shuttle into Puerto Argentino. Alerted to the presence of three British CAPs on the prowl in the vicinity, it turned back. The last KC–130 tanker returned to base, touching down at 1825 hours, thus ending the action of that first full day of war.

Analysis of the Day's Action

Brigadier Thompson, aboard the *Fearless*, and Admiral Woodward, aboard the *Hermes*, spared no effort in evaluating the day's events. Despite the sweeping effort of the carrier-based Sea Harriers, they had failed to blunt the massive Argentine air offensive, which had exacted an unexpectedly heavy toll on the Amphibious Force. The Rapier missile system had proven to be a disaster when put to use. The Sea Wolf missile system also had not performed up to expectations, for it was a weapon designed for use in open spaces, and the waters of San Carlos are lined with hills, bluffs, and inlets that interfere with their flight. Neither had the Sea Cats proven effective, while the Sea Dart, in light of the Argentine tactic of coming in at ground level between elevations, could not be used at all.

Paramount was the concern that the Argentine Air Force was far from grounded. Admiral Woodward conferred with Northwood for over an hour that evening. He emphasized that none of the transports had been hit by the Argentine air offensive. Brigadier Thompson was still nonplussed by the fact that the enemy had concentrated their offensive on the frigates instead of carpet-bombing the beachhead, which had been his foremost fear.

It is one thing to huddle about a table in an operations room, listening to staff briefings and mulling over tactical question marks, and quite another to be a pilot sitting in the cockpit of an aircraft, sorting out in split seconds the myriad dangers arrayed before him, his snap decisions dictated as much by his instinct for survival as by logical reasoning or his will to fulfill the mission. In this battle scenario, there was no time to be choosy, to favor one target over another. Once the silhouette of a ship loomed up, all his soul would go into that supreme high every pilot experiences as he plays for keeps, praying to last long enough to hit the trigger releasing his weapons and then, God willing, pull out in one piece.

This situation was not due to any shortsightedness on the part of the planning staff. Argentine Operations Plan 2/82, titled "Maintaining Sovereignty" and dated April 7, 1982, established priorities for the use of combat aircraft: (1) offensive against landing craft and troops on the beach; (2) offensive, if feasible, against troop transports. In the absence of precise intelligence with regard to the whereabouts of such desirable targets, squadron leaders were given a broad initiative to select their targets as they appeared. Strict orders had been issued against reruns, because they were so fraught with peril.

Admiral Woodward felt, wrongly, that his Sea Dart missiles were the main reason for Argentine treetop flying tactics, which, in turn, were seen to be the main cause of his foes' bombs not exploding. The fact is that the Sea Dart proved to be less offensive than the Sea Wolf, and that the low-flying tactics were due more to the need for the element of surprise than to fear, for surprise, against sophisticated arrays of electronic and ballistic air defenses, was his weaker foe's best tactic, taking his warships off guard.

As has been stated elsewhere, Argentina's lack of preparedness upon engaging in these hostilities, and not the low-flying tactics, was the chief reason for the unaccountable number of nondetonating bombs. Had it been otherwise, the bombs would have been equipped with the proper fuse to enable them to detonate regardless of the altitude from which they had been dropped.

Admiral Woodward, as well as Sir John Fieldhouse and Admiral Halifax, were confident that although the toll taken by the Argentine Air Force had been high, the lost frigates could be replaced. The beachhead, as well as the troops spearheading the landings, had yet to be tested under fire; but the determination of the enemy air force, as well as the intensity of the attacks, bore heavily on their minds. The fate of the task force and the beachhead was at stake.

As things turned out, it was extremely fortunate for the Amphibious Force that no Argentine submarines had put in an appearance at such a crucial juncture and that, on landing, resistance from Argentine ground forces had been practically nil. By the same token, the British felt that the heavy price paid by Air Force South—20 aircraft shot down, by their own estimate—was such that no air force of its perceived makeup could absorb such losses and still be effective.

For the time being, and under cover of darkness, the British redeployed their naval assets. The light cruiser *Glamorgan* moved up to stand in for the crippled *Antrim*. The *Brilliant* escorted the *Canberra* out of San Carlos Strait even though it had yet to complete unloading. It was felt that the sinking of such a large ocean liner would cause a much greater military loss of face than whatever political advantage might be gained from the establishment of the beachhead. The unloading of ships was rescheduled for nighttime hours, in order to avoid bombing raids. This involved problems for the 3rd Commando Brigade, and delays in previously laid plans that particularly incensed Brigadier Thompson, who felt that once again Admiral Woodward had made a single-minded decision for the defense of his ships at the expense of the operational needs of his infantry. But from where Admiral Woodward stood, it boiled down to one simple issue: his ships had borne the full brunt of the battle until that moment. The needs of the 3rd Commando Brigade could wait. And so the logistics vessels were moved up to San Carlos in the dead of night and swiftly unloaded. By sunrise, they were far out to sea, out of range of the Argentine Air Force.

Meanwhile, in Puerto Argentino, General Menendez had set aside any idea of moving his troops toward the prospective landing sites. The difficulties of moving troops and gear over such hostile terrain ranked high in his rationale, but his main priority was both political and strategic. He would make his stand at Puerto Argentino. Vice-Admiral Lombardo, commander of SATO, kept close tabs on the day's operations. Use of Argentina's high seas fleet to counterattack the enemy beachhead was rejected because the risk of exposing his ships to enemy submarine action was deemed too high. In Comodoro Rivadavia, Air Force South command was feverishly going over every aspect of the day's action while preparations went forward for the following day's operations at first light. There was a good feeling about the results achieved by various weapons systems in what would prove to be the toughest engagement of the conflict. While serious losses had been sustained, the actual kill rate was well below expectations and the air force stood ready to carry on the fight. Damage to the British fleet—the exact extent of which was unknown—was felt to be considerable and telling. As for combat aircraft losses, the heaviest kill rate was sustained by the Mirage-V Dagger platforms: a loss of 5 aircraft out of 23 represented a casualty rate of 23.5 percent. At this point, the fate of the pilots who had been able to eject was unknown. Once they were picked up and returned, a picture of events could be fitted together and corrective measures taken. This was particularly crucial in the case of the Ratón squadron. All three had been shot down, and this in itself was one of Brigadier General Crespo's staff's biggest question marks.

What had happened to the Ratones, and what would continue to occur until the first rescued flyer was returned to Comodoro Rivadavia, was simple: the Sea Harriers were onto the avenue of approach used by the Daggers on their bombing runs over Falkland Sound. So much so that all they had to do was lie in wait for their prey to come down the flight path and knock them out of the sky. The Mirage-V was restricted by fuel limitations to flying the straightest path to its target, unable to select alternative routes or detours, or to engage in evasive action. This procedure had cost Air Force South several aircraft, but measures were quickly adopted to put an end to the British "feeding frenzy" in which Sea Harrier pilots fell over one another to fly these snap missions and chalk up easy victories at little risk to themselves.

The role of the Mirage-III interceptors was also the object of close scrutiny. These planes came home empty-handed, for the British flew low in wait for their prey while the Mirage-IIIs, with an even shorter range than the Mirage-Vs, stayed upstairs—unable, because of fuel restrictions, to come down and engage the enemy in combat.

The highest marks of the day went to the A4-Bs. They had penetrated to their objectives, inflicting heavy damage on enemy vessels and demonstrating their capability to pierce the defense perimeter erected by the task force, without the loss of a single one of their number. By and large, the men of Air Force South were grimly satisfied with their achievements. They had honed their skills, and there would be more to come. In-flight refueling was down to a science, and the problem of salted-up canopies had been solved. They had yet, however, to prove their effectiveness in carrying the offensive to the transports. A heavy net of British warships bristled protectively about them, and this obstacle had to be overcome in order to attain a high kill ratio. And the enemy was also clever in protecting its own during daylight hours against Argentine Air Force attacks. But the bottom line for the men of Air Force South was the high price to be exacted from the enemy in return for snatching back "their" islands.

On that day alone, the British suffered the loss of one warship (*Ardent*), heavy damage to four more (*Argonaut, Antrim, Broadsword*, and *Brilliant*), varying degrees of damage to five others, and six aircraft brought down. In his action report for that day, Defense Secretary Nott owned up to " . . . light damage to three warships, all remaining operational while undergoing repairs" (*Latin American Newsletter*, p. 701).

THE ENGAGEMENTS OF MAY 22

The day dawned bright and clear over the Malvinas. San Carlos Bay was the scene of intense activity as the British sought to secure their beachhead. Not so in Patagonia, where a cold front, with accompanying low ceilings, limited visibility and snow flurries kept part of Air Force South grounded. These units were forced to face, as they flew in and out of the combat zone, the possibility of encountering foul weather on the return leg. They could not head for alternative ports and, under the best of circumstances, they had just enough fuel for one go-around on instruments.

Scouting operations that day continued to track the advance of British ships into the operations zone. Warships, transports, and tankers were plying the Atlantic waters at 30° south latitude. At 31° 46'S/30°43'W, an air force Boeing 707, flying about 1,375 miles east of the coast of southern Brazil, was attacked by Sea Dart missiles at an altitude of 10,000 feet. The heavy four-engine jet was able, in spite of its size and weight, to execute a skillful maneuver to avoid six of these oncoming missiles, in all probability fired by the 7,200-ton light cruiser *Bristol* and the Class 42 destroyer *Cardiff*, which were two days' sailing time from Malvinas.

News from abroad included reports that the 11,000-ton container ship *Contender Bezant*, along with a ferry-type craft, had weighed anchor in Great Britain with cargo that included more Harrier aircraft and Chinook helicopters. At the same time, the United States was picking up the slack left by the British RAF Victors, which were being used for in-flight refueling in the South Atlantic, by sending their own KC–135 tankers to NATO. At the same time, Pentagon officials were poring over ever-lengthening British requests for war supplies.

At 0930 hours, four RAF Harriers raided Condor air base and the Darwin-Goose Green Base as a preemptive measure against any possible action that might be brought to bear against the newly established beachhead at San Carlos by the Mercedes or Pucara aircraft stationed there. The attackers were met with heavy antiaircraft fire, with one presumed damaged, for it was seen to lose altitude as it headed for its carrier. Whether it made it home is not known.

Operation Corporate

This was the code name for the British operation to retake the Falkland Islands. On D-Day + 1, the landing forces secured their positions. This decision was hastened by the previous day's Argentine Air Force attacks and the total absence of Sea Harrier aircraft over the area. British ground forces lost no time digging deep into the soft peat that abounds in the landing zone. Progress was made not so much inland as underland. Only the 2nd Airborne Battalion made any noticeable progress toward Mount Wickham (Rivadavia Highlands), leaving behind what the British came to call "Bomb's Alley," San Carlos. Meanwhile, Brigadier Thompson had begun to feel the need to leave behind his floating command post aboard the *Fearless* and take up positions on the recently recaptured beach.

As invariably is the case with landing parties, British personnel underwent some hardships that were particular to the circumstances. For openers, their field rations were designed for use in Arctic climates, and snow was a necessary ingredient for their preparation. It had yet to snow in the San Carlos area, and readily available sources of soft water are exceedingly rare within that perimeter. The British Quartermaster Corps had also incorrectly figured the proper number of calories for fighting men on the ground. The constant red alert, brought on by diversionary overflights, subjected the men to living conditions similar to that of moles, for most of the time they had to stay huddled in their trenches, and suffered grievous privations as a result. Out in the bay, the RFA *Stromness'* deck bristled with automatic weapons. The men had orders to shoot straight up, if necessary, in case of enemy attack; the captain was heard to say that the only problem was that if all the men fired their weapons at the same time, the ship would capsize from the recoil.

Air Force South flew 14 sorties that day. During one of them, the *Fort Austin*, which was at anchor near the *Stromness*, was shaken by a booming explosion, followed by a geyser of water, as the bombs fell short of the ship's hull, to the horror of its crew, who knew it was loaded with munitions. A similar incident befell the *Norland*, which lay nearby with a damaged bow. Two bombs had detonated fore and aft of the vessel, which was laden with personnel and military gear waiting to be unloaded.

The coast guard cutter *Rio Iguazu* (82-ton displacement) and a sister ship, the *Islas Malvinas*, had been carrying out vital assignments covering a broad range of activities since their unexpected arrival through the British blockade. At 0430 hours on May 22, it set sail with a load of supplies for the army on what proved to be its last voyage. It steamed under cover of darkness. At first light it entered Choiseul Channel, where it was set upon by a flight of Harriers. As the attack commenced, at 0832 hours, the Rio Iguazu resorted to its lone weapon, a 12.7mm machine gun, with which it succeeded in inflicting damage on an enemy aircraft, which made away trailing a plume of smoke. But the Harriers' 30mm cannon took their toll. Its superstructure riddled with bullet holes, one crew member killed in action, and three wounded, the brave company was forced to abandon the *Rio Iguazu*.

RAF GR-MK–3 Harrier Squadron I: Mission Impossible

Making the GR–3 ready for action in the South Atlantic theatre of operations demanded not only a considerable technical effort, in order to enable the aircraft to operate under these unfamiliar conditions, but also special training for RAF personnel, who were not qualified to fly off aircraft carriers. It had become painfully clear to the British that the squadrons of Sea Harriers deployed to the South Atlantic during the early phase of the war, following the battle of May 1, would not be enough to do the job. They thus decided to call up and deploy a fresh squadron of Sea Harriers, Squadron 809, and another of Harrier GR–3s.

Since the container ship *Atlantic Conveyor* had already sailed from Liverpool on its voyage to the South Atlantic, plans were made for catching up with it by flying the aircraft into Wideawake and transshipping them from there by surface transport. One of the aircraft had to set down in Dakar (Senegal), because of mechanical problems. The following day, three more were sent out. Two made it to their destination but a third, beset with fuel system problems, had to seek an alternative landing site in Europe. The last four aircraft made Ascension on May 5. On May 7, room was made aboard the *Atlantic Conveyor* for the six Harriers, in addition to the eight Sea Harriers, four heavy Chinook helicopters, and a squadron of 12 Wessex 5 helicopters already on board. The giant ship set its course for the Malvinas, from whence, along with the bulk of its precious cargo, it would not return.

Three Harriers remained behind on Ascension to bolster air defenses about the island and prevent any Entebbe-type commando raid by Argentina. They were relieved by Phantom jets detached from an RAF base in West Germany, and were then redeployed to carrier-borne groups. On May 18, the Harriers were moved by their pilots from the *Atlantic Conveyor* flight pad to the carrier *Hermes*. They were followed by a fifth plane the next day, and by the others on May 20, the date the first RAF GR–3 Harrier joined a raid over the islands.

On May 21, Squadron I sustained its first casualty. One aircraft, registry XZ–963, went down, and the pilot, 1st Lt. Geoffrey Glover, was taken prisoner. It was not the last casualty. Heavy losses incurred during the conflict forced Britain to scrape the bottom of the barrel.* Aircraft scrounged from as far away as Canada and Germany were pressed into service, being flown perilously to the decks of the *Hermes*, in marathons that left no margin of safety.

If the transfer of the *Harriers* was a miracle of logistics, professionalism, and devotion by flyers, at great risk to themselves, the operational requirements of flying missions over the Falkland Islands were no less formidable, for they arrived on the scene just as the naval air operations of this action were reaching their apex. To begin with, the RAF GR–3s were assigned the most dangerous of missions: carry the attack against heavily defended Argentine positions—which had already exacted their toll from the Royal Navy's FRS–1 Sea Harriers. To the latter went the safer, more comfortable, and higher-yielding role of inter-ceptors, in view of their having been fitted with the Sidewinder missile, a "noble and unique weapon" for such a task. It is not the same to accumulate victories over enemy aircraft under such conditions as to make a direct attack against a target, no matter how difficult. If the Harriers had set themselves the mission of destroying the landing facilities at Puerto Argentino, it would have proved to be "Mission Impossible."

THE ENGAGEMENTS OF MAY 23

Once again, weather conditions were favorable to the United Kingdom's land-ing force. The cold front that had moved in over Air Force South bases throughout Patagonia began to reach the islands on May 23. It would hamper—but not ground—air operations.

At 0015 hours, a lone C–130 lifted off from Comodoro Rivadavia as part of the task of preserving that thin lifeline to Puerto Argentino, the shuttle between the mainland and the islands. It reached its destination without mishap at 0355 hours and, having emptied the holds and taken on 30 seriously wounded men, it undertook the return leg at 0420 hours. A second flight was attempted later but was grounded because of the weather.

At 0827 hours, the small requisitioned freighter *Monsumen*, which ensured the link between Puerto Argentino and Fox Bay, was attacked by helicopters, sustaining heavy damage and a serious casualty. Taken under tow by the *Forrest*, it was salvaged the next day at Port Darwin.

At about 1130 hours, a flight of four helicopters (three Pumas and one A–109) assigned to the Argentine land forces, transporting a load of supplies and heavy mortars for the 5th Infantry Regiment at Port Howard, was sighted by a British CAP flying at 8,000 feet over the straits. They were able to reach the east coast of West Falkland (Gran Malvina), where, in an attempt to evade the Harriers, they tried to land. The lead helicopter was damaged in the attempt,

---

*In Argentina, rumor had it that U.S. Marine Harriers had been pressed into the fight.

and the British opened fire on the A–109 and one of the Pumas that had landed successfully, its crew scurrying for shelter. The third Puma, which was undamaged, picked up the crews of the other three craft shortly thereafter. Three precious helicopters had thus been lost, but their crews sustained no casualties.

In the afternoon, Super Etendard aircraft armed with Exocet missiles sortied in search of targets. They found none. As of May 15, the P–2 Neptunes, which were the backbone of the navy's scouting team, were grounded for repairs, thus imposing a serious limitation on the operational use of the weapons system that had gained such notoriety following the sinking of the *Sheffield*.

The Beginning of the End for the Frigate HMS *Antelope*

Air Force South, in an all-out effort, issued flying orders and made ready 64 aircraft to be sent against British shipping and the beachhead. Some of the squadrons were armed with 500-pound delayed-fuse parachute bombs, in an attempt to improve the score on bombing runs.

The first wave of attackers, comprised of a four-aircraft flight and led by Captain Carballo, set a heading for "Bomb's Alley," coming over at 1330 hours. As they approached Falkland Sound, they came across a Sea Lynx helicopter, flying off the frigate *Antelope*, in Grantham Sound. As luck would have it, as the chopper came into the cross hairs of the attackers, their cannon jammed. The Sea Lynx beat a hasty retreat, after sounding the warning to its mother ship. Shortly thereafter, the lead man and his wingmen executed a turn as two frigates—the *Antelope* and the *Broadsword*—hove into view at the entrance to San Carlos Bay. They flew their attack run from the north branch of the bay, circling behind Fanning Head (Guemes Promontory) as they went. Two of the aircraft broke formation unexpectedly, following a different path of attack, while the first section drew a bead on the *Antelope*, which cut loose with everything it had as its assailants closed. As the lead man came in over Fanning Island, he received the full brunt of *Antelope*'s air defenses. A Sea Cat missile exploded beneath him, producing an enormous cloud of smoke and causing temporary loss of control. As the pilot was about to eject, his control surfaces responded and he returned, wounded, to base.

Wingman 2 saw his leader swallowed up in a ball of smoke and a shower of rocks kicked up by the blast, which scooped out a crater in the north bank of the bay. His speed took him into the smoke on a prayer. Coming out, he saw the ship before him, took aim, released his bomb, and made a swift getaway. The MK–17 came to rest in the stern of the *Antelope*, imbedding itself without detonating. Hours later, it sealed the doom of the frigate.

The other members of the squadron, having set a different course, attacked from the northeast, zeroing in on the two vessels lying at the entrance to the bay. Lieutenant Rinke, of the second section, faced off with the *Broadsword* as both frigates threw up a desperate shield of artillery fire. The Class 22 frigate shuddered under the impact of the 1,000 pound bomb that pierced its hull but, miraculously, failed to detonate. At the same time, 1st Lt. Luciano Guadagnini homed in on the *Antelope* through a withering hail of air defense artillery and tracers. His left wing sustained hits by 20mm Derlikon cannon shells, causing a partial loss of air surface control. He managed to adjust, and initiated a steep climb just as it seemed he would smash into the side of the ship. But his Skyhawk caught the main antenna, snapping it in two and disintegrating his aircraft, which spewed over the starboard side in a burning shower of hundreds of fragments, a fiery funeral pyre for a brave young pilot. He did not trade his life for naught: just before his plane was caught in the hail of antiaircraft fire, he had managed to release his bomb, which ripped through the port side of the vessel and came to rest in the officers' wardroom, where it lay, undetonated. Though it did not go off, it would prove to be a second and very serious headache for the ship's company.

The remaining three members of the squadron turned back toward the mainland. They made it to base, ragged and battered, but ready to go again, if the call came down.

The *Antelope* swiftly turned toward the safety of the inner waters of the bay to seek shelter from further attack and to nurse its wounds. Coming alongside the damaged *Argonaut*, it made a detailed assessment of the damage sustained: mainly two large, unexploded pieces of ordnance within its hull. Two task force bomb defusing experts, who had been performing a similar task aboard the *Argonaut*, were ferried to the *Antelope* by helicopter in order to neutralize the imminent danger presented by the large amounts of live explosives contained within the deadly MK–17s. They concentrated their efforts for hours, unsuccessfully, on the bomb dropped by Nene Squadron's no.2 man. Then they tried a tactic used successfully aboard the *Argonaut*, where an MK–17 had not detonated in spite of the explosion of a rack of Sea Cat missiles all about it. The remainder of the crew was removed to the stern of the ship, anxiously awaiting their fate.

The small charge used to deactivate the fuse went off uneventfully, as before. As the bomb experts cautiously sidled up the passageway to examine the results of their handiwork, the fuse primer, set for 20 seconds, had ignited. As they opened the bulkhead door to enter the compartment, the MK–17's explosion reverberated through the ship. One died in his tracks; his companion suffered grievous injury.

The crew stood horrified as flames shot through the passageway and spread about the vessel. As some fought a losing battle against the growing holocaust, others took to the waters of the bay. All available small boats turned about in an all-out effort to pick up the survivors. Moments after the ship's captain, Nick Tobin, and the last crew members had left the ship, the fire reached the magazines, and there ensued a dazzling display of fireworks as the exploding munitions arced into the sky. Like the *Ardent*, the *Antelope* was in flames throughout the night. At dawn's early light the British ship, broken in two, silently disappeared under the mantle of the sea.

Tábanos over San Carlos Bay

About 15 minutes after the A4-Bs had completed their bomb run, the combat zone was again awhine with jet aircraft. Three A4-Qs, refueled en route by the KC–130, came in over the target area. Their code name: *Tábanos*. It was their second run. The A4-B squadron had pinpointed the position of the British ships, including a capital vessel (possibly the *Canberra*), at the tip of the south branch of the bay, while the remainder—some seven—lay within its confines. The A4-Qs came down low over the coast of West Falkland and penetrated San Carlos Bay, on the west coast of East Falkland. No Sea Harrier disturbed them either on their incoming or on their outgoing leg.

They achieved penetration at 1348 hours. Boring through a seemingly impenetrable storm of missiles, cannon, and artillery fire, the lead man released his bombs against the largest vessel in sight. He was buffeted by the shuddering explosion. Number 2 sent his bombs whistling into the Class 21 frigate, but heard no explosion. Number 3 was unable to confirm or even hear his hits. Number 4, Lieutenant Commander Zubizarreta, then made his run. Four 500 pound BRP bombs slung from their struts. Due to some malfunction, they failed to release. As he was coming in on final approach on return to his base at Rio Grande, a control failure caused Zubizarreta to lose his rudder. Faced with the danger of clipping his landing gear and bellying in on a load of live explosives, he chose to eject. It was a fatal choice, for his parachute had not fully opened when he hit the ground. He sacrificed his life in the line of duty. As fate would have it, his plane rolled on down the runway, sustaining only light damage; it would live to fight another day.

Harrier and Sea Harrier in Action

Flying off carriers stationed at a safe distance from the islands, the task force's two carrier-based groups went about their work with fierce determination. The Sea Harriers, now veterans of the theater, operated off the *Invincible*, and were able to maintain at least three CAPs in the air at all times, to intercept incoming enemy aircraft. They were not always successful. The RAF Squadron I Harriers, operating off the *Hermes*, flew reconnaissance and attack sorties.

On May 23, this squadron flew a bombing run against the airstrip at Puerto Argentino but inflicted no damage of consequence. It also flew two reconnaissance missions over Port Howard, where it attacked a target of opportunity, the 5th Infantry Regiment, without causing casualties. Between 1630 and 1725 hours, four more aircraft sortied on bombing missions over facilities on Pebble Island, dropping MK–17 1,000 pound bombs. They had assumed that the landing strip there was still being used by the Pucaras, or even the Hercules, since the latter had been seen to drop low at this point and disappear off British radar. The assigned target was the runway, which was to be made unusable, and thus unavailable to any Argentine aircraft. The fact was that the whole area had been abandoned following the successful action carried out by special forces on May 15. The bombs destroyed the local residents'storehouse, the school building, and a carpenter's shop, injuring several of the local population but leaving the targeted runway intact.

It is quite probable that, in the wake of their experience in the Falklands, the British may have beefed up their bombing crews'target practice. Argentine pilots were to remark jokingly that their British colleagues had been unable, throughout the whole of the conflict, to "hit the broad side of a barn,"said "barn" (the landing strip at Puerto Argentino) having been 1,300 yards long and 50 yards wide.

Sea Harrier activity ran below expectations. Numerous Air Force South squadrons had encountered weather problems in their attempts to rendezvous with their tankers and had been forced to abort their missions. All of this notwithstanding, out of the five formations that penetrated to their targets, only one Mirage-V, code-named Punal 2, was intercepted at 1510 hours. Its pilot was unable to eject, and the plane went down in the vicinity of Calderon base on Pebble Island. Punal 1 returned safely to base. The other two Mirage-V formations that were over the target area at the same time heard the attack on preceding flights and observed, as they passed over the far end of San Carlos Bay, a dense thicket of surface-to-air missiles being fired by infantry positioned on the flats and surrounding hills. "It looked like a cloud of flying organ pipes," was the description of one pilot. They were the British Blow Pipes—also being used by Argentina—and the U.S. Stinger missiles, whose baptism of fire had been less than auspicious. The heights surrounding the perimeter had also been studded with eight British Rapier batteries, which, in spite of their vaunted sophistication, put on a sorry show indeed. Having been launched against an aircraft that had come in at an altitude below the elevation of the battery, the missile had hit the side of a hill in the midst of a British position, causing an estimated eight casualties (which the British have never officially acknowledged).

Brigadier Thompson's prophetic words—"It is clear now we do not enjoy air superiority"—had come back to haunt them. The crews of British ships in San Carlos Bay, as well as the marines and paratroops ringing the perimeter, had felt the stinging bite. In testimony to this, let the men on the battlefield bear witness in their own, often uniquely British, style:

Alan Gibson, intelligence officer, 40th Commando Battalion on San Carlos: One of these days, the "Argies" are going to realize that their bombs are not properly armed. Had everything they dropped exploded, they would have wiped us out.

Overheard between two Marines on the beach at San Carlos: Not to worry [pointing out a flight of fast-approaching jet fighters], according to what we have been told, they can't be unfriendlies. What we are seeing is proof positive that the Harriers are as good as we are at camouflage.

From the book *Don't Cry for Me, Sergeant Major*:

Understandably, the impending arrival of the enemy air forces' aircraft instilled fear in all members of the Task Force, but most were confident that the British Harriers would stop them. After all, Rear Admiral Woodward had promised them almost complete air superiority on D-Day, to allow the troops to secure their positions on the ground.

Error.

The foremost lament heard above the din of "bandits in the sky" reverberated throughout the length of the beachhead: "Where are the bloody CAPs?"

This reference to Woodward's air cover, the Combat Air Patrol, seldom found a satisfactory answer. Those who knew it, were not there, those who did not, were running full cover.

Instead of friendly Harriers, the sky seemed to brim with Skyhawks and Mirages. (pp. 104–5)

Total Disagreement

On May 23, the numbers seemed to be 10 British ships sunk or damaged by unexploded bombs, and 14 Argentine aircraft shot down, if one were to include the Pucaras chalked up on May 21. Such figures were enough to instill terror in the heart of the commander of any naval task force. However, at the highest echelons of the Argentine Air Force there was one unshakable truth. It did not matter how much sacrifice the air forces were willing to make; if their own land forces did not engage in the battle to break up a beachhead of such growing dimensions, sustained by land, sea, and air, the outcome would be unfavorable. There are many things a pilot can do, but one thing he cannot do is fight on foot.

In spite of this, the morale of the Argentine Air Force combat units had never been higher. Even if defeat was a foregone conclusion, the watchword was "Make them pay the price, send as many to the bottom as you can." The lack of air superiority was not, however, the problem of the British alone. Argentine land forces would soon lament the "full air superiority" enjoyed by the enemy over the Malvinas theater of operations. In this game of winner take all, in which both sides appeared to have lost air superiority, the answer lay basically in a very poor grasp of the significance of this concept. Both the pilots of the carrier-based aircraft of the British task force, and the men of the Argentine Air Force gave their all, making do with the scarce assets available to them. If they did no more, it was because they could not do more.

Staffs aboard British task force vessels began to reveal discouragement following the sinking of HMS *Antelope*. Some officers felt that the situation could drift into a stalemate, since they could not go on sustaining such frightful losses. Admiral Woodward, who later acknowledged his error in underestimating the Argentine Air Force, held a telephone conference from his flagship, the *Hermes*, with all of his ships' commanders. They believed they had brought down seven Argentine aircraft that day, a figure deemed insufficient. The intercepting aircraft had to improve their kill rate. The captains of the carrier *Invincible*, home to the interceptors, and of the *Brilliant* were of the opinion that Admiral Woodward should move his carriers a bit closer to the ''hot seat''so as to allow the CAPs more flying time in the battle zone. Then as many as four Sea Harrier groups could be maintained in the air at a given time, instead of the current three. The captain of the *Coventry* proposed edging in further west, the better to make use of the fancied prowess of the Sea Dart. The position of the two carriers continued to be the thorniest issue of contention between staff officers, as much of the task force as of the ground forces.

Woodward's decision, in the face of Argentina's undaunted will to carry on attacks from the air, was not to move up his carriers, for fear of putting them in harm's way. The loss of a single one of these units could spell disaster for the task force, so he decided to continue operations as before. He did not approve the *Coventry's* bid for a move further west, for were it to encounter serious trouble, he would be unable to come to its assistance.

THE ENGAGEMENTS OF MAY 24

The sun rose over the most favorable weather conditions throughout the area since the initial engagements at San Carlos. Ceiling and visibility from the mainland to the islands were good for air operations. A misty fog hanging over West Falkland would burn away toward noon, dissipating a partial low and medium cloud cover. The time was right for the offensive, but it was no less so for the defenders.

The first CAP was seen over the Malvinas at 0745 hours, thus beginning the long vigil that would slowly wear down the Sea Harrier pilots, who faced six hours at the controls of their planes on a daily basis, as the ever-increasing need for a British air presence over the area made itself felt. There they lay, in wait for their assailants as they came in, wave upon wave. The British advantage lay in the time-over-target factor, for they could afford the luxury of keeping their aircraft in the combat zone for so long at one time that each Sea Harrier became worth ten Skyhawks or Daggers—while the British could remain on station for up to 30 minutes, the Argentine craft had at the most 2 or 3 minutes of effective time over the target to fulfill their mission and get out. The implicit danger for Argentine pilots was thus immeasurably greater than that for the Sea Harrier crews, since the latter ran little risk of being attacked during their interception runs: Argentina's aircraft were not configured for air-to-air combat, and if the choice had to made, they were forced to jettison their ordnance and face off with cannon, as the Daggers had done over West Falkland on May 21, or to do their best to elude enemy Sidewinders and cannon fire.

There could have been dogfights had the British decided to face off with the Mirage-IIIs, which were fitted with Magic or Matra missiles, and flew daily sorties in the hopes that some Sea Harrier might fly high to meet them. It was not to be. The British interceptors were after Air Force South and its bombers, which came in buzzing the ground, and not the Mirage-IIIs, which had the advantage at altitudes above 15,000 feet. The Mirages stayed high to save fuel; the Sea Harriers kept low, because it was in their perceived interest to do so.

On the ground, the 3rd Commando Brigade's biggest concern was to receive sufficient logistics support to enable the landed ground forces to launch the final thrust toward Puerto Argentino. They set up numerous missile battery emplacements, grumbling all the while about the lack of air superiority and the snail's pace at which the task force was apparently delivering their supplies.

Meanwhile, both London and the task force flagship were wondering why Brigadier Thompson was waiting to order the advance of his troops toward the positions held by the Argentine defenders, and thus avoid an assault and the ensuing losses, as well as the further loss of British ships, which was an increasing source of alarm in both political and military circles, at Whitehall as well as at Northwood. What Brigadier Thompson was lacking was a more efficient line of supply. He was being held back by the task force's reluctance to ask further transports during daylight hours. To make the vicious circle complete, this could not be changed, for Admiral Woodward did not have air superiority with which to repel his Argentine tormentors.

At Malvinas Military Air Base

The most saturated target area in the whole theater of operations was the air base at Puerto Argentino and its landing strip, which survived as the naval and air components of the task force threw their full weight, night and day, unceasingly at that facility. During the whole engagement, 237 bombs, 1,200 artillery shells, and 16 missiles were launched against its perimeter. The commanding officer had the responsibility of keeping his facility operational, in order not to break that slim thread of communication linking him with mainland: the shuttle.

Argentine air defense artillery had earned the profound respect of the enemy, which simplified the commander's task somewhat. He had achieved a resounding intelligence coup by simulating bomb craters, creating circular mounds of earth on the surface of the paved runway, which in high altitude reconnaissance photos appeared to be the real thing. But on May 24, an enemy attack took the base by surprise and almost achieved the prized objective: damaging the runway. Following 23 days of high-altitude missions, this day appeared to be business as usual. Two aircraft came in high over their target and dropped their bombs, thus distracting the air defense batteries, while two Harrier GR–3s streaked through on a west-northwest course, lobbing 1,000-pound bombs from a very low altitude. Their feint had succeeded in fooling the antiaircraft batteries, which were never able to take aim. Their bombs hit the side and the west end of the runway, without causing major damage. The British must have been less than happy with the result, for following reconnaissance flights, further bombing attacks were mounted from a safe altitude.

The main task carried out by base personnel was to service the C–130s, which were operating at night only and with almost no ground lighting, in order not to reveal the arrival of a flight or the precise location of the runway. Puerto Argentino radar played a vital role in guiding the pilots. As they approached at low altitude, under cover of darkness, and generally in bad weather, the radar operators talked them in to final touchdown. The whine of the props never ceased as the ground crews hastily unloaded crucial supplies and reloaded the big birds with wounded, breaking all previous turnaround times for this type aircraft, which could bring in 14 tons of materiel at a shot. They had it down to 25 minutes.

Bomb's Alley or Missile Pass?

Air Force South issued 12 sets of orders to mount the attack against the beachhead and the ships at San Carlos. The first aircraft over the combat zone were five A4-Bs at 1015 hours. It was a combined formation of two flights, the Chispas (Sparks) and the Nenes (Babies) that, defying a barrage of missiles and artillery from both land forces and ships in the bay, broke through from the east and dropped their bombs on any target of opportunity, large or small. The *Sir Lancelot* was struck by an MK–17, which failed to explode, and the *Sir Geraint* was splintered by cannon fire. Two A4-Bs pulled up as their bombs homed on a landing craft loaded with 100 men. Once over, the squadron pulled out without suffering more than numerous bullet holes from ground defenses, and landed safely at Rio Gallegos. The two British logistics vessels had been in the process of unloading. Halfway through their task, they hastily closed up shop, evacuated all personnel, and proceeded to defuse the undetonated ordnance.

At 1102 hours, it was Azul (Blue) flight's turn to run to the fearful gauntlet. The Mirage-Vs penetrated San Carlos from the south branch, hugging Rivadavia Heights on their way into the bay. As they broke out over the water, they were face to face with a large ship moored at a pier, surrounded by some eight frigates. Completely surprised, the latter were unable to swing their weapons to meet the Daggers, which bore in, cannons ablaze, dropping down and flying between ships so that if the latter brought their defenses to bear, they would hit each other. The *Sir Bedivere* sustained damage from a 1,000-pound bomb that glanced off without exploding. It ricocheted off the foredeck and imbedded itself in the *Sir Galahad*, still undetonated. On their way home, the Azules came upon a Sea Harrier that raked them with cannon fire. They returned to base at 1159 hours, none the worse for the few bullet holes sustained by wingmen 2 and 4.

The Azules were followed into San Carlos by a flight of three Daggers, code-named Plata (Silver). Five minutes had elapsed since the first wave, and the air was thick with British missiles and artillery, both land- and sea-based. There was so much ordnance flying about that they had difficulty in homing on a given target. The ships inside the branch of San Carlos joined the fight, and confusion reigned. They were unable to confirm the effect of their 500-pound bombs and their cannon fire. As they made their escape northward, they observed two ships lying about 12 miles off Pebble Island, one of which launched a salvo of Sea Darts. The ships were HMS *Conventry* and *Broadsword*. The Platas made it home at 1155 hours, after having written a new chapter on the art of missile evasion. One frigate sustained damage during this attack.

Three squadrons having successfully and successively penetrated the beach-head without having been intercepted by British aircraft fairly evened the odds. The next would not be so lucky. Three Mirage-Vs code-named Oro (Gold) met their fate at the hands of interceptors guided in by the *Broadsword*, by now alerted to their presence and lying in wait for their prey. The interceptors climbed high and dived on the unsuspecting Daggers, swooping in with Sidewinders. The Daggers attempted to jettison their external loads, but too late. All three were obliterated by the Sidewinders. One pilot died at the stick; the others, having been able to eject, were picked up later.

The next mission was flown by three A4-Cs, code-named Halcón (Falcon). Prior to reaching the the target area, they were intercepted by a CAP. Executing skillful evasive maneuvers, they succeeded in shaking off their pursuers, and were able to dodge their missiles and cannon fire as they returned, unharmed, to base.

The final mission of the day was flown by another three A4-C formation: the Jaguars. Each carried three 500-pound delayed-fuse parachute bombs. The target: San Carlos. Estimated time of arrival: 1130 hours. As they arrived over the combat zone, the lead man selected a frigate and bored in through a hell fire of exploding shells and withering cannon fire. Guns ablaze, the aircraft released six bombs over the target. As they pulled out, the lead man noted that his two wingmen were trailing fuel, the result of myriad hits during the attack that had riddled their airfoils and fuel tanks. Number 3 radioed that the lead plane was leaking, too. Number 3 (Lieutenant Bono) was losing the largest amount of fuel and was ordered to eject. He responded that he could make it as far as the tanker. Suddenly, as they had begun their climb and were over Queen Charlotte Bay, southwest of West Falkland, Bono went into a slow spin and, without responding to his comrades' radio calls, went down into the water off the north coast of Weddell Island.

Jaguars 1 and 2 searched for the parachute that would indicate a successful ejection. There was none to be seen. They turned in search of the tanker. The KC–130, alerted to the emergency, banked toward their heading and, pushing the throttles full open, coaxed every mile of speed possible to meet them, coming dangerously close to the perimeter patrolled by the CAPs. The booms locked in successfully, and the two aircraft sucking fuel all the way home, were nursed back to a safe landing at San Julian. Number 1 took on the unbelievable amount of 8,000 gallons of jet fuel, escaping what would have been certain death.

The frigate targeted by the Jaguars could not be identified positively, since British forces did not acknowledge the attack. Subsequent analyses have enabled researchers to ascertain almost positively that the ship was HMS *Arrow*, which had put into San Carlos the morning of May 24 to replace the *Antelope*. It was assisted by the repair ship *Stena Seaspread*, which set about reriveting its hull plates after it was withdrawn from the combat zone.

The result of the day's attacks was a source of small consolation to the British high command, who were unnerved that the Argentine bombs had begun to do their job. One MK–17 had ricocheted off one ship and, in an acrobatic somersault, had bounced onto a neighboring vessel. Although the frisky bomb did not go off, it was the bane of the crews aboard the transports, three of which had been penetrated by duds, and a fourth of which, the *Sir Geraint*, had been raked by 30mm cannon fire. *Sir Lancelot* had an MK–17 lodged in its starboard side, which caused damage to the plumbing system and knocked out part of the 59th Commando Engineer Squadron's gear, but failed to detonate. *Sir Galahad* had been pierced by an MK–17 that had lodged in its battery room, causing the crew to abandon ship, thus leaving it out of commission for several days. Neither did *Sir Bedivere* come through May 24 unscathed. The amphibious assault vessel HMS *Fearless* took 25 30mm cannon shells from Argentine fighter-bombers, to the consternation of the 3rd Commando Brigade and Amphibious Force command headquarters, located aboard that vessel.

Statistical analysis of the day's actions showed that a maximum number of sorties had been flown as well as passes over the targets—in the face of an increasingly dense and lethal defense thrown up by the enemy.

May 24 has been dubbed "Day of the Knights of the Round Table."

THE ENGAGEMENTS OF MAY 25

This was Argentina's National Holiday—a unique Fourth of July.

British forces were wondering how the Argentines might mark the anniversary of their first national government, established 172 years earlier over territories that remained to be consolidated, such as the Malvinas Islands. From a tactical standpoint, it would be business as usual for Air Force South. Every day there was an all-out effort, so on May 25 efforts would be made in accordance with available means and worthwhile targets, just as on previous days. Some British Marines were heard to joke that a good way to celebrate that particular date would be by sinking the *25 de Mayo*. A pipe dream, even for the British forces, for the ship was moored under close guard at its home port, Puerto Belgrano.

Weather conditions that morning were perfect for flight operations, both on the mainland and in the islands, marred only by the presence, in the early hours of the morning, of mists caused by a high-pressure zone, which would generate good weather conditions until noon, with light southwesterly winds.

The British task force had its carriers on station between 80 and 90 NM northeast of Puerto Argentino, with a light escort. The remaining warships were at San Carlos or escorting transports that had to be withdrawn from the beachhead area before first light, to seek safety on the high seas to the east. At sundown, they made their nightly shuttle into the bay to proceed with landing Brigadier

Thompson's 3rd Commando Brigade's men and materiel. The *Canberra* had been withdrawn from San Carlos to the more peaceful waters around Cumberland Bay at South Georgia Island, where it served as a holding area for task force reserves. The ships riding at anchor in San Carlos Bay bristled with a profusion of automatic weapons and portable rocket launchers on their decks. Firing at will at the oncoming swarms of intruders had begun to take its toll, for every time they came over, they flew a gauntlet of improvised and jerry-rigged anti-aircraft defenses that included the rifles and even the side arms of those brave enough to stick their necks out in the heat of battle.

On this day again, a C–130 shuttled into Puerto Argentino for a record-breaking turnaround. Off-loaded at the blacked-out terminal were shells for the 155mm Sofma artillery pieces, rations, miscellaneous spare parts, surgical equipment, mail and packages from home, and seven passengers. The whine of the turboprops faded into the distance as the craft winged its way back. British aircraft retaliated with a vengeance. The worst attack was mounted at 1000 hours. Six Harriers, bearing in at low altitude, released their bombs along the runway, again in vain. They made their bomb runs so low that their ordnance failed to explode.

At 1407 hours, another aircraft made a high-altitude approach, on what appeared to be a reconnaissance mission. At 11,000 feet, the pilot must have felt he was out of range of the perimeter's fearsome air defenses. Not so! A skillfully aimed Roland missile found its mark. As the intruding aircraft disintegrated in flames, a parachute blossomed, and its pilot landed in the waters around Port William (Port Groussac). At 1538 hours a second aircraft was shot down over Cape San Felipe (Pembroke), caught in the stream of 35mm fire from the batteries at the end of the runway, as well as cross fire from 20mm batteries. It went up in a ball of fire as it neared the water. A companion aircraft must have sustained damage during this action. Follow-up attacks, at 1715 and 1900 hours, were repulsed by the antiaircraft emplacements. By now, the plucky RAF pilots had gauged their enemy's defenses, which had earned their respect. But they, too, had a job to do. Duty-bound to the bitter end, they tried again and again to put that airstrip out of action.

The Sinking of HMS *Coventry*

The destroyer HMS *Coventry*, the *Sheffield, Exeter*, and *Glasgow*, comprised the task force's first line of destroyers in the South Atlantic deployment. They were the latest in state-of-the-art warships, on which the Royal Navy pinned its highest hopes, as much for their fighting capability at sea as for their modern design and construction. This particular vessel had seen action on May 3 during the attack on the *Alferez Sobral* by Sea Slug-fitted helicopters flying off it and the *Glasgow*. One of the *Coventry*'s Sea Dart missiles had brought down the Argentine helicopter that had gone to render assistance to the survivors of the *Narwal* following the action of May 9. It also had had a support role in the landings, lying on station near the class 22 *Broadsword* as an early-warning radar picket.

On the morning of May 25, the *Coventry* was on station 20 NM north of Pebble Island when the first waves of Air Force South squadrons appeared at first light. Until then, it had played a limited role in the operations at San Carlos, its job being to mount surveillance over the north flank of the sound, where few Air Force South planes had ventured. The first section over the operations area, code-named Marte (Mars), comprised two A4-Bs. They had left Rio Gallegos before daybreak and had made part of the crossing under cover of darkness, the better to take the British CAPs by surprise.

The target area was covered by a thick fog, which caused the attackers to lose contact with the terrain and depart from their originally established flight path. They passed up the plainly marked hospital ship *Uganda* and executed a turn into Darwin. Unknowingly, they made a pass over their own positions, firing as they went, and were promptly repelled by their own air defenses. The lead plane was hit but could still fly. Believing he was over San Carlos, the pilot initiated his withdrawal northward, as his wingman broke formation and headed south. In so doing, he blundered into the heaviest British defenses along the north of the sound. His plane was blasted to bits by two sea-air missiles. He was never found.

They were followed at 1225 hours by a four-Skyhawk formation code-named Toros (Bulls). They came in low over Rivadavia Heights toward the south branch, where they saw 12 ships, heavily armed and firing at will, as they came into view. As they shot over, one took a hit and went down, the pilot ejecting into the bay, where he was picked up by British forces and transferred abroad the *Fearless*, where he received prompt medical attention for his wounds. Of the three remaining aircraft, only the formation leader was still in full fighting trim. As he streaked north over the bay, he took lethal hits over Green Beach and lost control of his aircraft. He died at the stick. Meanwhile, No. 4, his fuel tanks riddled and spewing his aircraft's lifeblood, gambled against ejecting and put out a call to the KC–130, which came to meet the disabled plane. Toro 4 made base, coupled to the life-giving fuel boom trailing from the big Hercules. The Toros were unable to confirm positive hits on British ships. Perhaps one had sustained some damage, possibly the *Sir Lancelot*.

HMS *Coventry*, escorted by the *Broadsword*, mainstay of Admiral Wood-ward's "destroyer 42/frigate 22" tandem, was making 12 knots, steaming off the north coast of Pebble Island, when its radar picked up bandits to the south. They were Vulcano Section, two Skyhawks piloted by the star flying team of this war, Captain Carballo and Lieutenant Rinke, who had strayed a bit from their established flight path due to cloudy conditions over the islands. The time was about 1520 hours. The Vulcanos caught sight of the two enemy ships just as general quarters and battle stations were being sounded on the vessels, their air defense crews scrambling to move the rocket launchers into position to sight the target and launch a salvo of Sea Dart missiles. The naval artillery, though the foe was still beyond range, began pounding away as fast as the guns could be reloaded; but the bandits, seeking refuge behind the elevations of Pebble Island, dropped off British radar. The *Coventry* and *Broadsword*, full speed ahead, churned up the sea as they prepared to meet the foe. Captain Carballo banked for the attack, zeroing in on his target, the *Broadsword*.

Aboard the frigate, the radar was locking in on one of the targets in order to launch a Sea Wolf. But the planes were flying such a tight formation that the machine could not resolve this unforeseen situation its designers had overlooked. Precious seconds ticked by as the Vulcanos—defying the barrage of artillery cannon raised by the vessels in their desperate bid for safety—released their bombs. The ship's crew watched helplessly as the Sea Wolf system blinked its electronic ''I do not compute''signal, its circuit breakers snapping in unison to the ''off'' setting. A flying ''bombola'' pierced the bow of the vessel, destroying the hangar and a helicopter, crippling the engines, and sparking a fire as it tore through. The pilots of the Skyhawks pulled up and out, elated at finding themselves still whole. Then they picked up the pitched scream of a second wave of aircraft diving to the attack against the same targets.

The Zeus Squadron was comprised of a team of A4-Bs piloted by First Lieutenant Velazco and Second Lieutenant Barrionuevo. Each was armed with three 500-pound bombs. Their original targets had been at San Carlos, but upon observing the action initiated by Captain Carballo against these two targets of opportunity, they decided to join the fight, following the first flight barely two minutes later. As they faced off, the first thing they saw was the frigate at a dead stop in the water and the destroyer coming up from astern. As HMS *Coventry* caught sight of the fresh wave of attacking aircraft, it heeled toward them, coming between the frigate and the attackers.

The *Broadsword* had lost its engines, but all systems were now go, and the Sea Wolf missiles were being swung into firing position. The fire-control computer banks had acquired the targets, and the missiles were ready for launch. But *Coventry*'s protective maneuver aborted the shot. The *Coventry* fired cover with its own missiles: two Sea Darts blazed from the decks and climbed skyward on a tail of flame, while Zeus 1 and 2 dodged under them and took a bead on the destroyer, which was lobbing everything it could muster against them. The lead plane's three bombs penetrated into the very heart of the ship, below the bridge. Two of the wingman's three weapons stubbornly clung to their struts, but the third whistled true, smashing into the stern of the ship. This time all detonated, sealing the doom of the proud *Coventry*.

One bomb went off just below the operations room, killing nine crew members and causing widespread damage. Chaos reigned as fire spread throughout the *Coventry*. Its engines useless, it began to list heavily. As the skipper, Capt. David Hart-Dyke, directed emergency operations, the order was given to abandon ship. Almost at once, helicopters began to stream in from San Carlos, moving wounded and survivors to the *Fort Austin*. Nineteen crew members lost their lives in the holocaust. In less than 25 minutes, the *Coventry* capsized, going keel up, then slipping beneath the waves.

Thus a third Class 42 destroyer had gone down in this conflict, leaving serious doubts with regard to its weapons systems and the supposedly fail-safe electronics systems.

Both Vulcano and Zeus squadrons returned uneventfully to base at Rio Gallegos. They touched down at 1601 and 1621 hours, their spirits buoyed by that best of all feelings: mission accomplished!

The Sinking of the *Atlantic Conveyor*

The 14,946-ton container ship *Atlantic Conveyor* had been requisitioned from the Cunard Container Ship Company to transship Harrier and Sea Harrier aircraft, and Chinook helicopters to the theater of operations. Its deck had been specially fitted for VTOL operations, thus giving the task force greater flexibility, since aside from serving as a conveyance for such aircraft to the battle area, it could also stand in as an aircraft carrier.

The aircraft had left the *Atlantic Conveyor's* flight pad on May 19, 20, and 21. The Wessex 5 Squadron 848 helicopters (12 in all), as well as Squadron 18 (four heavy RAF Chinook helicopters), along with gear for the landing troops, and spare parts for the carrier-based groups aboard the *Hermes* and the *Invincible*, had remained aboard for future use. Also among the inventory were tents, aluminum landing mats, and desalinization plants. This equipment had been sent by air and surface transport from the United States to Ascension Island, then transferred to the *Atlantic Conveyor* for the final leg of the voyage.

On May 25, the giant vessel was awaiting nightfall north of Puerto Argentino, to make a run into San Carlos Bay to unload equipment for the 3rd Commando Brigade to spearhead their advance toward the Argentine garrisons. But at Rio Grande, a second mission with Exocet-armed Super Etendard aircraft had been planned for several days. There were three of these weapons left in Argentina's arsenal, and they had to be used against the most worthy targets the British had to offer: their aircraft carriers. With this in mind, the unit (2nd Fighter-Attack Squadron) had engaged in intense daily practice to get the system just right for their next strike against the British fleet.

Two aircraft left the runway at 1434 hours, each carrying one of the precious missiles. At 300 NM from their target, they refueled in flight and continued their mission according to plan. As they came in over West Falkland, they dropped down to evade detection by enemy radar. Shortly thereafter, they executed one of the most crucial maneuvers of the operation: gaining altitude to seek the target, in order to enable the Exocet's on-board avionics system to home in on the target. Fortunately, the latter was in the same position that had been reported earlier that morning. Their course set, the two aircraft dropped to wave-top level and skimmed their way toward the task force vessels. At shooting distance, the pilots pressed the missile release triggers and turned for home. Following another rendezvous with the tanker, the two Super Etendard jets touched down at Rio Grande without mishap.

The Class 21 frigate *Ambuscade*'s radar first spotted the incoming missiles and sounded the alarm throughout the fleet, which included, besides the *Ambuscade*, the *Atlantic Conveyor*, the carrier *Invincible*, and three more vessels. There were 2 minutes and 45 seconds left for the missiles to home in on their targets. The warships and the carrier's helicopters immediately scattered chaff to confuse the missiles and divert them. The *Atlantic Conveyor* was not equipped with chaff. The crew of the *Ambuscade* watched the missile streak past, as they fired all her available weapons. The Exocet executed a turn and homed on the looming container ship. Perhaps it had locked onto this target from the beginning, and perhaps the second missile spent itself over the sea. It is exceedingly difficult to determine exactly what happened. It is known, though, that at least one missile found its mark, pierced the hull, exploded, and started what proved to be an uncontainable fire, spelling a fiery end to both the ship and its precious cargo except for a single Chinook, registry ZA–768, which happened to be in the air at the time.

It was a close call for the *Invincible*, which had been steaming nearby. The target, which had become a mass of flames, was not to be ignored: it would prove the largest logistics setback sustained by the British expeditionary force, for its holds had contained equipment deemed vital by Brigadier Thompson— mainly the helicopters. Twelve men perished in the disaster. The last to leave the ship, her gallant skipper, Capt. Ian Norton, on seeing the lifeboats overloaded, swam off, never to be seen again.

High Noon

If the British staffs, following analysis of the action of May 24, were concerned, the people at Whitehall and Northwood, not to mention those aboard the task force, must have been bordering on panic at the results of May 25. For Brigadier Thompson, the loss of the *Atlantic Conveyor* meant the loss of priceless helicopter squadrons, especially the hefty Chinooks, each capable of carrying 44 men in full combat gear, or heavy cargo such as artillery pieces. Considering the nature of the terrain in the islands, the Chinooks were the only effective way of moving men and materiel. It was also a serious setback for the continuous supply of the men in the field: there would be a shortage of tents, ammunition, field rations, and even water. Potable water is not in ready supply in the islands, and the container ship had been scheduled to unload at San Carlos a water-treatment plant obtained from the United States. None of this was conducive to a successful thrust against a firmly entrenched garrison that had had weeks in which to make ready.

For Admiral Woodward, the situation was becoming untenable. The loss of yet another Class 42 destroyer, along with several of his carrier-based aircraft, increased his vulnerability to the probing attacks of the enemy air force and was bringing the survivability of his vessels to the crucial test point. Both he and his command at Northwood were increasingly concerned over the fact that both the landed marines and airborne troops were becoming spectators to a war of attrition involving the British fleet in the waters of San Carlos. The landed troops perceived an unfinished struggle that the task force should have wrapped up prior to sending them in to the beachhead.

On the previous day, Brigadier Thompson had met with his unit commanders to explain that they should initiate preparations for the eastward thrust, tempering the impatience of some while soothing the concerns of others. Every available helicopter was used to ferry rations, munitions, and equipment from the ships to the positions on the ground. In the meantime, special air and boat squadrons would soften up the route to Puerto Argentino, scouting and reconnoitering the terrain, as well as evaluating Argentine defenses. Junior commanders returned to their units less than happy, at a loss to resolve what was becoming a pressing problem: how to keep their men occupied. The 16-hour Falklands nights under complete curfew—no lights, no cooking fires, no reading, no heating—was making life unbearable for men squeezed into squalid and limited living spaces.

During the meeting, not a word was said about Darwin-Goose Green. The only issue was the march to Port Stanley (Puerto Argentino). Under the circumstances, the exchanges of criticism between the task force commands and the forces on the ground were generating an ever-growing antagonism.

Nor was all well in London. The politicians were tightening the screws on Northwood to report some concrete task force results in its struggle to retake the islands. There was growing fear that a U.N.-imposed cease-fire would leave those troops as the sole stewards of a narrow slice of remaining British territory. But if the intent of the high command in London had been to launch an immediate thrust against Argentine positions as soon as they hit the beaches, nobody aboard the landing craft had been given the word.

Whitehall felt things might have taken a turn for the better had Gen. Jeremy Moore been at the helm of the brigade during those early days at San Carlos. Such feelings were not shared by military experts or by Brigadier Thompson's subordinates, who were of the opinion that the 3rd Commando Brigade could not have moved a single yard before it did so. In an exceedingly tense atmosphere, the commander of the task force made one of his most debated and unpopular decisions of the conflict: instead of moving his carriers closer to the action, he would move them further east. This generated such skepticism and hostility that surely Admiral Woodward did not let it pass unnoticed.

But history was to prove him right. Argentine land forces were hampered by a lack of mobility, to such an extent that they were incapable of exerting any pressure against the beachhead, which was quite free of any danger of being neutralized. Had it been otherwise, the outcome of the battle of San Carlos might have been a British Waterloo.

THE ENGAGEMENTS OF MAY 26

Nightly British naval bombardment became increasingly persistent against the Argentine garrisons. British ships sneaked in under cover of darkness to elude their enemy's air forces, but in return for this relative safety, they lost all accuracy in their shelling, for seldom did they inflict any telling damage on the defenders.

Unfavorable weather conditions caused Air Force South to scrub its flying orders. It did, however, ponder the renewed employment of the Canberra bombers, this time in nighttime raids, in order to pull yet another surprise on British forces. The plan was shelved for lack of a good opportunity. One Mirage-V squadron sortied and, from between cloud layers, made a dead-reckoning bombing run over the target area. They were met by no enemy fire, and were unable to confirm any hits with their 500-pound BRP bombs. A single Harrier mounted an attack on the garrison dug in at Port Howard, killing six and wounding six.

The day was also marked by the arrival, at 1400 hours, at Puerto Argentino, of First Lieutenant Esteban's Guemes special combat team, who had successfully faced British troops at San Carlos and had eluded their pursuit.

The air force's long-distance scouting sorties, following a long and uneventful day, turned up nothing new in the way of any shipping in the areas they scoured. For the flyers and their crews, May 26 was almost a day of rest and recreation.

The Defenders Attempt to Hold

Argentine commando teams, which had been deployed toward the perimeter of the beachhead, ran afoul of an enemy worse than anything the British could have sent their way: the environment was so hostile that they were able to advance only at a cost of great exhaustion to personnel and conveyances, which, under such unfavorable conditions, could not be resupplied.

On May 24, faced with the expanding beachhead at San Carlos, the commander of Group Litoral at Puerto Argentino, who had Task Force Mercedes under his orders, issued an order code-named Defense that ordered the commander of the task force at Darwin to undertake the following:

—Recognize the defenses.

—Keep the enemy pinned down by hostile fire to the north and northwest of Darwin.

—Interdict the Darwin isthmus.

—Employing an infantry company, mount a nighttime attack on British forces that very evening.

—Proceed, in accordance with the results of the prior action, to mount a second attack during the night of May 27, backing it up with scouting parties.

Far from achieving the objective sought, this order had a negative effect on Argentine forces, for it wore them out needlessly. Straining at the ropes, they mustered their last bit of strength moving the artillery pieces into the emplacements by hand, since they had no vehicles to assist them. At length, the pieces were set in place and considerable ammunition was expended shelling the hillsides, causing at the most light casualties to the enemy.

About 2330 hours, a hospital ship answering the description of the *Uganda* was spied landing troops at Brenton Branch on Grantham Sound north of Darwin. This obvious violation of the rules of the Geneva Convention was promptly denounced by the Argentine government.

Argentine Company A pushed toward the northern quadrant of the Darwin isthmus, under extremely difficult conditions, without making contact with the enemy. Exhausted, they withdrew at 0500 hours on May 27. The enemy had passed a mile and a half from them, at 0300 hours, over the same hill. They were Company D, 2nd Airborne Battalion, who had received orders, shortly after noon on May 26, to launch the thrust toward Darwin.

At 0400 hours, a telephone conference was held with General Menendez from Mount Wickham (Rivadavia Heights). The need for Argentine troops to go on the offensive to limit the enemy initiative, as well as the necessity for a significant number of men, was stressed.

The British Move Out

Brigadier Thompson's determination to ensure an adequate supply of military equipment prior to initiating a thrust toward enemy lines found few takers in London, where consternation over what the 3rd Brigade could possibly have been doing during five days of total immobility in the San Carlos perimeter was complete. In fairness, neither Whitehall nor Northwood had the slightest inkling of conditions on the beachhead, or of the responsibility that now bore down so heavily on the shoulders of the commander of the 3rd Commando Brigade. Brigadier Thompson had endured the consequences of the exceedingly slow delivery, under chaotic conditions, of the bare essentials needed for survival in this environment, not to mention engaging an enemy in combat. If his large combat unit was not up to snuff for the big push, then Great Britain would fail in its attempt to retake the islands. Too many of his colleagues had underestimated the enemy, at a great cost to their own. He was not to repeat their mistake.

At this juncture, no one could be sure if Argentina's ground forces were in the process of putting the final touches on a devastating counterattack against British troops advancing in the field, or even against the beachhead, where, a full week following the first landings, the logistics people had yet to see to the adequate and full supply of all the land forces for a proper engagement with the enemy. Not all the blame could be laid at the feet of the task force. The management of the helicopter squadrons also came under some harsh criticism.

But the winds in London were now blowing on a new heading. In the wake of a blizzard of disturbing reports, the politicians were in urgent need of quick victory both to lift the spirits of the public and to keep the pro-government polls up, as well as to muzzle the swell of opposition. The closest objective was Darwin.

As the staff of the 3rd Commando Brigade was laying plans for a direct push on Puerto Argentino, feeling that Darwin-Goose Green was of no strategic or tactical relevance, Brigadier Thompson was called to the satellite communications station rigged at Ajax Bay. There he learned that Northwood felt that the landing force should engage the Argentines at the earliest opportunity, and that that engagement should take place on the Darwin isthmus. No matter that it could be bypassed in the push eastward, at a savings of numerous lives. No matter that Brigadier Thompson was certain that Darwin would lay down its arms at the surrender of Puerto Argentino. The politicians had other, more pressing concerns on their minds. General Dick Trant, Admiral Fieldhouse's second in command at Northwood, issued Brigadier Thompson his marching orders.

The honor of taking Darwin-Goose Green fell to the 2nd Airborne Battalion, under the command of Lt. Col. Herbert Jones. The 45th Royal Marines Commando Squad and the 3rd Airborne Battalion were to undertake the overland march to Mount Kent, to the west of Puerto Argentino. Deprived of their helicopters, the men were to trek over the boggy, spongy terrain. A bitter pill indeed, even for the best-trained and best-equipped elite troops of the British forces.

The British marines and paratroopers were speechless. The proud image of their coming in by helicopter to engage the enemy, spit-and-polished, dry as a bone, shouldering only the arms needed for the fight, dissolved into a soggy reality that raised some serious doubts in their minds as to whether they would be up to the task. But in the army you march to the commander's drum. So off they trudged through mud and bog on a long and arduous march. Lieutenant Colonel Whitehead, battalion commander of the 45th Marines, put it best:

> In order to achieve our victory, we must fight a three fold enemy:
> The real one out there in the field,
> The frightful climate and terrain,
> And our equally frightful logistical muddle.

THE ENGAGEMENTS OF MAY 27

The day's activities commenced with the sighting of a ship coming up Brenton Branch at 0010 hours. Soon thereafter, beginning at 0359 hours, the Darwin garrison came under heavy naval gunfire.

On the mainland, Air Force South decided to tweak the enemy once more. Since the enemy was unused to such tactics, two MK–62 Canberra bombers sortied with a load of BRP bombs in the dead of night, arriving over the operations area at approximately 0430 hours. Their mission: take out the ships that were subjecting the Darwin garrison to naval bombardment. The salvo from the first aircraft whistled in from 1,000 feet over the Ajax Bay area—on the south branch of San Carlos Bay—and the second aircraft dropped its rack of bombs north of San Carlos harbor.

The bombs, which thudded rhythmically across British lines in a rapid-fire succession of detonations, caught the marines like a bolt out of the blue. They had been told "The Argies don't fly at night." As they heard the approaching whine of jet engines through the dark, they thought that—at last!—their own Harriers were flying air cover over their positions. As the area reeled under the explosions and mud spattered the air, they had second thoughts, and dived for cover in foxholes. The attack left in its wake the shattered remnants of the brand-new earth satellite station antenna. It also damaged a hospital facility at Ajax. This attack elicited no response from the British defenses. The bombers returned to base without having to evade missiles or elude prowling Sea Harriers.

At 1110 hours, the Harriers raided the air facilities at Puerto Argentino, again ineffectively. Between 1345 and 1445 hours, incoming naval shells thumped into the Darwin-Goose Green compound, with a view to softening up the perimeter for the forthcoming attack against the garrison. A Harrier, flown by Group Commander R. D. Iveson, fell to ground fire. Iveson ejected and was soon picked up by his own men.

The air defenses at Condor base also exacted final tribute during the latter action, thanks to battery no. 1, equipped with a Rheinmetal 20mm antiaircraft cannon operated by Cpl. 1st Class Galanti, a musician who had been commandeered from the army band and quickly taught the rudiments of an instrument of a different brass.

At 1724 and 2014 hours, two C–130s droned up to the ramp with a priceless cargo: the 602nd Commando Company. The daily shuttle was becoming an increasingly risky business for the brave crews of the Hercules Squadron. In addition to this already perilous undertaking, the Herkies were assigned yet another mission, which would prove to be the most death-defying of all. Their latest and most dangerous mission: long-range scouting. (The Neptunes were down for maintenance.) This cumbersome aircraft was now flying a mission for which it was not designed: seeking out enemy ships and reporting their positions so that attack bombers would have specific targets. This meant exposing the barn-sized C–130s to the enemy fleet. The risk was all the greater because the enemy vessels, as they concluded their rounds into San Carlos Bay, became increasingly difficult to ferret out. The scattering of the larger targets, such as ships or concentrations of enemy troops and supply dumps, would become a major problem for Air Force South. As the British fanned out from the beachhead, their infantry made ever more difficult targets, which did not justify sending in aircraft to drop ordnance with dubious or no results at all, especially since the odds of their safe return were stacked in favor of the enemy.

In the waning hours of the afternoon, two formations of A4-Bs were winging their way toward San Carlos. Their mission was to drop parachute bombs on enemy troops on the beachhead. Poker Section, flown by Captain Carballo and his wingman, Lieutenant Rinke, came in over the target from the south at about

1658 hours, as twilight was fading. As they entered "Missile Pass," they were met by heavy concentrations of ground fire. The two Skyhawks released their four bombs each as they passed over San Carlos Settlement. The members of the 40th Marine Squadron held their breath as the eight bombs, each swaying gently from a blooming parachute, came straight to their positions. A minute later, a second flight code-named Truco (a cards game) flown by First Lieutenant Velazco and Lieutenant Osses, came center stage. Their configuration and mission were the same, but they aimed their lethal ordnance at Ajax Bay, across the south branch. Their eight bundles of mayhem floated gently onto their targets, parachutes blossoming, as the British took cover.

Both formations had taken the defenses by surprise, and no enemy CAPs rose to challenge them; but as they passed through, the toll was collected for the air rights over the bay: Poker 1 was riddled with enemy canister, knocking out his radio and his instruments, and ripping a large hole in his canopy. He flew home blind, guided by his wingman, who talked him safely to the runway. On the ground, a gaping hole was found in the nose section of the Skyhawk. The following formation was not so lucky. One aircraft was mortally wounded by enemy fire. As it went into its death plunge, the pilot—First Lieutenant Velazco—ejected safely, and was picked up later on West Falkland.

Two of Poker section's bombs came directly into British positions where the marines had dug in, killing one as he fired at the oncoming bomb with his automatic weapon. Three others were wounded. Damage was limited because of the characteristics of the soft bogs, which absorb the blast wave, making all but direct hits ineffective. A third came down on the squad's main bunker, where it could have done great harm. It failed to detonate, but they were forced to evacuate the area for 24 hours, until it could be defused.

It was a different story on the opposite side of the south branch, where Truco section bombs came to rest. The maintenance and supply dump of the 3rd Brigade took a direct hit. In the ensuing explosion, 6 men were killed, 27 were wounded, and the 45th Commando Squad's main powder dump was set ablaze. For the next several hours, often under the personal direction of Brigadier Thompson, the men fought to evacuate the wounded and contain the raging flames. The vulnerability of his brigade's supply dump to enemy air attack was not lost on the commander. He was rightfully concerned that the whole operation could be jeopardized. Ammunition dumps and supply areas were on land because those items could not be stored aboard ship, where the danger was even greater. There was no safe haven on land or sea for any of their gear. The Falklands night was lit up with the red glare of Milan rockets, mortars, and munitions of various calibers bursting in air, lending a festive Fourth of July aura to a fireworks display that served to mask the cruel facts of life.

Truco Squadron had dealt a severe blow to Operation Corporate. All the same, and without either side realizing it, the battle of San Carlos was coming to a close. The beachhead may not have been entirely secured, but General Trant's decision to move inland was the signal that, for better or for worse, at whatever the cost, that beachhead was serving the purpose for which it had been established: to be the jumping-off point for the infantry thrust against the enemy positions.

The decision to advance, in the absence of opposition other than from the air, underscored all too clearly that the all-out effort of the air force, which had given full measure, had proved insufficient to break the enemy's back. How could it have been otherwise? By selecting San Carlos Bay, a place of difficult access to Argentine land and naval forces, the British had dealt themselves the royal flush of the war. Nevertheless, the decision to stage the bulk of the amphibious force from that treacherous perimeter at San Carlos might well have proved to be the greatest folly of the war. Had the Argentine Air Force had even short notice of the impending conflict, our aircraft would have seeded that bay with mines, and had on hand enough torpedoes. Even absent that precaution, had all the MK–17 ordnance that failed to detonate upon finding their mark been properly set and done their job, that British beachhead might well have gone down in history in a very different way.

Those who would seek to draw conclusions based on hard data should be aware of the losses sustained by both sides, especially by the British, for they were largely attributable to the action of the air forces of their enemy. The Argentine Air Force would have kept the heat on, there and wherever viable and significant targets may have been found. It threw in everything they had. Victory eluded them at San Carlos, but, by the same token, it prevented the enemy from achieving air superiority. In so doing, it caused the enemy to sustain grievous losses; it delayed the securing of the beachhead; it was the source of endless wrangling within the British high command; it wrought logistical havoc, thereby hampering the enemy's capability to do battle, not to mention lowering morale; and it made the advance to Puerto Argentino a muddy march through hell on earth.

The mighty British fleet, notwithstanding the support of the United States, came close, in this perilous fight, to meeting, at the hands of a few good men, its own waterloo.

Total Losses in the Battle of San Carlos

Argentine forces:

—21 combat aircraft (9 Mirage-V, 5 A4-C, 3 A4-Q, 2 A4-B, and 2 IA–58) shot down/ destroyed

—6 helicopters (3 Pumas, 1 Chinook, 1 Augusta, and 1 UH–1H shot down/destroyed

—11 pilots killed in action

Map 6
The Battle of San Carlos, May 21–27

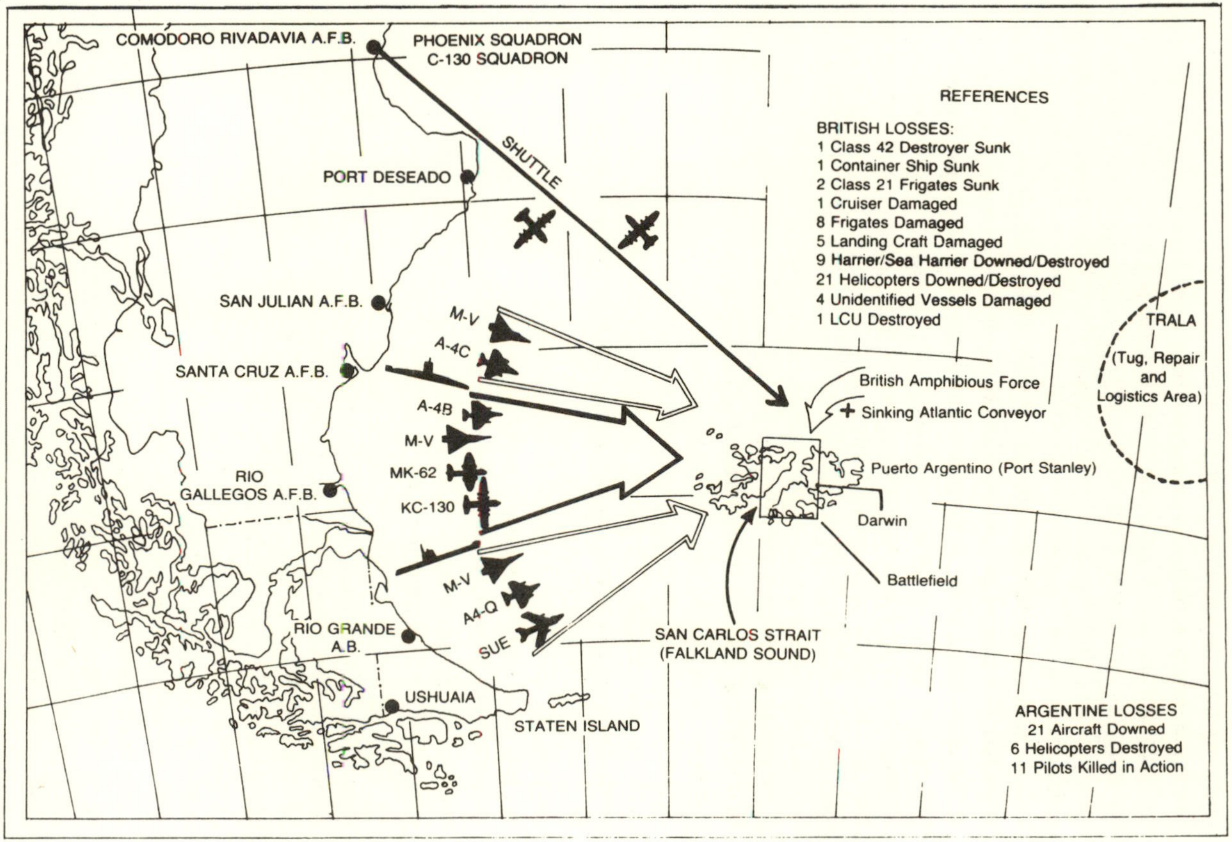

REFERENCES

BRITISH LOSSES:
1 Class 42 Destroyer Sunk
1 Container Ship Sunk
2 Class 21 Frigates Sunk
1 Cruiser Damaged
8 Frigates Damaged
5 Landing Craft Damaged
9 Harrier/Sea Harrier Downed/Destroyed
21 Helicopters Downed/Destroyed
4 Unidentified Vessels Damaged
1 LCU Destroyed

ARGENTINE LOSSES
21 Aircraft Downed
6 Helicopters Destroyed
11 Pilots Killed in Action

British Amphibious Force

Sinking Atlantic Conveyor

TRALA
(Tug, Repair and Logistics Area)

Puerto Argentino (Port Stanley)

Darwin

Battlefield

SAN CARLOS STRAIT
(FALKLAND SOUND)

SUE

STATEN ISLAND

USHUAIA

RIO GRANDE A.B.

RIO GALLEGOS A.F.B.

SANTA CRUZ A.F.B.

SAN JULIAN A.F.B.

PORT DESEADO

SHUTTLE

COMODORO RIVADAVIA A.F.B.

PHOENIX SQUADRON
C-130 SQUADRON

M-V
A-4C
A-4B
M-V
MK-62
KC-130
M-V
A4-Q

British forces:

—1 Class 42 destroyer (HMS *Coventry*) sunk

—2 Class 21 frigates (HMS *Ardent* and *Antelope*) sunk

—1 container ship and its cargo (*Atlantic Conveyor*) sunk

—1 LCU (landing craft) destroyed (unconfirmed by Great Britain)

—1 Cruiser (HMS *Antrim*) heavily damaged

—1 Class 22 frigate (HMS *Brilliant*) heavily damaged

—2 Class 21 frigates (HMS *Argonaut* and *Arrow*) heavily damaged

—1 Class 22 frigate (HMS *Broadsword*, in three different actions) damaged

—2 Class 21 frigates (HMS *Alacrity* and *Avenger*) damaged

—2 Class 12 frigates HMS *Playmouth* and *Yarmouth*) damaged

—4 logistical landing vessels (HMS *Sir Tristram, Sir Galahad, Sir Geraint*, and *Sir Bedivere*) damaged

—1 amphibious landing vessel (HMS *Fearless*) damaged

—1 transport (HMS *Norland*) damaged

—4 unidentified vessels damaged (unconfirmed by Great Britain)

—21 helicopters (including those on the *Atlantic Conveyor*) shot down/destroyed

—9 Harrier/Sea Harrier aircraft shot down/destroyed (not including another five presumably lost aboard the *Atlantic Conveyor*, unconfirmed by Great Britain)

—76 men killed in action (according to British sources; Argentine estimates are somewhat higher).

11

The Fight for Darwin-Goose Green

Men do not usually conduct themselves in accordance with the abstract notion of pure reason. They have to see their ideal embodied in a man who by his very example can inspire them to follow him.

U.S. Army Field Manual 100–1

THE ARGENTINE BATTLEMENTS

At 0800 hours on May 27, Argentine ground forces dug in around Darwin isthmus were made up of Task Force Mercedes, under the command of Lt. Col. Italo Piaggi. The task force was comprised of a reinforced infantry regiment numbering 643 men, which was joined by the 43-man Guemes Combat Team. There were also air force personnel numbering 202, whose assignment was to man and service Condor air base. (These men are not included in the figures for the ground combat forces.) The physical layout of Task Force Mercedes and its morale were far from the best, since the obstacles the team had to overcome during their deployment, added to the hostile environment, had taken their toll. The men's heavy gear had been left aboard the transport at Puerto Deseado. For fire support they had four field guns with 1,860 shells, for mortars with 234 shells, and anti-aircraft artillery.

Another company, 132 men strong, was dug in on Mount Kent, overlooking Puerto Argentino. When the action began at Darwin, they were moved by helicopter to that location, once the situation had been defined, by May 28. They were not all members of the same unit, most of them were poorly trained conscripts, and their only support weapon was an MAG machine gun.

The tactic followed by the task force was based on an in-depth deployment that swung on Goose Green, across from Condor air base. The group was spread over four miles, and initially had been organized to face an attack coming from the west. The first defensive positions had been placed north of the isthmus, where they laid booby traps and mine fields throughout the area, using mines, 250-pound aerial bombs, and electric detonators. The facilities and communications were sadly lacking, since most of their gear was on the mainland. When the enemy was met, some of the men had a single clip of ammunition (seven cartridges) for the weapon they had been issued. A chain of events and circumstances was to lead these unfortunate men to a tragic date with destiny. It was under circumstances such as these that the Argentine Army prepared for its first battle of this century, against a highly professional enemy.

THE BRITISH ATTACKERS

When Brigadier Thompson selected the unit to carry out the raid against the Darwin isthmus, he left nothing to chance. If the politicians back in London wanted a quick victory, it had to be assured. He decided to send in a single battalion, since it would have been difficult for him to assure supplies to two units simultaneously. Paratroop units have not enjoyed the greatest popularity within the Royal Army, although they have earned a well-deserved respect. The two battalions that had been deployed to the Malvinas were the best professionals the Royal Army could muster; their military philosophy was that there was no such thing as impossible, and that the key element of a unit on the battlefield was its capability to generate mayhem. Their armament comprised the most automatic weapons available, rounded out with U.S. M–79 grenade launchers. This balanced out a broad range of firepower, and enabled them to carry out a wide variety of missions. The 2nd Battalion used its final days on British soil for intense combat training. They were led by a man who loved his chosen profession, was quick-tempered, would brook no inefficiency, and was an inspiration to his men.

British infantry battalions are 600 men strong. They are divided into a command company and four rifle companies. Each company has about 120 men, and the rifle companies are identified as A, B, C, and D. Each company is subdivided into platoons of about 30 men each. British battalions differ from their Argentine counterparts in that the latter have three companies each, and do not have as wide an array of heavy and automatic weapons. For the attack against the Argentine garrison, the British 2nd Battalion had the following backup groups: one engineering squadron; three field pieces with 960 shells; two air defense detachments; one Milan rocket detachment; one helicopter squadron; and, as of May 28, a marine infantry company. They also had air support provided by GR–3 Harrier squadrons flying off the *Hermes*, the 3rd Commando Brigade Air Wind (Sea King helicopters), and naval artillery support provided by the frigate HMS *Arrow*.

It can easily be appreciated that this was a force of considerable strength. While they were comparable in numbers with the troops available to Task Force Mercedes, both their firepower and their maneuverability were considerably superior to those of the Argentines. When the order to move out was issued, their morale was high, and they were well equipped and well trained. They found solace in the fact that theirs was an important mission that involved some real action.

FIRST LAND CONTACT

Around midnight on May 26, Company D, 2nd Airborne Battalion, moved out toward the north of the Darwin isthmus. They were quickly followed by the rest of the unit. By 0620 hours on May 27, they had advanced and secured the way, and directed the companies following them. The battalion halted in the houses scattered about this semideserted area, to rest and regain their strength for the final assault.

About this time, the paratroops were tuning their portable radios to the BBC news reports. To their great consternation, they heard that the 2nd Airborne Battalion was advancing toward Darwin, and at that very moment was less than five miles from Argentine positions. Lieutenant Colonel Jones, visibly irritated, ordered his men to leave their comfortable lean-tos and disperse throughout the neighboring terrain, where they proceeded to dig foxholes in the expectation of an onslaught by enemy artillery. This announcement was disregarded by the Argentine intelligence services, which felt that this was in keeping with the enemy's proved tactic of "psychological action,"misinforming in order to veil its true aims. They refused to accept that the enemy was on the march.

The first skirmishes occurred when British troops attempted to reconnoiter an area held by Argentine troops. The former withdrew. At 1240 hours, an Argentine scout team made contact with the British. Following a brief firefight, outflanked by superior numbers and lacking communications with which to call in fire support, they were overwhelmed. Their leader fell prisoner to the British.

The British had planned to advance Company C to prepare the way south in case the remainder of the battalion was ordered in that direction. The plan was rounded out by the overrunning of defense positions in night actions; the troops remaining in the area would be mopped up during daylight, to avoid unnecessary civilian casualties. By the morning of May 28, the operation was to be wrapped up. Under cover of night, Sea King helicopters moved three 105mm guns from Battery 8, 29th Regiment, Royal Artillery, along with ample shells, to the north of the isthmus.

In the meantime, Argentine positions came under attack from Harrier aircraft. As they made their third run over Condor air base, at 0830 hours, one of them was shot down. Their group commander, Lieutenant Colonel Iveson, was picked up later.

At 2100 hours, British Company C moved out toward the south under a persistent drizzle. They were preceded by engineers from Squad 59. Theirs was the sensitive job of ferreting out mines along the trail and under the bridges. The squad had sustained a casualty following the A4-B attack on Ajax Bay, and part of their gear had remained aboard the *Sir Lancelot*, which, having an armed but unexploded 1,000-pound bomb within its sides, had been evacuated. They were followed an hour later by the rest of the battalion, as they got the range of the Argentine positions. Shortly thereafter, at 2305 hours, following an exchange of fire, British troops occupied Burntside House, to the north of the isthmus. Meanwhile, British Company B was faced with an Argentine machine gun nest that had to be taken out. The latter withdrew under heavy British fire.

Argentine mortar fire rained down on the enemy rear guard, even though there was no precise data for pinpointing their range. The naval barrage paused momentarily, because of a technical foul-up, and the pressure was relieved, if only briefly. To facilitate their advance, British rifle companies had left behind their two-inch mortars. This proved to be an error; they would have to defend their position with portable arms.

At about 0320 hours on May 28, following heavy fighting, defending Company A initiated a withdrawal to rearguard positions, coming very close to the British airborne forces. Their support section (three mortars and one recoilless gun) had run out of munitions and had to be abandoned for lack of transport. Company A moved east along the isthmus without encountering resistance as they approached Darwin Settlement. By this time, they were convinced they would achieve their objective, which was to wipe out Argentine opposition before midmorning.

But the Argentines began to lay precision fire from their well-dug-in positions against the Red Berets, who were completely in the open. At that time, every one of Task Force Mercedes' few heavy pieces was aimed straight at the British units deployed throughout the isthmus. As Airborne Company A attempted to move on Darwin, they were taken by surprise as machine gun fire swept through their platoons, forcing them to scramble for cover. They sustained casualties. Things were so bad that they ceased firing and devoted their full efforts to extricating themselves from this quagmire.

The Argentine platoon, commanded by Lieutenant Estevez, which had fewer men than its British counterpart, entered the fray. Ahead of them was British Company B, advancing from the west. The lieutenant reached the first line and was able to block the enemy by penetrating to Boca Hill, from which, although wounded, he starting calling his artillery's range. He thus succeeded in holding up the advance of the British paratroops, inflicting heavy casualties, as he covered the withdrawal of the 12th Infantry Regiment. Estevez fell, mortally wounded by enemy fire, but not before he had proved himself in combat. His dying order was to his squad leader, who continued to call the artillery's range. The position was being riddled by British fire, and the squad leader soon succumbed to the withering hail. A private took up the position and soon joined his companions. But the heroic sacrifice of these brave men proved not to have been in vain. At 0930 hours, the enemy broke off the attack and began to withdraw.

British commanders, confused by the unexpected intensity of the opposition, added to what they regarded to be the contradictory behavior of their foe, for while some held and counterattacked, others fell back in disorder. It was now clear to Lieutenant Colonel Jones that daylight had substantially changed the fortunes of war, and that his troops were dangerously exposed to well-entrenched riflemen who could take their aim with leisure. His own forces could ill afford the luxury of wasting ammunition, for fear of running out and having to break contact, and could not expose themselves to a frontal assault against their enemy's battlements.

In spite of appearances, the circumstances of the Argentine defenders were far from ideal. Company A had taken 50 percent casualties. The remainder had abandoned their positions and scattered, seeking shelter in the settlement. Estevez's reserve platoon had sustained high casualties and had used 60 percent of their ammunition. The heavy weapons support section had ceased to exist.

AIR ACTION OVER THE ISLANDS ON MAY 28

As the situation of the Darwin-Goose Green garrison grew increasingly desperate, Air Force South command in Comodoro Rivadavia began to feel deep concern. The remaining aircraft were scrambled. But the weather proved to be their enemy. A low-pressure system hung over the islands, which made for precipitation, low ceilings, fog, and limited visibility. Not a single squadron was able to take aim on a target, and they returned to base without having achieved their objective. The only noticeable effect of the approach of Argentine aircraft was the withdrawal of the frigate engaged in naval bombardment. Its orders had been to keep up the fire absent enemy aircraft. The frigate was obliged to seek shelter in San Carlos Bay.

The *Uganda* again came into the cross hairs of Skyhawks flying northwest of the north entrance to Falkland Sound. Although hard data were now available that this hospital ship was being employed for tasks not provided for under the Geneva Convention, the aircraft passed up the target as its plainly visible red crosses came into view.

The RAF sortied the fourth run of Operation Black Buck. The objective was to destroy a vital enemy radar emplacement. The Vulcan bomber was fitted with two struts mounted with U.S. Shrike missiles, which home in on the wavelength of the targeted radar. As the bomber rendezvoused with its Victor tanker for in-flight refueling, a malfunction in the fuel transfer boom caused the mission to be scrubbed.

The Pucara squadron that would see the most action was moved to Puerto Argentino, in view of the increased vulnerability of the Condor airstrip at Darwin. During the support missions flown during the day, these aircraft took a considerable number of hits, and many had to be withdrawn from action for repairs. The sturdiness of this plucky aircraft, undergoing its first test under combat conditions, proved surprising, for it demonstrated its ability to take considerable punishment and yet remain airworthy. That morning, in spite of bad weather, two Pucaras sortied at 1030 hours, flying under a thick cloud cover with limited visibility. As they made a pass over enemy positions, firing as they went, they spotted a British Scout helicopter heading for a staging area where other aircraft were unloading gear, in the vicinity of Darwin Settlement. The IA–58s, quickly redubbed "antihelicopter gunships," made a beeline for their prey. At the controls of the lead aircraft, Lieutenant Cimbaro caught a Scout in flight with a salvo of rockets, in spite of its pilot's best efforts at evasive action. The wingman, Lieutenant Gimenez, closed in on the aircraft sitting on the ground, destroying one and damaging the other. Brigadier Thompson observed in his memoirs that the Pucaras pursued Niblett (the helicopter pilot) from every possible angle and altitude, and at various speeds, firing deadly combinations of armament: rockets, cannons, and machine guns. They employed every imaginable tactic for fixed-wing aircraft, and became feared by the helicopter pilots. The Pucaras could throttle back and match the helicopters' every move, thus proving to be a deadly foe.

As Gimenez pulled out, he penetrated the low cloud cover. Coming out over the top, he found himself flying over a white blanket stretching the breadth of the sky below him, which must have confused his senses. The remains of his aircraft and his body were found on West Falkland two years later. It is not known if he was shot down or if he crashed as he attempted to come down through the overcast.

At twilight, after 1630 hours, the Pucaras sortied again. A flight took off from Puerto Argentino in order to cover Task Force Mercedes with close-in fire support. They banked for an all-out attack on Airborne Company D, coming in from Brenton Loch, launching a hail of cannon, rockets, and bombs, in that order. They were met by the Red Berets, who raised a barrage of defensive fire. Although riddled with ground fire, the lead man was able to release his bombs. His wingman was caught in a blizzard of small arms fire, which caused him to eject behind enemy lines, where he was taken prisoner.

Shortly after 1640 hours, a flight of Aeromacchi MB–339 navy aircraft left Puerto Argentino, on a mission to give air support to the beleaguered Darwin-Goose Green garrison. They homed in on enemy positions along the isthmus and unleashed the full fury of their cannon and rockets. The British reaction was immediate and heavy: a storm of tracers zeroed in on the attacking aircraft and found their mark. One of the MB–339s peeled off and went into a slow spin, as if its pilot had been hit. The plane spun into the ground near the landing strip without its pilot ejecting.

The last word of the day had yet to be said. By that time, the whine of turbines crescendoed at the perimeter. This time it was the Harriers, which in spite of the frightful losses they had taken in this sort of action, tried one more low-altitude run over Condor air base in the hope of taking out the air defenses, especially the 35mm guns, which were being used with devastating effect, not as antiaircraft artillery but against British troops on the ground. The cannon and rockets from aircraft that had been knocked out of action were pressed into service for the ground defense of the perimeter. A rocket launcher was hastily mounted on a tractor. This jerry-rigged contraption, which with some fine tuning was able to achieve a 4,000-yard range, proved to be an extremely effective weapon against the British, who suffered heavy casualties that day. As the Harriers made their run, a lucky shot disemboweled the generator, leaving both radar and batteries useless. The base defenders, who had held their position so tenaciously, stood by helplessly. Under cover of darkness, they withdrew to Goose Green, where Argentine forces in the area would make their last stand.

A C–130 succeeded in shuttling into Malvinas base at 1850 hours and, in a record 15-minute turnaround, lifted off on the return leg to Comodoro Rivadavia. It was followed by two more Hercules, which touched down at 2000 and 2210 hours, challenging the ocean waves as they bore in over the whitecaps.

Calls for fire support pouring into Brigadier General Crespo's headquarters at Comodoro Rivadavia soon overwhelmed Air Force South's dwindling capability to sustain them, as the irreversible fortunes of war began to turn against them.

THE DEATH OF LT. COL. HERBERT JONES: THE STUFF OF HEROES

By 1030 hours that morning, the situation was as follows:

1. Northwest sector of the isthmus: British attack repelled
2. Northeast sector of the isthmus: British Airborne Company A arrived in the vicinity of Darwin Settlement
3. Goose Green-air base sector: Second Lieutenant Gomez Centurion's second platoon in the area, and First Lieutenant Esteban's Guemes combat team in position. Other remnants of Task Force Mercedes covering the approaches to Condor base and Goose Green Settlement

At this point there was a lull in the fighting in which the capability of each side to regain its momentum would play a vital role in the action yet to come. From both a logistical and a morale standpoint, the ball was in the British court.

Shortly after 1030 hours, Lieutenant Colonel Piaggi decided to launch a counterattack aimed at preventing the enemy from taking an elevation known as Darwin Hill. This difficult task fell to Gomez Centurion's platoon. At 1100 hours, the platoon moved over the trail linking Goose Green and Darwin. As the men initiated their penetration, they spotted an enemy platoon moving up the same path, at a distance of about 1,000 yards. Faced with this situation, Gomez Centurion ordered his men to fan out to attack the British column. The British kept to the trail, since they assumed the adjoining areas were mined. This allowed the Argentine contingent to take aim and open fire. There ensued a 30-minute firefight, after which five British soldiers started waving their helmets and their rifles from the center of their position, as if in a bid for a truce.

The guns fell silent, and Gomez Centurion advanced to parley with his counterpart, who moved out from his own position. The lieutenant, in view of the tight spot the British were in, thought the latter were seeking terms of surrender.

As the two met, the British officer—Lieutenant Jim Barry—presented himself as the emissary of the British paratroop battalion commander, and demanded the surrender of the Argentine platoon and the laying down of their weapons. The Argentine officer told him to withdraw immediately to his own position, for his platoon would resume firing in two minutes. Both hurriedly returned to their respective strongholds. In the meantime, British troops had secured a position to the southeast of the Argentines, and opened fire. There ensued a heavy firefight, which ended as the British officer fell to the ground, hit.

The British state that there was a confusing incident during this action in which the Argentine platoon apparently waved a flag of truce. It was under these circumstances, they say, that Lieutenant Barry came out to parley and was wounded by fire from the opposing position, which claimed it did not know why the officer left cover and came out in the open. Subsequent investigation has determined that none of the commanders of the Argentine party had intended to surrender. They were at a loss to understand the British contention that a flag of truce had been waved. If there had been such a flag, it was not authorized, nor was any such order issued.

By 1100 hours, British troops still had not achieved a breakthrough of what appeared to be a solid circle of defenders. As the perimeter narrowed, a growing shortage of ammunition forced the survivors to salvage munitions and weapons from their dead and wounded comrades. All the while, Lieutenant Colonel Jones looked with increasing impatience on the apparent ineffectiveness of his artillery. Every measure provided for in the field manual had been tried with less than auspicious results. It was up to him to find a novel solution, an unconventional tactic to overcome the unexpected.

Observing Darwin Hill, he ordered the commander of Company A—Maj. Dair Farrar-Hockley—to try for that hill. Farrar-Hockley started inching up the flank with a squad of 16 men, including his second in command and the battalion adjutant. Minutes later, the latter two fell, mortally wounded, soon followed by others who brought up the rear. Having sustained heavy casualties, the squad was forced to withdraw. Accompanied by two other men, automatic pistol at the ready, Jones, with total disregard for his own safety, launched a personal attack on his entrenched foe. It was 1330 hours. His objective was a machine-gun nest. When he was within 25 yards of that obstacle, he came into the cross fire of another machine-gun position he had not reckoned with. Hit in the neck, he slumped to the ground. The assault had failed. In bare minutes, the battle for Darwin Hill had cost the lives of the battalion commander, his adjutant, the second in command of Company A, and nine others.

The circumstances of Lieutenant Colonel Jones's death have been scrutinized from various angles. The tactical value of the targeted position has been debated, and the action has been labeled "foolish bravery." Others hold that the men were braced by his example, that in spite of their professional reservations and their sagging morale following the death of their commander, the 2nd Battalion was propelled into action, in an all-out assault, in which Maj. Chris Keeble, second in command, led his men through a deadly gauntlet, thereby achieving the final objective. One thing is certain. Lieutenant Colonel Jones died in battle, leading his men. He gave his full measure of devotion and was awarded Britain's highest military honor, the Victoria Cross, posthumously.

Far from being demoralized, the men of the 2nd Airborne Battalion were inspired to carry on the fight and change the fortunes of war. British troops solved the problem of the Argentine emplacements by employing, with singular success, the 66mm Milan guided missiles, which ripped gaping holes in the defenders' redoubts.

Falling back under withering enemy fire, Gomez Centurion's platoon withdrew southward, dragging their wounded and fighting every inch of the way, until they reached the defense perimeter at Goose Green. Here, too, the powerful Milan missiles took their toll. One by one, the British wiped out the defenders' positions and secured their advance.

The Red Berets now held the high ground at Boca and Darwin, following an engagement in which they met an enemy determined to fight. The positions were taken at great cost to the British, who succeeded in achieving their objective as much by their professionalism as by their awesome firepower. Major Keeble took careful stock of the situation. His men had won a hard-fought victory, but they were exhausted, they were low on ammunition, they had numerous wounded, and the battlefield was littered with their dead. No less fearsome opponents were the cold, the unrelenting rain, and the terrain. It was 1700 hours. Before them lay the gently rolling moors leading to the last Argentine stronghold, and the coveted objective: Goose Green Settlement. It would not be a snap for any infantry battalion in the world. But the 2nd Airborne Battalion was no ordinary unit.

Major Keeble bided his time. His was not an easy decision, but it was essential. He would await the arrival of reinforcements, which apparently had been called in by Lieutenant Colonel Jones with his dying breath. When the British moved out, it was hard going all the way. The defenders opened up with everything they had left. The 35mm antiaircraft guns at Condor base, which had been turned against the British troops advancing on the ground, were lethally effective as they raked the perimeter with columns of fire and showers of steel. Major Keeble himself felt the effect of these guns. One discharge churned up a tangled patch of thorny plants, from which the major was able to free himself with the greatest of effort. Many British soldiers fell to the canisters spewed out by the 35mm Oerlikon antiaircraft guns. About this time, Argentine Macchi and Pucaras momentarily slowed the advance of the Red Berets. But as the Harriers flew their avenging runs into Condor, they silenced the antiaircraft guns that had been turned on the ground troops.

At nightfall, the commander of Task Force Mercedes was surrounded by the British. To secure the defense perimeter of the settlement, all he had left were two platoons, and the remnants of other units who were too exhausted to be effective. British heavy artillery swung around and spoke resoundingly again and again as it pounded this last redoubt.

Meanwhile, behind British lines, the battalion commander witnessed yet another turning point of the battle. His troops had reached the outskirts of Goose Green Settlement. Were he to order the final charge against Argentine positions that night or early the following morning, his men would sustain grievous losses to the well-entrenched defenses and to the mine fields. There were, furthermore, 114 civilians there, and he did not wish to answer for their fate.

Major Keeble contacted Brigadier Thompson. The commander of the 3rd Commando Brigade agreed to the immediate dispatch of Company J, 42nd Marine Commando Battalion, to reinforce the 2nd Airborne. This would be backed up by three 105mm field pieces and six mortars, with ammunition, along with a mortar-locating radar, two tracked vehicles for moving the pieces, light weapons ammunition, and two helicopters. It was agreed that a show of air and ground firepower would be made at first light in an attempt to convince the Argentine defenders of the futility of holding out. This was what Major Keeble wished above all else, for otherwise the way would be hard indeed. There was the grim prospect of destroying the homes of numerous Kelpers in the process. His orders had been to proceed at whatever cost, even the lives of these defenseless civilians. Anything to ensure the defeat of this defiant Argentine outpost.

The politicians back in London wanted a victory at all costs. What were 114 Kelpers—men, women, and children of British descent—whom the task force allegedly had been sent to liberate? Principles espoused to rationalize government decisions to the public are one thing; the true designs for which men are sent to fight and die are quite another. The British decision with regard to the local inhabitants at Goose Green was, for all intents and purposes, a sentence of death. The sentence was stayed, for Argentina decided to avoid a senseless butchery. There would be no Little Big Horn in the South Atlantic. At 1100 hours on May 29, on instructions from headquarters, the Argentine garrison at Goose Green laid down its arms.

And so it was that units of the British task force retook Darwin-Goose Green. According to British sources, 50 Argentines and 17 Britons were killed in action, the latter buried on the spot. No one who fought at Darwin believes those casualty figures, but be that as it may, London had achieved victory in the nick of time. The 3rd Commando Brigade had at that point run out of rations and ammunition, thanks largely to the lack of British air superiority at the beachhead. But the British propaganda machine rose to the occasion, finding effective methods of covering up these and other shortcomings.

The first releases crowed that "450 paratroops . . . trounced 1,600 Argentine regulars." And while these figures changed as time passed, the truth was never established. The *London Times* stated on its front page (June 2, 1982) that "Argentina lost 250 men [killed] in the Battle of Port Darwin and Goose Green."

No mention is made of the myriad problems, of hand-to-hand combat, of casualties sustained by the Red Berets. (According to confidential British sources, about 120 were killed in action.) Nor was any explicit mention made of the fact that the 2nd Airborne had had to call for reinforcements, and that, from a logistics standpoint, it had been oversupplied for its artillery and fire needs.

There is no wish to detract from the victory gained by the Red Berets at Darwin. They did what they were sent to do. They are blameless for the shortcomings of the enemy they met on the battlefield. At all times they conducted themselves professionally and honorably, and are deserving of our respect and admiration. Neither can they be held responsible for the fudging of the truth and the fiddling with the facts of which their superiors in London are guilty.

In the final accounting, Task Force Mercedes gave full measure. Angels could have done no more. Had its men been properly prepared and trained, as those they faced that fateful day had been, the story of the battle for Port Darwin and Goose Green might have read, for Argentines, like the battle of New Orleans.

12

The March to Fitz Roy and Mount Kent

The courage and spirit that propel an army have been for all time, and shall continue to be for all time, a powerful factor behind its physical strength.

Clausewitz

THE BRITISH BATTLE ORDER

British ground forces were organized as follows:

The 3rd Commando Brigade, with the 40th, 42nd, and 45th Royal Marine Commandos; the 59th Regiment, Royal Artillery Command; and the 59th Squadron, Royal Engineers Command

The 5th Infantry Brigade, with the 2nd Battalion, Scots Guards; the 1st Battalion, Welsh Guards; the 1st Battalion, Gurka Riflemen; the 4th Regiment, Royal Field Artillery; and the 36th Regiment, Royal Engineers

Joint forces, with Platoons 3 and 4 of the Blues and Royals Armored Reconnaissance Squadron; and the 2nd and 3rd Airborne Battalions.

The 3rd Battalion of Red Berets moved out on their long march east to Puerto Argentino on May 27. They were followed by the Royal Marine 45th Battalion, which marched from Port San Carlos. The lack of helicopters hampered the British as they struggled over some of the worst terrain that infantry can encounter; burdened down with full field gear weighing over 70 pounds per man, they slogged through the mushy Falklands peat bogs.

The 40th Marine Battalion was held back at San Carlos Bay in order to ensure the defense of the beachhead until the arrival of Gen. Jeremy Moore, who was sailing in with the 5th Infantry Brigade under the command of Brig. Anthony Wilson, aboard the *Queen Elizabeth II*. Following transfer to lighter transports, they were faced again with the perilous approach into enemy waters with their vital cargoes.

This decision followed lengthy debate over whether to establish a second beachhead on East Falkland in order to land the 5th Brigade. It was governed by the lack of enough Rapier antiaircraft missile batteries to fend off enemy air raids. The makeup of the 5th Brigade differed considerably from that of the 3rd. The Defense Ministry had apparently intended it as a backup for the latter, which had been handpicked to do the job. There is no rational explanation for the presence, in an environment such as Malvinas, for the Scots and Welsh Guards, battalions usually employed for ceremonial duty.

THE ARGENTINE ORDER OF BATTLE

The fall of Port Darwin-Goose Green was cause for great concern among the defenders at Puerto Argentino. The fact that Argentine troops had laid down their arms added to the effectiveness of the British psychological warfare being waged and further deepened the ominous clouds gathering over General Menendez's troops, clouds that could no longer be dissipated. Faced with the British thrust from the west, the Argentine commander ordered that approach beefed up. Battlements had already been erected around the airport (to the east), and in the quadrants north and south of Puerto Argentino.

Argentine ground forces were arrayed as follows:

Army Group Puerto Argentino was comprised of the 10th Mechanized Infantry Brigade, with three regiments of mechanized infantry; one infantry regiment; one marine battalion; and two artillery groups.

Army Group Litoral was comprised of the 3rd Infantry Brigade (at Puerto Argentino), with the 5th Infantry Regiment (Port Howard); the 8th Infantry Regiment (Fox Bay); and the 601st Aviation Battalion.

Joint formations included one infantry regiment; two commando companies (601 and 602); one company of the National Gendarmerie; the 10th Armored Cavalry Squadron (Panhard vehicles); and one company from the 1st Infantry Regiment Patricios.

THE ENGAGEMENTS OF MAY 29

In the political field, New York continued to be the scene of intense Argentine efforts aimed at achieving enough support to push through a cease-fire in the South Atlantic as a prelude to negotiations while the meeting of consultation of foreign ministers, called under the terms of the Rio Treaty, went forward in Washington. In London, the visit of Pope John Paul II was the object of close media scrutiny, and the requisition of yet another tanker for deployment to the war zone was announced.

In the battle zone, two Air Force South Canberras carried out a night bombing raid over the San Carlos Bay perimeter, harassing the beachhead. In the dead of night, at 0208 hours, members of the 3rd Airborne were shaken up as they began their long march east.

Meanwhile, Air Force South command and its staff had been working on a plan to mount an attack on one of the enemy carriers, employing navy Super Etendard's, and therefore were watching the target ships' movements. The position of both carriers, as well as that of the QE II, had been pinpointed by May 29. The intricacy of such an operation, as well as the limited availability of the KC–130 tankers, made it impossible to move on that date.

By 0900 hours, the air was thick with British aircraft. As many as six CAPs, a total of 12 aircraft, were flying simultaneously. At 0920 hours, the Harriers flew persistent raids against the airfield, employing air-surface rockets with some measure of success, since casualties were sustained. At 1108 hours, the Harriers turned their attention to Calderon (Pebble Island) airstrip. Six delayed-fuse bombs were dropped, but the runway remained intact. In spite of all this enemy activity, Air Force South authorized the sortie of a DH–6 Twin Otter search-and-rescue aircraft from the mainland to evacuate Argentine personnel. It came in at 1405 hours as the beleaguered base was under full red alert, and succeeded in picking up two ejected flyers. The Twin Otter, a slow-flying, vulnerable, and defenseless aircraft, defied the odds and landed safely at Puerto Deseado at 2040 hours. At 1205 hours, two Harriers executed a bombing run over the airport but failed to achieve results. One plane was hit by a Roland missile, and air defense confirmed the kill. The British reported the loss of a Sea Harrier that skidded off the frozen flight deck into the sea as its pilot ejected.

By noon that day, several air force squadrons were in the air, winging their way to San Carlos in search of targets. The British ships were nowhere to be seen, and the first formation of Mirage-V Daggers turned for home empty-handed. As they flew over the north of San Carlos Strait, just as they caught sight of a target, one of their number was blown from the skies by a Rapier. The pilot was listed as missing. They were followed by a formation of A4-Bs, which scoured the straits for a target, sighting one north of West Falkland. Short on fuel, they were forced to turn back without engaging. Another formation of three Daggers entered the area at 1410 hours and were met by a Sea Harrier CAP that hit no targets. Not an even score. While night bombing had proved its worth, for targets had been hit, bad weather at that time of year severely limited this sort of operation. Air Force South was further concerned about the absence of enemy ships. Its aircraft lacked the range to go out in search of the enemy, and what they did achieve was thanks to the precision timing of the in-flight refueling operations.

During the night, the paratroops of the 3rd Battalion, followed a 25-mile march from San Carlos, pitched camp at Teal Inlet; the 45th Marines did the same further north, at Douglas Settlement. By this time, the British had figured that it would be all over by June 6 or 7, with Puerto Argentino secured.

THE ENGAGEMENTS OF MAY 30

From a political standpoint, recently adopted U.N. Resolution 505 would do little to alter the course of events or thwart British resolve. An article reprinted from the *London Times* in New York stated that Mrs. Thatcher had done everything but actually demand surrender of the Argentine garrison in so many words. This was the general impression within the United Nations, since British intractability had doomed the secretary general's mandate, embodied in Security Council Resolution 505, to failure. In London, *The Guardian* pointed out, in an extensive article, that a solution should be sought based on the principles continuously upheld by the government. To go on for years under the threat of Argentine interference with British ships, and the possibility of air attacks, was no formula for peace. Neither was the total isolation of the continent a long-term solution. These would prove to be wise words.

By this time, the Argentine Foreign Ministry was concentrating on an upcoming meeting of the nonaligned countries that had been expressing their support for Argentina's position on the Malvinas since their Lima conference in 1975. For want of better allies, Argentina had nothing to lose by attending this function. Others had been tried and found wanting. The Reagan administration, the U.S. Congress, and the Pentagon had all slammed the door shut over the issue.

In the battle zone, action on May 30 was marked by a sustained naval bombardment against Argentine positions, as well as the movement of helicopters west of San Carlos in a concerted effort to support the British advance on the Malvinas garrison at Puerto Argentino, and lay the groundwork for a second troop landing on East Falkland. The Harriers paid their regular calls on the airstrip at 0850 and 1030 hours, damaging two MB–339 aircraft. During another action, an enemy aircraft fell victim to the 601st Air Defense's 35mm batteries. The plane came down in the water and its pilot, Maj. Jerry Pook, was rescued shortly thereafter. At about 1000 hours, an Argentine Army Puma was brought down by enemy fire in the vicinity of Mount Kent. Several casualties were sustained.

In the meantime, the British troops struck camp and moved out. In a relentless march unpunctuated by rest breaks, they slogged on with grim determination. In time, they came into sight of the first ridges around Mount Kent. This elevation, which had been lightly manned by lookouts and occasional Argentine patrols, was of vital tactical value to Brigadier Thompson, who earnestly wished to take it before General Menendez decided to beat him to the punch.

According to plan, the task force was to carry out a second landing in the Fitz Roy area with the 5th Brigade, since landing them at San Carlos would force these men to follow their mates in the long overland trek to Puerto Argentino, thus delaying the retaking of the island capital by several days, a delay the politicians in London, pressed by other concerns, were not inclined to grant. With Darwin-Goose Green now in British hands, and Fitz Roy lying a third of the way to the island capital, this appeared to be the logical solution, since troops landing at Fitz Roy would incur no risk of hostile action from the rear but would be a threat to Puerto Argentino as they approached the south perimeter of the garrison's defenses from a shorter distance.

Jeremy Moore, 53, enjoyed great prestige. He was Britain's most decorated general, and had the most combat experience of the Royal Marines. His arrival in the theater of operations, which came at a critical juncture for the political situation facing the sitting government in London, allowed him to conduct himself in such an evenhanded way as to instill great confidence in his men.

The task force arrayed its assets for the landing, and prepared the 5th Infantry Brigade to the beach at Fitz Roy. In so doing, it also afforded itself a primary role—instead of a secondary one—in the action to come. But something happened that day that forced the high command to rethink their plans entirely.

THE ATTACK AGAINST HMS *INVINCIBLE*

May 30, 1982, will probably go down in the annals of the conflict as being the day of the most daring, unthinkable, and risky operation of the South Atlantic War. Air Force South, well aware that the enemy was holding a winning hand, decided to risk its trump card. It would mount an all-out attack on the very nerve center of the British task force: it would go for the jugular, the light carriers!

David versus Goliath

The problems implied by an operation of this scope, not to mention the risks, were overwhelmingly complex. The prospects for success were just a glimmer. The odds against the pilots who would carry it out coming back alive were almost unfathomable. For openers, the distance at which the British carriers usually operated was a formidable obstacle. Getting to the target and back would require more than one in-flight refueling operation; therefore, the KC–130 tankers had to be placed with pinpoint precision. The slightest glitch would send the assailing aircraft to a watery grave for lack of fuel.

The second problem lay in the position of the two prospective targets. They had to be located precisely. Scouting the vast reaches of the ocean, whether by air, surface or undersea means, and pinpointing two tiny dots in the process, amounted to a technical challenge that would normally be regarded as beyond the resources of a developing nation. Radar at Puerto Argentino could give approximate locations of the enemy carriers by plotting the headings of the Harriers or Sea Harriers, but this procedure offered neither certainty, precision, nor the lead time such an operation would require.

The third problem arose from the dilemma of which aircraft to use. Because of the pinpoint navigational requirements, the navy Super Etendards would lead the way to the target and fire their missiles. The Mirage-V Daggers, which could not be refueled in flight, were unusable. The MK–62 Canberras, which might have been ideal because of their range, were discarded because of their relatively slow speed, lack of maneuverability, and mainly their large, telltale radar signature. The aircraft most suited for the job was the Skyhawk. It brought together in a single airframe all the required characteristics: it could be refueled in flight, it matched the Super Etendard in speed and maneuverability, its ability to penetrate naval electronic and weapons systems had proved superior, and it could carry three 500-pound bombs per aircraft.

The mere suggestion of such a use for this small plane, designed by Douglas Aircraft and first flown in 1954, would have brought a smirk of incredulity from even the most earnest of its boosters. It would be more in keeping with the wry sense of humor among British staff officers than anything Air Force South would seriously attempt to do. And yet . . . .

The commander issued his decision on May 28. A modern-day David would face off with a Goliath of the high seas. The mission was GO! The order was to attack.

Flight Order OF/1268, which included transfer of a squadron of A4-Cs to the base at Rio Grande, from whence the attack would be mounted, was issued and sent down. As of May 29, an all-out effort was made to pinpoint the exact positions of the targeted British carriers, which had been tracked from the onset of the conflict by the air force's operations electronics center. By May 30, the center had locked onto the *Invincible*, plotting its position and headings. The aircraft carrier, which was poised for the offensive, was sailing a tight east-west loop at about the latitude of Puerto Argentino, 100 NM off the coast.

The two KC–130 tankers, which had been prepared for this particular mission down to the very smallest detail, sortied at 1125 hours, heading for their carefully calculated rendezvous points. By 1243 hours, the final member of the formation was off the ground. The historic mission was on. Section Ala, comprising the two Super Etendards, and Flight Zeus, with the four Skyhawks, flew out for an uneven battle with Britain.

As the coast of Tierra del Fuego dropped behind them, every pilot was at one with his thoughts. What fate awaited them could only be surmised. Maintaining complete radio silence, the two Super Etendards led the formation, and the Skyhawks brought up the rear. Their flight path was to take them south of the islands on an easterly heading to a point just beyond the position of the task force vessels. They would execute a turn northward and, coming in on the targeted ship from behind, would close for the attack in what they hoped would be a surprise action, for that vital element was their only hope for survival. There was no way they could give battle to the Sea Harriers if they detected their presence and flew out to meet them. The lone Exocet A/S 39 was slung along the underframe of the lead Super Etendard, whose backup flew cover. Following close behind, each Skyhawk had nestled under its wings three 500-pound bombs. Perhaps not enough to deep-six an 18,910 ton man-of-war, but surely enough to give it food for thought. The six aircraft executed their two in-flight refueling operations without a hitch. As they approached the target area, they dropped

Map 7
The Attack against HMS *Invincible*

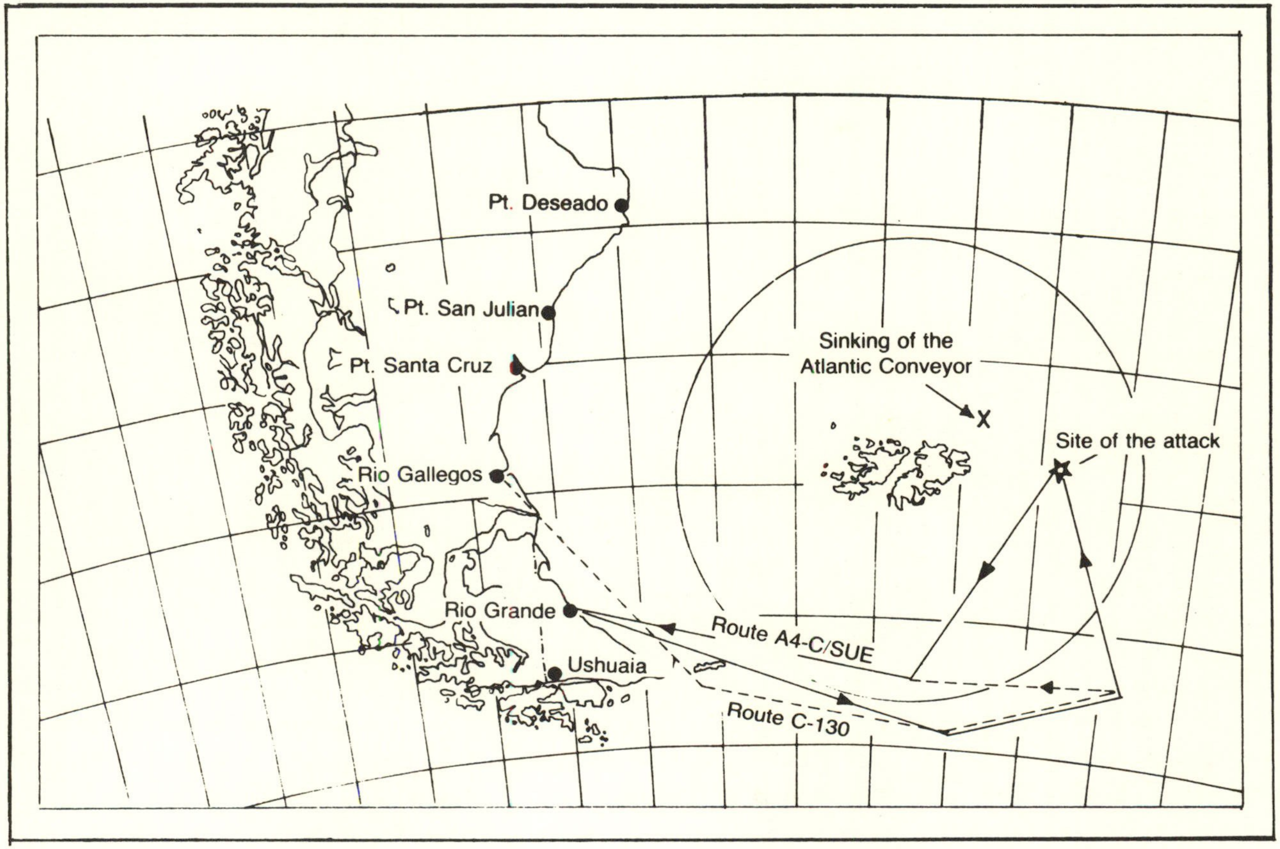

Pt. Deseado

Pt. San Julian

Pt. Santa Cruz

Rio Gallegos

Rio Grande

Ushuaia

Route A4-C/SUE

Route C-130

Site of the attack

Sinking of the
Atlantic Conveyor
X

down to wave-top level. A single malfunction would have scrubbed the whole mission. Thus far, it was all still GO!

Breathlessly, the formation approached the target acquisition point: if it was not where it was supposed to be, the mission would have to be aborted, since they had no leeway for a search operation. The two Super Etendards edged ever so slightly up over the water to switch on their radar at the preestablished point. The target's signature gleamed true, right where it had been plotted. A split second later the last Exocet whooshed from its launcher and undertook its short, but lethal, flight. The two pilots immediately executed a hard turn to the left and headed for home. It was 1424 hours. Following the path of the missile as it blazed its trail to the target, the four Zeus locked in and held on for dear life. At this very moment, the men plotting the shadow of the attackers looming ever larger on their radarscopes must have been powering up the electronics and swinging the ship's formidable array of defenses into battle positions; the fast moving-flying object followed by four smaller and slower ones had not gone undetected.

The carrier's defenses must have been overwhelmed by the Exocet, for reaction time was measured in seconds. Complete surprise for the missile, but not so for the squadron of Skyhawks that had been homed in on by the Sea Dart missile system's 909 radar detector, which lost no time in automatically firing a first salvo of two of the deadly warheads, riding a tail of flame. Up and down the length of the massive grey hull, antiaircraft emplacements were cranking into the firing position, bristling on full alert to the impending fight being brought to them at "three o'clock" by the invading marauders.

Their hearts pounding with all the pent-up excitement of the moment, the pilots of Zeus flew into battle. This was *High Noon* on the high seas! Would they live to tell the tale or go down to a watery grave? Launched 24 miles from the target, Exocet would reach its mark in 109 seconds, while the A4-Cs would take a seemingly endless 153 seconds, losing the element of surprise, as they closed to meet the ship's massed air defenses. Halfway to the target, the hulk of the carrier was a looming silhouette against the horizon. Seventy-six seconds to go! Instants later, Zeus No. 3 watched part of his squadron leader's (1st Lt. Jose D. Vasquez) left wing break off, following almost at once by the explosion of his engine. The plane broke in two, cartwheeling off to the left and exploding into the sea, taking its pilot with it. Sea Dart had scored a victory.

The other three Zeus pilots saw an orange blur rush past as they pressed in on the aircraft carrier. They homed in on the black smoke billowing from both sides of the flattop's control tower, surely the handiwork of the Exocet. As they closed, No. 2 disintegrated in a spinning shower of flaming debris as he fell to the barrage of antiaircraft fire tracing out from the ship. Its pilot, 1st Lt. Omar J. Castillo, joined his companion. Zeus No. 3, piloted by 1st Lt. Ernesto Ureta, made it through the storm of fire and aimed his salvo of bombs aft of the flight deck, making his escape by zooming up past the right flank of the control tower, then hugging the sea in his bid for safety. One final look at his target showed it enshrouded in a pall of smoke. Zeus No. 4, 2nd Lt. Gerardo Isaac came face to face in the next seconds with all the contingencies entailed by bringing up the rear of a formation of attack aircraft in action. Undeterred by the toll exacted against his two lead companions, he bore in on the wounded vessel. But at his angle, he was surrounded by smoke, as was the ship, and he was unable to take sharp aim. He released his salvo and pulled out over the stern. Following the escape path of Zeus No. 3, he was able, from about four miles out, to appreciate the spectacle of the carrier, totally hidden from view by billowing black smoke.

The *Invincible* soon faced its most crucial hour. According to unofficial British sources, its flight control center took a hail of 200mm cannon fire and the Exocet, which pierced the starboard side reportedly exploded in the inner compartments, causing grievous damage. Three 500-pound bombs hit the flight deck, two of them detonating and causing heavy damage to that part of the ship. Fire soon reached the underdeck where several Sea Harriers were undergoing repairs. As a final touch, the careening remains of one of the Skyhawks damaged the port engine room, causing serious fire damage.

Word was flashed posthaste to the commander of the task force and the commander of the British ground forces. They called off the landings at Fitz Roy and reassessed the whole situation. Aircraft flying off the *Invincible* were reassigned to other platforms. General Moore immediately decided to remove to San Carlos and plan the landing there. On arrival in the perimeter, he set up his command post aboard the *Fearless*. There he took stock of the day's disastrous news and the all-too-inauspicious opening performance of his first day as commander of British ground forces. His presence in the theater of operations, as well as his experience, mettle, and professionalism, not to mention the confidence he instilled in his men, steadied Great Britain at that crucial juncture, in what was proving to be a possibly decisive setback.

The two surviving Skyhawk pilots, who had just performed the greatest single feat of arms of the war in a mission that would become the symbol of the struggle to reclaim our Malvinas Islands, regrouped and returned safely to base. They touched down at Rio Grande at 1620 hours, and there, finally, they could give unbridled vent to their emotions.

The Search for the Truth

If the British War Cabinet had carefully concealed the outcome of the battle of May 1, it was not about to acknowledge that one of its carriers had been successfully attacked by Argentine aircraft, forcing the second task force landing operation to a dead halt. In terms of military and political loss of face, the aftermath of this latest event could be much more disastrous than its real effect in the tactical field. Mission 1268 had put the very survival of Mrs. Thatcher's government at risk.

The problem was no easier for the Argentine side. It would not be enough to have crippled an enemy carrier if such an act could not be acknowledged and

confirmed with certainty. The surviving pilots were submitted to intense de-
briefings; only an in-depth analysis would determine the accuracy of their accounts, and that the vessel was indeed the *Invincible*. The nature of the
intelligence defied the senses, and there were only two eyewitnesses: First Lieutenant Ureta and Second Lieutenant Isaac. When Argentina made public the fact
that the *Invincible* had been hit by Argentine aircraft, the British Defense Ministry, aware that an outright denial was impossible, issued a report to the effect
that Argentine aircraft had attacked the hulk of the *Atlantic Conveyor*, and that
a single aircraft had been brought down in the course of that action. This announcement can be shot down with three simple and verifiable facts:

1. The *Atlantic Conveyor* had been abandoned by its crew on May 25 at a position about
   40 NM northeast of Puerto Argentino. The derelict had drifted aimlessly in that general
   direction over the following days.
2. The target of the attack by the A4-Cs had been fully armed and manned, and had
   brought down two of its assailants.
3. The still-smoking hulk of the container ship had gone down on May 28, at 51°07'S/
   57°34'W, a position 60 NM from that of the *Invincible*, which was at 51°35'S/55°34'W
   when it came under attack.

The British later altered their version of events; stating that the action had
been carried out against the *Avenger*—which claimed to have destroyed the
Exocet with its guns—and the *Exeter*, which had brought down the two Skyhawks
with its Sea Darts. This tale is so farfetched as to defy the imagination (Ethell
& Price, p. 109). Something very odd that did not go unnoticed at Puerto
Argentino bears underscoring at this point: Shortly after the action against the
Invincible, there was a flurry of helicopter activity out of San Carlos, heading
north over East Falkland and then east. The CAPs then in the air climbed
unexpectedly to 35,000 feet, most likely to conserve fuel in response to the
emergency that had arisen. That same afternoon, both Harrier and Sea Harrier
aircraft landed at an improvised airfield at San Carlos Bay.

As for Air Force South command, there was little doubt as to the type of
vessel that had sustained the attack. The only room for question arose from the
debriefing of the pilots: whether they had nailed the *Invincible* or the *Hermes*.
That they had attacked a carrier there was no doubt, since it had the typical
configuration of a ship fitted with a flight deck—a flattop. The choice was
narrowed to the *Invincible*, since it, unlike the *Hermes*, does not have a curve
at the end of the launching deck.

Furthermore—aside from the eyewitness accounts—the fact that one plane
had been destroyed by a missile almost ten miles from its target signifies that
these were not warheads such as Sea Cats, carried by the *Hermes* and the smaller
frigates, nor were they the Sea Wolf, for the range of both types is considerably
shorter. What is certain is that the vessel that came under attack was a capital
ship with a flat deck. It carried Sea Dart missiles and was equipped with heavy

caliber antiaircraft defenses. The latter were not normally carried by the *Invincible* and *Hermes*, but once Air Force South had made its tactics and effectiveness felt, the task force had hurriedly issued 20mm, 35mm, and 40mm antiaircraft guns, which were even mounted aboard requisitioned merchant vessels. Based on all of the above, only one ship of that configuration came under attack by the Squadron that day: the light carrier HMS *Invincible*.

To add to the mystery surrounding these events, *Invincible* was the last of the British task force vessels to quit the South Atlantic. It steamed north on July 29 and, following an inexplicably long voyage (51 days), finally dropped anchor at Portsmouth on September 17, 1982. It was immediately placed off limits to reporters and all other personnel, except the queen. Apparently the extent of the damage wrought by the attack was such that even the prolonged stay at sea was insufficient for proper repairs. Once safely in port, *Invincible*'s spent five months in dry dock.

Great Britain may persist in denying that its carriers fell prey to Argentina's puny air force, but *Invincible*'s 166 days at sea, without calling at a single port, is a world record for continuous sea duty for a vessel of its class. It broke the previous record—held by the nuclear attack carrier U.S.S. *Eisenhower*—by 13 days. A strange record indeed for a light carrier, in a conflict that lasted only 45 days.

Zeus Squadron lost two members, who went down in flaming glory, but Flight Order 1268 went down as "mission accomplished."

THE ENGAGEMENTS OF MAY 31

The London press swallowed up the previous day's events and parroted the Defense Ministry as if its official spokesmen. Any attack against the *Invincible* was flatly denied. Accounts were published of the downing of two Mirages and two Skyhawks as they attempted to attack the fleet. British public opinion was being made ready for the next onslaught: the battle to retake Port Stanley. Prospects of heavy losses and forecasts of the "toughest battle for British Forces since Hill 327 in Korea" were being aired. The *London Times*, in its main article of the day, took Mrs. Thatcher strongly to task and underscored her differences with Foreign Secretary Francis Pym in the following terms:

Relations between the Prime Minister and Mr. Francis Pym, her Foreign Secretary, have reached such a low ebb, that some of Mrs. Thatcher's senior ministerial colleagues have begun to vilify Mr. Pym in the most disparaging personal terms, in private commons conversations. . . .

Mr. Roy Hattersley, the shadow spokesman on home affairs, said in a T. V. interview yesterday that the Prime Minister was being both "short-sighted and foolish" and withdrawing all offers of negotiation . . . semi-war with Argentina for a decade or more, is clearly absurd.

In the United States, the *New York Times* labeled the OAS resolution as "a significant setback for the U.S. in the Western Hemisphere. The U.S. was the target of the most emotional and sharp attacks ever heard within that body." An argument between Secretary of State Haig and U.N. Ambassador Jeane Kirkpatrick was also rumored, in which the latter has been quoted as saying, "The Secretary of State and his aides are amateurs with no feel at all for Latin cultures," and even to have added, "Why don't we just disband the State Department and let the Foreign Office run our policy . . . ?"

Meanwhile, at the front, actions on May 31 could be characterized as routine except for unusual air activity and a replay of Operation Black Buck that, mounted at 0540 hours with AGM–45 Shrike missiles, endeavoured—unsuccessfully— to take out the radar facilities at Malvinas ground control. British CAP activity dropped considerably below previously recorded levels, most notably in the number of flights in the air at the same time. There were, however, intermittent enemy sorties, the Malvinas air base being the target of choice. At 1040 hours, two Harriers bore in, in a low-altitude run that was vigorously repelled by air defenses. Both aircraft sustained confirmed damage. At 1118 hours, one of the crippled Harriers crashed as it attempted to land on the *Hermes'* flight deck. The other was presumed lost at sea. As of 1540 hours, Argentine radar operators began picking up unusual British aircraft and helicopter activity. For the first time in the war, British CAPs comprising a single aircraft made two passes, at 1617 and 1619 hours.

Air Force South launched two MK–62 Canberra bombing missions over the beachhead at San Carlos. Four aircraft dropped their bombs without eliciting any enemy response. Minor damage apparently was sustained by Naval Air Squadron 846.

In more daring action, the nuclear submarine *Conqueror* patrolled close to the Argentine mainland. It remained on station 25 miles out, while two other units kept a sharp eye on the surrounding sea. These operations were kept up until June 17.

During the afternoon of May 31 there was further intense British helicopter activity. Troops, as well as two 105mm guns and 300 shells, had been moved into place. For the first time, General Menendez's defense perimeter felt hostile fire.

At 2015 hours, the *Canberra* was sighted sailing into Falkland Sound. The 5th Infantry Brigade would be landed in the bay, moving up in this ship, the *Norland*, and other vessels.

At dawn, British troops were in position atop Mount Kent. Their sleeping bags were crunchy with frost, but the vista that lay before their sleepy eyes was comforting indeed. To the east, lay General Menendez's positions. The British held the high ground. Ahead and below stretched before them what would become the battlefield for the possession of the heights around Puerto Argentino: Mount Longdon, Two Sisters Hills, and Mount Harriet.

THE ENGAGEMENTS OF JUNE 1

On the morning of June 1, the U.N. secretary general spelled out Great Britain's conditions for a cease-fire, couched in the terms of a one-sided withdrawal by Argentina from the island chain, with no mention of future sovereignty. Later, the British delegation informed Dr. Perez de Cuellar that the only admissible cease-fire would be whatever might be agreed by military commanders in the field. Numerous influential persons tried to coax the United States into pressuring Great Britain to agree to a cease-fire. But the die was cast. Nothing would bring about an end to the conflict on any but British terms.

At the front, Air Force South mounted a bombing raid over British positions on Mount Kent. As the two MK–62s were on the return leg, a missile, apparently launched from a ship to its right, homed on the second aircraft. Rapid evasive action successfully thwarted the oncoming device.

The hospital ship *Bahia Paraiso* made port in Malvinas to evacuate Argentine wounded.

At 0620 hours, another C–130 foiled the blockade on its daily shuttle into the base. It was quickly followed by a Sea Harrier, which fell to the air defenses and their Roland battery. Its pilot, navy Lt. Ian Mortimer, hit the water and was picked up shortly thereafter by a Sea King helicopter.

General Moore arrived during a tense command situation between Admiral Woodward and Brigadier Thompson. General Moore's most pressing problem was to deploy his large combat units in the field though there was a critical shortage of helicopters. The 3rd Brigade had managed to advance overland to Puerto Argentino, with all the logistics problems that entailed, while the 5th Brigade was bogged down at its landing point at San Carlos Bay, so far from the objective of Puerto Argentino that the whole operation could be jeopardized by the delays. At first light on June 1 the 5th Brigade was still unloading at San Carlos. The Gurka battalion debarked from the *Canberra* and immediately began the march to Darwin, where it was to relieve the 2nd Airborne. It was followed onto the beach at San Carlos by the Scots and Welsh Guards, artillery units, army helicopters, and assorted other personnel and gear.

Brig. Anthony Wilson removed to Goose Green, where he met with Major Keeble, now commanding the 2nd Airborne, to discuss the brigade's next move. It was decided that the march to Puerto Argentino had to be undertaken posthaste. The brigadier was in no mood to be left behind when the prize was plucked, for the British Green Berets held a strong advantage for the taking of the capital. Major Keeble immediately moved two companies by Chinook helicopter to Fitz Roy, where they took up positions. When General Moore's staff learned of this, it was deemed "highly imprudent," for the unit was too far away for fire support, and thus lay exposed to an Argentine counterattack. This further complicated the picture, for the lack of helicopter transport had forced General Moore to establish priorities for their employment. During the ensuing days, the 5th Brigade proved an endless source of headaches for General Moore's staff as they tried to grapple with the problems arising from its scattered units.

In the afternoon of June 1, some Argentine POWs at Darwin were moving ammunition from a large dump to a more secure location. As they lugged the munitions over the terrain, an explosion killed five of them and wounded several more. The event was protested by Argentine officers, and the men were relieved from further duty of this sort.

That evening, a navy group headed by Commander Perez, which had made their way to the islands in a C–130 with a naval-type Exocet S/S–38 missile launcher scrounged from a ship for use on the ground against British naval units, fired its first salvo. Because of technical problems, the missile went wild.

FO 2258 assigned a four-engine Hercules to a scouting and reconnaissance mission some 30 NM north of the islands. Although this was far from an ideal aircraft for such a task, it was all that was available to Air Force South. The Argentines felt that the British were becoming desperate in their attempt to recapture the islands, whatever the cost.

Similar missions had been flown on May 27, when shipping disappeared from San Carlos Bay. Encouraged by initial success, follow-up sections had sortied on May 28, 29, and 31, all in the face of an increasing risk of meeting a cunning enemy head-on in full daylight. The Hercules pilots had often put themselves in the Harriers' position. Would they shoot down a defenseless aircraft? They were less than objective in their evaluations. What chance would any hunter, however ruthless, give to his prey? The C–130 is a cumbersome, heavy, bulky aircraft. It carries no offensive or defensive armament. If hit by an enemy attacker, there are no ejection seats to get the crew out alive. Its speed is half that of any jet, and the crew carry no parachutes. The only honorable, sporting way to put a C–130 out of action would be to damage it in such a way as to preclude its reuse, thus giving the crew a fighting chance to come out alive, or to call for help, or to ditch in the sea.

That day the leader of Royal Navy Squadron 801, Commander Ward, with a wingman, was flying patrol when he was advised by the frigate *Minerva* of a radar blip to the north of the islands that might be an Argentine C–130, judging by its speed. The constant shuttling back and forth of these lumbering craft, which had the audacity to cross the exclusion zone without a single one having thus far been intercepted by a British CAP, was becoming a point of honor for the Sea Harrier pilots, who did not hesitate to boast of their numerous victories in aerial combat.

At 1140 hours, the C–130 was going about its business when its friend-foe transponder device warned of enemy radar acquisition. Evasive action was immediately undertaken to depart the area, but the two Sea Harriers had been vectored in on their cumbersome foe. They hove into view of the four-engine craft just as they were redlining their fuel supplies, jeopardizing their safe return to their platform. Perhaps this explains why one attacker's missiles were fired from beyond range, falling into the sea. But the Hercules took a third Sidewinder in its right airfoil, between the no. 3 and no. 4 engines. The commander, Captain Martel, radioed an SOS but lost contact before giving a detailed account. The CAP leader, even though his prey was crippled and obviously would not make it back to base, joined the chase in hot pursuit. As the wounded plane came within his cross hairs, he fired his 30mm cannon, keeping up the stream of lead until the craft began to break up over the water. It went down at 50°28'S/59°55'W.

Commander Ward fired 240 rounds in his attack run. He had crippled the big plane, enough to put it out of action for good. His mission had been accomplished; he had done his duty. Why did he go for more? The whole crew of the C–130, registry TC–63, was lost at sea. Commander Nigel Ward was decorated with the Distinguished Service Cross. The words of his citation included the following:

As a pilot, Commander Ward flew over 50 combat missions under both daytime and nighttime conditions, in marginal weather conditions, thus giving a splendid example to his squadron . . . by his determination, skill, and disregard for his own safety. He personally shot down three Argentine aircraft: a Mirage, a Pucara, and a Hercules. The destruction of the Hercules, the only success achieved against this significant target, was the result of his absolute determination, a total show of professional team-work between Cdr. Ward and his wingman, whose aircraft suffered grievous problems on their long return flight, due to lack of fuel.

THE ENGAGEMENTS OF JUNE 2

On the morning of June 2, Foreign Minister Costa Mendez left for Havana, to attend the nonaligned countries'meeting. In New York, Dr. Perez de Cuellar reported to the Security Council on the outcome of his initiatives in the wake of Resolution 505, aimed at achieving a cease-fire between the contenders. He was followed by Argentina's representative, Dr. Ros, who charged Great Britain with seeking to establish on American soil yet another shameful example of colonial imperialism by means of aggression. He went on to propose the implementation of a cease-fire and the reopening of talks. He wrapped up his presentation by stating:

The Republic of Argentina will never negotiate the reestablishment of colonialism on Argentine or American soil . . . . The . . . war that has been forced upon us will by and large be their responsibility, since they turned their backs on the avenue of peaceful negotiation, for there can be no other historical outcome than that of the definitive incorporation of those islands into Argentine territory.

The British representative in turn raised a barrage of hurdles to any type of accommodation through his systematic rejection of any cease-fire that might imply the staying of further military action, or any U.N. say in any future government. The British government was underwriting the reestablishment of a colonial status quo, backed by force of arms; any forces to be employed were not to be U.N. forces, but either U.S. or NATO forces, since it was thanks to the latter that Britain had been able to "finance"this outrage.

At the front, the day opened at 0020 hours, with the first exchange between naval and land gunnery emplacements. Air operations were severely restricted due to unfavorable weather conditions, except for heavy British helicopter activity on and about Mount Kent and Mount Wall.

The *Atlantic Causeway* entered the operations zone with vital cargo for the landing party, especially some helicopters, so desperately needed by General Moore. British forces on the ground numbered over 9,000 at this point. The Scots and Welsh Guards were landed that day at San Carlos. They took over the battlements left behind when the marines and the 3rd Airborne pulled out. These units were given a rousing welcome by the 40th Commando Battalion, for now they could move against Puerto Argentino. However, General Moore had other ideas. Concerned that Argentina might launch an airborne brigade against the perimeter, he felt the area should be defended by an experienced unit. The 40th Battalion remained behind while the recently landed battalions moved out. The idea looked good on paper. Implementing it was something else.

Meanwhile General Menendez, having noted the increasing strength of the positions around Mount Kent, requested Air Force South to commence bombing the area as soon as possible.

THE ENGAGEMENTS OF JUNE 3

The news of the day concentrated on the death of Argentine POWs forced to handle explosives and the landing of a Vulcan bomber at Rio de Janeiro. To round things out, the London papers were underscoring the fact that Australia, a country that had had an option to purchase the *Invincible* prior to the conflict, was having second thoughts.

In Washington, Argentine diplomats sought to keep the United States from vetoing the proposed resolution aimed at a cease-fire in the theater of operations, since that would represent an act of such gravity that continued diplomatic relations between the two countries would be jeopardized. Secretary of State Haig was in Paris at the time, and Thomas Enders would attempt to make him see the need for the United States not to deteriorate their relations in the hemisphere further, and abstain when the resolution was put to a vote. Surely Great Britain would not raise objections, for it had its own right of veto, and did not need the United States to torpedo the initiative. Furthermore, opposing a cease-fire would be a difficult position to justify, in light of the principles of the U.N. Charter, and of the U.S. Constitution.

In New York, the Security Council was preparing to vote on the draft resolution proposed by Spain and Panama, which read:

The Security Council

Reaffirming its Resolutions 502 (1982) and 505 (1982) and the need for implementation of all parts thereof,

1. REQUESTS the parties to the dispute to cease fire immediately in the region of the Falkland Islands (Islas Malvinas);

2. REQUESTS the parties to initiate, simultaneously with the cease-fire, the implementation of Resolutions 502 (1982) and 505 (1982) in their entirety;

3. AUTHORIZES the Secretary General to use such means as he may deem necessary to verify the cease-fire;

4. REQUESTS the Secretary General to report to the Security Council on compliance with this Resolution within 72 hours. (Doc. S/15156/Rev. 1, June 3 1982)

The United States requested a 24-hour delay in order to seek to convince Mrs. Thatcher of the need to approve this draft resolution. The British representative also requested a 24-hour postponement in order to consult his government. The Security Council recessed until the following day.

Back on the front, Operation Black Buck 6 was carried out, again targeting the radar facilities operated by the air force at Puerto Argentino. The aircraft was unable to complete its mission, for the radar operators, warned of the impending attack, had shut the whole system down. The Shrike missile had no signal on which to home. The missile did, however, pick up the signal of a secondary radar facility, which sustained several casualties. The Vulcan turned for home. As it rendezvoused for refueling, the fuel delivery nozzle at the end of the boom snapped upon coupling. With five minutes of fuel left, the only option open was to land at Rio de Janeiro, where both aircraft and crew were promptly taken into custody by Brazilian authorities. They were sent home a week later.

During the afternoon, the Welsh Guards undertook a hard march to Goose Green. Following 12 hours of exhausting slogging, the march was called off. These improvised infantrymen were in miserable shape. They could not contend with the terrain, and the weight of their packs surpassed anything for which they had received training in the past. The group returned to their staging area, to the further consternation of General Moore, for whom this represented a possible postponement of the whole operation, or having to attempt a landing at a location more convenient to Puerto Argentino.

THE ENGAGEMENTS OF JUNE 4

The proposed resolution was put to a vote in the Security Council on the afternoon of June 4, at 1755 hours, New York time. Great Britain had already stated it would not vote for a cease-fire, so the objective was to achieve nine yeas, which would oblige Britain to use its veto. At the hour of truth, nine countries stood to be counted: Spain, Panama, Poland, Japan, Ireland, China,

Zaire, Uganda, and the Soviet Union; two stood against: the United States and
Britain; four abstained: France, Guyana, Togo, and Jordan. But the unsettling
events of the day were not yet over. When the votes were counted, Mrs. Kirkpatrick, representing the United States, stated:

Mr. Chairman, the dilemma continues right up to the vote on this issue. I am told that
it is impossible for a government to change its vote once it has been cast, but my
government has requested that I go on record to the effect that, were it possible to change
our vote, we would like to change from a veto, a no, to an abstention. Thank you.

The delegate from Great Britain was speechless. The rest of the members
could not fathom the reasons governing the U.S. ambassador's statement. The
delegate from Argentina requested the floor and made the following statement:

Through the proposed resolution submitted by Spain and Panama, the Council would
have taken upon itself a minimum expression of the responsibility with which it is entrusted
by this organization's charter, in the field of international peacekeeping and security,
which is to request a cease-fire, to spare human lives and halt a war so that the United
Nations may effectively serve the cause of peace.

The United Kingdom, who is both a permanent member and a party to this conflict,
has made use of her veto, in order to frustrate this intent and the obligations that are the
responsibility of this Council.

Let the record show before the whole of the international community, before history
itself, that by her veto, the United Kingdom assumes full responsibility for all battle
deaths, be they Argentines or Britons, yet to come, in the conflict over the Malvinas
Islands.

Let the record also show that the provisions of the charter for a just keeping of the
peace and international security can only lose their effectiveness when a power with the
right to veto decides to wield it in consonance with its own colonial interests, which is
what has happened here today. It is deplorable that this organization must sit with its
hands tied, unable to act, in the face of such dramatic situations.

As for the United States, Great Britain cried foul, as if the last-minute change
of heart concealed some cunning treachery. The U.S. vote rang hollow in Latin
America. For the rest of the hemisphere, it was as useless as it was irritating.

On the battlefront, meanwhile, Brigadier General Crespo and Air Force South
staff and command sought to give top priority to the call for fire support coming
from Malvinas garrison. In spite of the bad weather, three MK–62 sorties were
sent out, backed up by a squadron of Mirage-Vs. The Canberras were armed
with six 1,000-pound MK–17 bombs each, and 500-pound BRP bombs were
loaded aboard the Daggers. This represented enough firepower to pack a heavy
wallop against enemy concentrations, if they could be dropped with precision.
The Daggers came in over the target areas at 1630 hours, dropped their bombs,
and returned uneventfully to base. They were followed by the first formation of
three Canberras, which unleashed their lethal loads over the target area. The

second formation came through a minute later, and they counted the flashes as the MK–17s hit home. Puerto Argentino reported that accuracy appeared to be good, but there was no way to confirm the extent of losses, if any, sustained by the enemy.

This operation was pulled off undisturbed by British CAPs. One carrier out of action, another damaged, and the toll thus far taken on Harrier and Sea Harrier aircraft made the skies over the Malvinas eerily silent.

On the ground, the situation was different. British land forces were engaged in fierce competition as each unit struggled for the honor of being first into Puerto Argentino. The men of the 5th Brigade complained bitterly that the few available choppers were being used to move the 3rd Brigade, which, in turn, was upset because the only available heavyweight ship, a Chinook, was being used by Brigadier Wilson's men. General Moore, with his 83-man staff, tried to coordinate the needs of his brigades as they advanced toward the objective.

THE ENGAGEMENTS OF JUNE 5

In the political arena, the world press gave broad coverage to the events that had unfolded within the Security Council, especially the vote change. The *New York Times* said it best:

Mrs. Kirkpatrick had been deeply concerned about the consequences of a veto for American relations with Latin American. . . . According to American diplomats, Secretary of State Alexander Haig, Jr., and Defense Secretary Caspar W. Weinberger have both insisted that the U.S. stand with Britain, a NATO ally . . . .

. . . These diplomats said the change in instructions could have been deliberately late in an effort to please the Latin Americans, stand with Britain, and embarrass Mrs. Kirkpatrick . . . .

. . . Mr. Reagan, Mr. Haig and other Americans have generally confined their public comments about restraint to appeals that Britain be "magnanimous in victory." But Mrs. Thatcher, when asked in a T. V. interview Wednesday . . . replied, "It is a word I use in connection with the Falklands . . . ."

Before leaving the American embassy, Mrs. Thatcher told reporters, "The United States is firmly on our side, and we are very grateful to them for being staunch allies" (p. 4).

History may take note of the U.S. waffle at voting time in the Security Council as evidence of a lack of consensus within the U.S. government regarding a clear policy in the face of such a crisis: U.S. interests in the Atlantic Alliance conflicted with hemispheric commitments, the former supported by certain positions within the government, the latter by certain influential circles.

In the theater of operations, Air Force South sent out yet another early morning twin mission of MK–62s, in order to keep up the pressure against the staging area atop Mount Kent. The area around the islands was covered by low clouds, but the Canberras flew in clear skies. Suddenly they saw the bright flash of two

Sea Dart missiles clearing the cloud cover and heading for them. They had been launched by the Class 42 destroyer Exeter, which had gone on station at this strategic point in order to intercept Argentine aircraft, thus far with little success. The Argentine pilots took evasive action and aborted the mission, returning to their home base.

The follow-up Gaucho formation had no better luck, since they were flying close behind the lead planes. This time the Sea Darts were closer, and coming straight at them. Gaucho no. 1 executed a sharp maneuver that no. 2 was unable to follow and, as a consequence, was caught in the slipstream of no. 1. This caused one of his engines to flame out, sending the aircraft into a tailspin. By this time, both aircraft felt the blast of the missiles, which caused them no damage, but as Gaucho no. 2 regained control of his Canberra, and was seeking to set course for a return to the mainland, Gaucho no. 1 pointed out two more missiles homing in on him. They took further evasive action and, finally, were able to make their way safely out of range of the enemy ship. They had failed in their mission, but disappointment aboard the Exeter was greater, since it had not brought down a single enemy aircraft with six missiles. Air Force South ordered offensive reconnaissance missions in search of the Exeter, in hopes of putting it out of action, but by this time it had moved safely out to sea.

A detailed analysis of British task Force air activity showed 16 Harrier/Sea Harrier raids during daylight hours, but no night action. This figure indicated the scarcity of serviceable aircraft and platforms from which to launch them. Of the total 16 sorties, 12 appeared to have been flown off a single carrier, and four seemed to have headed for a landing area in the San Carlos perimeter.

Ground activity for the day was punctuated with artillery duels, and the continued massing of troops west of Mount Kent, which became a spreading city of tents as men poured in. Following the failure of the British attempt to march the 5th Brigade to Darwin, it became obvious that if they were ever to link up with the 3rd Brigade, which was already positioning itself for the final assault, they would have to be moved by helicopter to a perimeter closer to Puerto Argentino, from which they could spearhead an attack from the southern flank.

In the face of the utter unavailability of sufficient helicopters, it was decided to move the men aboard the amphibious assault ship Intrepid. Under cover of darkness, the ship weighed anchor at San Carlos and, groping along the coast, put in near Bougainville Island, where the troops were transferred to landing craft, under the expert guidance of Maj. Ewen Southby-Tailyour, whose mission was to get them safely ashore. But no sooner had they set sail than heavy winds began to blow in from the west, whipping up 20-foot waves. In the foaming brine, the cold, the yawing swells, and the darkness, the frail boats sought not only to stay on course but to remain afloat. Adding to the confusion, a recently arrived British destroyer—HMS Cardiff—which had not received word of this troop movement, opened up against them with a barrage of gunfire. By the time the ship's gunnery crew got the word that they were firing on their own men, the occupants of the bobbing boats were totally unnerved. Finally, at a speed of two knots, following a seven-hour ordeal, they at last made landfall at Fitz Roy and Bluff Cove Settlement, where they were received by the recently appointed commander of the 2nd Airborne, Lieutenant Colonel Chaundler.

For Air Force South, the presence of a landing strip in the San Carlos perimeter that enabled the Harrier/Sea Harrier aircraft to operate was the source of grave concern. It meant that the enemy aircraft, which had been limited to ten minutes for patrol and intercept activities, would now enjoy over 35 minutes per sortie for the same duty, since they were spared the shuttle between their floating platforms and the operations area. For the task force, this meant a quadrupling of its air presence over the islands.

THE ENGAGEMENTS OF JUNE 6

On the political front, Dr. Perez de Cuellar pursued his efforts to achieve a cease-fire. With this aim in mind, he drew up a proposal that was rejected by both London and Buenos Aires. The U.S. vote in the Security Council continued to be front-page news in the world press, an unusual coverage, for never had the Security Council enjoyed such a high profile.

In Buenos Aires, hard feelings against the United States for its role in the conflict were reaching their height. This sentiment was especially strong within the armed forces, for many of their number had received military training and education from the great nation to the north. These links were not shared by all. A growing number of officers began to return decorations or other citations they had received from the United States. This chapter includes the full text of the letter written, with regret, by the author of this book to the chief of staff of the U.S. Air Force, for it illustrates the feelings prevailing at the time. The head of the U.S. Air Force, a highly trained, professional general officer, must have been unsettled upon reading it. The position espoused by his government, as well as the feelings stirred up by the main players in the Malvinas crisis, could well have been a source of misgivings. He and the vast majority of his countrymen were at a loss to grasp the problem and all of its ramifications and significance, no small thanks to the one-sided reporting of the U.S. mass media, which had sought to rationalize the British intervention and Washington's support of it.

At the grass-roots level, only the Latin communities scattered throughout the United States had a broader understanding of the unfolding events, and threw their unwavering support to Argentina. In the halls of government, those who shared similar feelings fought a losing battle, in a minority stand against the well-orchestrated pro-British stance taken by a crushing majority in Washington.

As for events unfolding at the front, Northwood was shaken by the Cabinet wrangling over what was happening in the field. The deployment of the 5th Brigade along the southern flank of the attack was the object of no small controversy. With the greatest reluctance, Northwood gave the nod to a second landing in the Fitz Roy area, to be launched that night. At dawn on June 6, the *Intrepid* returned to the waters of San Carlos without its four landing craft, since it had been planned that the *Fearless* would conduct a campaign at the same location during the night hours, and would use its own four landing craft in conjunction with those left behind at Fitz Roy. Totally unfavorable weather conditions would keep them from putting out to sea. The assault ship returned to San Carlos at first light on June 7, with 300 men in the holds. Land activities were a replay of the day before. Both naval and ground artillery fire reverberated throughout the area.

The activity of Argentine troops, as intense and risky as it was, was no less so than that of the British, for each side made every attempt to infiltrate behind enemy lines in order to reconnoiter their position, layout, units, and any other intelligence that would prove vital to staffs in planning the battle that was to come.

Bad weather, punctuated by high winds, squalls, low ceilings, limited visibility, and cold continued to prevail throughout the islands, keeping mainland-based aircraft socked in. At nightfall, the British ships drew in close for their nocturnal round of bombardment against the defenders. While the British task force ruled the waves undisputedly, the lack of air superiority kept it from operating close in during daylight hours. This in turn made it exceedingly difficult to get the range.

To the south of Malvinas air base, on the narrow land bridge linking the peninsula with the rest of East Falkland, a team was putting the Exocet battery in fighting trim.

To conclude the chronology for the day, an Army Gazelle helicopter was shot down west of Fitz Roy by a missile, a loss later acknowledged by the British. Considering the absence of Argentine forces in that area, and the fact that none claimed the kill, the helicopter must have fallen prey to one of its own units.

THE ENGAGEMENTS OF JUNE 7

There was not much to report from the diplomatic front on June 7 and, judging by the results thus far achieved, this could be regarded as business as usual. Here, in all its magnitude, was the significance of the frustration experienced by Argentine diplomacy on April 3, when the Security Council adopted Resolution 502. As of that fateful moment, nothing was to deter Great Britain from its military victory, the scope and weight of which were now looming ever more obvious.

On the military front, one or two British CAPs flew patrol over the islands, ensuring air cover for troops on the ground. Their origin around Darwin or San Carlos was obvious, and their activity was quite limited. At 1630 hours, a British aircraft bombing positions held by the Argentine 5th Marine Battalion was hit by heavy fire from that unit. It withdrew, trailing smoke. At 2030 hours, two C–130 aircraft were on final approach to the landing strip at Puerto Argentino when they were sighted and attacked by the destroyer *Cardiff*, which launched its Sea Darts from too far out. The missiles were spotted by the lead aircraft, and the two C–130s returned to the mainland, making good their escape but not having been able to land. The crucial shuttle operation was becoming ever more fraught with danger, for the landing of British troops at San Carlos, along with their advance to the north, south, and east of Puerto Argentino, was slowly tightening a noose on the avenues of approach.

The ongoing amphibious operation aimed at landing the men of the British 5th Brigade around Fitz Roy suffered yet another setback that day, this time at London's behest. No further Fearless Class vessels should be risked, since they were deemed to be of capital importance, and the loss of just one could entail a political risk for the government that it was not in a position to take. As a result, members of the landing parties were to be moved to less strategically vital logistics vessels such as the *Sir Galahad* and *Sir Lancelot*, which had demonstrated their battleworthiness by taking four MK–17 bombs at San Carlos, not one of which had detonated. It now appeared that London was banking heavily on the fact that these ships, which were part of the auxiliary fleet, were manned mostly by civilian personnel under contract, and were therefore a problem of lesser importance to the War Cabinet.

The movement of British ships near Fitz Roy had not gone unnoticed by Puerto Argentino radar, which, as early as the night of June 5, had picked up the blips of ships moving into that area from the north. There was repeat performance on June 7; at 0715 hours, the *Fearless* appeared to be making full speed ahead on a return heading to the safety of the quiet waters of San Carlos. At 1100 hours, observation posts sighted a logistics ship, accompanied by smaller craft, making landings in the Fitz Roy area. It was the *Sir Tristram*, which was carelessly unloading munitions in full daylight. Not a single warship oversaw this operation. The news was flashed to Air Force South, which set about planning a strike in that area. All the necessary elements for a major British tragedy were present on a stage that, ironically, bore the name of Pleasant Bay.

For June 7, Air Force South had planned a series of operations spearheaded by two Lear jets, code-named Phoenix Squadron. The numerous, unsung, and vital tasks carried out by the Lears had gone unnoticed by the public and those who did not take part in the daily operations. But they made a vital contribution to the effectiveness of the attack aircraft.

FO 2309 ordered two LR–35s to the islands, northwest of West Falkland. They came in over their assigned reconnaissance area at 0900 hours, and this was, at least on paper, to be their furthest penetration east. It should be noted that in spite of this aircraft's not having been designed for warfare, carrying neither defensive nor offensive weapons for combat, no ejection seats and no parachutes—in other words, they were flying coffins—certain liaison hitches impelled their pilots to go beyond the bounds of safety and, in so doing, to go above and beyond the call of duty.

The destroyer *Exeter*, the British fleet's first line of defense, lay on station off West Falkland. It had begun its patrol from the south, hugging the coastline as close as its fathometers would allow. As it was returning east, perhaps to reprovision, its radar picked up two bandits, flying high. Gongs sounding full battle stations, it turned to meet the enemy.

At 0907 hours, the lead aircraft decided to cease penetration and turn for home; as it banked to turn, the wingman warned of the flame trail of two missiles, which the lead locked onto instantly. They lost sight of one missile, which precluded their taking evasive action against both. One went wild, but the other found its mark. The wingman watched as the lead man's aft section disintegrated while the fore went into a spin. The pilot, Lieutenant Colonel de la Colina, was heard shouting over the radio, "We're hit! We've had it! We're in a spin!" The aircraft crashed on the west end of Pebble Island, killing all five crew members. De la Colina became Argentina's most senior officer to be killed in action.

As the personal effects of Major Falconier, the copilot of that ill-fated mission, were gathered for delivery to his next of kin, a letter addressed to his children was found:

To Nequi and Mononi:

Your Dad has not left you, he has simply laid down his life for his friends, for you, and for your children . . . and for the unborn heirs to my country.

You will no doubt sorely miss my companionship and advice, but I leave . . . you the best companion, and the wisest adviser there is: God. Hold Him close, feel His love until your chests burst with joy. And may your love be pure: for this is the only "right way" to live. Every time you find yourselves fighting off temptation to leave Him aside, do not flinch, for I will be there, standing side by side with you, radiating love.

Be a family. Respect and love your mother, whatever her perceived shortcomings. Always be one, always be united.

I leave you our family name, Falconier. May you always bear it with pride and dignify it, not through money or material wealth, but through culture, love, the beauty that purity of soul brings. Be ever more men, and ever less animals, and most of all, face life squarely, with the truth ; take responsibility even though you may suffer the consequences, perhaps with your very lives.

I leave behind:

Materially, very little.

The name of Falconier, and

God (before Whom nothing more is of importance)

(Signed) Daddy

May my children read this as youngsters, and even as oldsters, for as time goes by, as they gain experience, or as they have children of their own, they will find ever increasing significance in these words, into which a father's love is poured.

Major Falconier was the father of four boys, aged eight, six, three, and two. He had found his way, and was showing the way to those who came after. His wife, who was expecting their fifth child at the time, bore another son in October 1982. Although this book has not sought to delve into the personal lives, nor tell the personal stories, of those who lived this experience, this letter has been included in order to throw a clearer light on the spiritual sense of those Air Force crews who saw action in the war.

THE ENGAGEMENTS OF JUNE 8

Great Britain was absorbed by the visit of Pope John Paul II, who in every exchange with the British public called, again and again, for peace in the South Atlantic. British Roman Catholics gave witness to their faith by attending all of the pope's public appearances in large numbers thus lending a significant pastoral meaning to his presence in the British Isles. The cancellation of his audience with Prime Minister Thatcher was also the subject of broad media attention.

During his visit to London, President Reagan threw his full support behind the British government's policy, insofar as its refusal to seek a peaceful solution to the conflict was concerned. He stated in his address to Parliament that the United Kingdom was not fighting for territory, but to enforce the principle that aggression should not bring rewards to those who resort to it, while emphasizing the values held by democratic institutions in the face of totalitarian forms of government.

On the following day, after the carnage at Pleasant Bay, the London press had ample opportunity to observe that Britain's veto in the Security Council would end up costing the lives of too many young soldiers for a cause that was surely not in keeping with the ideals that had led them to their chosen calling.

On June 8 there was yet another event that has yet to be satisfactorily clarified. The foreign press reported on a Liberian-flag, U.S.-owned, Italian-captained tanker named *Hercules*, which, it was said, sustained aerial bombardment from a four-engine amphibious aircraft as it was steaming at approximately 46°S/49°W. According to its owners, the 270,000-ton vessel was sailing from the eastern United States to Alaska round the Horn. The captain reported that the ship had been damaged at the waterline; that it was heading back to Rio de Janeiro, to put in for repairs; that it was not in distress; that the situation was under control; and that there were no wounded aboard.

Hercules had been given a coastal routing in keeping with its draft, which it chose not to follow. The *Hercules* continued making headway at fifteen knots. On June 9, an Argentine Air Force B–707 flew over the tanker to assess the situation, and saw nothing unusual. Argentine authorities suggested it put in at Puerto Belgrano, but it maintained course for Rio de Janeiro. Since the presence of undetonated ordnance aboard had been revealed, it was denied entry to the port. As soon as the ship arrived off Rio the crew was shielded from the press and flown to Europe—all except the captain, who denied access to the press in spite of having promised otherwise. Some time later, worldwide media gave ample coverage to the fact that the *Hercules*, with the armed but unexploded bombs still aboard (efforts to defuse them having proven futile), was to be towed to a deep area of the ocean and deliberately sunk. This was a strange outcome indeed, for it has been amply demonstrated by experience that experts are capable of disarming unexploded ordnance.

The front pages of many newspapers showed photos of the sea, with the bow of a ship reaching skyward as it slipped beneath the waves. Confidential reports subsequently revealed that the *Hercules* was heavily insured, for more than it was worth. Claims filed against Argentina, charging that one of its C–130s had bombed the ship, were dismissed for lack of evidence. That would have been a truly unique feat for the 1st Air Brigade's Hercules Squadron! It is more rational to speculate that the ship—however unconscionable this may be—was sunk for its insurance.

TRAGEDY BEFALLS THE BRITISH AT PLEASANT BAY

London's decision not to risk amphibious assault vessels at Fitz Roy forced the removal of men and materiel from the *Fearless* to the RFA *Sir Galahad* prior to sailing from San Carlos. Company 3 of the Prince of Wales's Regiment boarded, followed by a mortar platoon and support units for the Welsh Guards. Another unit was also to be transferred from the other vessel. By the time all had been made ready, several hours had elapsed, and the opportunity to make the crossing and unload under cover of darkness had been lost. All of those with command responsibility on location felt that the sailing had to be put off until nightfall the following day. They were overruled by their superiors in London, who were being pressed, and could brook no further delays. This was caused in part by the sense that the Argentine Air Force had sustained such disastrous losses that their squadrons would no longer be able to muster the strength necessary to launch a replay of their sustained attacks against San Carlos. The ship would set sail immediately.

Meanwhile, at Fitz Roy, the *Sir Tristram* had been unloading munitions and ordnance at Pleasant Bay since the previous day. That morning, *Sir Galahad* pulled alongside, in broad daylight, dropped anchors, and commenced unloading. The arrival of this logistic vessel took the group already there by surprise, since they had received no advance notice of this movement. They certainly had not expected any such operation in broad daylight. Major Southby-Tailyour had been preparing to send *Foxtrot–4* one of the landing craft, to Darwin, in order to bring back the communications gear that the unit needed so much. In the meantime, a Rothesay Class frigate had been moving up from the south toward Pleasant Bay to support the operation. It tried to sneak in unnoticed.

Aboard the *Sir Galahad*, the Welsh Guards, who had yet to experience combat, waited. They remained on board, hoping to be moved by water further north to join their mates. They lounged in the main mess of the ship, watching a videotape. It was a few minutes to 1400 hours.

A squadron of Air Force South Skyhawks was approaching the bay. The Guards were minutes away from their baptism of fire. It would be sudden, swift, and tragic.

PACK TO THE ATTACK

At 1026 hours on June 8, Air Force South received confirmation of the movement of enemy ships in the Fitz Roy area. The weather was right. Nine sets of flight orders were issued, quickly followed by five more. Aircraft were scrambled, streaking into the air. Following rendezvous with the tanker, five A4-Bs headed into the target area, screaming over Bluff Cove Settlement. No ships were in Fitz Roy Inlet. As they executed a turn to the right, they came upon *Sir Galahad*, and *Sir Tristram*. Surprise was complete.

The lead—First Lieutenant Cachon—bore in on the transport, his bombs whistling into the ship's superstructure, followed in lightning succession by his wingman, whose bombs clung stubbornly to their struts. Number 3—Lieutenant Rinke—confirmed the leader's hits and launched his own bombs, which whizzed 18 inches over the startled heads of some crew members who were still lounging on deck, ricoheted two or three times off the surface of the water, and slithered onto the beach, which was thick with men, materiel, and vehicles. The bombs went off in their midst, causing a pandemonium of flame and flying debris, not to mention heavy casualties. *Sir Galahad* took a lethal blow to its innards. One of the bombs smashed through to the mess and blew up, while its twin did the same to the fuel tanks of the Rapier batteries. The spectacle of exploding munitions, in various stages of unloading, was a sight to behold. The two remaining members of the five-plane formation watched as the ship was rent by explosions. Through the billowing smoke and leaping flames they zeroed on *Sir Tristram*. The bombs pierced its sides at the waterline by the stern, causing irreparable damage but few casualties, since it was not loaded with troops. The load of munitions, however, sealed its fate.

In the few seconds between the appearance of the first A4-B and the disappearance of the last attacker in a trail of vapor, the placid scene at Pleasant Bay had been transformed into a burning hell of fire and brimstone. *Sir Galahad* was engulfed in a ball of flame; the racking explosions spewed fuel over the water, spreading tongues of burning oil over the bay that overtook many survivors as they desperately sought to escape the sheet of flame, grasping at the fleeing dinghies, the thrashing life jackets.

In a heroic effort, and at great risk, some British helicopters hovered above the flames in an attempt to divert them from the clusters of survivors riding the swells. Many owe their lives to this gallant action. The men of the 2nd Airborne rushed down to the beach to assist the Welsh Guards and the crew members as they made shore. Grievously wounded, their clothes still smoldering, burned skin hanging in shreds, they were a pitiful lot. All helicopters in the area were diverted to lend assistance in rescuing and evacuating the numerous wounded, who lay suffering from exposure on the frigid sands of Pleasant Bay. The gruesome task went on all day.

Brigadier Anthony Wilson and his men, who were conferring with General Moore at San Carlos, came to the hard realization that war is not a semisporting game, but the most brutal and senseless action of which mankind is capable. Those who shouldered the burden of these events back in London were looking askance.

We had not yet begun to fight.

Map 8
The Attack on Pleasant Bay

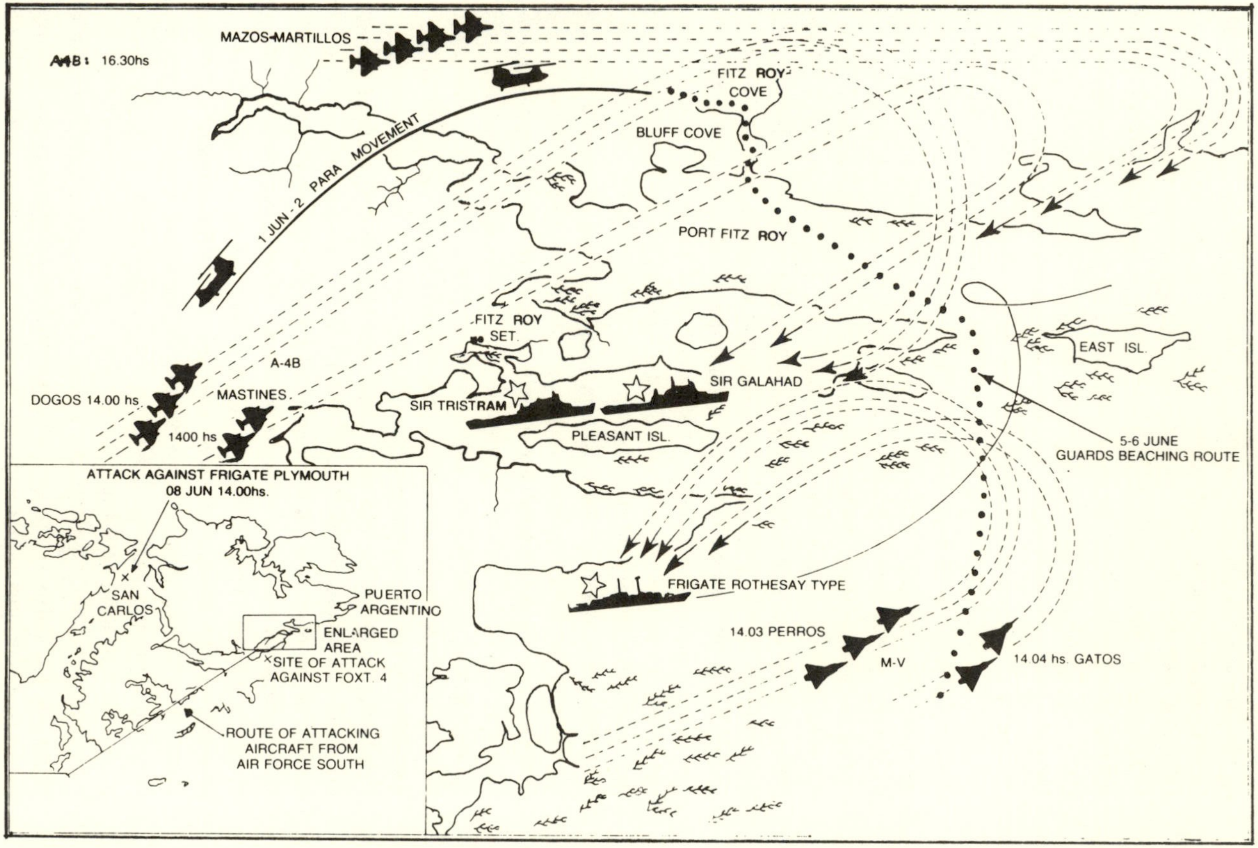

MAZOS-MARTILLOS

AMB 1 16.30hs

1 JUN - 2 PARA MOVEMENT

DOGOS 14.00 hs.

MASTINES

1400 hs

A-4B

FITZ ROY SET.

SIR TRISTRAM

SIR GALAHAD

PLEASANT ISL.

FITZ ROY COVE

BLUFF COVE

PORT FITZ ROY

EAST ISL.

5-6 JUNE GUARDS BEACHING ROUTE

14 04 hs GATOS

M-V

FRIGATE ROTHESAY TYPE

14 03 PERROS

ATTACK AGAINST FRIGATE PLYMOUTH 08 JUN 14.00hs.

PUERTO ARGENTINO

ENLARGED AREA

SITE OF ATTACK AGAINST FOXT. 4

ROUTE OF ATTACKING AIRCRAFT FROM AIR FORCE SOUTH

SAN CARLOS

The Mystery of the Frigate *Plymouth*

Just after all hell had broken loose in the wake of the A4-B blitz, two formations of Mirage-Vs Daggers, code-named Perro (Dog) and Gato (Cat), screamed in over Pleasant Bay, bristling with 500-pound bombs, gunners' trigger fingers at the ready on 30mm cannon. They bore in from the west, and as they came in, they spotted a frigate on the inlet that was going to great lengths to conceal its presence. But it proved to be too late. The planes hugged the elevations around Pleasant Peninsula, then lunged for the prey, coming in at 30° on both the bow and the port side. Again bombs fell and cannon blazed as they made their attack run over the hapless vessel, whose gunners cut loose with everything they had in a vain attempt to drop their tormentors from the skies. The attackers returned to base without a single loss. Where had the British CAPs been at the moment of truth? Something was strangely amiss with the Sea Harriers.

The wounded frigate turned about and, making slow headway (three knots), left the bay on an easterly heading. Apparently, four of the eight bombs hit the ship's structure. Initial reports from Great Britain indicated that none of them detonated, but later reports from the same sources told a different tale.

At the same time, the armed forces' operations electronic center picked up a source of infrared radiation, similar to that given off by a vessel afire, in the Falkland Sound area. There was no logical explanation for this, since there had been no Argentine attacks in that area. Then, unexpectedly, Hasting and Jenkins revealed in late 1983 that the Rothesay Class frigate *Plymouth* had been attacked by Argentine aircraft (Mirage-V and A4-B) at the exact point where the infrared radiation had been detected in Falkland Sound. A later publication (Ethel and Price) restates the *Plymouth*'s position at the same location.

What really happened? British officials seemed to waffle in the days immediately following the June 8 attack. Argentine analysts could be certain only of the events reported by their own men: that a Class 12 frigate had sustained an attack in Pleasant Bay by air-launched 500-pound bombs. This was confirmed by aerial photographs. Data provided on the attack against the frigate report serious damage by the bombs from the Mirage-Vs, which had not been revealed by the infrared radiation, thus agreeing with the original British report that the bombs had failed to detonate.

The process of deduction has enabled the following events to be surmised:

1. The frigate targeted by the Daggers in Pleasant Bay was similar to the *Plymouth*. One of the Argentine pilots saw the Marks F–16 during the attack, indicating that the frigate would be the HMS *Diomede* (similar to the *Plymouth*).

2. The *Plymouth* may have fallen victim to a mistaken attack by a Harrier squadron flying cover against Argentine troops at Port Howard, under adverse weather conditions and poor visibility.

The Royal Navy has sought to explain the events by attributing to Argentine flyers ''an understandable navigational error,'' which is not borne out because of the distances involved and the pinpoint precision of the Mirage-V's navigational system.

The Second Wave

The surprise and success achieved by the first wave of attacking aircraft encouraged Air Force South to send three other formations of A4-B and C aircraft, all armed as their predecessors had been.

This time the British were waiting. Following the first wave, British troops had lined the elevations surrounding the landing perimeter with everything they could muster. The Rapier batteries, the Blow Pipe units, anything that could be fired vertically was pressed into position to repel the onslaught of enemy bandits. Topping off this array, CAP lay patiently in wait, prowling the area along the approach path of the Argentine attackers.

At about 1630 hours, the A4-Bs—Mazo (Mace) and Martillo (Hammer)—came in over Choiseul Channel, straight into the cross fire of antiaircraft guns, light weapons fire, and surface to air missiles. The leader spotted the smoke-engulfed *Sir Galahad*, and almost at once came upon the heavily laden *Foxtrot–4*. He banked for the attack just as the CAP came in, bent on keeping the Skyhawks from baring their talons. In the ensuing melee, three of the four aircraft went down to the Sea Harriers, two before they were able to launch their weapons, but not before the leader scored a direct hit on the landing craft with a 500-pound bomb—which caused grievous casualties—as a Sidewinder homed in on him. He died leading his mission bravely into action, causing the enemy to sustain heavy losses. His wingman, nipped by an air-to-air missile, managed to eject. He was seen going into the water with a partially opened parachute. The British were unable to rescue him. The third airplane went into the bay as its pilot rode it down. A single aircraft managed to live to tell the story. That ill-fated formation was followed into action by four A4-Cs of the second squadron. They were faced with the spectacle of a ship in flames in the bay, and a withering barrage of antiaircraft ordnance. They decided to carpet the enemy staging area with their bombs. They made a successful withdrawal, with a swarm of missiles in hot pursuit.

Back at Air Force South command, and down through the ranks, morale was at a peak. Three brave pilots and three vital aircraft had been the price, but the grievous losses to the British were the payoff. Whatever the figures the latter released, one knew things had been worse.

Meanwhile, on the ground at Fitz Roy, British forces went about alleviating the sorry state of their men. Not only did they have to tend to the numerous wounded, but they also had to turn their immediate attention to the many men who came ashore, their clothing burned, in tatters, or gone altogether, half frozen from being in the frigid waters. They were evacuated to San Carlos for recovery, while men from the 40th Marine Battalion were moved up to replace them at Fitz Roy, all of which represented an additional burden that further hindered the advance on Puerto Argentino. The British acknowledged that it was the good fortune of their troops that General Menendez's defenders had not been in a position to take advantage of the ensuing turmoil and overwhelm them.

As the Dust and Smoke Settled

Air Force South's raid on Pleasant Bay proved to be the biggest setback of the war for the British. It has been dubbed the "Blackest Day of the Fleet." Had Argentine troops had greater strength and mobility, it could also have proved to be Britain's darkest hour. It was a textbook example of what can happen when there are command mixups and political and military interference in the unfolding of an operation in the field. The landing should have been conducted with the amphibious assault vessel designed for the purpose, instead of delaying the operation. The task force ordered the *Fearless* and *Intrepid* replaced by civilian craft, thereby dooming the men aboard ship at the time of the attack.

Following some hemming and hawing, the British acknowledged losses of 57 killed in action and 48 wounded as a result of this attack (a strange ratio, since casualty figures usually run at about four wounded for every death). Such figures are at odds not only with higher Argentine estimates but also with that of British analysts. At that time, the Defense Ministry in London admitted: "Five British sailors were wounded last night when the Argentine Air Force carried out its first big raid in over a week on ships of the Task Force" (*London Times*, June 9, 1982, p. 1, Col. 1).

The lack of air and naval cover during the landing was not due as much to a British shortcoming as to the successful campaign by Air Force South. By carrying the attack to the enemy, the British had either lost or suffered damage to over 23 vessels and 50 aircraft. With what remained available, there was no way they could preempt the well-planned and successful surprise thrusts mounted by Argentina's air forces. The scarcity of task force assets was evidenced not only by the paucity of CAPs in the air but also by the refusal of the latter to engage in aerial combat, not for any lack of aircraft capability or pilot skill, but because they felt the results were not worth the risks. Britain had scraped the bottom of the barrel. There were no aircraft left in the home islands or in the European garrisons to press into service in the Malvinas theater of operations.

The notion of "kill ratio" prevailed on both sides of the battle lines. It served to justify the resistance of the task force against any type of operation that involved exposing its ships during daylight hours at locations within enemy flying range. This situation was made worse when the carrier *Invincible*, thought to be stationed safely out of harm's way, was caught in Air Force South's clutches. Neither did Air Force South command wish to risk its aircraft in ground support missions, in view of the concentrated ground fire available to the British, who may well have whittled Argentina's air forces down to a few wafting feathers, without a visible or meaningful "kill" with which to justify such a loss.

In this light, once the task force had removed its vessels to the safety of its TRALA zone, and Air Force South had no more suitable targets within grasp, the final outcome would inevitably prove to be governed by the facing off of the opposing sides' ground forces. If General Menendez's forces had lacked the means to mount an attack on a disorganized and disarticulated British beachhead less than 15 miles from its furthest outposts, they would be hard put to defend themselves when they made their last stand.

LETTER FROM THE AUTHOR TO THE CHIEF OF STAFF, U.S. AIR FORCE

Buenos Aires, June 6, 1982

Dear General ALLEN:

By means of this letter, I wish to return the enclosed CERTIFICATE OF APPRECI-ATION conferred on me in 1962 by General CURTIS E. LE MAY, Chief of Staff, U.S.A.F., in acknowledgment of my participation, as a member of the Argentine Air Force, in the Combined Task Force which was formed at that time to respond to the "Cuban Missile Crisis," during which I served as a crew member aboard an *Albatross* aircraft, contributed by my Air Force.

It is with great pride that I have thus far held this certificate, moved by feelings both of satisfaction and esteem toward your great Nation and her Air Force, to the assistance of which the Armed Forces of my country went at one of her most crucial hours.

Now, those same Armed Forces, with the support of all ARGENTINA, are struggling to reclaim a small but beloved part of our Country, which, over 149 years ago, was illicitly taken over by the United Kingdom. By the same token, we are carrying on a struggle for the dignity of the Hemisphere.

The decision to follow this course of action has certainly not been taken lightly.

Your Government's resolve to support the designs of GREAT BRITAIN in this part of AMERICA surpass all bounds of comprehension, not only in light of the America-for-Americans tradition espoused by President MONROE in 1823, but also in the light of those bold words, so proudly inscribed in 1776 in the U.S. Declaration of Independence, when you first shook off the colonial shackles of London: "He has looted our seas, devastated our coasts, burned many of our towns and destroyed the lives of our people. At this moment, he is moving great armies of foreign mercenaries to conclude his works of death, desolation, and tyranny, already started under conditions of cruelty and perfidy unmatched in the most barbarous of times, and unworthy of a Civilized Nation."

General, I have taken the liberty of quoting the whole paragraph, not to enlighten you, but to remark on the present-day currency of these lines, written over 200 years ago, for all the citizenry of modern day Argentina. I would be remiss in not concluding with a thought which concerns us all:

> Faced by the position of the leading Western Powers, it is safe to note, with deep trepidation, the downfall of the values which have been the cornerstone of our civilization. Peace, Justice, Equality, Liberty, Truth. Who now, and by what right, shall become their standard-bearer?

With the assurance that you will fully grasp the reasons which have compelled me to write these few lines to you, as Chief of Staff, United States Air Force, and to return to its safekeeping the honor which General LE MAY was kind enough to bestow upon me on December 10, 1962, I remain

Very sincerely yours,

Rubén O. Moro
Vice-Commodore,
Air Force of Argentina

13

The Last Stand at Puerto Argentino

A minister sitting with his cabinet, far removed from the action, is
in no position to make battlefield decisions. Only the commander
in the field can be the final arbiter of events as they unfold.

Napoleon

THE ENGAGEMENTS OF JUNE 9

The attack carried out against Pleasant Bay reverberated to such an extent that
Secretary of State Haig issued a statement in support of the British government,
if only to salve the wound. In Buenos Aires, the chief of staff of the Malvinas
joint command, General Americo Dahler, made a detailed presentation to the
top military brass regarding the situation in the islands. At the end of the meeting,
those present came away with the feeling that the military situation of the Malvinas garrison was less than critical, and that they had a clear picture of what
was going on. In New York, the United Nations was being sounded out as to
the results to be achieved by Argentina from the convening of the General
Assembly.

For General Moore and his two commanders, Brigadiers Thompson and
Wilson, the disaster at Pleasant Bay was yet another setback. From a tactical
standpoint, the extent of the setback would depend very much on what the
enemy's next move would be. As General Menendez's troops held their positions
without taking advantage of the turmoil created by Air Force South, it became
clear to the British that their plan was to lie in wait in their battlements for the
final thrust. Faced with this prospect, as well as the pressure being exerted by
London and the arrival of winter, which would be a tough test of the troops'
steadfastness and morale, the only possible decision was to push on to Puerto
Argentino, and lose no time about it.

The second item discussed with the two brigade commanders was how the attack should be carried out. Three courses of action lay before them: form a narrow and strong attack wedge in the Mount Longdon, Two Sisters, or Harriet area; attack from the south, skirting the fortified hills; or initiate an assault along the whole front, using each battalion to take a specific objective. This last option became the 3rd Brigade's assignment.

For General Menendez and his subordinate commanders, General Jofre and General Parada, there was but one alternative: absent naval support—the fleet was bottled up because of the submarine threat, and the air force was seriously limited in its ability to provide close-in ground fire—they must hold their fortified position in the hopes that the enemy would wear themselves down trying to overcome them. Most of their available troops were no match for the enemy they were to face. Two units stood out for their high level of training and the command capability of their officers: the 5th Marine Battalion, on the west salient, and the 25th Infantry Regiment in the eastern sector, near the airport.

THE ENGAGEMENTS OF JUNE 10

In the House of Commons, Defense Minister Nott explained to the members of Parliament that during the attack of June 8, the frigate *Plymouth* had sustained "light damage" but remained "operational," and the *Sir Tristram* had been "slightly damaged." He concluded by stating that, for security reasons, he could not make public any British casualty figures. Faced with this situation, the Labourites repeated their demand to the government that a proposal be submitted to the Security Council in order to achieve a cease-fire and, by and large, a peaceful solution to the conflict.

In the islands, June 10 was not a good day for the British Special Forces. Compelled to obtain intelligence on the Argentine layout, the SBS and SAS carried out incursions and raids, mostly at night. On West Falkland, the SAS troops encountered resistance and, during this action, lost one of their best officers, Capt. Gavin John Hamilton. This officer, a veteran of the two helicopter crashes on Fortune Glacier on South Georgia at the opening of the conflict, had also taken part in the attack against Calderon naval air station. He was a member of an observation team 2,500 yards from Argentine positions when they were taken by surprise by a patrol from the 601st Commandos, and was killed in action following a gallant struggle. A British sergeant was taken prisoner.

The artillery duels continued as on previous days, Argentine Artillery Group 3 having caused serious problems for the British. A ship firing from Annunciation Bay on positions around Puerto Argentino made a direct hit on a local house, causing the deaths of three inhabitants and injuring several more. Mrs. Doreen Burns, Sue Withney, and Mary Goodwin perished in this action.

While the use of professional troops in action brought about more balanced results, the same was not true of the larger combat units, which on the Argentine side were comprised mostly of poorly trained conscripts. The telling difference was not only the superior training of the British troops but also the mobility afforded them by the vastly greater availability of helicopter transport.

There is no such thing in current air inventories as an antihelicopter aircraft, but the future of such a development would be assured. Unfortunately for Argentine forces, the Pucara aircraft, which proved to have the maneuverability for this type of action, had not been equipped to do the job, for its gun sights had been calibrated for air-to-surface and not air-to-air combat. Even so, they had been able to knock down some British helicopters, such as those on May 28, in spite of all the latter's expert evasive maneuvers.

A flight of Pucara aircraft left Malvinas air base at 0840 hours to rake the Mount Kent area with machine gun, rocket, and cannon fire. Two of the aircraft returned with bullet holes throughout their structures, testimony of the effectiveness of ground fire. This worked both ways: British Harriers sustained similar damage. In the final stand for Puerto Argentino, infantry on both sides lacked close-in fire support from their aircraft, except in isolated instances when specific major targets were being attacked. But the IA–58 Pucara aircraft proved itself very well in combat. Some of its newfound qualities were true revelations, since they had never before been sought. The squadron was forced to operate under extreme conditions. Their base facilities were rudimentary at best, for lack of support. They had been further weakened by a successful enemy thrust. They had been unable to make full use of the Pucara's capabilities as a strong, agile airframe with superior firepower, able to operate under the worst possible conditions.

One of the Pucara's major qualities was its ability to sustain enemy fire and remain in flight, thus ensuring, in most cases, the survival of the crew. Such characteristics are revealed only under combat conditions, and therein lies the importance of the aircraft, since it had been designed for ground support and thus was subject to exposure to close-range, small-caliber ground fire. The second capability that the Pucara demonstrated was its adaptability for air-to-air combat, especially against highly maneuverable helicopters. Had the Pucaras been properly fitted for such a mission, their performance might have been outstanding, given the numerous helicopters deployed by the British in the theater of operations.

The joint operations center at Comodoro Rivadavia set about studying the feasibility of carrying out an airborne operation against the rear flank of the British battle array, using paratroops and the men already deployed on West Falkland. The launching of an airborne operation had previously been shelved as a high-risk venture of difficult feasibility. On further analysis, it was again discarded.

General Moore's troops were now poised for the final push that would net Great Britain the military victory sought by its government from the very outset.

THE ENGAGEMENTS OF JUNE 11

The War Council met one last time before the fall of Puerto Argentino, giving General Moore a broad initiative for conducting the battle in accordance with the conditions in the theater of operations.

The day was marked in Buenos Aires by the arrival of Pope John Paul II, on the first papal visit ever to Argentina. Argentines looked up to this fatherly figure as if in prayer for the life of a critically ill patient. They were in search of peace, of a solution to the war that was casting a dark pall over the whole country, as British forces prepared their final attack to retake the Malvinas Islands. Perhaps following his departure from Rome and his visit to both contending nations, the message of Christ's vicar on Earth might sink through to those who still had ears: that the best peace of all is peace of mind, for pride is not only a cardinal sin but the worst among them, because it alone faces man off with God.

THE FIGHTS FOR MOUNTS LONGDON, TWO SISTERS AND HARRIET

Following their experience at Darwin-Goose Green, British forces—which have the reputation of being one of the best trained armies for night fighting— decided to carry out the greater part of the final assault under cover of darkness, when they could depend on the support of naval gunfire.

All that afternoon, helicopters had been ferrying shock troops up to the positions from which they would advance to meet the enemy. The 2nd and 3rd Airborne Battalions would strike at Mount Longdon and along Wireless Ridge. The 45th Marines would do likewise at Two Sisters, while the 42nd Marines would hit Mount Harriet, along the southern flank. Mount Longdon and Wireless Ridge are located northwest of Puerto Argentino. These ridges were held by the Argentine 7th Infantry Regiment, commanded by Lt. Col. Omar Gimenez.

Commencing at 2030 hours, British heavy artillery began softening up the positions on Mount Longdon, with support from naval gunfire. Close-in combat initiated at 2130 hours. At 2300 hours, Company B of the British 3rd Airborne became trapped in a mine field as they started up the hill, and sustained casualties. The ensuing firefight was so heavy that each side thought it was up against a much larger force. The defenders unleashed a hail of mortar, machine gun, and small arms fire against the British assailants as they struggled up the hill, hauling their 66mm mortars and Milan antitank missiles with them as they fought doggedly, position by position, for possession of Mount Longdon. They achieved their objective following a costly 12-hour fight.

About midnight, Major Carrizo, subsector commander, ordered an attack to block the British advance. The enemy was engaged in hard fighting, including hand-to-hand combat, made all the more treacherous by the total darkness. Casualties were heavy on both sides. British Sgt. Ian John Mackay, Company B, Platoon 4, died a heroic death, having assumed the position of a fallen mate in an attempt to take out a machine gun nest. He was awarded the Victoria Cross for his gallantry.

By 0100 hours on June 12, Major Carrizo, seeing his positions about to fall into enemy hands, called in fire from the 5th Marines as he readied his withdrawal. The request was answered immediately. Shortly thereafter, British paratroops joined the fight, which quickly spread throughout the area. Prior to this, Brigadier Thompson had decided to call in the 2nd Airborne reserve units and the 40th Marines to reinforce the charge, in the face of stiff Argentine resistance.

The commander of the Puerto Argentino group, General Jofre, ordered up reinforcements for the southeast sector of Mount Longdon and sent in the 10th Cavalry scouting squad, which came under immediate and heavy enemy mortar fire. By 0500 hours, the situation of the subsector manned by the Argentine 7th Infantry became critical. Having sustained heavy casualties and low on ammunition, their lines had been pierced at several locations, and they had no reserves to plug the gaps.

By 0800 hours on June 12, the remnants of Argentine Company B, 90 of the 300 men who had gone into battle, arrived on Wireless Ridge. Mount Longdon had fallen to the enemy, but at a heavy cost: 23 paratroops killed in action and 47 wounded, according to British sources. On the Argentine side, the count was 31 killed in action and 152 wounded, following 12 hours of nonstop fighting. They were all members of the 7th Mechanized Infantry Regiment, which, of all the units moved to Malvinas for the showdown, took the heaviest casualties, particularly the men of Company B, who made their stand on the flanks of Mount Longdon.

The Two Sisters lie west of Puerto Argentino. They were held by Argentina's 4th Infantry Regiment. Brigadier Thompson ordered the 45th Marines to take the hills. Applying the principle of pressing against the weakest points, they mounted their assault at about 2300 hours, almost simultaneously with the offensive against Mount Longdon. The men holed up on the south peak of Two Sisters held out until the early hours of June 12, when, their ammunition almost exhausted, a withdrawal was ordered by the battalion commander. They proceeded to an orderly fallback, fighting a holding action as they joined positions held by the Argentine 5th Marines. The north peak came under attack at 0100 hours on June 12. Held by a scant two platoons, the position fell to the British Green Berets in little more than an hour.

At 0300 hours, the battalion's command post fell to the enemy in the absence of a sufficiently spirited defense. Faced with this tactical situation, with both Two Sisters and Longdon in enemy hands, the troops in the depression between these elevations were in a dangerously exposed position. The Puerto Argentino group commander therefore ordered the withdrawal of the remaining units of the 6th Infantry from the area, to take up fresh positions at Mount Tumbledown.

The third British objective was Mount Harriet, on the south flank of the perimeter. The task fell to the 42nd Marines. The defenses were manned by Company B, 4th Infantry Regiment, on the west of the crest of the hill. The north and south sides were held by the Service and Command Company, while the east was defended by a reserve platoon from the 12th Infantry Regiment. Following a heavy naval and field bombardment, the attack against Mount Harriet was initiated at 2300 hours on June 11. British troops concentrated their thrust from the south, outflanking the forward positions that proved the least combat-ready. In spite of individual acts of bravery by the defenders, the position, which was outmanned and outgunned, and unprepared for night fighting, was soon surrounded by the enemy, who took Mount Harriet shortly thereafter. A few men, although encircled, kept up the fight until they ran out of ammunition; others were able to break out and, fighting as they fell back, reformed in combat strength further east.

Brigadier Thompson's 3rd Marine Brigade took the high ground west of the Argentine battlements. Although the marine battalions did not fight as fiercely or with as much spirit as the paratroops, they achieved their objectives at a lower cost. The 42nd Marines sustained a single combat death and 13 wounded, while the 45th had four killed in action and eight wounded (according to British sources).

Phase 1 of the British plan was now complete. Brigadier Thompson's efficiently led, trained, and equipped men always attacked at battalion strength, coming up against companies. The ratio in manpower was four to one. This ensured not only the outcome of the actions for Mount Longdon, Two Sisters, and Mount Harriet but also the final outcome of the battle for Puerto Argentino.

THE ENGAGEMENTS OF JUNE 12

As British infantry advanced toward their objectives, three British ships moved in close at sundown on June 11 to bombard Puerto Argentino.

On the beaches on Freycinet Peninsula, a group of Argentine Navy men set up the launching ramps for the Exocet surface-to-surface missiles that had been hastily removed from ships for a daring experiment. The emplacement was fixed, which did not allow the jerry-rigged weapon to be aimed. It was pointed in a likely direction, in hopes that a ship would sail into its range. At about 0338 hours, the *Glamorgan* was supporting the advance of the 45th Marines with its 115mm guns as they headed for Mount Harriet, when the navigation officer reported an incoming missile. Two Sea Cats were fired off to intercept the interloper, and chaff was scattered in its path. The missile bore through this barrage and hit *Glamorgan's* stern as it heeled about, churning out 24 knots in a vain bid for safety.

Both the British 42nd Marines on Mount Harriet and the Argentine troops on Mount Tumbledown witnessed the ensuing explosion aboard the vessel. Its swift maneuvering had spared it more extensive damage, but the modern cruiser sustained structural damage and lost 13 men. Nighttime naval superiority was no longer a free ride for the task force.

The Second Line of Defenses at Puerto Argentino

The second line of defenses encircling the island capital was as follows: north, along Wireless Ridge, two companies from the 7th Infantry Regiment were in position, along with two scouting platoons. In the center of the perimeter were two groups from the Argentine 5th Marines. The avenue of approach south from the sea lay wide open.

Brigadier Wilson requested a postponement of the attack by General Moore, whose 5th Brigade was held up by the lack of helicopter transport. The request was a source of irritation to Brigadier Thompson, for it meant that the 3rd Brigade had to stand by without advancing. General Moore, realizing that Brigadier Wilson's men had had no time to reconnoiter the terrain and sound out the objectives, accepted the suggestion. The attack would be launched at sundown on June 13, in accordance with phase 2 of the plan.

Noteworthy among the actions on June 12 was the seventh run of the now veteran Vulcan XM–607, which in spite of its best efforts, failed to produce tangible results during its farewell performance. Black Buck thus took its final bow.

A 155mm 3rd Artillery Group cannon position came under attack by a squadron of Harriers one of which was brought down by light weapons fire from the 5th Marines. The artillery piece was knocked out of action, but was replaced by a backup brought to Malvinas by C–130 shuttle that same night. The C–130 returned to Comodoro Rivadavia without incident although it had been picked up and pursued by a single British CAP, which had been too far away to be effective.

June 12 also marked the debut of the laser beam Paveway smart bombs, which can be guided to their targets. The device's first showing was relatively effective.

June 12 proved to be the toughest day for the artillerymen on both sides. The Argentine 5th Marine positions received heavy softening-up fire, in preparation for the coming assault. The battlements of the 7th Infantry Regiment also came in for some hard punishment. The fire became so deadly and precise that the commanding officer of Company A withdrew from his splintered redoubts to a more protected location. Company C also took heavy artillery fire, sustaining heavy losses in both personnel and materiel.

During the morning, a Canberra, guided by Malvinas radar control, succeeded in dropping bombs on the flanks of Mount Kent, greatly startling General Moore—so much so that he made a swift exit to safer ground.

Naval Air's Last Sortie

The Tábanos, in what would be the final sortie of the war for the A4-Qs, ran into enemy aircraft and were forced to break contact and return to base at Rio Grande. Thus the A4-Q squadron wrapped up its showing in the Malvinas campaign, flying not from their carrier but from a land base. They saw action nine times during the campaign, and inflicted serious damage on task force vessels. They lost three aircraft, two to British CAP action, with the death of one pilot. The third crashed on arrival at Rio Grande, also with the loss of the pilot.

The Super Etendards operated on various occasions. They were notoriously effective with the Exocet missile, which caused grievous damage to the enemy fleet, without losing any of their number.

Not to be forgotten is the performance of the Navy F–28 transports, which ran the blockade to Puerto Argentino, in addition to the C–130 shuttle, on 15 occasions. The Macchi MB–339s stationed at Puerto Argentino also fought during three sorties (May 21 and 28), and carried out a variety of other missions. One of them was shot down with the loss of the pilot, and another suffered an equally fatal accident. Four were damaged on the ground. Four T–34Cs (small trainers) were lost in the commando attack against Pebble Island.

As for helicopters, the navy lost one that was aboard the *General Belgrano*, and two others to accidents. The Argentine Naval Prefecture lost a Skyvan in the Pebble Island attack, and another Skyvan, as well as a Puma helicopter, sustained minor damage in other incidents.

THE FIGHT FOR WIRELESS RIDGE AND MOUNTS TUMBLEDOWN AND WILLIAM (JUNE 13/14)

The coming showdown proved to be a tremendous challenge for the Argentine troops manning the second line of defense on these elevations and on the intervening low ground. They were obviously outgunned and outsoldiered. General Moore deployed his forces in accordance with the following general layout: The north sector would fall to the 2nd Airborne. Mount Tumbledown would be entrusted to the 2nd Battalion of Scots Guards, which finally had been moved up by helicopter. The south sector would be taken by the Duke of Edinburgh's Gurkas. The British 5th Brigade would thus join the last battle, going against Argentina's best-trained and -equipped outfit, the 5th Marines.

From the north, the Paratroops mounted the attack with a formidable array of firepower, two full artillery batteries backed by naval gunfire, which was topped off by the front-line machine gun section. The precision and concentration of the fire was such that as of 1900 hours, six of the ten recently delivered Argentine machine guns were out of action; the unit's communications were inoperative; and the positions had been decimated with casualties. In the preceding 12 hours, British artillery had fired 6,000 rounds with their 105mm pieces, and as they began their push, they were further backed by naval fire and the 76mm guns mounted on their armored vehicles. The casualties sustained by the 2nd Airborne in the fight for Mount Longdon had induced the British not to take any unnecessary chances the second time around.

At 2330 hours, a diversionary action was fought to the northeast in order to divert attention from the 2nd Airborne's main thrust. The incursion was carried out by the SAS and SBS, who were harshly repelled, sustaining so many casualties they were obliged to withdraw. If the intent had been to divert the Argentine 7th Infantry Regiment, it had been unsuccessful, for by this time the British 2nd Airborne were closing on their true objective, and there could be no doubt in the minds of the opposing troops as to the main thrust of the enemy attack. The two Argentine artillery groups sought to slow the advance of the 2nd Airborne, but in spite of their best efforts, and the precision of their fire, Wireless Ridge was in British hands as numerous Argentine troops fell back. At 0450 hours, the commander of the 7th Infantry was ordered to withdraw. They had been fighting at close quarters. A heavy snow began to fall on the barren Falklands hillsides.

Further south, action was initiated shortly after 1600 hours as the Scots Guards carried out a diversionary attack, advancing with Blues and Royals armored columns. The attack proved unsuccessful, for the British chose an approach route that had been mined. Just as the British column came into the range of the Argentine Marine brigade, one of their Scorpion armored vehicles was blasted out of action by a mine. A hail of metal rained down on the hapless intruders, who halted their advance in spite of their doctrine, which would have had them continue. They decided to fall back toward the south, but the defenders had foreseen that possibility and had carefully sown the area with mines, just in case it was employed as an escape route. The Guards were then caught in a well-timed cross fire from the massed pieces of the 3rd Artillery Group, mortars, and other weapons. They sustained grievous casualties. Not only had their attack been disjointed, but a platoon had been wiped out. They withdrew, leaving over 60 men littered about the field.

Meanwhile, to the north of these positions, a company of Argentine 5th Marines lay entrenched. At 2200 hours, they started to receive unusually heavy incoming fire. At 2250 hours, they were attacked from the west and northwest: it was the 2nd Battalion, Scots Guards, and the 1st and 7th Gurka Rifles. The 5th Marines directed the 3rd Artillery to fire on the advancing enemy. The Guards faced off with the well-trained Argentine Marines, sustaining numerous casualties. The employment of the Milan missiles, as well as the 66mm mortars, did not prove as effective for the British as they had at Darwin-Goose Green. The 5th Marines were well dug in, and succeeded at holding up the enemy advance.

However, the fall of Wireless Ridge and the heavy expenditure of ammunition rendered the situation of the defenders very tenuous. At about 0100 hours on June 14, the commander of the 5th Marines ordered his troops, who had fought so well along the south of the perimeter, to withdraw in order to stand in reserve. By 0300 hours, the approach of more British regulars, to reinforce those already engaged in the field, was detected. They were the 42nd Marines. The men of the 5th Argentine Marines, about two companies strong, were thus facing off with three battalions. The arrival of these forces beefed up the British attack. The situation of the defenders became uncertain; their ammunition supplies, critically low.

At 0520 hours, the commander of the 5th Argentine Marines reported his command post had come under enemy fire. By 0700 hours, part of the high ground was in enemy hands. As the 5th Marines awaited reinforcements, they received permission to withdraw. They stood their ground. About 0800 hours British forces, supported by massive artillery fire, launched the final assault against the hill. By 0900 hours, the Argentine unit had been ordered to withdraw. They continued to hold out. In a daring action, and in spite of the numerous casualties sustained, Brigadier Wilson's troops succeeded in overrunning the hill while the Argentine Marines carried out an orderly withdrawal toward Sapper Hill, from which they continued the fight. At 1100 hours, Cmdr. Carlos Hugo Robacio, battalion commander, 5th Argentine Marines, reported the news to his superior.

This unit had held its positions with bravery and professionalism. Its men, a battalion-strength group reinforced by two companies, had taken on the bulk of the British 5th Marines (2nd Battalion, Scots Guards; 1st and 7th Gurka rifles; and the Welsh Guards Battalion) and the 42nd Marine Commandos. These British units sustained the largest share of the casualties incurred by the infantry in the retaking of the islands.

By 1300 hours, the 5th Marines had initiated their withdrawal, after destroying their munitions and heavy equipment. Minutes later they were attacked by a British column jumping off from eight helicopters, two of which were brought down by the retreating Argentine Marines, who were successful in shaking off their pursuers. At 1430 hours, the battalion marched into Puerto Argentino in parade order, carrying their weapons. They felt far from defeated. They had made the British pay a disproportionately heavy price for the sector they had been assigned to take. The 5th Argentine Marines took 84 casualties (16 killed and 68 wounded) while inflicting over 300 casualties on the enemy, as was verified when the dead and wounded were removed from the battlefield, a cleanup that lasted through June 19.

AIR FORCE SOUTH SORTIES ITS FINAL RAIDERS

Air Force South, in what would prove to be its last and supreme effort to assist the beleaguered garrison at Puerto Argentino, went all-out to put as many aircraft up as possible, to carry the fight to the enemy, in spite of the now certain outcome. A flight of A4-Bs, after having dropped their bombs and hit a helicopter in flight, became aware that they did not have enough fuel to enjoy a relaxed return to base. Number 2, Second Lieutenant Dellepiane, whose fuel supply was so low he could not make base, was faced with a decision: try for the tanker, or eject over the islands. He decided to go for the tanker, for this way he could save the aircraft. It turned out to be one of the most dramatic episodes in the KC–130's refueling record. The Hercules came out to meet the fuel-starved Skyhawk, and in so doing, came too close to the islands, and thus into range of British radar. There was no way it could fly low. The two defenseless aircraft came in sight of each other as the A4-C fuel gauges rested on 0. If he missed the boom on his first try, he would not get another chance. The boom nozzle and intake inched closer until the connection was locked in and the life-giving liquid began to flow. The A4-C's fuel tanks were riddled with holes. The C–130 nursed it all the way to a safe landing at San Julian, where the pilot touched down, elated, at 1320 hours.

This squadron was followed by another formation of A4-Cs. The objective: the 3rd Royal Marine Brigade's command post! Fortunately for the British, the closest bomb detonated 50 yards from brigade headquarters, moments before the final battalion commanders' meeting, chaired by General Moore, was to be held, to put the finishing touches on the plan for the final assault on Puerto Argentino. Brigadier Thompson reflected in his memoirs on the seriousness of this incident. He felt that a closer hit would have caused severe losses to the command post. Most of the 3rd Brigade's key personnel, including the battalion commanders, might have been killed or wounded.

The squadron left three helicopters destroyed on the ground, and senior British commanders wiping the mud from their chins following their dive for cover in the mushy terrain. For General Moore and his brigade commanders, how Air Force South was repeatedly able to pinpoint and attack their command posts would remain an unanswered question.

Thus the Skyhawks chalked up their final scores and closed out the chapter on their action over the Malvinas. There would be no further sorties against the enemy. This aircraft, which had proved to be the workhorse of the South Atlantic conflict, had accumulated a battle record in which the bravery and professionalism of its pilots were exceeded only by the renewed virtues of this venerable war bird. The two units that flew it saw more action, carried out more missions, fought the hardest against the invading enemy, and caused the most grievous losses.

The A4-Bs flew 133 missions and took on the enemy in 86 of them. Ten of them were lost. Only one pilot made it back. The A4-Cs flew 86 missions and engaged the enemy 41 times. Their losses were nine aircraft. Again, only one pilot came home. These two weapons platforms proved to be both the vehicle and the offering of the greatest sacrifice in blood. As a footnote, it should be pointed out that the A–4s all flew with outdated ejection seats. No updated replacements were available because the United States, as a consequence of the Humphrey-Kennedy amendment, had refused to supply them.

The Mirage-Vs flew 133 sorties and engaged in combat 81 times, inflicting serious losses on the enemy, even though they were not fitted for in-flight refueling, which seriously hampered their capability to attack or to evade enemy interceptors. This was the system that took the biggest beating of the war. Eleven Daggers were lost in action. Seven flyers ejected and were picked up, and four gave their lives in the line of duty.

The C–130 Squadron Flies the Last Shuttles

The steady deterioration of the situation did not deter the Malvinas shuttle flown mainly by the C–130 squadron, although the risk of falling prey to the British increased in like proportion. Until the establishment of the beachhead at San Carlos Bay, the approach routes for the Hercules were unlimited. Their headings were governed by the positions of British vessels along the way. The time of day was a compromise: flying in daylight meant threading one's way through heavy British CAP traffic; night flights entailed the possibility of being targeted by a guided-missile frigate. The latter was opted for, even though this meant landing on an unlit airfield. Operating under such conditions was a tremendous challenge, for switching on the runway lights would betray the arrival of a flight. In addition, there was the almost constantly unfavorable weather.

The establishment of a British base of operations at San Carlos and increased task force activity north of the islands created the first serious obstacle to the Hercules' approach routes. After the fall of Darwin, the southern approach also became risky. The circumstances compelled a flight east past the islands, followed by a turn into Puerto Argentino, with the risk of flying over some British vessel.

Some of the flights were made under minimal weather conditions, far below the usual ceilings for normal flight operations. Neither the low visibility caused by fog, nor the strong cross winds at the runway—as high as 45 knots in some instances—nor 150-foot cloud ceilings kept these pilots from their appointed rounds, without radio-electrical aids (to foil discovery by the enemy) and the bare minimum of lighting to indicate the end of the runway. They flew fully loaded aircraft, which required the use of maximum effort procedures, which required a slower approach speed, afforded less maneuverability, and called for final approach and touchdown at the very head of the runway, since its length left no margin for error. Yet not a single crew decided to abort a landing attempt on its own initiative. Each incomplete approach was cut short in strict compliance with orders. The shuttle was Puerto Argentino's lifeline. It ensured the flow of supplies, and was a vast morale booster to the troops: every successful operation meant that there was a thread of hope, that all was not lost.

The capture of Mount Kent and the emplacement there of enemy artillery within range of the strip would have been a legitimate reason to cancel the flights. The shuttle flew on. After the fall of Mount Longdon, Two Sisters, and Mount Harriet to the British, it came to be regarded as "Mission Impossible." Doing the impossible just takes longer. The flights kept coming in.

At 0605 hours on June 13, a Hercules flew in with a full load of munitions for the 155mm Sofmas. That same evening, between 1930 and 1950 hours, under full red alert and as the British 3rd and 5th Brigades were mounting their final assault against the second Argentine line of defense, one last Hercules operated into the beleaguered garrison. The British thus had visual evidence that the task force had been unable to make one of their government's most important missions—the blockade—stick!

June 13 was also the day of the final KC–130 tanker operations for in-flight refueling of the Skyhawk formations, rounding out the record with the nursing home of a last crippled aircraft, just as they had done throughout the conflict. Thanks to them, not a one went into the sea. They were the cornerstone that made possible the flights that sealed the doom of the *Sheffield* and the *Atlantic Conveyor*, and without them, the attack against the *Invincible* could not have been made. Their record was as noble as it was saddened by the loss of an aircraft—with all hands—as it flew reconnaissance in the face of overwhelming odds. It was their finest moment.

Between May 1 and June 13, the Hercules squadron operated 33 flights into Malvinas, carrying 434 tons of cargo and 514 men, and bringing home 264 wounded. The entire 3rd Infantry Brigade, the 155mm Sofmas and all their munitions, the 602 Commandos, the S/S 38 Exocet missile system, and the Roland missile batteries, to mention just a few, were transported in the cargo bays of the Hercules.

The MK–62 Canberras Do Their Bit

At 2135 hours on June 13, two MK–62s took off on a final mission, laden with a full complement of MK–17 1,000-pounders that, when dropped from a horizontally flying bomber, explode upon impact. Two Mirages escorted the bombers. After dropping their loads on British staging areas, one of the bombers was hit by a missile fired by HMS *Exeter*. One of its crew members was unable to eject, and perished just hours before the end of hostilities. The aircraft went down over Bougainville Island. It was the air force's last casualty.

The Canberra squadron thus wrapped up its active participation in the war effort. It pushed the antiquated and inadequate MK–62 to the very limit while going up against the modern, sophisticated missilery of the enemy. Undaunted, they flew 46 missions, dropped their bombs, and hit the enemy where it hurt. Two aircraft and three crew members were lost.

The Mirage-III squadron was hampered by serious operational limitations over Malvinas. Their short range kept them from flying low-altitude interception, but they flew nonetheless. To them fell the duty of flying backup to the rest of the attack fleet and as an air defense platform that would deter enemy raids against mainland targets (which never materialized). The unit lost two aircraft and one pilot (the latter was picked up).

Other Units

The British expressed amazement upon discovering, at conflict's end, the existence of the Phoenix Squadron, comprised mainly of Lear jet aircraft, as well as other civilian aircraft. They were well aware of the headaches generated by radar signatures of aircraft similar to Mirage-Vs or A–4s appearing day and night, triggering alerts, and constituting a general nuisance for the task force's defense systems. The loss of one Lear jet, with the squadron leader aboard, further demonstrated the dedication and selflessness with which the crews went into battle, flying unarmed, defenseless aircraft.

The Boeing 707 squadron also flew its last long-range scouting mission on June 13. They had picked up the task force as it sailed from Ascension, and had had the honor of making the first face-to-face air contact with an enemy aircraft, a Sea Harrier that flew up from the Hermes to challenge it.

Army Aviation

The Argentine Army deployed a total of 21 helicopters (7 Pumas, 2 Chinooks, 9 UH–1H, and 3 Augusta 109s) to the Malvinas theater of operations. It lost nine of these craft (six Pumas, one UH–1H, one Chinook, and one A–109), and two Pumas were damaged in noncombat incidents. Two other UH–1Hs sustained enemy fire in combat that put them out of action for the duration. These units were all flown by the 601st Army Aviation Battalion, which carried out 796 various missions. Three crew members were killed in action.

GENERAL MENENDEZ LAYS DOWN HIS ARMS

The few remaining Argentine heavy artillery pieces were silenced, one by one. Cannon barrels overheated by repeated use and breaches jammed into the bog by the constant recoil became unable to respond to the calls for fire cover.

The 5th Argentine Marines' withdrawal from Sapper Hill marked the end of General Jofre's organized resistance. The last remnants of the other forces had quit their positions and were straggling back into Puerto Argentino, many with their weapons still in hand but having lost the will to go on fighting. Many marched alongside their British counterparts, who did not even bother to disarm them. Five Argentine regiments never saw action, which means that less than 50 percent of the troops deployed to Malvinas were effectively employed, whereas every available British trooper had been pressed into service. The difference was not just in quality, it was in the numbers.

Generals Menendez and Jofre, following a quick conference, agreed that to continue resistance would entail the useless loss of lives. The bulk of their units on the western front had ceased to exist as such. The two British brigades ruled the perimeter through their firepower, their movement, and their physical presence. By this time, a de facto cease-fire was in effect. The first British regulars appeared along the main road into town, Ross Road West. There they halted.

General Menendez contacted General Galtieri and gave him an update of events. Following a terse exchange, General Galtieri issued, in spite of General Menendez's report, a direct order that resistance be sustained. General Menendez reminded his commander of the inevitability of events, and promptly assumed a true commander's responsibility for the consequences. There was to be no further bloodshed.

General Menendez sent an aide to parley with the British, to set a meeting to discuss terms. Like Lee at Appomattox, he was offering his sword. During this preliminary meeting, the British underscored the need for an immediate cessation of all hostile action by Air Force South. The situation at Puerto Argentino was radioed to General Crespo: It was over, cease all further action! Air Force South, however, could not—would not—accept the idea of quitting. They had borne the main burden of the battle, and theirs would be the last fight. The men sitting in their cockpits were incredulous. Quit now? Hell, no! They had not given in; the ground troops had been overwhelmed! As truce talks went forward, it took radio communication, and finally an unsecured telephone call to the commander of Air Force South, to stay his final thrust. The attack was called off.

The truce team recessed to consult their superiors. A second meeting was set for that evening, with General Moore himself. At 1945 hours, the commander of British forces stepped down from a helicopter, followed by seven of his staff officers. Dressed in combat fatigues, he presented a document spelling out the terms, which were harsher than had been agreed upon. A further meeting was held to hammer out final details. General Moore nodded his acceptance. The final laying down of arms would be less than unconditional. There would be no public ceremony; Argentine officers would remain in command of their troops; and they would keep their colors. The cease-fire became effective at 2359 hours, June 14.

With this, the curtain rang down on the final act of Argentina's ill-fated attempt to make its territory whole again.

14

Recapitulation and Food for Thought

> Never has so much been owed *to* so many, *by* so few.
> Paraphrase of Sir Winston Churchill

THE ROLE OF THE UNITED STATES IN THE CONFLICT

In order to gain a proper perspective on the share and influence of the United States in the South Atlantic conflict, we should examine the action of men in key positions and the means provided to Great Britain to enable it to carry on its war effort.

In Washington, the political-diplomatic stage was shared by two men from President Reagan's cabinet: Secretary of State Haig and Secretary of Defense Weinberger. Alexander Haig's performance was given preferential coverage throughout the world. He took charge, replacing Vice-President Bush, who had at first been assigned by President Reagan to assist the contenders in the negotiations. This was apparently a ripe opportunity for the secretary of state to enhance his political prestige, for he must have felt that the situation concealed no underlying traps, and that the Argentine military junta would bend easily enough to pressure exerted from Washington. In regard to the latter, Haig was caught short. He had no grasp of the significance of the island chain for Argentines, nor of the pledge their president had made as he backed the junta's decision to reclaim a territory regarded by every inhabitant of that South American nation as unredeemed. Further, he sadly overestimated his ability to pressure the "Iron Lady" in London.

Neither did Haig take into account the historical facts behind the dispute. The righteousness of Argentina's cause apparently never entered his mind, nor was it the subject of an analysis in such a light: International law and U.N. resolutions took a back seat to the common interests binding the United States and Great

Britain, the United States' staunchest European friend and ally, the Conservative government of which was to be maintained in office. British officials were well aware of this, and acted accordingly. They gained U.S. support for Security Council Resolution 502, as well as permission to operate out of a U.S. facility on Ascension Island, Wideawake. With this blank check in hand, London had the means of unleashing a conflict in all its breadth. Once this had been set in motion, Mrs. Thatcher had to be sustained in power; her political and logistical requirements had to be met.

It is most probable that Secretary of State Haig offered his good offices as go-between with more objective intentions than those he wound up demonstrating at the negotiating table, where the fate of the islands and of several hundred men was at stake. His stiff one-sidedness lost him the confidence of the government in Buenos Aires, which he certainly enjoyed at the outset, and he steered the talks to a final breakdown. Perhaps his biggest error was that in acting as mediator, he failed to evaluate the facts rationally and fairly. If his primary goal was to uphold the interests of the United States, it was a resounding failure, for Latin America will not soon forget the outcome. Fortunately for his own political future, Vice-President Bush remained on the sidelines for the duration of the conflict.

The secretary of defense, on the other hand, played a much more vital and decisive role. Caspar Weinberger was unabashedly pro-British, and acted accordingly. Pledged to the United Kingdom both emotionally and intellectually, his actions were felt not so much in the political as in the military field, and in the long run proved to be lethal for Argentine attempts at self-defense against the task force while a negotiated solution was being sought. This was confirmed in early 1988, when the British government bestowed upon him an honor usually reserved for British subjects: he was dubbed a Knight of the British Empire. He joined Dwight D. Eisenhower and Henry Ford II in sharing that rare distinction for an American. In a statement, the Foreign Office described Weinberger as a staunch friend to Britain "who will be remembered most of all for his unfailing support and assistance during the Falkland War" (*Washington Post*, February 24, 1988, p. C–4). This is a strange distinction indeed for an American who helped hone the sword against the Americas. May the Lord grant that if some day the tables are turned, the United States finds itself in the position to bestow high honor on a British subject for defending America.

The British expeditionary force would never have been able to operate effectively in the South Atlantic had it not been for the almost unrestricted support the United States threw behind the British war effort, and Weinberger was the chief engineer behind such assistance. This was acknowledged by former Secretary of the Navy John F. Lehman, Jr., in an interview on BBC-TV in May 1988, when he stated: "Britain would have withdrawn from the Falklands if the United States had cut off the aid" (*Philadelphia Enquirer*, May 30, 1988, p. 3).

Weinberger's acting with such determination against Argentina's aspirations is strange, in light of the fact that it did not appear to be consonant with President

Reagan's stated intentions, or with the initiatives being taken by Secretary Haig in the course of his shuttle diplomacy. Rather, his action served to discourage any goodwill the president may have received for seeking a peaceful solution to the conflict, for it moved him onto a track that made him the agent of London's designs. By the same token, it undermined the efforts of the secretary of state, for his announcements had the effect of sapping the confidence of the Buenos Aires government in those efforts.

Weinberger's decisions emanated neither from the White House nor from Congress, nor were they based on any ideal that could be upheld by a statesman desirous of a better America. Pentagon assistance to London began well before the announcement of the failure of the Haig initiative, predating April 2, 1982. It was initiated without the knowledge of Congress and the White House, and sometimes flowed beyond the bounds provided for by law, which spell out how the secretary of defense should go about providing assistance to the government of a third country.

The British Admiralty and the U.S. fleet held frequent and close secret talks outside official channels, with the knowledge and consent of the secretaries of defense and the navy. Great Britain would have been hard put to send a fleet to the South Atlantic, and in a worse position yet to support a war effort at a colossal distance. U.S. Navy experts entertained serious doubts as to British prospects for achieving a victory in the South Atlantic, doubts that were shared by British naval analysts.

Unrestricted use of the base at Wideawake was the first step. Absent these facilities, it would have been impossible for the task force to operate in the South Atlantic. Most of the fuel for British vessels, aircraft, and helicopters was shipped in from the United States, for Great Britain was unable to keep up the flow at those latitudes. Admiralty materiel requests were mind-boggling. Equipment was made available to Northwood on 24-hour notice—as opposed to the usual two-week lead time—skipping over 15 different official formalities. Requests were channeled straight to Weinberger. Missiles such as the Sidewinder, the Stinger, and the Phalanx arrived in British hands in this way. In most cases, the equipment was delivered directly to Ascension. Ninety percent of British intelligence requirements regarding Argentine military capabilities were provided by U.S. sources. Satellite communications facilities were made available so that London could have instant contact with task force units. All of this serves to underscore the accuracy of the West German news weekly *Der Spiegel* (March 11, 1984) when it stated: "Without Caspar Weinberger, England might have lost the war."

Neither President Reagan nor Secretary of State Haig appeared to be fully aware of the scope of this assistance. The National Security Council decision of May 1, practically railroaded through by the secretary of defense, came in for criticism from both the State Department and the Pentagon. It meant scrapping patient efforts by Washington to improve relations with Latin America, a policy that was beginning to bring in positive results for President Reagan for the first time in many years. This involved both opposing and overriding Washington policy, as summed up in the statement "In the issue of sovereignty over the Falkland Islands the U.S. stance is neutral."

Washington's support to its ally was bound by two restrictions: U.S. ships and aircraft would not operate south of Ascension; and Britain was enjoined from operating against the Argentine mainland. Without such restrictions, it is entirely within the realm of possibility that the Vulcan bombers might have attempted missions over Argentine air bases, or the latter could have come under attack by SAS or SBS troops. There are serious grounds for not discarding such an intention.

The United States should pause to reflect on its friend and ally's recognition of its assistance during the conflict. Great Britain, far from expressing gratitude, railed against the restrictions imposed on its designs and requests, and when it came time to pass out the "well dones" to those who carried the day, British success in retaking the island chain was attributed almost entirely to the professionalism of British troops. It was the virtues of British soldiers, and not the flow of supplies, that enabled them to operate in the South Atlantic, that had decided the outcome.

Nor did Great Britain repay the favor in the political arena when the United States decided, in 1983, to intervene militarily in Grenada, to eradicate a leftist regime in that small Caribbean country. In this instance, London fell back on the line used by Washington during the Falklands crisis: one should not resort to the use of force to change the political status of states.

The effect of the Weinberger-Haig policy surfaces every time Washington seeks Latin American support in international bodies on issues involving the Central American conflict. If the United States is overwhelmed with a feeling of loneliness at voting time in hemispheric councils, it should be mindful that there was a South American government that had cooperated decisively with the Reagan administration in the struggle against subversion in Central America— the Argentine military junta of 1982, whose members are now languishing in jail. By granting unbridled support to a European ally, at the expense of its allies within this hemisphere, the United States took an extremely dangerous step regarding its national security, as can be noted in the words of former Secretary of the Navy Lehman, who admitted during an interview that "U.S. involvement in the South Atlantic conflict led indirectly to the Iran-contra scandal last year" (*Philadelphia Inquirer*, May 30, 1988, p. 3). Lehman stated that when Latin American countries learned of the U.S. aid to Britain, they withdrew support for the Nicaraguan rebels, forcing Washington to find other means for backing them. Lehman said that Latin American countries "still don't quite understand the extent" of the U.S. aid and its effect on that war's outcome (Ibid.). "But we certainly did, and we knew the price we would be paying," he said. "The Argentines and all the other Latin Americans abruptly stopped supporting the efforts of the Salvadorans and the contra forces against the communists in Central America, and that led to 'Contragate' " (Ibid.).

The lesson to be learned from these truths is that U.S. defense strategy is on target when it prescribes that the enemy should be deterred from starting a war; that if war comes, the United States should be prepared to win; and that the battlefront should be as far from home as possible. However, by strengthening its political and strategic ties in far-removed lands, the United States has neglected its own hemisphere, which is more than just its "backyard"; it is its shelter of last resort. Its enemies are well aware of this, and will spare no efforts to carry their fight as close to the U.S. homeland as possible, but by much more subtle means: by taking advantage of the social, political, and economic ills of a Latin America whose confidence in the one who should be its natural ally and brother in the hemisphere, the United States, has been gravely undermined.

And how could it be otherwise? For as long as men born in America receive the Order of the British Empire, and are dubbed Knight Grand Cross, for having aided and abetted an extra-hemispheric colonial power at the expense of an American republic that was attempting to exercise its claim on that which it regards as its own, the sacred trust has been broken.

The United States can square its debt to Argentina and the rest of Latin America by demanding that Great Britain comply with the U.N. resolutions regarding the Falklands and colonialism. That is Washington's responsibility. Not only will Washington regain the confidence of its next-door neighbors, but it will strengthen its own strategic line of defense. The price of such action: nothing. It will cost the United States no more than it did in 1956, when, by staying Britain's action at Suez, it showed its upper hand, and the British bowed gracefully, if unwillingly. Why should the Falklands be any different? Should Britain risk its special relationship with the land of George Washington and Abraham Lincoln, which has infinitely more value than any benefit those desolate islands in the South Atlantic wastes might bring?

We earnestly hope that Washington will help wipe the slate clean—not only for the righteousness of a cause, and hemispheric security and solidarity, but also for the whole West, as well as its principles, which are sometimes allowed to go astray by the two leading powers of the free world.

THE WAR IN FIGURES

1. The Argentine Army suffered the loss of 186 men: 13 officers, 35 NCOs, and 138 troops; 918 sustained varying degrees of wounds. Total casualties (killed and wounded) were 1,104 officers and men. Decorations or citations were awarded to 650 army personnel.

2. The Argentine Navy suffered the loss of 394 men: 16 officers, 211 petty officers, and 167 seamen; 105 were wounded. Total casualties were 499 officers and men. Decorations or citations were awarded to 596 navy personnel.

3. The Argentine Air Force suffered the loss of 55 men, most of them pilots: 36 officers, 14
   NCOs, and 5 airmen; 47 sustained wounds. Total casualties were 102 officers and men.

The Air Force limited decorations to special commendations for "killed in
action" or "wounded in action," and gave unit citations to all those who played
a role in the war. The reasoning was as follows:

1. It was deemed best, in order to allow for an evenhanded analysis of the historical
   record, not to proceed further at this time.
2. It was felt best not to engage in any type of speculation that might tend to color
   objectivity and the judgment of history.
3. Almost all air force units played an active role in the battle. Each did its share. It
   was decided, therefore, to "avoid self-glorification."

The preceding figures reveal that 635 Argentine officers and men were killed
in action in the South Atlantic conflict and 1,068 were wounded, for a total of
1,703 casualties for all Argentine armed forces. These figures are subject to
verification, and they are not colored by any type of propaganda or psychological
action.

Argentine Aircraft Losses

The Argentine armed forces lost a total of 57 aircraft during the war: 47 air
force, 9 navy, and 1 coast guard. The air force lost 10 A4-Bs, 9 A4-Cs, 2
Mirage-IIIs, 2 MK–62s, 11 IA–58s, 1 C–130, and 1 LR–35. The navy lost 3
A4-Qs, 2 MB–339s, and 4 T–34Cs. The coast guard lost a Skyvan. Of the 57
aircraft put out of action, 2 were shot down by our own antiaircraft fire, 6 were
lost to operational accidents (including 1 IA–58 at Comodoro Rivadavia), and
49 to enemy action. Following are the various causes for the losses—according
to British sources, which claim 60 aircraft—as well as the number of rounds
fired or missiles expended by each weapons system.

1. To Sidewinder: 17 (68 launched)
2. To commando action: 10 (Pebble Island raid)
3. To 30mm cannon fire: 4 (average 350 rounds expended per aircraft downed)
4. To naval antiaircraft artillery: 3 (average 2,500 rounds expended per aircraft downed)
5. To Sea Cat: 5 Class 12 and 21 frigates (108 missiles launched)
6. To Sea Wolf: 3 Class 22 frigates (96 launches)
7. To Sea Dart: 6 (Class 42 destroyers, HMS *Invincible*, cruisers) (76 launches)
8. To Rapier: 4 (100 launches per battery, over 8 batteries in operation)
9. To Blow Pipe: 5 (140 launches per firing unit, between 22 and 25 operational)
10. To light weapons: 2

11. To Stinger: 1 (40 launches)

12. To aerial bombardment: 1.

These figures do not include damaged, salvageable aircraft or those captured on the ground by British forces at the end of the conflict, most of which were out of action:

Air force: 13 IA–58s

Navy: 3 MB–339s

Coast guard: 1 Skyvan.

Argentine Helicopter Losses

Total helicopter losses to enemy action were ten: nine army and one navy (not including three operational accidents). Of these, six were shot down in flight (three by Sea Harrier, two by light weapons fire, and one by Sea Dart); three were destroyed on the ground during air raids; and one went down with the General Belgrano.

At the conflict's end, the following helicopters remained in the islands:

Air force: 2 Bell 212s

Army: 1 Chinook, 2 Augustas, and 9 UH–1H

Coast guard: 1 Puma.

Total Argentine Aircraft Lost in the Conflict

In December 1982, a Defense Ministry report entitled *The Falkland Campaign: The Lessons* was submitted to Parliament by order of the queen. This report outlined the losses allegedly inflicted on Argentine forces by the British forces. Annex B, page 45, of this official report lists aircraft losses. (The figures in parentheses are Argentine figures for aircraft lost to enemy action, not including operational accidents.) A total of 117 (59) Argentine aircraft were destroyed (the last three types are helicopters):

45 A4 Skyhawks (17)

27 Mirages (12)

21 Pucaras (10)

4 Mentors (4)

3 Aeromacchis (1)

3 Canberras (2)

2 Skyvans (1)

1 C–130 (1)

1 Lear jet (1)

6 Pumas (6)

2 Bell Hueys (3: 1 Allouette, 1 UH–1H, and 1 A–109)

2 Chinooks (1)

The author will venture to admit error with regard to losses incurred by British forces for lack of hard data, but there are no mistakes as far as our own are concerned. The reader may accept the figures given here as being the true count. Unfortunately, British fudging with their own loss figures while exaggerating ours has cast doubt on the true extent of the damage they sustained. It also demonstrates that concealment of the truth has been systematic on their part.

Argentine Naval Vessels Sunk, Destroyed, or Damaged

The listing of Argentine naval losses is not a record of which British forces should be proud. For openers, the only Argentine warship sunk by the task force was the *General Belgrano*, attacked from behind as it was sailing away from the war zone, in violation of Great Britain's self-imposed rules of engagement, at a deplorable, unnecessary, and irreparable cost in human lives, and for reasons that have yet to be satisfactorily clarified by Great Britain.

The second vessel sunk was the trawler *Narwal*, in another gratuitous act of cruelty, since it was a completely defenseless commercial fishing vessel that, even had it been operating as a lookout, did not merit the unresisted attack of British warplanes. Not content with doing in the unarmed ship, the British went after the crew in their lifeboats, a despicable act that is at all odds with maritime traditions, and cost one crew member his life and grievous wounds to several more. Also, a search-and-rescue helicopter that had gone to that crew's assistance was destroyed during this action. At no time did Argentine forces challenge the British during this action, although they had a number of opportunities to respond in kind during the conflict but refrained from doing so.

The submarine *Santa Fe*, which was a more likely candidate for a place in a naval museum than in combat, was taken by surprise under the worst possible conditions for a submersible facing an enemy: on the surface in shallow waters. It was defenseless. Weeks later, as the British were attempting to move it to better moorings—a museum in Britain, ironically enough—it sank off the coast of South Georgia Island.

The transports *Buen Suceso*, *Rio Carcarana*, and *Isla de los Estados* were unarmed freighters. They had not so much as a naval escort. Their assailants were safe from the defenses our own people had to face when they attacked the cream of the Royal Navy.

The two coast guard vessels attacked by British aircraft were small, 81-ton craft, mounted with a single 12.7mm machine gun, a defense more symbolic than real. Nevertheless they plied the islands waterways, one of them for the duration of the war.

British reports state that the picket *Comodoro Somellera*, having characteristics similar to the *Alferez Sobral*, was attacked during the action against the latter. This is inaccurate. The *Somellera* did not come under attack. The British Sea Lynx pilots who took credit for its sinking must have attacked the *Sobral*, which had already been damaged by aircraft from the destroyer *Coventry*.

In summary, Argentina suffered the loss of the following ships:

1. By sinking—one cruiser, the *General Belgrano;* one trawler, the *Narwal;* and a transport, the *Isla de los Estados*. The submarine *Santa Fe*, initially damaged and captured, sank later while under tow

2. Damaged—the escort *Guerrico*, the picket *Sobral*, the cutter *Islas Malvinas*, the freighters *Rio Carcarana* and *Bahia Buen Suceso*

3. Captured—the cutter *Rio Iguazu*, following the surrender at Puerto Argentino, along with the British freighters *Monsumen, Forrest,* and *Penelope Stanley*, which had been taken over in the islands by Argentine forces. All were shallow-draft vessels.

British Casualties during the Conflict, and Decorations Bestowed

Official British figures establish the death toll for the task force during operations at 255, with another 777 wounded. Although such figures should be sufficiently straightforward, it should be pointed out that the circumstances do not guarantee absolute credibility for such statistics. This is based on two underlying factors:

1. The falsehoods to which the British government resorted as the conflict unfolded, which were noted by Argentine forces on numerous occasions, and acknowledged by unofficial British sources on others

2. The analysis and evaluation of events in the tactical area do not agree with official British figures, since both estimates and hard facts indicate a considerably higher figure.

Taking into account the fact that such losses were sustained in a conflict not with an adversary of like potential but with one of much more modest means, such a victory not only was Pyrrhic but also revealed to friend and foe alike unfathomable shortcomings. Therefore, concealing the true figures became of vital importance. And the British Conservative government had its ways: the lid of military secrecy precluded any proper analysis of the situation based on hard figures. Only after a great many years have elapsed will we be able to judge the full extent of the political-military absurdities of 1982. By then historians can wax poetic rather than face the hard realities.

As for scruples that may keep a government from concealing the truth, it is obvious that in this day and age, the important thing in politics is results; moral aims have been set aside, in both East and West, by material aims. A government that would have no qualms about sending the crew of a ship such as the *General Belgrano* to their death, especially if its own survival were at stake, could hardly be accused of ethical queasiness. Unfortunately, this tendency of British governments to equate bad news with no news is not the exclusive turf of the current prime minister, Mrs. Thatcher. In 1957, the Windscale nuclear plant in northern England burned out of control, producing radioactive pollution in a class with the disasters at Three Mile Island and Chernobyl, causing numerous deaths from leukemia. Harold Macmillan, prime minister at the time, and his successors kept this terrible truth under wraps.

Getting back to numbers, it becomes difficult to play with figures under the guise of reality. It is known that in the common graves at Goose Green many more than the 17 officially counted British war dead share a final resting place. The same can be said of Pleasant Bay. It has been rumored that the taking of Port Stanley cost Gen. Jeremy Moore over 300 men, and that some of his units, particularly the 5th Infantry Brigade, returned home dismally decimated. Calculations worked out in West Germany show British casualties as being in the neighborhood of 700 battlefield deaths and over 1,500 wounded. This figure is more in consonance with Argentine estimates.

The official casualty figure announced by the British Defense Ministry has been called into question by British authors and publications. For example, the body count at Pleasant Bay was made public only on June 13, after several days of secrecy. Defense Minister Nott acknowledged 50 killed and 60 wounded. Yet British author Anthony Preston states in his book *Sea Combat of the Falklands* that following that attack, the hospital ship *Uganda* received (according to "highly reliable sources") 159 wounded within a four-hour period. Such official accountings also have been questioned by British authors William Fowler, James Ladd, and Patrick Bishop and John Witherow, all of whom affirm that the British government fudged the figures in order to tone down the bad news.

There is, however, no need to speculate over dubious numbers, for even the official toll of 255 dead and 777 wounded tells the tale of the exceedingly high price the United Kingdom paid for its last successful colonial stand. To put this into perspective, let the figures for previous British battlefield engagements during the postwar era speak for themselves: Korea, 1950–1953—537 killed in action; Malaya, 1958–1961—525; the Suez campaign 1956—32; Cyprus, 1954–1959—105; Palestine, 1945–1948—223. Leaving aside whatever the true figure for Britain's action in the South Atlantic was (which would surpass the total of the above), the acknowledgment of 255 battle dead in a 45-day operation indicatives the highest daily casualty count sustained in any war Great Britain has been involved in since World War II.

With regard to decorations and titles granted, the British government was exceedingly generous to those whose greatest personal risk was running the gauntlet of political intrigue in London, more so than those whose feats of arms achieved the objective sought.

British Losses in Aircraft

Any attempt to determine the exact number of aircraft losses sustained by the task force, and how they came about, comes up against a great big blank. Here the difficulty of ascertaining the truth is compounded by the fuzziness of official British data and the impossibility of providing absolutely trustworthy data from our own sources.

Air Force South feels safe with the following figures: in action with Harrier/Sea Harrier aircraft—14 confirmed downings, 7 probable, 2 damaged. Further investigation provided these final figures: 17 confirmed, 11 probable, 11 damaged.

The official British figures were the bottom-line minimum, and some losses reported as due to operational accidents whitewashed some Argentine kills. In the final analysis, based on the law of probabilities, it can safely be assumed that 22 British aircraft were downed during the action. Unofficial reports coming out of London from trustworthy sources allow for the following British aircraft losses during the conflict, including accidents:

—Aircraft downed/destroyed: 31 (19 Sea Harrier and 12 Harrier)
—Damaged aircraft successfully landed: 16 (10 Sea Harrier and 6 Harrier)

This accounts for the difference of 9 aircraft between the 22 officially confirmed and the 31 unofficially reported by reliable sources. Perhaps the answer lies in the saga of two of the vessels that came under Argentine air attack: the container ship *Atlantic Conveyor* and the light carrier HMS *Invincible*.

British Helicopter Losses

Great Britain has officially acknowledged the loss of 24 helicopters during the war. Our own sources come up with a higher figure, which includes the 12 Wessex helicopters lost when the *Atlantic Conveyor* went down. Unofficial British sources have revealed a total loss of 46 units with many more laid up for repairs, due mainly to salt-water damage.

Total British Aircraft Losses during the Conflict

A balanced figure for all aircraft lost by British forces would be the following:

1. According to official sources—35 (11 fixed-wing and 24 helicopters)
2. According to our own figures—66 (28 fixed-wing and 38 helicopters)
3. According to unofficial British sources—77 (31 fixed-wing and 46 helicopters).

If there is any truth in these figures, the Conservative government, which had called up every available aircraft in its arsenal, had to conceal the true extent of the losses, for the armed forces and the very security of the kingdom had been compromised in a colonial war it would be hard put to justify before history.

British Vessels Sunk, Destroyed, or Damaged

Had any Argentine military analyst (or, for that matter, one from any country) been asked, prior to the conflict, his estimate of prospective losses to be sustained by the British fleet in such an action, his wildest "guesstimate" would have fallen pitifully short of the true figure at conflict's end. British staffs, as it turned out, shared the Argentine belief that perhaps one ship, two at the most, could have been lost. This modest figure was also what the air force surmised, even though it was ready to sacrifice three-quarters of its assets in order to achieve it. These estimates were in keeping with what both war theorists and guided-missile frigate builders felt were the odds for surface vessels equipped with leading-edge-technology antiaircraft electronic and defense systems.

On the very first day of action, the Torno Squadron upset this balance, for in the aircraft-surface vessel standoff, the latter came out the losers, in spite of our antiquated weapons platforms (with the notable exception of the Super Etendard). If only a single virtue stood out in this lopsided engagement, it was the full viability of the airplane as an irreplaceable weapons platform in modern warfare, even when obsolete antiques were flown against one of the world's most modern fleets.

Here is the price tag for the task force's intervention in the conflict:

1. Vessels sunk or destroyed (salvageable)—9 (Class 42 destroyers *Sheffield* and *Coventry*, Class 21 frigates *Ardent* and *Antelope*, landing transports *Sir Galahad* and *Sir Tristram*, heavy containership *Atlantic Conveyor*, 2 landing craft (1 LCU and 1 LCVP)

2. Vessels sustaining heavy damage (salvageable following extensive overhaul performed away from the operations area)—12 (carriers *Hermes* and *Invincible*, cruisers *Antrim* and *Glamorgan*, Class 42 destroyers *Glasgow* and *Exeter*, Class 22 frigate *Brilliant*, Class 21 frigates *Argonaut* and *Arrow*, Rothesay Class frigate *Plymouth*, one unidentified Class 12 frigate, and 1 LCU)

3. Vessels sustaining moderate damage (salvageable following routine repairs in operations area)—11 (Class 22 frigate *Broadsword*, Class 21 frigate *Alacrity* and *Avenger*, amphibious assault vessel *Fearless*, logistics transports *Sir Lancelot, Sir Geraint*, and *Sir Bedivere*, transport *Norland*, and three unidentified vessels).

A total of 32 British vessels sustained varying degrees of damage, due to the following causes:

1. Air attack—29
2. Other causes—3.

To round out the figures for vessels struck one or more times by Argentine weapons systems, 46 attacks against naval targets were successfully carried out, inflicting varying degrees of damage. What would the toll have been had our MK–17 ordnance detonated on impact? The facts show that out of all the 1,000 pound bombs dropped that hit targets, only two exploded within the bowels of their naval targets: HMS *Ardent* on May 21, and HMS *Antelope* on May 23, the latter as attempts were being made to disarm the bomb. In both instances, the vessels were sunk. On the other hand, as least 11 MK–17s pierced or became embedded in various vessels without detonating: the destroyer *Glasgow* (May 12), the cruiser *Antrim* and the frigate *Argonaut* (May 21), the frigate *Broadsword* (May 23), logistics ships *Sir Lancelot, Sir Galahad,* and *Sir Bedivere* (May 24/25). Three of these vessels were hit by two bombs, but all saved by the failure of the ordnance to explode. The detonation of an MK–17 proved to be fatal for any ship hit. Others also were struck by MK–17s, but they have not been identified.

Any analysis of the ensuing events, had all those bombs gone off as they should have, can only be the object of conjecture. Every act of war brings a counteraction. It is quite possible the British might have lost the war unless the United States became directly involved in the conflict. Perhaps the best answer to all these questions was given by a high-ranking West German official during a diplomatic gathering in Bonn: "The best thing that could have happened to Argentina was that the bombs did not go off." Queried about this apparent contradiction, he elaborated: "otherwise, Mrs. Thatcher's government would have resorted to the use of nuclear weapons against the mainland."

THE AIR FORCE'S PERFORMANCE: SOUR GRAPES AND TESTIMONIALS

In order to achieve a better grasp on the realities of Argentina, the reader should be aware of the fact that, after all was said and done, the air force's performance during the conflict came in for some criticism, some examples of which follow:

—The shuttle was not effective in meeting the logistical needs of the Malvinas garrison.

—The Pucaras sortied on only two occasions.

—The San Carlos beachhead was consolidated due to the ineffectiveness of the air force.

—The air force did not achieve air superiority.

—The air force carried on its own private war with the "little frigates."

—The air force acted very independently during the conflict.

—The air force issued faked and overblown combat reports.

—The air force conducted itself in this fashion in order to garner a larger share of political power, and to create heroes not justified by the facts.

—The air force should have lengthened the runway at Puerto Argentino.

—The air force did not provide ground support.

—The air force failed to operate during the last days of the conflict.

This is not the proper medium in which to rebut such statements or to justify what the service did, or left undone, during the hostilities for reclaiming the Malvinas Islands. Neither does the author wish to be a party or a judge by stating his own opinion. Let the reader, and history, be the judges. Nonetheless, some clarification is due, if only to honor the memory of those who fell in battle, for those who bravely gave their lives did so out of a simple but high ideal, and out of their sense of duty: they gave their lives in defense of their country.

Such criticism brings to mind the story of the skillful swimmer who reaches safety following a shipwreck and calls out encouragement to the others to follow him, but does not attempt to go to their assistance. The men of the air force swam, as it were, the best they could to keep the dignity both of a nation and of a continent afloat.

TESTIMONIALS

If you wish to know how you did in war, ask your enemy.
                    San Tzu (Chinese philosopher, fifth century B.C.)

Following the mind-boggling air war over San Carlos Bay, the news media throughout the world began to publish items describing the conduct of Argentina's pilots during the action of May 21. In honor of our fallen brethren, and that their kin may ever be proud—and for this reason only—a few of these testimonials appear below:

British Defense Minister John Nott before Parliament: "I believe that the Argentine pilots are showing enormous bravery. It would be fool of me not to acknowledge it."

Admiral John Foster Woodward, in an article published by *La Estrella de Panama* (January 3, 1984): "The Argentine pilots were most brave. They gave me no end of headaches, but I admire them nonetheless." In reference to the attack at Pleasant Bay, he stated: "We had already received sufficient proof of what they were capable of doing. They came in skimming over the surface of the water. We would never have expected that."

Statement by Gen. Kelly Aguilera Nessi, of the Venezuelan Air Force:

Baron von Richthofen is not just a German hero, he is a hero for all mankind, especially for those of us who wear the blue; the heroic feats of Douglas Bader, the legless British flyer, belong to the ages; and when mention is made of the recent conflict in the South Atlantic, the outcome of which has caused such heartache in this part of the Americas, which rejects colonialism with all its might, the most moving pages of this chapter in history were written by the glorious and heroic air force of Argentina. (speech delivered at Caracas, August 18, 1982)

The Guardian, May 25, 1982, p. 1:

CREWS APPLAUD ENEMY PILOT BRAVERY—By Gareth Parry, with the landing forces at San Carlos Bay

It is 2 P.M. on a sunny day, and we are under attack by Argentine Mirages and Skyhawks. A bomb has just thrown up a gigantic column of water barely 100 yards away, between our boats and a logistics ship loaded with gear.

We watched as the coastal batteries and the ships' missile systems opened fire, along with the deafening noise of the deck cannon and machine guns.

. . . The crewmen all about us pay tribute to the courage of the Argentine pilots.

The Miami Herald, May 27, 1982: "The Argentine pilots are winning the hearts of their countrymen, and the admiration of their foes."

Kenneth Freed, *Los Angeles Times Service*:

Buenos Aires. Almost daily they fly into battle, and each time, only a few return. But the Argentine pilots are becoming the heroes of the Falklands war, admired almost as much by their enemies as by their countrymen.

They are the only thing standing against a total defeat, said a European military expert.

I do not not believe that there are finer pilots in the world.

To date, the British confirm that Argentine flyers have sunk two destroyers, two frigates, one logistics ship, and some landing craft. Argentina claims that the air attacks have put at least five more ships out of action, and damaged another five.

But while Britain refuses to acknowledge some of the damage sustained, she recognizes the skill and courage of her opponents in the air.

This article was reprinted in other papers in English-speaking cities round the world under the title "The Golden Boys of Argentina."

Another article, coming from closer to home, by Brazilian air analyst Milton Loureiro, of Rio de Janeiro's *Jornal do Comercio*, praised the bravery and courage demonstrated by Argentine flyers in the Malvinas conflict.

In an article entitled "The Incredible Argentine Air Force," in *Jornal do Comercio*, Loureiro stated: "Whatever the outcome of the conflict, the unwavering courage of the Argentine pilots will remain forever etched in history." He went on to say that the principles of naval-air engagements had been proven outdated by the daring and technique shown by the Argentine pilots, both air force and navy. He added:

When this undeclared war ends, the world's navies will have to revamp their tactics, because the daring and bravery of Argentina's flyers have trashed all the currently existing theory.

The enemy himself has been stunned by the cool and daring of Argentina's pilots, and has recognized the South Atlantic conflict to be as unreal as a fairy tale.

Chilean radio station Diego Portales news bulletin:

Argentine flyers have earned worldwide recognition, even by the British themselves, for their bravery. They have been described as boring through a veritable wall of missiles, shells, and antiaircraft machine gun fire, inflicting damage upon the enemy.

The Venezuelan ambassador to Argentina, on bestowing one of his country's decorations on Air Force General Lami Dozo:

I have the honor, as Venezuelan ambassador, on behalf of our own air force, to thus distinguish the heroic and glorious Argentine Air Force, of which all Venezuelans especially, and Latin Americans in general, can be justly proud, for the glory and the feats achieved in this action, for the Americas, and for their own dignity.

Statement by Col. Jonathan Alford, vice-director of the International Institute for Strategic Studies in London, during a conference in the United States:

Compared to those of many countries, Argentina deployed a relatively modest and aging air force, which operated for the most part up to the limits of its range. And yet there were moments of great anguish for the fate of the British fleet. Perhaps with just a bit more luck at the critical junctures, the Argentine Air Force might have succeeded in forcing Great Britain to abort her expedition. . . .

What really shook us up was learning that the Argentines had flown their Hercules into Port Stanley right through the last day of the conflict.

Not less moving was a cable received from France, from the Argentine embassy in Paris, which read as follows:

Mr. Ambassador. There are many Frenchmen, more than you could imagine, who are standing wholeheartedly alongside Argentina during her hour of trial.

As you may know, I am an old friend of your country. In the struggle in which Argentina and England find themselves locked, my fellow flyers in Argentina have earned my unabashed admiration. I hold many in high regard, I feel a moral obligation, for many of them chose their calling somewhat because of me, and my book *The Great Circus*.

Mr. Ambassador, I would be most grateful to you if you could forward this message to your air force chief of staff, for transmittal to all the pilots. The Argentine government has my permission to use it as it sees fit. I have always stood behind everything I have ever written.

Please accept, Mr. Ambassador, the assurance of my highest consideration, as well as my wishes for a timely and least possible tragic outcome of this terrible conflict.

(signed) Pierre Clostermann*

Pierre Clostermann's Message to Argentine Combat Pilots:

To you, my young Argentine fellow combat pilots, goes the full expression of my admiration. Against the most sophisticated electronics, surface-to-air missiles, the most

*Pierre Clostermann is a French World War II flying ace.

dangerous targets possible, ships, you have achieved success. You have not hesitated to fly out against the worst prevailing weather conditions in the world, with fuel reserves measured in minutes, to the very limit of your range, in raging storms, in your Mirages, your Etendards, your A4s, your Pucaras, all emblazoned with your blue and white roundels. In spite of antiaircraft defense arrays and SAM missiles launched from powerful ships, which enjoyed the early warning of both AWACs and U.S. satellites, you have gone unwaveringly through. Never in the history of warfare since 1914 have flyers come face to face with such a terrifying convergence of lethal obstacles, not even those of the RAF over London in 1940, or those of the Luftwaffe in 1945.

Your courage has enlightened not only the people of Argentina. Many of us throughout the world are proud to call you our fellow aviators.

To the fathers and mothers, to the brothers and sisters, to the wives and children of those Argentine pilots who met death with unflinching, unfathomable courage, I say all honor and glory is theirs, both for Argentina and for the Latin world.

Alas! Truth is sealed only in the shedding of blood, and the world believes only in those causes whose champions are willing to lay down their lives for them.

(signed) Pierre Clostermann

Jean Pierre Gillet, a French expert and author of the book *Les Combattants de Mai*, stated in his work: All has been said about Argentine steadfastness. Let us but add that we should like to see that courage matched in certain NATO countries'' (p. 28).

La Estrella de Panama (August 10, 1984), on a double centerfold complete with photographs of pilots killed in combat, on Air Force Day:

I wish to pay moving tribute to these heroes who gave their lives for their country during the heroic quest for Malvinas. They fought for an ideal that nobody can change, and that we Panamanians share as our own: The Malvinas Islands were, are now, and shall be forever Argentine.

Jorge E. Illueca
President of the Republic of Panama

At the close of hostilities, General Lami Dozo sent Pierre Clostermann a model of the Pucara as a token of his appreciation. The French ace responded as follows:

General:
The Argentine air attaché in Paris has forwarded me the model of the Pucara along with the dedication, for which I am honored.

Please be assured how moved I am by this souvenir, which will remain on my desk, before my eyes, as a constant reminder, as if I could someday forget, of what a battle all Argentine flyers fought over Malvinas.

The fact is, whether it was the C–130 pilot taking off under hostile fire with his load of wounded, or the pilots of the A–4s, the Mirages, the Daggers, or the helicopters, all made a brilliant showing of their outstanding professional skills, as well as of a courage that has elicited the admiration of the whole world, including that of your adversaries.

In this Western world, where cowardice competes with need, the heroism of the Argentine aviators is likened unto a light in the darkness, toward which all those who still believe in the virtues of patriotism, in the philosophic values of our Latin world, and in the destiny of mankind should strive, for all men can be justly proud to be of the same strain as that of your crewmen. With my best wishes—and I learned from General De Gaulle that to lose a battle is by no means to lose a war—for your country, for yourself, and for all those under you, please accept, General, the renewed assurance of my highest consideration and deepest respect.

Not to be outdone during the heat of the fight for San Carlos, Jose Maria Carrascal, correspondent for Madrid's daily *ABC*, filed the following moving account:

The Daring of Argentina's Flyers in Combat over the South Atlantic

They are but a few hundred—or at least they were—but they bear on their shoulders the heaviest burden of this war, which is no less the bloodier for its being undeclared. They appear undaunted by the death of their comrades, or by the prospect of their own on the next sorties. Seldom has such gallantry been shown in life, or such self-assurance in the face of death, such feeling for their own, such daring before the unknown.

They fight under extreme conditions against objectives 300 miles away, with just enough fuel for three or four minutes over the target and then to make it home. One eye glued on their prey, the other on the fuel needle, they are oblivious to the missiles swarming at them from all sides, from the enemy's array of aircraft and ground batteries.

Most of their jets are not equipped with all-weather radar, which forces them to come out in broad daylight, to avoid clouds, to flee fog. Others, such as the Super Etendard, have to be refueled in flight, so limited is their range. But no matter. Just like the prince of yore who increased the length of his sword by moving ahead a step, they drop down ever further—they *graze* the British masts—even though by so doing, they greatly increase fuel consumption. They do it again and again, as if it were some sort of drill.

Each time they sortie, they gamble their very lives, in a game often played for keeps. They fly machines that are refurbished by ground crews on the run. These are the ones who reload the bombs, rack the rockets, top off the fuel, who check everything out, who say GO! The pilots have barely the time for a quick nap, a cup of coffee, a briefing on the silhouettes of the remaining enemy vessels. And off they go again. The 1940 RAF would have been proud!

No bragging, no talking. Let the enemy tally the kills and hits. They just answer their cues and fly into center stage—no fuss, no muss—as if it were business as usual.

The romanticism of feats of arms, of military glory, is no longer of our times, and I begin to wonder if this report is from another time, another place. It is inspired by the human qualities of the Argentine aviators. In a world such as ours, where the rule of thumb is to demand but not to give, the shining example of these flyers, who gave their all, asking nothing in return, not so much as a pat on the back, is so moving as to blind the senses. A modern mind has to strain to make sense of it all, and it still comes up short.

They are not, by any manner or means, laying down their lives for the junta. Not even—one would think—for lofty notions such as honor or country. They do so for something very tangible, something of value to them; they do it for their community, which has entrusted them with its defense. And yes, when you get down to it, they do it out of a sense of commitment, of duty. It is men such as these who ennoble all mankind.

In this particular instance they ennoble all those of Spanish, of Latin descent, to whom the world has been less than kind in modern times. Our breasts swell with pride, and yes, our eyes with tears of grief, as we read the roll of those two-tiered Spanish and Italian family names, which somehow have the ring of another age.

Will the sacrifice of these brave flyers return Malvinas to their country? I cannot say. But one thing I do know, something more important, and that is that Malvinas, in this swiftly spinning world of ours, will one day be Argentina's. I do know that down the line when one thinks of Argentina, the image will no longer be the typical gaucho, the slicked-haired tango crooner, or some latter-day figurehead president. What will come to mind will be these pilots, who knew how to die because they knew for what they lived. This is a privilege shared by a precious few in this day and age.

It has oft been said that Argentina is a land blessed by every gift of Heaven and Earth. She has been further blessed, as we have been shown, by those of her sons whose calling was with the eagles.

The testimonials are endless. Almost all came from abroad. Especially moving was the letter from the U.S. air attaché in Buenos Aires at the time of the conflict, Col. Robert W. Pitt, in view of its deep significance:

EMBASSY OF THE UNITED STATES OF AMERICA
Office of the Air Attaché—Buenos Aires—Argentina

June 25, 1982

To the Commander in Chief, Air Force
General Basilio A. I. Lami Dozo
Air Force Command HQ

Dear Sir:

By means of this letter I wish to convey the expression of my personal esteem and consideration, both for you and for the Argentine Air Force, in recognition of your professionalism and unwavering courage during the recent armed conflict with the United Kingdom.

I would be further honored if you were, on behalf of all those who fell or were wounded in action in service to the Argentine Air Force, to accept my Purple Heart as a sincere personal token of my esteem. Of all my decorations, the Purple Heart, which was bestowed on me for wounds sustained in action over North Vietnam on October 5, 1965, is the one I cherish the most.

The Order of the Purple Heart was authorized by order of General George Washington, almost 200 years ago, on August 7, 1782. Following over a century of suspension, the Order of the Purple Heart was reestablished in the early thirties by General Douglas MacArthur. Years later, General MacArthur wrote:

"No single action carried out by me as Chief of Staff has given me greater satisfaction than reestablishing the Order of the Purple Heart. . . . This decoration is unique in many ways: First: it is the oldest in U.S. history. . . . Second: it came down to us from the greatest American of all, George Washington . . . . Third: it is the only decoration which is totally unbiased in that it is not dependent on the approval or the favor of any individual. It is granted solely to those who are wounded in battle, and it is thus enemy action alone that determines its bestowal. It is a true badge of courage, and each chest that bears it can beat with pride.''

It is thus clear why the Purple Heart is my most cherished decoration. From one military flier to another, I would respectfully request that you accept this decoration on behalf of all the brave officers and men of the Air Force who fell or were wounded in action during this recent conflict.

Remaining ever at your service, I take this opportunity to renew the expression of my highest consideration and esteem.

> (signed) Robert W. Pitt
> Colonel, USAF
> Air Attaché

And so the air force received its baptism of fire. It has blazed a path of glory to be followed. It will serve as a beacon to future generations of Argentine fliers as time goes by. Their fallen comrades will not be forgotten.

FOOD FOR THOUGHT

The purpose of this work is not to delve into the lessons learned from the conflict. There are, of course, many—so many that they could be the subject of a separate book. Rather, this study centers on the facts, the reality of events as they were lived day by day; as they are known; and as they have thus far not been reported throughout the rest of the world. As of now, those who devote time to analyzing these events will have a point of view other than that of the British to ponder, and from which to draw up their studies. Everything that has thus far been written on the subject has a serious flaw: events have been reported solely from the British perspective, a viewpoint that has often been at odds with the truth, both during and after the war.

It is therefore proper to digest some reflections based on what has thus far been stated here, in order that those faceless people who are in one way or another the victims of unfair practices—something that appears to be getting ever more ingrained in contemporary society—may know where they are coming from, and where they are headed.

In the Military Field

Based on the final score of the match, we were not quite so soundly thrashed as some would have us believe. The achievements of British psychopolitics, based on the final outcome, are one thing, while the objective analysis of events as they unfolded, is quite another.

Let us first take a glance at the final tally, in both human and materiel losses. Argentina suffered 1,703 casualties, dead and wounded. Leaving aside the 323 men who went down with the *General Belgrano*, who could be better classified as victims of a backhanded act than as true war casualties, this figure drops to 1,380. The official British casualty figure for dead and wounded is 1,332, which just about evens the score. Now, we know these figures to be flawed, so we are convinced that the losses sustained by the British expeditionary force were greater than our own.

Going on to losses sustained in materiel, according to our figures, the British lost 66 aircraft, while their own unofficial sources put the count at 77. Add to this the wear and tear of an ocean environment on aircraft and helicopters, and one can surmise losses in excess of 100 aircraft, which again establishes a parallel that is colored by a substantial qualitative difference. Our own aircraft were far from being modern, sophisticated, first-line assets. Many of them were acquired reconditioned from the United States at prices more attuned to the scrap heap than to operational employment. These same "junk" aircraft produced a much greater kill yield than their British counterparts.

As for naval vessels, the count must cause a lordly share of high-ranking Admiralty officials endless sleepless nights. The loss of seven capital vessels, four of which were modern guided-missile platforms—not to mention the various degrees of damage sustained by numerous others—is a price no fleet in the world, even in a major engagement, can afford. It is all the worse for having been in support of a "colonial venture" aimed at maintaining a minute governing faction in power. Surely Britain's military professionals—who are first rate, and who were trained to take on the Warsaw Pact countries—must be less than overjoyed at having been employed in a confrontation of this sort, for it proved to be exceedingly costly.

Argentina's naval losses are of far lesser significance. Two of the warships that were lost would have been better off in a naval museum—or on the scrap heap—than in a war. The rest were defenseless merchant or private vessels. Their demise could elicit modest applause for their conquering heroes only through an intense propaganda effort.

The bottom line is that Great Britain has had to face some cold, hard facts arising from the conflict. The weaknesses proved on the field of battle, when analyzed from a NATO standpoint, are of great significance. Weapons systems, many of which had never been tested under true combat conditions, were found wanting. None of this has been lost on the Warsaw Pact countries, which established the most sophisticated intelligence network of any power in the theater of operations. There was a tailor-made proving ground for all the latest in modern Western weaponry, in a little "family squabble" among Westerners. Soviet military and political analysts must surely have drawn conclusions that allowed their staffs to breathe a bit easier. The Act of Military Secrecy was not aimed at the Soviet Union or the Iron Curtain countries; its purpose was, and is, quite another: to conceal the truth from Britain's allies, from its own public.

Finally, in the area of naval and air operations during the conflict, experts should capitalize on experience gleaned from events, that could be applicable in any future war, especially if they are able to draw on the mainline concepts that could guide strategy in wars to come, ever mindful that the only museum of military art is found in the ledgers of history.

In the field of naval air operations, the battle for the Falklands again emphasizes the need for, and the preeminence of, two main prongs above all others: air and submarine forces. Land-based air forces inflicted the bulk of the losses on their opponent, in a lopsided engagement, since our attack aircraft had to operate at the very limit of their range. In sorting out lessons learned, it should be noted that in this action, an air force ranking about thirtieth in the world faced off with the third-ranking naval fleet. In this light, they did quite well, in spite of the uneven odds, especially since this battle had to be fought far from any bases of support, in complete isolation. Also noteworthy is the fact that aircraft operating with weapons systems of the same generation as their naval opponents proved to be much more economical, and at the same time more lethal, than their surface counterparts. This was so because a warship, however advanced its technology, is always more vulnerable to attack by aircraft or missiles, since it is bigger, heavier, and slower than the former.

With regard to the submarine weapons platform, one thing stands out incontrovertibly: The presence of British nuclear submarines discouraged our high seas fleet from making an active contribution to operations in the war zone; it held to the protected, shallow waters near the mainland. Submarine detection continues to be a difficult science, and they are therefore hard to neutralize. Their range, their ability to penetrate defense, and their weapon, the torpedo, make them the deadliest of enemies to surface vessels.

Aircraft carriers demonstrated their usefulness for any nation with the means to maintain and protect them, and that has war hypotheses at the ready that call for operations outside their home waters. They are, however, extremely vulnerable, for their defense requires superiority in the air, on the surface, and underwater. All of this entails a vast array of protective assets. Great Britain, which was in the process of decommissioning its remaining carrier group, succeeded in mounting a well-balanced force, but was unable to prevent its flattops from coming under enemy attack. Only the great powers can justify the operation of such assets, but at such an exorbitant cost that even the United States has encountered stiff resistance to this budget item. For the armed forces of the rest of the world that would consider investing in such platforms, the big question is this: With what it costs to maintain an operational carrier force, how many land-based aircraft equipped for in-flight refueling, or how many submarines, could they buy for the same capital outlay?

The Argentine Navy found itself incapable of properly defending the carrier *25 de Mayo*, and thus was obliged to withdraw it to its berth from the very outset. Its complement of aircraft as deployed to land bases from which they operated with support and weapons systems that were completely independent of their mother ship. To sum it up, Argentina's naval air arm operated as a pocket land air force, not as a naval air force.

The foot soldier proved his continued viability in modern combat. Technology, however, as more and more sophisticated weapons are made available, causes an ever increasing demand for high-level technical training, so much so that the concept of the draftee who does a one- or two-year hitch and returns to civilian life is gradually giving way to that of the professional, career military man. It is a change in quality that is added to the need for superior mobility, along with independent air defense teams, considering the proven effectiveness of modern portable weapons in neutralizing air attacks. As for surface forces, specialized commandos can play a vital role in a broad variety of situations, some of which acquire true strategic significance, such as a failed Argentine frogmen operation at the Rock of Gibraltar.

In closing, events show that Argentina's armed forces went into battle against the following odds:

—The enemy was a powerful nation that enjoyed the support of a world superpower, NATO, and the EEC.

—There were no war hypotheses on the books to cover a contingency with Great Britain, nor were any such plans considered.

—There was no lead time, no time to make proper arrangements, not even in the field of psychological warfare.

—The battle was fought single-handedly, despite the possibility of receiving assistance from other world powers.

Although the deck was heavily stacked in Great Britain's favor, the final cost of achieving victory proved so high that it was, and continues to be, grounds for deep concern. In this light, Argentina was defeated in relative, rather than absolute, terms. This will not bring back to life those who died for their country, nor will it change what is perceived to be a temporary setback for the objective sought—which will continue to be sought—but it should give Great Britain food for thought.

For next time—and may God grant that diplomacy will preclude any such next time—London will not enjoy the same advantages (except, possibly, U.S. support): our bombs *will* go off, our torpedoes *will* work, and our men *will* be properly trained for such a battle. A symbolic statement, perhaps, for future generations of weapons systems will take the place of those employed in 1982.

Argentina would not fight to reclaim or retain a little-known colony, but to reclaim a piece of its country that was taken by force first in 1833, then again in 1982. Therein lies the difference. The war has not been lost, for defeat is a psychological element quite apart from the outcome on the battlefield, and comes about only when the objective to be achieved is abandoned.

And, just like the Phoenix, from the ashes of the historical events narrated here a new April 2, 1982, will arise that will find the people of Argentina united behind a cause they will never renounce.

In the Political and Strategic Fields

When Jacques Clostermann, son of Pierre and an officer in the French Air Force expressed his admiration and amazement at the Argentine pilots' thrusts against the arrays of British ships, he cried out "Fous! Fous!" (They're mad! Mad!) It is probable that a similar thought crossed his mind when he first heard of the Argentine government's decision to reclaim the southern island chains.

Perhaps no other nation in the world might have the audacity to challenge a stronger country to a war, acting entirely on its own, however righteous the cause. Argentina holds an important position within its own region, but in the world concert of nations she is but a small country. Great Britain, in spite of its numerous problems, is still a power to be reckoned with, and it is allied with the United States and Western Europe.

The pragmatism with which international relations are conducted, putting interests ahead of numerous and highly touted principles, should have led one to surmise what Washington's response would have been in the face of a threat to the stability of the British Conservative government. When the members of the military junta—or at least two of its members—spread the issue of reclaiming our Malvinas Islands on the table, they sadly underestimated the scope of Britain's response. This proved to be the lesser of two errors, for alone Britain would have been powerless in the South Atlantic. The big mistake was misreading how the United States would respond.

This was followed by the debacle in the diplomatic arena brought on by Resolution 502. Our government also allowed its final opportunity to slip by, complying with it as the task force sailed into sight of Ascension Island. The outcome became inevitable, and Argentina could not, under such circumstances, achieve the political objective sought. Nevertheless, and without its ever having been suggested in any of the armed forces' operational command missions, they were able to exact an exceedingly high price from the United Kingdom for the retaking of the islands, in an escalation unleashed by Britain through its order to sink the cruiser *General Belgrano*. The colonial venture carries a human, materiel, and moral price tag, the shock waves of which are still rippling out. It will not be one of the prouder chapters in British history.

The decision to face off against Great Britain with heavily unbalanced forces and without proper planning not only cost the members of the military junta their jobs, but also spelled the beginning of the end of the National Process for Reorganization, and set the country back on the path to democracy and the rule of constitutional law.

In the United Kingdom, on the other hand, there was pomp and ceremony to welcome the conquering heroes home from the South Atlantic that would have been more fitting for the cessation of hostilities in a conflict such as World War II. The raw truth is that all that had been achieved was the retaking of a small, unknown colony from a South American nation that had been claiming sovereignty for years. This resounding triumph, trumpeted by the British government-controlled mass media, elevated Mrs. Thatcher to the pinnacle of her popularity, which in turn gave her a record-breaking showing in the next elections.

A brief reflection should be made at this point on the effectiveness of psychological action on world society. There are few places left on the globe where one can find safe haven from such action. It serves not mankind as a whole but small power groups that use it and monopolize it to enhance their own interests, which are less than philanthropic. It is a terrible new weapon. It does not destroy the body, but it can control ideas and, what is worse, the will of men. In so doing it tends further to divert mankind from a worthy and transcending objective: God.

Mrs. Thatcher's punitive expedition did what it came to do. It "set things right" in the face of the excesses and pretensions of an obscure South American "military dictatorship." But the military junta that bore responsibility for taking this conflict far beyond established bounds paid the price. It answered for its shortcomings, not only in the political arena but also in the halls of justice. Argentina now enjoys a government elected by all the people. But has London changed its attitude, now that the objective is firmly in its clutches? Quite the contrary. It has erected a formidable military redoubt aimed at discouraging Argentines from any ideas about asking for the return of what is rightfully theirs. London's attitude has been one of haughty nonnegotiation of any such Argentine claim. In this regard, a *New York Times* editorial, published on April 8, 1988, states under the head "Talks, not Maneuvers on the Falklands":

On the matter of the Falkland Islands, Britain behaves with an arrogance worthy of the Juntas that used to rule in Argentina. . . . At stake are lucrative fishery and mineral resources in adjacent waters, as well as the rights and welfare of several thousand islanders of British stock. It is hard to fathom how either side's interest is advanced with provocative maneuvers and repeated rejection of negotiations. It is also hard to believe Britain is prepared to spend hundreds of millions indefinitely on Fortress Falkland, rather than hear the dread word sovereignty in mixed company with Argentines.

As London has slowly begun to grasp the staggering current and future cost of its military adventure, it has attempted to interest partners and allies in the "strategic importance" of the islands, even to the point of citing the "need" for creating a SATO (South Atlantic Treaty Organization), along NATO lines. This proposal appears to be a thinly veiled maneuver aimed at finding someone else who might be willing to share the cost and further rationalize the British Conservative government's decision, since it would be:

1. A multilateral defense organization bringing together one group of Western nations against one—or more—members of the same group. The political incongruity of such a scheme is of not inconsiderable significance.

2. The consummation of such an alliance would achieve, in the long run, the military security of the islands and their area of influence while turning the coastal powers of the adjacent continent against them—a juicy state of affairs for the Soviet Union. This would be a strategic absurdity of mind-boggling proportions for any Western analyst.

And lest we forget, there are those 1,800 silent Kelpers and their proclaimed rights, in whose defense Mrs. Thatcher bore the standard at the head of the task force. The Franks Report points the finger squarely at the intractability of the representatives of these very pseudo-British subjects as being one of the basic causes of the conflict, and states that the thousands of Argentine and British soldiers who fought and died in the South Atlantic had an even more sacred right: the right to life. And either here or in the hereafter, someone will assuredly be compelled to answer for them.

The punitive objective of the British expedition loses its currency in light of the heavy human and materiel cost of the venture to Great Britain. Had there but been in all the Anglo-Saxon world a statesman of the stature of Sir Winston Churchill, with the fortitude to paraphrase one of that great man's sayings, crying out: "Never has so much been owed to so many by so few."

THE WAY

If this armed conflict had any positive fallout, it served to unmask a series of fallacies that govern the world in which we live. We have seen how international organizations come to be manipulated to give the upper hand to the interests of the mighty, whatever their high-sounding principles may be. In that club called the United Nations, there are two levels of membership. There are five first-class members, and the rolls are forever closed. The remainder fight over their relative shares of the spotlight in the shadow of the powerful, in hopes that one of the latter will champion their cause—for a price—when their rights are trampled on.

It therefore becomes transparent that the battle lines separating the whole of mankind are drawn along a north-south axis. The more chaotic and wretched the producers of raw materials become, the cheaper they can be had by the developed world, the better to compete for markets for their finished products, complete with value added, and credit for their purchase at interest rates the developed world sets. Loans may well never be paid off, because the "have nots" cannot establish the price for their own raw materials.

The OAS should have responded more than just emotionally, mindful of the existence of the Rio Treaty to defend the rights of each and every signatory. It should remain aware that an extra-hemispheric power has erected a fortress in the treaty's zone of influence. It costs that power money, and the price will go up—but it is there nonetheless. Our area countries go about their business unconcerned. They appear to prefer to look the other way, wanting to believe that nothing really happened down here.

Defeat is not so much the result of a contest as of the attitude of indifference that, like a boomerang, will come back to strike down those who have yet to grasp the facts that the struggle against colonialism has not ended in this hemisphere, that our world is one where human dignity counts for something, and that the New Testament calls for joy in brotherhood, fair price for fair measure, and goodwill among men.

In defense of a piece of our America, Argentina took up the implements of war while its soldiers instinctively grasped their rosaries. Thus they carried the battle to the British intruder, to the very limits of their aircraft's range. In so doing, they stunned the world with their daring.

The heroics of this contest may herald the birth of a renewed political philosophy based not on the love of material wealth but on love of one's fellow man. They laid the foundation of a true fraternocracy that will enable an ever more lost humanity to find its way toward God.

Bibliography

Books

Andrada, Beningo H. *Guerra Aerea en las Malvinas*. Buenos Aires: Emcee Editora, 1983.

Bishop, Patrick, and Witherow, John. *The Winter War*. London: Quartet Books, 1983.

Burden, Rodney A., Draper, Michael I., Rough, Douglas A., Smith, Colin R., and Wilton, David L. *Falklands—The Air War*. London, New York, Sydney: Arms and Armour Press, 1986.

Caillet-Bois, Ricardo R. *Una Tierra Argentina, las Islas Malvinas*. Buenos Aires: Academia Nacional de la Historia, 1986.

Calvert, Peter. *The Falkland Crisis, the Rights and the Wrongs*. London: Frances Printer, 1982.

Carballo, Pablo M. *Dios y los Halcones*. Buenos Aires: Ediciones del Cruzamante, 1985.

Cardoso, O. R., Kirschbaum, R., and Van der Koy, E. *La Trama Secreta*. Buenos Aires: Sudamericana Planeta, 1984.

Child, Jack. *Geopolitics and Conflict in South America*. New York: Praeger Publishers, 1985.

Cockerell, Michael, Hennessey, Peter, and Walker, David. *Sources Close to the Prime Minister*. London: Macmillan, 1983.

Coll, Albert R., and Arend, Anthony C. *The Falklands War*. Boston: Allen & Unwin, 1985.

Comunicados Oficiales de Gran Bretaña y de la Argentina. *La Historia Oficial de la Guerra*. London: Latin America Newsletter, 1982.

Dalyell, Tam. *Thatcher's Torpedo—The Sinking of the Belgrano*. London: Cecil Wolf, 1983.

Del Carril, Bonifacio. *La Cuestion de las Malvinas*. Buenos Aires: Emece Editora, 1982.

———. *El Futuro de las Islas Malvinas*. Buenos Aires: Emece Editora, 1982.

Destefani, Lauro H. *Malvinas, Georgias y Sandwich del Sur ante el Conflicto con Gran Bretaña*. Buenos Aires: Edipress, 1984.

Ethell, Jeffrey, and Price, Alfred. *Air War South Atlantic*. London: Sidwick & Jackson, 1985.

Ferns, H. S. *Argentina*. London: Ernest Benn, 1969.

Foulkes, Haroldo. *74 Dias Alucinantes en Puerto Argentino*. Buenos Aires: Ediciones Corregidor, 1984.

Fowler, William. *Battle of the Falklands*. London: Osprey, 1983.

Fox, Robert. *Eyewitness Falklands*. London: Methuen, 1982.

Franks Report. *Estudio de Antecedentes sobre las Islas Malvinas*. Buenos Aires: I.G.A., 1982.

Gamba, Virginia. *El Peon de la Reina*. Buenos Aires: Editorial Sudamericana, 1984.

———. *The Falklands/Malvinas War*. Boston: Allen & Unwin, 1987.

Gavshon, Arthur, and Rice, Desmond. *El Hundimiento del Belgrano*. Buenos Aires: Emece Editora, 1984.

Goebel, Julius. *The Struggle for the Falklands*. New Haven and London: Yale University Press, 1982.

Harris, Robert. *Gotcha. The Media, the Government and the Falklands Crisis*. London: Faber & Faber, 1983.

Hastings, Max, and Jenkins, Simon. *The Battle for the Falklands*. New York and London: W. W. Norton & Co., 1982.

Heathland, Robert. *The Island of South Georgia*. Cambridge: Cambridge University Press, 1984.

Informe Oficial del Ejercito Argentino. *Conflicto Malvinas*. 2 vols. Buenos Aires, 1983 and 1984.

Koburger, Charles W. *Sea Power in the Falklands*. New York: Praeger Publishers, 1983.

Ladd, James. *Inside the Commandos*. London: Osprey, 1984.

Lafin, John. *Fight for the Falklands*. New York: St. Martin's Press, 1983.

Lanchar, Roger. *La Guerre du Bout du Monde—Isles Falklands*. London: Willow Books, 1983.

McGowan, Robert, and Hands, Jeremy. *Don't Cry for Me, Sergeant Major*. London: Futura McDonald and Co., 1983.

Marriot, Leo. *Royal Navy Frigates*. London: Ian Allan, 1983.

Momyer, William W. *Air Power in Three Wars*. Washington, DC: U.S. Government Printing Office, 1985.

Muller Rojas, Alberto A. *Las Malvinas, Tragicomedia en Tres Actos*. Caracas: Editorial Ateneo, 1983.

Palazzi, Ruben O. *El Transporte Aereo Militar durante el Conflicto del Atlantico Sur*. Buenos Aires: ESGA, 1984.

Perrett, Bryan. *Weapons of the Falkland Conflict*. London: Biddles of Gilford, 1984.

Pitman, Howard T. *Geopolitics in ABC Countries*. Michigan and London: University Microfilms International, 1979.

Portela, A., J. Godoy, R. O. Moro, and P. Toma. *Malvinas, su Advertencia Termonuclear*. Buenos Aires: AZ Editora, 1985.

Preston, Anthony. *Sea Combat of the Falklands*. London: Willow Books, 1982.

Quellet, Ricardo L. *Historia Politica de las Islas Malvinas*. Buenos Aires: ESGA, 1982.

Rodriguez Motino, H. *La Artilleria Argentina en Malvinas*. Buenos Aires: Clio, 1985.

Romero Briasco, Jesus, and Maffe Huertas, Salvador. *Malvinas, Testigo de Batallas*. Valencia: Editorial Federico Domenech, 1984.

Scheina, Robert L. *The Malvinas Campaign*. Washington, D. C.: Proceedings, 1983.

Sunday Times of London Insight Team. *War in the Falklands*. London: Harper & Row, 1982.

Thompson, Julian. *No Picnic*. London: Butler and Tanner, 1984.

Tinker, David. *Cartas de un Marino Ingles*. Buenos Aires: Emcee Editora, 1983.

Underwood, Geoffrey. *Our Falkland War*. Cornwall: Maritime Books, Buenos Aires: 1982.

Villarino, Emilio. *Exocet*. Buenos Aires: Editorial Abril, SA, 1983.

Watson, Bruce W., and Peter M. Dunn. *Military Lessons of the Falkland Islands War*. Boulder, Colo.: Westview Press, 1984.

Journals and Newspapers

ABC (Madrid).

Aeroespacio (Buenos Aires)

AIAA Journal (U.S.A.)

Air Combat, Special Report (Canada)

Air Force Magazine (U.S.A.)

Air Sonic (Barcelona).

Armada Internacional (Spain)

Armas y Geoestrategia (Buenos Aires)

Armed Forces Journal International (France)

Aviation Week and Space International (U.S.A.)

Clarin (Buenos Aires)

Conviccion (Buenos Aires)

Cronica (Buenos Aires)

Current News, Special Edition, USAF (U.S.A.)

Daily Telegraph (London)

Defence Special (U.K.)

Defense (France)

Defense and Foreign Affairs (U.S.A.)

Defense Week (U.S.A.)

Department of State Bulletin (U.S.A.)

Diario Popular (Mendoza, Argentina)

L'Express (France)

Financial Times (London)

Flight International (U.K.)

Gente (Buenos Aires)

Geopolitica (Buenos Aires)

The Guardian (London)

The Guardian (Montreal)

The London Gazette

Mendoza (Mendoza, Argentina)

Miami Herald

Military Electronics (U.S.A.)

Military Technology (U.S.A.)

Naval War College Review (U.S.A.)

New Statesman (London)

Newsweek (U.S.A.)

New York Times

The Observer (London)

Philadelphia Inquirer

The Scotsman
Der Spiegel (G. F. R.)
Strategic Review (U.S.A.)
The Sun (London)
Sunday Times (London)
10 (Buenos Aires)
Tiempo Argentino (Buenos Aires)
Time (U.S.A.)
The Times (London)
U.S. News & World Report
Washington Post
Washington Times

Index

About the Author

COMMODORE RUBÉN O. MORO was born in Buenos Aires Province, Argentina in 1936. He graduated from high school in 1953 and started his career in the Argentine Air Force, receiving his commission as second lieutenant from Military Aviation School in 1959 and being promoted to military aviator the following year.

He was posted to Reconnaissance and Strike Group I at the Mar del Plata air force base and in June 1962 was assigned to a training program with HU–16B Albatross aircraft in the United States, taking part in search-and-rescue operations during the Cuban missile crisis late that year. Later he took part in Long-Range Maritime Reconnaissance Group I, Search-and-Rescue Squadron, at Tandil air force base and Airlift Groups I & II at El Palomar I Air Brigade Buenos Aires Province. He was awarded the Antarctic Badge and Certificate for missions accomplished on the antarctic continent.

In 1974 Commodore Moro completed the basic Staff and Command School course, and the following year, as a major, he graduated from that institution and was awarded the Air Force Medal for the highest point average in the exercise section of that course. In 1977 he was appointed U.N. observer in the Middle East, where he held several posts in Damascus and Jerusalem; served in the Golan Heights and the Sinai Peninsula; and received the U.N. Award in 1978.

In 1979 Commodore Moro was appointed to the Department of Policy of the general staff of the Argentine Air Force. He completed a course in geopolitics at the Buenos Aires University School of Social Sciences. Also, the System of Cooperation of the Air Forces of the Americas awarded him the medal and diploma in recognition of his performance as liaison officer of the Argentine Air Force. In 1982 he saw action as a member of the C–130 squadron in the South Atlantic conflict.

In 1983, Commodore Moro was appointed chief rapporteur to the Rattenbach Commission, which was nominated to assess the responsibilities in the South Atlantic conflict. He was named chairman of the Drafting Committee on the History of the Air War in the Malvinas Islands. He was voted ranking member of the Jorge Newbery National Institute of Air Force History and was awarded the Newbery Order of Merit, chevalier degree in 1985.

Among Commodore Moro's academic activities are the advanced leadership course at the Air War School, Air Force of Argentina, 1985; the joint military planning course at the Ministry of Defense; and the advanced military strategic course of the joint chiefs of staff of Argentina during 1986.

Commodore Moro has lectured extensively and published many papers related to his professional activities, which include his chairing of the geopolitical course at the Santa Maria Catholic University School of Law and Political Sciences in Buenos Aires. He also has published papers on the Vietnam war, the Middle East conflict, geopolitics of the Americas, and the antarctic. His most recent book is *The History of the South Atlantic Conflict—The Unprecedented War* (in Spanish). In 1987 he was assigned to the Inter-American Defense Board, in Washington, D. C., where he served as a member of the international staff until January 1989.